Meditation as Spiritual Therapy

Meditation as Spiritual Therapy

Bernard of Clairvaux's *De consideratione*

Matthew R. McWhorter

The Catholic University of American Press
Washington, D.C.

The paper used in this publication meets the minimum requirements
of American National Standards for Information Science—
Permanence of Paper for Printed Library Materials, ANSI Z39.48-1992.

Cataloging-in-Publication Data is available from the Library of Congress

ISBN: 978-0-8132-3800-5 | eISBN: 978-0-8132-3801-2

Book design by Burt&Burt
Interior typeset with Garamond Premier Pro and Solitas Serif

In memory of Fr. Matthew Lamb, OCSO

List of Abbreviations

Treatises of Bernard of Clairvaux

Csi	*De consideratione*
Dil	*Liber de diligendo Deo*
Gra	*Liber de gratia et libero arbitrio*
Hum	*Liber de gradibus humilitatis et superbiae*
Mor	*Ep de moribus et officiis episcoporum*
Pre	*Liber de praecepto et dispensatione*

Sermons of Bernard of Clairvaux on the Annual Liturgical Cycle

Adv	*Sermo in adventu Domini*
Nat	*Sermo in nativitate Domini*
Pent	*Sermo in die sancto Pentecostes*
Quad	*Sermo in quadragesima*
Res	*Sermo in resurrectione Domini*

Other Sermons of Bernard of Clairvaux

Conv	*Sermo de conversione ad clericos*
Div	*Sermo de diversis*
QH	*Sermo super psalmum Qui habitat*
SCC	*Sermo super Cantica canticorum*

Works by Gregory the Great

Hiez	*In Hiezechielem*
Mo	*Moralia in Iob*

Other Scholarly Works and Critical Editions

ASOC	*Analecta Sacri Ordinis Cisterciensis*
CCCM	Corpus Christianorum Continuatio Mediaevalis
CCSL	Corpus Christianorum Series Latina
CF	Cistercian Fathers Series
CS	Cistercian Studies Series
CSQ	*Cistercian Studies Quarterly*
GW	*Gesammelte Werke* (Hans-Georg Gadamer)
PL	Patrologia Latina (ed. J.-P. Migne)
RB	*Regula monachorum sancti Benedicti*
SBO	*Sancti Bernardi Opera*
SC	Sources Chrétiennes
SW	*Sämtliche Werke* (Bernhard von Clairvaux)
TM	*Truth and Method* (Hans-Georg Gadamer)
VP	*Vita prima* (Geoffrey of Auxerre)

Introduction

Contemporary interest in meditation has led to the development of numerous resources for persons who desire to integrate mindfulness-based practices into everyday life. Similar resources have been developed for integrating such practices into various forms of civil psychotherapy.[1] Among some Christian persons, however, the perceived origin of mindfulness-based practices in Buddhist monasticism might lead to the expression of spiritual concern.[2] Is it possible to integrate such Buddhist exercises into Christian religious practice? Or, alternatively, are there similar meditation resources to be found in the monastic traditions already at the heart of the Christian religion?

Bernard of Clairvaux's mature work *De consideratione* (1148–53) provides one such resource in the Catholic-Christian monastic tradition.[3]

1 Regarding the meaning of civil psychotherapy, I am referring to state-licensed health care providers who offer psychological services such as clinical psychiatrists, psychologists, and mental health counselors. The reference of the word 'civil' in this sense functions in the same way as reference to civil law, the civil common good, and civil educational degrees in the Catholic-Christian intellectual tradition. See, e.g., J. Brian Benestad, "Civil Society and the Church," in *Church, State, and Society: An Introduction to Catholic Social Doctrine* (Washington, DC: The Catholic University of America Press, 2011), 215–53.

2 That mindfulness practice in a civil treatment modality such as MBCT is discerned to originate from Buddhism, see Joshua J. Knabb, "Centering Prayer as an Alternative to Mindfulness-Based Cognitive Therapy for Depression Relapse Prevention," *Journal of Religion and Health* 51, no. 3 (2012): 908–24. Regarding the possible concern on the part of Christian clients with the Buddhist origin of the practice, see, e.g., the clinical scenario described in Philip Brownell, *Spiritual Competency in Psychotherapy* (New York: Springer Publishing, 2015), 95.

3 For a Latin edition of *De consideratione* (hereafter *Csi*) see Bernhard von Clairvaux, *Sämtliche Werke, lateinisch/deutsch*, Bd. I (hereafter *SW*), ed. Gerhard B. Winkler, Alberich Altermatt, Denis Farkasfalvy, and Polykarp Zakar (Innsbruck: Tyrolia, 1990), 611–841. *SW* 1 reprints the Latin for *Csi* from Bernardus Claraevallensis, *Sancti Bernardi Opera*, vol. 3 (hereafter *SBO* 3), ed. J. Leclercq, C. H. Talbot, and H.-M. Rochais (Rome: Editiones Cistercienses, 1963), 393–493. The *SBO* is currently reprinted by Brepols (1993–2017). For an English translation of *Csi*, see Bernard of Clairvaux,

The work is, as Benedictine scholar Jean Leclercq observed, the "crown" of Bernard's literary career.[4] Spanning five books, Bernard outlines for his primary reader (Pope Eugene III) a path for Christian meditative reflection that has perennial value.[5] In particular, the monastic exercises concerning mental self-regulation that Bernard prescribes to Eugene III can serve as a resource for contemporary persons who might be interested in cultivating a specifically Catholic-Christian approach to meditative practice. Bernard's emphases on *vigilance* (taking custody of one's thoughts)[6] and *self-recollection* (recalling one's thoughts from distraction) are central elements of his teaching on mental self-regulation.[7] While Bernard recognizes that mental self-regulation in this regard is a character of a healthy mind, developing such mental qualities is not for Bernard an end in itself, but rather a preparation for the contemplation of God.

Leclercq characterizes Bernard's teaching on meditation as a program of *spiritual therapy*.[8] I agree with Leclercq when he observes with respect to Bernard that "his writings manifest a kind of teaching which many can put into action and realize in their daily life."[9] The study of Bernard's teaching in this regard will be especially helpful for persons interested in an approach to meditation that is based upon sources indigenous to the Catholic-Christian religious culture.[10] Such a 'spiritual therapy' might be employed in Catholic

Five Books on Consideration: Advice to a Pope, trans. John D. Anderson and Elizabeth T. Kennan, Cistercian Fathers Series no. 37 (Kalamazoo, MI: Cistercian Publications, 1976) (hereafter CF 37).

4 Jean Leclercq, "L'Art de la Composition dans les Traités de S. Bernard," in *Recueil D'Études sur Saint Bernard et Ses Écrits*, vol. 3 (Rome: Edizioni di Storia e Letteratura, 1969), 105–62, at 118.

5 That *Csi* was written for Pope Eugene III, see CF 37:5.

6 *Csi*, IV, 6.17 (CF 37:131; *SW* 1:764; *SBO* 3:462).

7 *Csi*, V, 2.4 (CF 37:143; *SW* 1:778; *SBO* 3:469).

8 Jean Leclercq, *A Second Look at Saint Bernard*, trans. Marie-Bernard Saïd (Kalamazoo, MI: Cistercian Publications, 1990), 74 (hereafter CS 105). This is a translation of Jean Leclercq, *Nouveau Visage de Bernard de Clairvaux: Approaches psycho-historiques* (Paris: Les Éditions du Cerf, 1976).

9 Jean Leclercq, "St Bernard and the Christian Experience," in *Aspects of Monasticism*, trans. Mary Dodd (Kalamazoo, MI: Cistercian Publications, 1978), 251–65, at 264 (CS 7). This chapter reprints an essay found in *Worship* 41, no. 4 (1967): 222–33, with the original French in *La Vie Spirituelle* 116 (1967): 182–98. See also CS 7:327–43, at 332–33, reprinting Jean Leclercq, "The Role of Monastic Spirituality Critically Discussed," *Worship* 39, no. 10 (1965): 583–96, at 587.

10 My perspective in this regard is influenced by what is called indigenous religious psychology (a psychology that develops out from within religious praxis, rather than as an exterior study of religious praxis that does not participate in such praxis). See Timothy A. Sisemore and Joshua J. Knabb, "Seeing Religions and Spiritualities from the Inside: Problems for Western Psychology That Can Be Addressed with an Indigenous Psychological Perspective," in *The Psychology of World Religions and Spiritualities: An Indigenous Perspective*, ed. Timothy A. Sisemore and Joshua J. Knabb (West Conshohocken, PA: Templeton Press, 2020), 3–28.

spiritual direction as well as serve as an auxiliary resource for Catholic persons undergoing spiritually-integrated civil psychotherapy.

Some contemporary spiritual direction treatises on Catholic meditation already draw on Bernard's teaching. Thomas Merton, for example, exhibits familiarity with Bernard's *De consideratione* in his work *Spiritual Direction and Meditation*; yet Merton does not attempt to discern and consolidate the various detailed topics found in Bernard's teaching. Similarly, writing from an evangelical Protestant perspective, clinical psychologist Joshua J. Knabb recognizes that the medieval literature discussing meditative practices can serve as a resource for integration with contemporary clinical practice in civil psychotherapy, yet Knabb does not explore Bernard's teaching in a focused way. As such, I discuss in the final chapter of this study how Bernard's teaching might undergo a recontextualization for contemporary Catholic spiritual direction and for Catholic persons receiving spiritually-integrated civil psychotherapy.

Readers who are primarily interested in this recontextualization might move ahead to review the final two chapters of this book, where I explore the contemporary relevance of Bernard's teaching for spiritual direction and civil psychotherapy. However, I encourage such readers to return to the historical and interpretive parts of this study in order to appreciate the original formulation of Bernard's teaching and the context of the monastic tradition from which it derives. While it is possible to benefit from Bernard's teaching by proceeding directly to this summary, understanding his account primarily involves one taking up his spiritual perspective more so than following a step-by-step method or technique. In order to grasp his spiritual perspective, it is important that one become familiar with the historical context and the interpretive content that is provided in the first two parts of this study.

The historically-grounded presentation of Bernard's spiritual and moral psychology differentiates the current study from similar studies that proceed by first adopting a contemporary psychological perspective. For example, Robert Stepsis aimed to derive from the works of Bernard a general theory of personality development in dialogue with the self-actualization psychology of Abraham Maslow.[11] Leclercq however questioned whether Bernard's actual monastic practice conformed to any specific personality theory in this regard.[12] On the other hand, Leclercq also developed a research approach

11 Robert P. Stepsis, "Fulfillment of Self and Union with God in the Writings of Bernard of Clairvaux," *The American Benedictine Review* 24 (1973): 348–64, citing Abraham Maslow, *Motivation and Personality* (New York, 1954) and *Toward a Psychology of Being*, 2nd ed. (Princeton, NJ: Princeton University Press, 1968).

12 CS 105:xiv.

similar to that of Stepsis.[13] For example, Leclercq similarly suggests that scholars might examine Bernard's understanding of monastic ascesis in light of the psychological theory of Carl Jung.[14] Leclercq also proposed in certain studies that scholars approach Bernard's spiritual practice from a "psycho-history" perspective where, by "applying psychological methods," a historian might be able to come to "some sort of clinical judgment" regarding Bernard's degree of self-integration.[15] Leclercq later came to emphasize that such an approach might be more specifically characterized as a *religious* psycho-history.[16] In particular, Leclercq refers to the medieval psychology present in Bernard's writings as a monastic or *claustral* psychology (as distinct from the "Scholastic psychology" associated with the medieval urban schools).[17]

In parallel with such a religious psycho-history (without the clinical diagnostic dimension), Leclercq also approached Bernard's works in a *descriptive* way, as found in his general introduction to the multi-volume *Opere di San Bernardo*; there, Leclercq describes common themes that he discerns throughout Bernard's writings.[18] Cistercian scholar Bernard McGinn likewise undertakes an "investigation of the dominant psychological themes through which the Abbot expressed [a] very pragmatically oriented theory of man."[19] Similarly, Bernardine scholar John R. Sommerfeldt sought to explore various topics found in Bernard's teaching on meditation in connection with where

13 Jean Leclercq, "General Introduction to the Works of Saint Bernard (III)," *Cistercian Studies Quarterly* (hereafter *CSQ*) 40, no. 4 (2005): 365–93, at 384.

14 Leclercq, "General Introduction (III)," 382. Leclercq cautions elsewhere that not all Jungian archetypes can be projected back into past eras by a researcher. See Jean Leclercq, *Monks and Love in Twelfth-Century France: Psycho-Historical Essays* (Oxford: Oxford University Press, 1979), 3. For discussion of Catholic theology and Jungian psychology, see Victor White, *God and the Unconscious* (Providence, R.I.: Cluny Media, 2021); Victor White, *Soul and Psyche: An Enquiry into the Relationship between Psychotherapy and Religion* (New York: Harper, 1960).

15 CS 105:xiv. Proceeding chronologically, Leclercq describes this research program in the following works: Jean Leclercq, "Modern Psychology and the Interpretation of Medieval Texts," *Speculum* 48, no. 3 (1973): 476–90; "Psycho-history and the Understanding of Medieval People," *The Hanoverian* 6 (1975): 6–9; "Psycho-history and the Understanding of Medieval People: Part III and Conclusion," *The Hanoverian* 7 (1975): 7–10; *Nouveau Visage de Bernard* (1976); "Psycho-history and the Understanding of Medieval People," *CSQ* 11 (1976): 269–89 (reprinting the two articles from 1975); *Monks and Love*; "Prayer at Cluny," *Journal of the American Academy of Religion* 51, no. 4 (1983): 651–65, at 659; CS 105 (1990).

16 Leclercq, "Prayer at Cluny," 662.

17 Leclercq, "Psycho-history," *CSQ*, 288.

18 Leclercq, "General Introduction (III)," 378.

19 Bernard McGinn, "Introduction," in *Three Treatises on Man: A Cistercian Anthropology*, ed. Bernard McGinn (Kalamazoo, MI: Cistercian Publications, 1977), 1–100, at 79 (hereafter CF 24).

these topics reappear in Bernard's other writings.[20] When outlining these various dimensions of Bernard's thought, Sommerfeldt aimed to sketch the general structure of what he referred to as "Bernard's method" of meditation.[21]

In the study that follows, I develop this type of inquiry modeled by Leclercq and Sommerfeldt, focusing in a special way on Bernard's discussion of meditation as found in *De consideratione*. While Leclercq and Sommerfeldt do not explicitly discuss their research approach, I find that the mode of research they model exhibits some similarities to qualitative research as found in the contemporary human sciences.[22] Such interdisciplinary approaches have also been adopted by other Bernardine scholars (e.g., John D. Anderson describes a portion of his study of Bernard's use of scripture in *De consideratione* as a "qualitative analysis"[23]).

Regarding the meaning of the word 'meditation' as used in the title of this book and throughout the discussion, one might note that in *De consideratione*, Bernard uses the words 'consideration' and 'meditation' as synonyms.[24] I predominantly use the latter word 'meditation' in the current study as a matter of preference.[25] The meaning of this word for Bernard is discussed in great detail in the second part of the present study.

I proceed in the first part with a historical representation of the context of *De consideratione*.[26] I assume Bernard's authorship of the treatise and I outline the chronological events surrounding the time period when he wrote the work (chapter 1). This outline is developed primarily as a literature review that is dependent on secondary sources who are familiar with the time period that situates *De consideratione*; I reference a number of primary sources as

20 John R. Sommerfeldt, "Meditation as the Path to Humility in the Thought of Bernard of Clairvaux," *Mystics Quarterly* 15, no. 4 (1989): 177–83; John R. Sommerfeldt, *The Spiritual Teachings of Bernard of Clairvaux* (Kalamazoo, MI: Cistercian Publications, 1991), 66–79 (hereafter CS 125).

21 Sommerfeldt, "Meditation as the Path," 180.

22 See, e.g., Janice M. Morse, "'Emerging from the Data': The Cognitive Processes of Analysis in Qualitative Inquiry," in *Critical Issues in Qualitative Research Methods*, Janice M. Morse (Thousand Oaks, CA: Sage Publications, 1994), 23–43, and Frederick J. Wertz, "Phenomenological Research Methods for Counseling Psychology," *Journal of Counseling Psychology* 52, no. 2 (2005): 167–77, at 172.

23 John D. Anderson, "Paul in Book 5 of the *De consideratione* of Bernard of Clairvaux," *CSQ* 42, no. 2 (2007): 137–50, at 140.

24 See, e.g., *Csi*, II, 6.13 (CF 37:61; *SW* 1:680; *SBO* 3:420); *Csi*, V, 14.32 (CF 37:179; *SW* 1:826; *SBO* 3:493).

25 Sommerfeldt frequently uses the terms 'consideration' and 'meditation' interchangeably when describing Bernard's thinking. See Sommerfeldt, "Meditation as the Path," 177–83; CS 125:66, 78n2, 223–24.

26 Qualitative research might begin with exploring the setting of the topic under consideration. See also Morse, "'Emerging from the Data,'" 26.

well. I next explore which historical events likely precipitated Bernard's authorship, focusing on the affairs of Pope Eugene III as Bernard's intended reader in order to infer Bernard's purpose for writing. I also investigate Bernard's selection of a literary genre (chapter 2). To close this first historical part of the study, I note the sources that influenced Bernard's thought, chief among which (with respect to the exercise of consideration) are the Rule of Benedict and the thought of Gregory the Great (chapter 3).

In the second part, I interpret the content of Bernard's *De consideratione* in a way that proceeds linearly through his five books, giving emphasis to certain key topics as they arise in his discussion.[27] I organize and explore these topics as they emerge in the five books of *De consideratione* and I compare these passages with other works by Bernard that contain similar content.[28] I begin the second part of the study by interpreting Bernard's introduction to the exercise of meditation as found in Book I. I examine the topics of leisure or quietude, how meditation is a spiritual exercise, and how this exercise might be understood in the context of a claustral psychology. This discussion allows the opportunity to briefly consider Bernard's anthropology as a whole. I then take up the topic of how meditation can be exercised as an act of religious piety in orientation to the Holy Spirit, as well as how the practice can lead one to humility that in turn provides a foundation for spiritual development (*aedificatio*), including personal growth in the Christian virtues (chapter 4). I gather together these topics by following a heuristic course of

27 I use the word "topics" in a manner similar to Aristotle in the *Rhetoric*. See Aristotle, *The "Art" of Rhetoric*, trans. John Henry Freese (Cambridge, MA: Harvard University Press, 1994). In II.22, Aristotle states that in any discourse, one must first select the elements or focal points of discourse (1396a6–8) and that the preferred mode of selection is the topical approach (1396b23–24). See also Eleonore Stump, "Dialectic in Ancient and Medieval Logic," in *Boethius's "De topicis differentiis"* (Ithaca, NY: Cornell University Press, 1978), 157–261, at 170–71.

28 Regarding the procedure of such a comparison, on one hand, Leclercq's analysis indicates that an interpreter should proceed chronologically with respect to discerning a thinker's development within the scope of any given topic (for example, Leclercq—when reflecting on the topic of free choice in Bernard's writings—proceeds from the early *Liber de gratia et libero arbitrio* to the mature *Sermones super cantica canticorum*). See also Leclercq, "General Introduction (III)," 381–82; "Psycho-history," *CSQ*, 288. Yet, on the other hand, when listing various works of Bernard in no particular chronological order, Leclercq also states "From these can be gathered his teaching" (namely, Bernard's teaching on the Holy Spirit): Leclercq, "General Introduction (III)," 391. As I organize this study according to the linear structure of the five Books of *De consideratione*, I follow this latter kind of comparative procedure when examining topics as discussed in other works of Bernard: "Not only must the text itself be questioned, but also any related or parallel texts which may help in the interpretation, taking into consideration the tradition on which they depend." Leclercq, "Psycho-history," *CSQ*, 273.

interpreting Bernard's texts that involved revisiting the same texts multiple times as Leclercq suggests.[29]

I continue this same procedure with respect to the remaining books of *De consideratione*. With respect to Book II of the work (meditation on oneself), I explore the topics of Bernard's distinction between meditation and contemplation, his emphasis on ordering the exercise of meditation toward one's religious salvation, and the topics that meditation should involve reflection on personal growth in self-knowledge, knowledge of one's human nature, as well as knowledge of one's personhood and moral character (chapter 5). In association with Book III of *De consideratione* (meditation on what is below one), I investigate the topics of stewardship and domination in relationships and, as occasioned by remarks in Bernard's text, the question regarding whether Bernard understood his prescribed exercises to comprise a Christian monastic philosophy (chapter 6). In connection with Book IV of *De consideratione* (meditation on what is around one), I examine the topics of bringing stability to one's relationships and cultivating desirable mental qualities—in other words, cultivating an undivided mind (chapter 7). Lastly, when proceeding through Book V of the work (meditation on what is above one), I again explore a number of topics that arise during Bernard's discussion, including the nature of theological meditation, meditative ascent (symbolized by Jabob's ladder), the steps of this ladder (which Bernard describes as practical and investigative), and the topic of contemplative self-recollection. I examine three kinds of belief that Bernard indicates are important for theological meditation (faith, reason, and opinion), his teaching that one should maintain an orientation toward God's unity, and lastly the topic of personal experiences of spiritual affection and prayer (chapter 8).

When seeking to understand these various topics, I frequently consult the scholarly tradition associated with *De consideratione*. My primary influence and guide in this regard is located in the numerous Bernardine studies of Leclercq, especially his essays collected in the multi-volume *Recueil d'etudes*.[30] I also draw heavily upon the insights of Bernardine scholars John D. Anderson, Jean Châtillon, Jean-Marie Déchanet, Gillian R. Evans, Elizabeth T. Kennan, and John R. Sommerfeldt. Throughout the interpretation of Bernard that is presented in the second part of this study, I frequently

29 Leclercq, for example, refers to "interviewing" hagiographical texts with respect to trying to understand the praxis of monastic prayer at Cluny. See Leclercq, "Prayer at Cluny," 662. Regarding the consolidation of themes or topics after a qualitative interview, see Steinar Kvale, *Interviews: An Introduction to Qualitative Research Interviewing* (Thousand Oaks, CA: Sage, 1996), 193–96.

30 See Jean Leclercq, *Recueil D'Études sur Saint Bernard et Ses* Écrits, 4 vols. (Rome: Edizioni di Storia e Letteratura, 1962–87).

consult the Latin critical edition of *De consideratione* as found in the *Sancti Bernardi opera*, reprinted in the Tyrolia Latin-German bilingual edition.[31]

I proceed in the third part of the study to provide a summative presentation of the overall structure of Bernard's teaching on meditation (chapter 9).[32] This summative presentation is not a theory but rather a descriptive consolidation of the various topics outlined in chapters 4–8.[33] I close the study by considering the contemporary relevance of Bernard's teaching on meditation as a program of spiritual therapy (chapter 10). His teaching is relevant not only for providers of Christian spiritual direction, but also for providers of civil psychotherapy who are assisting clients who desire the integration of Christian spirituality into the course of their therapy.[34] With respect to the three parts of this work, it is my hope that this study will interest not only theologians, medieval historians, and scholars of Bernard, as well as persons exploring Catholic spirituality in general, but also Christian spiritual directors who are interested in meditation resources, as well as civil mental health professionals who seek to integrate culturally and religiously appropriate spiritual practices into psychotherapeutic treatments for patients and clients.

31 See note above for publication documentation.

32 See, e.g., the discussion of themes being gathered into a unified pattern in Steinar Kvale, "The Qualitative Research Interview: A Phenomenological and Hermeneutical Mode of Understanding," *Journal of Phenomenological Psychology* 14, no. 2 (1983): 171–96, at 186.

33 Regarding how the abstraction of a "theory" might occur at this stage in qualitative research, see Morse, "'Emerging from the Data,'" 32–34.

34 On the integration of meditation practices into civil psychotherapy, see Kenneth I. Pargament, *Spiritually Integrated Psychotherapy: Understanding and Addressing the Sacred* (New York: Guilford Press, 2007), 87–88 and 256–59.

PART 1

A Historical Evaluation of the Treatise

1

Authorship and Historical Context

Bernard of Clairvaux (ca. 1090–1153) wrote the treatise *De consideratione* to his acquaintance Pope Eugene III (r. 1145–53).[1] It is helpful to begin an evaluation of *De consideratione* by examining the chronological events surrounding the period of Bernard's writing. This chronology will facilitate not only understanding the references that Bernard makes to contemporaneous events, but also the complexity of his setting and his relationship with Pope Eugene III. I develop this chronology primarily as a literature review that is dependent on existing historical scholarship.

The Election of Pope Eugene III

The future Pope Eugene III, Bernardo Pignatelli, met Bernard of Clairvaux at the Council of Pisa in 1135.[2] Seeking to become a Cistercian novice, Bernardo

1 For these dates, see Adriaan H. Bredero, *Bernard of Clairvaux: Between Cult and History* (Grand Rapids, MI: Eerdmans, 1996), 282–86; Brian Patrick McGuire, "Bernard's Life and Works: A Review," in *A Companion to Bernard of Clairvaux*, ed. Brian Patrick McGuire (Leiden: Brill, 2011), 18–63, at 21. For further discussion of Bernard's life, see also M. B. Pranger, "Bernard of Clairvaux: Work and Self," in *The Cambridge Companion to the Cistercian Order*, ed. Mette Birkedal Bruun (Cambridge: Cambridge University Press, 2013), 186–98; Peter Dinzelbacher, *Bernhard von Clairvaux: Leben und Werk des berühmten Zisterziensers* (Darmstadt: Wissenschaftliche Buchgesellschaft WBG, 2017); Brian Patrick McGuire, *Bernard of Clairvaux: An Inner Life* (Ithaca, NY: Cornell University Press, 2020); Bruno S. James, *Saint Bernard of Clairvaux: An Essay in Biography* (London: Hodder and Stoughton, 1957). For further discussion of Pope Eugene III, see Helmut Gleber, *Papst Eugen III (1145–1153) unter besonderer Berücksichtigung seiner politischen Tätigkeit* (Jena, Germany: Verlag von Gustav Fischer, 1936); Michael Horn, *Studien zur Geschichte Papst Eugens III (1145–1153)* (New York: Peter Lang, 1992).

2 Bredero, *Bernard of Clairvaux*, 146.

followed Bernard back to the monastery of Clairvaux[3] where he became a monk in 1138.[4] Around 1139 to 1140, Bernard sent Pignatelli to establish a new Cistercian monastery near Rome; Pignatelli eventually became abbot of Tre Fontane (also called the Abbey of Saints Vincent and Anastasius).[5] At some point between 1141 and 1145, Bernard wrote to the monks of the abbey concerning their experience of disease.[6] Around 1143, a popular revolt at Rome turned against temporal papal rule and instituted the alternative political form of a Roman commune governed by a senate.[7] When the military attempt of Pope Lucius II failed to retake Rome in February of 1145 and resulted in his violent death,[8] abbot Bernardo Pignatelli was called to assume the papal role as Eugene III.[9]

Bredero conjectures that the motive of the cardinals in selecting Bernardo was to elicit the involvement of Bernard of Clairvaux in the Roman political conflict so Bernard might exhort King Conrad III of Germany (r. 1137–52) to undertake a military campaign to help restore order.[10] Runciman notes that Eugene III also had political concerns with the

3 Thomas Merton, "Blessed Eugenius III, Abbot of Tre Fontane, Pope," *CSQ* 44, no. 2 (2009): 173–80, 176; John Anderson, "Reconsidering De consideratione: Transition from Book 1 to Book 2," *CSQ* 48, no. 2 (2013): 143–60, at 144.

4 John D. Anderson and Elizabeth T. Kennan, "Appendices," in CF 37:183–91, at 183.

5 Anderson, "Reconsidering," 144.

6 See Bernard, "Letter 388," in *The Letters of Saint Bernard of Clairvaux*, trans. Bruno Scott James (Kalamazoo, MI: Cistercian, 1998), 458–59. For a Latin edition, see Bernhard von Clairvaux, *Sämtliche Werke, lateinisch/deutsch*, Bd. III (hereafter *SW* 3), Ep 345 (Innsbruck: Tyrolia, 1992), 598–602 (SBO 8:286–88). *SW* 3 reprints the Latin for Epistles 181–547 from Bernardus Claraevallensis, *Sancti Bernardi Opera*, vol. 8, ed. J. Leclercq, C. H. Talbot, and H.-M. Rochais (Rome: Editiones Cistercienses, 1963). See also Merton, "Blessed Eugenius III," 176; Anderson, "Reconsidering," 144. Regarding Bernard's letters, Leclercq maintains that these were edited and carefully prepared with a contribution from Bernard's secretaries prior to their publication. See Leclercq, "Modern Psychology and the Interpretation," 482, citing also Jean Leclercq, "Lettres de S. Bernard: Histoire ou littérature?," *Studi Medievali* 12 (1971): 1–74, and Jean Leclercq, "Recherches sur la collection des lettres de S. Bernard," *Cahiers de Civilisation Médiévale* 14 (1971): 205–19.

7 Bredero, *Bernard of Clairvaux*, 146; Kennan, "Introduction," 10.

8 Bredero, *Bernard of Clairvaux*, 285; Kennan, "Introduction," 10.

9 Jonathan Riley-Smith, *The Crusades: A History*, 2nd ed. (New Haven, CT: Yale University Press, 2005), 121; Merton, "Blessed Eugenius III," 175; Anderson, "Reconsidering," 144. See also Arnold of Bonneval, *Vita prima*, Book II, Ch. 50 (hereafter *VP*), in William of Saint-Thierry, Arnold of Bonneval, and Geoffrey of Auxerre, *The First Life of Bernard of Clairvaux*, trans. Hilary Costello (Kalamazoo, MI: Cistercian Publications, 2015), 135 (hereafter CF 76).

10 Bredero, *Bernard of Clairvaux*, 147. For dating the reign of Conrad III, see Susan B. Edgington, "Albert of Aachen, St Bernard and the Second Crusade," in *The Second Crusade: Scope and Consequences*, ed. Jonathan Phillips and Martin Hoch (New York: Manchester University Press, 2001), 54–70, at 57.

advancement of King Roger II of Sicily.[11] The citizens of Rome immediately rejected Eugene III's temporal authority.[12] Because of this political conflict, Eugene III avoided Rome and was consecrated at the monastery of Farfa on February 18.[13] Eugene III then relocated his papal court north of Rome at Viterbo.[14]

From the outset of Eugene III's pontificate, Bernard expressed paternal solicitude concerning the new pope's well-being.[15] Bernard wrote to the College of Cardinals expressing concern with whether the pope's personal character rendered him well-prepared for the papal office.[16] Bernard also wrote to Cardinal Robert Pullen, asking Pullen to step forward in order to assist and guide Eugene III.[17] Arnold of Brescia, a former student of the philosopher Peter Abelard,[18] arrived at the papal court in Viterbo in 1145 to make peace with Pope Eugene III.[19] Yet Arnold soon began to promote the political cause of the Roman separatists, consequently exacerbating the conflict.[20] Arnold was outspoken against clerical property ownership and also developed a theological argument to support the commune's resistance of the papacy.[21] Like his teacher Abelard, Arnold incited Bernard of Clairvaux's ire; writing to Pope Innocent II around 1140, Bernard lamented: "Goliath advances tall of body, girt in the noble accoutrements of war, and preceded

11 Steven Runciman, *A History of the Crusades*, vol. 2: *The Kingdom of Jerusalem and the Frankish East 1100–1187* (New York: Cambridge University Press, 1951), 248.

12 McGuire, "Bernard's Life," 51.

13 CF 37:183.

14 Rudolf Hiestand, "The Papacy and the Second Crusade," in *The Second Crusade: Scope and Consequences*, 32–53, at 32; Riley-Smith, *The Crusades*, 121.

15 Bredero, *Bernard of Clairvaux*, 146.

16 Ep 315 (James, *Letters*, 385–86; Ep 237 in *SW* 3:266–70; *SBO* 8:113–15), See also G. R. Evans, "The *De Consideratione* of Bernard of Clairvaux: A Preliminary Letter," *Cîteaux: Commentarii Cistercienses* 35 (1984): 129–34, at 129. See also G. R. Evans, *The Mind of St. Bernard of Clairvaux* (Oxford: Oxford University Press, 1983), 201; Bredero, *Bernard of Clairvaux*, 146.

17 Ep 316 (James, *Letters*, 386–87; Ep 362 in *SW* 3:644–46; *SBO* 8:309–10); Courtney, *Cardinal Robert Pullen*, 17–19.

18 Antonio Suraci, "San Bernardo di Chiaravalle e Arnaldo da Brescia," *ASOC* 13 (1957): 83–91, 87. See also D. E. Luscombe, *The School of Peter Abelard: The Influence of Abelard's Thought in the Early Scholastic Period* (Cambridge: Cambridge University Press, 1970), 15.

19 Constant J. Mews, "The Council of Sens (1141): Abelard, Bernard, and the Fear of Social Upheaval," *Speculum* 77, no. 2 (2002): 342–82, at 376; Merton, "Blessed Eugenius III," 177.

20 Mews, "Council of Sens," 377; Merton, "Blessed Eugenius III," 178.

21 John B. Freed, *Frederick Barbarossa: The Prince and the Myth* (New Haven, CT: Yale University Press, 2016), 111–13.

by his armour-bearer, Arnold of Brescia . . . the bee that is in France has murmured to the bee in Italy, and they have joined forces against the Lord."[22]

In 1145, Bernard of Clairvaux wrote to Pope Eugene III to express concern.[23] In the letter, Bernard encourages the pope to meditate on his mortality and dwell upon the memory that he is human.[24] This letter serves as a prelude of the lengthier guidance that Bernard will later provide the pope in the treatise *De consideratione*. Bernard indicates in the preface of *De consideratione* that Eugene III may have requested that Bernard author the longer work.[25] Anderson maintains that this papal request may have been communicated to Bernard just after he wrote the shorter 1145 letter to the pope; if this is true, Bernard could have begun writing Book I of *De consideratione* as early as mid-1145.[26] However, others hypothesize that Book I may have been written after Book II in 1148.[27]

The Onset of the Second Crusade

Bernard embarked upon a preaching tour in the south of France during the summer of 1145.[28] Regarding this tour, Geoffrey of Auxerre, who had become Bernard's secretary around 1141,[29] states that Bernard had been asked by Alberic (bishop of Ostia and a former monk of Cluny) to tour the churches of the region.[30] During this summer journey, Bernard preached

22 Ep 239, §3 (James, *Letters*, 317–20, 318; Ep 189 in *SW* 3:64–72; *SBO* 8:12–16), as cited by Bernard McGinn, "St Bernard and Eschatology," in *Bernard of Clairvaux: Studies Presented to Dom Jean Leclercq* (Washington, DC: Cistercian Publications, 1973), 161–86, at 170. For dating this letter, see James, *Letters*, 545.

23 Ep 205 (James, *Letters*, 277–80; Ep 238 in *SW* 3:270–78; *SBO* 8:115–19). See also Anderson, "Reconsidering," 144.

24 Ep 205 (James, *Letters*, 280; Ep 238 in *SW* 3:270–78; *SBO* 8:115–19).

25 *Csi*, Preface (CF 37:23; *SW* 1:626; *SBO* 3:393). Excerpts of *Csi* are also translated in *The Cistercian World: Monastic Writings of the Twelfth Century*, ed. Pauline Matarasso (New York: Penguin, 1993), 84–92; Bernard of Clairvaux, *Selected Works*, trans. G. R. Evans (Mahwah, NJ: Paulist Press, 1987), 145–72.

26 Anderson, "Reconsidering," 145; Anderson, "Paul in Book 5," 137.

27 Wim Verbaal, "Bernardus Philosophus," *Revista Portuguesa de Filosofia* 60, no. 3 (2004): 567–86, at 579n51.

28 Beverly Mayne Kienzle, *Cistercians, Heresy and Crusade in Occitania, 1145–1229: Preaching in the Lord's Vineyard* (Rochester, NY: York Medieval Press, 2001), 91. See also John R. Sommerfeldt, *Bernard of Clairvaux: On the Spirituality of Relationship* (Mahwah, NJ: Newman Press, 2004), 80–81; Bredero, *Bernard of Clairvaux*, 285; Dinzelbacher, "Bernhards Leben," 40; McGuire, "Bernard's Life," 51–52; Mews, "Council of Sens," 374.

29 Mews, "Council of Sens," 369.

30 Geoffrey of Auxerre, *VP*, III, 17 (CF 76:163).

against Henry of Lausanne (also called Henry the monk) who had adopted the anti-Catholic teachings of Peter of Bruys.[31] Bernard had encountered Henry previously in 1135, when Henry was brought to charges before the Council of Pisa (where Bernard originally had met the future Pope Eugene III).[32] Deane maintains that Bernard in his summer 1145 preaching campaign against Henry was successful at Albi, but met resistance to the southwest in Toulouse.[33]

A subsequent and lengthier preoccupation soon engaged Bernard with the advent of the second crusade.[34] Historians at times disagree over the precise sequence of events, depending upon whether attention is given primarily to the chronicle of Otto of Freising (*Gesta Friderici primi imperatoris*) or to Odo of Deuil (*De profectione Ludovici septimi in orientem*).[35] Otto was a Cistercian bishop and historian present at Viterbo with Eugene III.[36] As recounted in his *Gesta* and reaffirmed in William of Tyre's *Historia* (ca. 1183), Otto was a half-brother of Conrad III who accompanied the Teutonic king during the second crusade.[37] Meanwhile, Odo was a Benedictine monk of

31 Kienzle, *Cistercians, Heresy and Crusade*, 91. See also Sommerfeldt, *Spirituality of Relationship*, 80–81; Bredero, *Bernard of Clairvaux*, 285; Dinzelbacher, "Bernhards Leben," 40; McGuire, "Bernard's Life," 51–52; Mews, "Council of Sens," 374.

32 Kienzle, *Cistercians, Heresy, and Crusade*, 91.

33 Jennifer Kolpacoff Deane, *A History of Medieval Heresy and Inquisition* (Lanham, MD: Rowman and Littlefield, 2011), 49.

34 See also Marco Meschini, *San Bernardo e la Seconda Crociata* (Milan: Mursia, 1998).

35 Regarding this observation, see George Ferzoco, "The Origin of the Second Crusade," in *The Second Crusade and the Cistercians*, ed. M. Gervers (New York: St. Martin's Press, 1992), 91–99, at 92. For Otto, see Otto of Freising, *The Deeds of Frederick Barbarossa*, trans. Charles Christopher Mierow (New York: Columbia University Press, 2004). For Odo, see Odo of Deuil, *De profectione Ludovici VII in orientem: The Journey of Louis the Seventh to the East*, trans. V. G. Berry (New York: Norton, 1948). A portion of Berry's translation is reproduced in *The Crusades: A Reader*, 2nd ed., ed. S. J. Allen and Emilie Amt (Toronto: University of Toronto, 2014), 135–40.

36 On Otto, see Karl F. Morrison, "Otto of Freising's Quest for the Hermeneutic Circle," *Speculum* 55, no. 2 (1980): 207–36.

37 On William, see William of Tyre, *A History of Deeds Done Beyond the Sea*, vol. 1, trans. Emily Atwater Babcock and A. C. Krey (New York: Columbia University Press, 1943), esp. 184. For dating William's *Historia*, see A. C. Krey, "William of Tyre: The Making of an Historian in the Middle Ages," *Speculum* 16, no. 2 (1941): 149–66, at 160.

St. Denis appointed as a chronicler of the crusade by Abbot Suger of Saint-Denis.[38] Odo's account understandably favors King Louis VII.[39]

The second crusade was initiated in response to the capture of Edessa by Muslim armies in December 1144.[40] Drawing on the testimony of Cistercian bishop and historian Otto of Freising, Hiestand notes that messengers from the east arrived at the papal court in Viterbo in mid-November 1145 seeking assistance.[41] On December 1, 1145, Pope Eugene III then issued the bull *Quantum praedecessores* to Louis VII, calling for crusaders and providing the incentive of an indulgence.[42] Odo remarks that Louis VII expressed his interest in embarking on the crusade that Christmas at court in Bourges and sent messengers to communicate his desire to Eugene III.[43] Yet locally Louis VII encountered a tepid response from the French nobility concerning such a campaign.[44]

The pope also continued to strive with political unrest in Rome; Bernard wrote to the Roman citizens, chastising their treatment of the new pope.[45] By this time, Arnold of Brescia had assumed a position of leadership among the Roman separatists.[46] According to Odo, while Eugene III "wished per-

38 On Odo, see Henry Mayr-Harting, "Odo of Deuil, the Second Crusade, and the Monastery of Saint-Denis," in *Culture of Christendom: Essays in Medieval History in Memory of Denis L. T. Bethel*, ed. Marc A. Meyer (Rio Grande, Ohio: Hambledon Press, 1993), 225–40. See also Allen and Amt, *The Crusades: A Reader*, 135.

39 For a critique of Odo, see Giles Constable, "The Second Crusade as Seen by Contemporaries," *Traditio* 9 (1953): 213–79, at 217–18. See also Runciman, *A History of the Crusades*, 274. On Louis VII, see *Louis VII and His World*, ed. Michael L. Bardot and Laurence W. Marvin (Leiden: Brill, 2018); Aryeh Graboïs, "The Crusade of King Louis VII: A Reconsideration," in *Crusade and Settlement: Papers Read at the First Conference of the Society for the Study of the Crusades and the Latin East*, ed. Peter W. Edbury (Cardiff: University College Cardiff Press, 1985), 95–104.

40 Evans, *Mind of St. Bernard*, 30; See Jonathan Phillips, *The Second Crusade: Extending the Frontiers of Christendom* (New Haven, CT: Yale University Press, 2007), 38.

41 Hiestand, "The Papacy and the Second Crusade," 33 and 35, citing Otto of Freising, *Chronica*, ed. Adolf Hofmeister (Darmstadt, 1960), 554–56.

42 Phillips, *The Second Crusade*, 37–60 and 280–82; G. R. Evans, *Bernard of Clairvaux* (Oxford: Oxford University Press, 2000), 16; Riley-Smith, *The Crusades*, 121; John R. Sommerfeldt, "The Bernardine Reform and the Crusading Spirit," *The Catholic Historical Review* 86, no. 4 (2000): 567–78, at 567.

43 Odo of Deuil, *De profectione Ludovici VII* (Allen and Amt, 136).

44 Virginia G. Berry, "The Second Crusade," in *A History of the Crusades, Vol. 1: The First Hundred Years*, ed. Marshall W. Baldwin (Madison: University of Wisconsin Press, 1969), 463–512, at 469; Runciman, *A History of the Crusades*, 252.

45 Ep 319 (James, *Letters*, 391–94; Ep 243 in *SW* 3:300–308; *SBO* 8:130–34).

46 Evans, *Mind of St. Bernard*, xiv. See also McGuire, "Bernard's Life," 52; Elizabeth Kennan, "The 'De consideratione' of St. Bernard of Clairvaux and the Papacy in the Mid-Twelfth Century: A Review of Scholarship," *Traditio* 23 (1967): 73–115, at 111.

sonally to give the initial blessing" to the crusade, he was impeded by this Roman conflict.[47] Bernard soon became involved in the crusading effort.[48] Some scholars claim that like the French nobility Bernard's initial reception of Eugene III's proposal was "lukewarm."[49] Apart from his preaching tour to the south of France in the summer of 1145, Bernard's biographer Geoffrey gives his readers the impression that Bernard had no interest in leaving the monastery during this period.[50] Bernard had previously confided to Peter the Venerable, Benedictine abbot of Cluny, that Bernard did not desire to leave Clairvaux at all aside from attending the annual chapter of Cistercian abbots at Cîteaux.[51] Yet Bernard acquiesced to Eugene III's request.[52] His eventual acceptance to undertake another preaching tour to promote the crusade would be instrumental in garnering support for the campaign. Bernard had been prepared for this task of widespread travel by his previous campaigning throughout France and Italy to support the legitimacy of Pope Innocent II (r. 1130–38).[53]

Promoting the Second Crusade

In March 1146, Eugene III re-promulgated *Quantum praedecessores*.[54] Perhaps inspired by Louis VII,[55] Bernard agreed to preach on March 31 in favor of the crusade before a large crowd at Vézelay in Burgundy.[56] Bernard is reported as distributing crosses to be worn by the aspiring crusaders in order that they might signify their work as one of pilgrimage.[57] Abbot Suger names in

47 Odo of Deuil, *De profectione Ludovici VII* (Allen and Amt, 136).

48 Runciman, *A History of the Crusades*, 252.

49 McGinn, "Bernard and Eschatology," 182, citing Fritz Radcke, *Die eschatologische Anschauungen Bernhards von Clairvaux* (Greifswald, 1915).

50 Geoffrey of Auxerre, *VP*, III, 8–9 (CF 76:154–55).

51 Ep 305 (James, *Letters*, 374–77, at 375; Ep 228 in *SW* 3:236–40; *SBO* 8:98–100). See also *The Cistercian World* (ed. Matarasso), 16.

52 Geoffrey of Auxerre, *VP*, III, 8–9 (CF 76:154–55).

53 McGuire, "Bernard's Life," 40; *The Cistercian World* (ed. Matarasso), 15.

54 Evans, *Bernard of Clairvaux*, 16.

55 McGinn, "Bernard and Eschatology," 182.

56 Geoffrey of Auxerre, *VP*, III, 9 (CF 76:155). See also Constable, "The Second Crusade," 239 and 244; Riley-Smith, *The Crusades*, 122; Evans, *Mind of St. Bernard*, 33; Bredero, *Bernard of Clairvaux*, 285; McGuire, "Bernard's Life," 53. On Louis VII convening the assembly at Vézelay, see Frank McMinn Chambers, "Some Legends concerning Eleanor of Aquitaine," *Speculum* 16, no. 4 (1941): 459–69, at 459.

57 Constable, "The Second Crusade," 239–40.

detail the members of the French nobility who committed to the campaign at that time.[58] Yet a year of military preparation would be needed in order adequately to develop the campaign and increase the number of committed crusaders.[59]

Bernard then traveled throughout France promoting the crusade.[60] Sommerfeldt, following Katzir, argues that Bernard's intention in this regard was to promote the crusade not merely as a military campaign but also and primarily as a spiritual campaign of ecclesiastical reform.[61] Constable also calls attention to the historical perspective that "Bernard's view of the crusade" should be interpreted as promoting "a pilgrimage undertaken by each crusader for the welfare of his soul."[62] If this is true, Bernard's understanding was not without cognizance of military realities. For example, Bernard sent a letter in August or September 1146 to "the people of England"[63] and also to all the clergy and peoples of eastern France and Bavaria that encouraged participation in the crusade.[64]

In this letter, one encounters the rhetorical character that Bernard's preaching would have had at the time. Bernard's thought process seems to be that if non-Christian peoples are politically subject to Christian rule, then they should not be bothered and Christians should wait for their religious conversion: "But as they have now begun to attack us, it is necessary for those of us who do not carry a sword in vain to repel them with force."[65] This response, Bernard argues, has in turn soteriological benefit for the crusaders:

58 Abbot Suger of Saint-Denis, "The Illustrious King Louis [VII], Son of Louis [VI]," in *Selected Works of Abbot Suger of Saint-Denis*, ed. and trans. Richard Cusimano and Eric Whitmore (Washington, DC: The Catholic University of America Press, 2018), 127–83, at 140.

59 Berry, "The Second Crusade," 469.

60 McGuire, "Bernard's Life," 53.

61 Sommerfeldt, "Bernardine Reform," 569, citing Yael Katzir, "The Second Crusade and the Redefinition of *Ecclesia, Christianitas*, and Papal Coercive Power," in *The Second Crusade and the Cistercians*, 3–11, at 8. See also Hans-Dietrich Kahl, "Crusade Eschatology as Seen by St. Bernard in the Years 1146 to 1148," in *The Second Crusade and the Cistercians*, 35–48; Bernard Flood, "St Bernard's View of Crusade," *The Australasian Catholic Record* 47 (1970): 130–43.

62 Giles Constable, "A Report of a Lost Sermon by St Bernard on the Failure of the Second Crusade," in *Studies in Medieval Cistercian History: Presented to Jeremiah F. O'Sullivan*, ed. M. Basil Pennington (Shannon: Irish University Press, 1971), 49–54, at 50 (hereafter CS 13).

63 Ep 391 (James, *Letters*, 460–63; for the Latin, see the French-Bavarian version—Ep 363 in *SW* 3:648–60; *SBO* 8:311–17). See also Constable, "The Second Crusade," 247.

64 Ep 363 in *SW* 3:648–60; *SBO* 8:311–17. The date is found in James, *Letters*, 549. See also Jean Leclercq, "L'Encyclique de Saint Bernard en Faveur de la Croisade," in *Recueil D'Études sur Saint Bernard et Ses* Écrits (Rome: Edizioni di Storia e Letteratura, 1987), 4:227–46.

65 Ep 391, §6 (James, *Letters*, 463; Ep 363, §7, in *SW* 3:660; *SBO* 8:317). See also Ernst-Dieter Hehl, "War, Peace and the Christian Order," in *The New Cambridge Medieval History, IV, c.1024–c.1198,*

"I tell you that 'God is trying you' . . . God has pity on his people and on those who have grievously fallen away and has prepared for them a means of salvation."[66] God, Bernard explains to his readers, "puts himself in your debt so that, in return for your taking up arms in his cause, he can reward you with pardon for your sins and everlasting glory. I call blessed the generation that can seize an opportunity of such rich indulgence as this, blessed to be alive in this year of jubilee, this year of God's choice."[67] In another letter authored later to Abbot Suger, Bernard again indicates that he believes the crusade was a campaign providentially ordained by God.[68]

Part of Bernard's preaching efforts during the summer of 1146 aimed to neutralize the anti-Semitic exhortations of a different Cistercian monk who had been preaching in favor of the crusade in parallel to Bernard.[69] Bernard's concern that the crusade might occasion the perceived legitimacy of anti-Semitic violence is indicated also in the same letter he sent to the English people and the peoples of eastern France and Bavaria.[70] Likely referring to the preaching of the other Cistercian monk, Bernard warns his readers "not to believe every spirit" and urges that "the Jews are not to be persecuted, killed or even put to flight."[71] He then presents a biblical argument for this exhortation that indicates that he has had to give some thought into how to counter the theological content found in the anti-Semitic preaching.

Expending a significant personal investment of time and energy, Bernard promoted the crusade from November 1146 to February 1147 throughout France, Flanders, and Germany.[72] In November, Bernard traveled to Frankfurt to exhort King Conrad III of Germany to join Louis VII in the crusade.[73] Conrad III initially did not agree; Sommerfeldt suggests that his

---

Part 1, ed. David Luscombe and Jonathan Riley-Smith (New York: Cambridge University Press, 2004), 185–228, at 211.

66 Ep 391, §3 (James, *Letters*, 461; Ep 363, §3, in *SW* 3:652; *SBO* 8:313), quoting Dt 13:3.

67 Ep 391, §3 (James, *Letters*, 462; Ep 363, §4, in *SW* 3:654; *SBO* 8:314).

68 Ep 404 (James, *Letters*, 475–76; Ep 377 in *SW* 3:706–8; *SBO* 8:340–41).

69 Ep 393 (James, *Letters*, 465–66; Ep 365 in *SW* 3:666–70; *SBO* 8:320–22). See also McGuire, "Bernard's Life," 53; Watkin Williams, *Saint Bernard of Clairvaux* (Manchester: Manchester University Press, 1952), 266–67.

70 Ep 391, §6 (James, *Letters*, 462; Ep 363, §6, in *SW* 3:658; *SBO* 8:316).

71 Ibid.

72 Phillips, *Second Crusade: Extending the Frontiers*, 81; Dinzelbacher, "Bernhards Leben," 41; Kennan, "Introduction," 9; Anderson, "Reconsidering," 146. See also Jonathan Phillips, "The Murder of Charles the Good and the Second Crusade: Household, Nobility, and Traditions of Crusading in Medieval Flanders," *Medieval Prosopography* 19 (1998): 55–75, at 63.

73 Riley-Smith, *The Crusades*, 123; Phillips, *Second Crusade: Extending the Frontiers*, 87; Dinzelbacher, "Bernhards Leben," 41.

reluctance was due to contending with conflict within his own household.[74] In December, Bernard continued to preach in promotion of the crusade throughout Germany—Freiburg, Basel, Schaffhausen, and Constance.[75] Bernard's efforts in the region seemingly caught the attention of Benedictine mystic Hildegard von Bingen in Disibodenberg.[76] In a letter to Bernard, Hildegard remarks: "In your intense zeal and burning love for the Son of God, [you] gather men into Christ's army to fight under the banner of the cross."[77] Bernard traveled back to Speyer at the end of December.[78] Conrad III at this point had a change of heart.[79] Some ascribe this change to Bernard,[80] whereas others argue that Conrad III's reversal was due to the influence of Louis VII.[81]

Bernard continued promoting the crusade in early 1147,[82] proceeding northwest to Cologne, then making his return to France where he met Louis VII at Châlons-sur-Marne.[83] Berry states that Bernard next reported to the French nobility gathered at Étampes on February 16 and then returned to Frankfurt for a diet on March 13.[84] Meanwhile, Pope Eugene III left Viterbo with numerous cardinals and traveled northward to cross the Alps to support the crusaders who would soon depart under Louis VII.[85] At the Frankfurt Diet with Bernard present, some parties proposed a supplemental crusade

74 Sommerfeldt, "Bernardine Reform," 568. See also Runciman, *A History of the Crusades*, 255.

75 Phillips, *Second Crusade: Extending the Frontiers*, 93–94. For Bernard's preaching locations, see Runciman, *A History of the Crusades*, 255.

76 Miriam Rita Tessera, "Philip of Flanders and Hildegard of Bingen: Crusading against the Saracens or Crusading against Deadly Sin?," in *Gendering the Crusades*, ed. Susan B. Edgington and Sarah Lambert (New York: Columbia University Press, 2002), 77–93, at 83, citing Hildegardis Bingensis, *Epistolarium*, Ep. I, §3, ed. L. van Acker, Corpus Christianorum Continuatio Mediaevalis (hereafter CCCM) 91 (Turnhout: Brepols, 1991).

77 Hildegard of Bingen, "Letter 1 to Bernard of Clairvaux," in Joseph L. Baird, *The Personal Correspondence of Hildegard of Bingen* (Oxford: Oxford University Press, 2006), 17–20, at 17.

78 Berry, "The Second Crusade," 474.

79 Constable, "The Second Crusade," 244; Phillips, *Second Crusade: Extending the Frontiers*, 95–96.

80 Berry, "The Second Crusade," 474. See also Jay T. Lees, "The Wenden Crusade and Exile to Havelberg 1145–1152," in *Anselm of Havelberg: Deeds into Words in the Twelfth Century* (Leiden: Brill, 1998), 70–97, at 74.

81 John M. Riddle, *A History of the Middle Ages, 300–1500* (Lanham, MD: Rowman and Littlefield, 2008), 298.

82 Phillips, *Second Crusade: Extending the Frontiers*, 97; McGuire, "Bernard's Life," 54.

83 Berry, "The Second Crusade," 477.

84 Ibid., 477–78.

85 Hiestand, "The Papacy and the Second Crusade," 41; Phillips, *Second Crusade: Extending the Frontiers*, 97.

against the Wends east of Saxony.[86] Constable suggests that the proposal originated from the Saxon nobility.[87] After the Frankfurt assembly, Bernard wrote an open letter endorsing this supplemental Wendish crusade.[88] Berry states that the content of the letter is "puzzling" on the part of Bernard because Bernard did not first confer with the pope and Bernard would not arrogate to himself the authority to confer crusader indulgences as the letter states.[89] For this reason, Constable, disagreeing with multiple other historians, argues that Bernard only issued the letter later, after consulting with Eugene III.[90] Regarding when such a consultation may have occurred, Hiestand maintains that the pope's entourage arrived at Cluny on March 26 and, after the pope met Louis VII at Dijon on March 30,[91] Eugene III then met with Bernard at Clairvaux in early April.[92] Between the meetings at Dijon and Clairvaux, the pope could have been informed of the proposal for a Wendish crusade. Eugene III confirmed the Wendish campaign from Troyes on April

86 Berry, "The Second Crusade," 479 and 492–93, also citing Helmod, Priest of Bosau, *Chronicle of the Slavs*, trans. Francis Joseph Tschan (New York: Octagon Books, 1966).

87 Constable, "The Second Crusade," 257; Lees, "The Wenden Crusade," 75–76.

88 Ep 394 (James, *Letters*, 466–68; Ep 457 in *SW* 3:890–92; *SBO* 8:432–33). Bernard writes: "The evil one . . . He has raised up evil seed, wicked pagan sons, whom, if I may say so, the might of Christendom has endured so long . . . at the council of the king, bishops, and princes who had come together at Frankfort, the might of Christians was armed against them, and that for the complete wiping out or, at any rate, the conversion of these peoples, they have put on the Cross, the sign of our salvation; and we, by virtue of our authority, promised them the same spiritual privileges as those enjoy who set out towards Jerusalem" (James, *Letters*, 467). Constable reports that similar language regarding some kind of forced conversion of the Wends may be found in other contemporaneous historical sources (Constable, "The Second Crusade," 224). McGinn, citing Ep 467 (he may mean Ep 457 as Ep 467 is not extant—see also *SW* 3:920; *SBO* 8:447), believes that Bernard adopted an "eschatological perspective" at this time that influenced his consent to the campaign against the Wends. See McGinn, "Bernard and Eschatology," 183. Lees notes two different interpretations of Bernard's reference to the conversion or destruction of the Wends, a literal interpretation and a figurative interpretation where Bernard is only referring to their national identity. See Lees, "The Wenden Crusade," 76n20. Regarding the literal interpretation, Lees cites Helmut Beumann, "Kreuzzugsgedanke und Ostpolitik im hohen Mittelalter," *Historisches Jahrbuch* 72 (1953): 112–32, at 125–27. Regarding the figurative interpretation, Lees cites: Friedrich Lotter, *Die Konzeption des Wendenkreuzzugs* (Sigmarigen: Jan Thorbecke Verlag, 1977). For other sources on this topic, see also Riley-Smith, *The Crusades*, 123; Mihai Dragnea, *The Wendish Crusade, 1147: The Development of Crusading Ideology in the Twelfth Century* (New York: Routledge, 2020), 5.

89 Berry, "The Second Crusade," 479n15; Lees, "The Wenden Crusade," 76.

90 Constable, "The Second Crusade," 256n222.

91 Hiestand, "The Papacy and the Second Crusade," 41.

92 Bredero, *Bernard of Clairvaux*, 285; Evans, *Mind of St. Bernard*, xiv; Riley-Smith, *The Crusades*, 123; Dinzelbacher, "Bernhards Leben," 41; Anderson, "Reconsidering," 144.

11 by issuing *Divina dispensatione*[93] and appointing Anselm of Havelberg to accompany the campaign as his papal representative.[94]

Declining an invitation to Strasbourg on Good Friday (April 18),[95] Eugene III traveled instead to Paris around Easter, attending a general chapter of the Knights Templar[96] and spending Easter itself at Saint-Denis with Abbot Suger.[97] The pope remained at the court of Louis VII for over two months until the French armies departed.[98] Louis VII and Eugene III were together at Saint-Denis on June 11 after which time the king himself departed for the east.[99] Louis VII installed Abbot Suger as his regent in his absence; Wibald of Stablo was similarly appointed by Conrad III.[100] Eugene III remained in northern Europe; according to Hiestand, his purpose was to support Abbot Suger and Wibald during the absence of the kings.[101]

These numerous historical details are noteworthy in that Bernard at times accompanied Eugene III and his entourage in their travels.[102] Evans, for example, reports that they were present together in Paris.[103] This close proximity gave Bernard ample opportunity to observe the pope's affairs and personal characteristics.[104] These observations will inform Bernard's recommendations that he will later communicate to the pope in *De consideratione*.

Some historians allege that Bernard's efforts in promoting the crusade gave rise to an unexpected outcome when a contingent of seafaring crusaders from England and Flanders landed in Portugal; the crusaders were pulled into the military campaign of Alfonso I, who sought to expel the Saracens from the Iberian Peninsula.[105] This detour culminated with the siege of

93 Riley-Smith, *The Crusades*, 124; Phillips, *The Second Crusade*, 134.

94 Berry, "The Second Crusade," 479. See also Lees, "The Wenden Crusade," 75–76; Pegatha Taylor, "Moral Agency in Crusade and Colonization: Anselm of Havelberg and the Wendish Crusade of 1147," *The International Review of History* 22, no. 4 (2000): 757–84.

95 Hiestand, "The Papacy and the Second Crusade," 41.

96 Ibid., 40. See also Anna Silvas, *Jutta and Hildegard: The Biographical Sources* (University Park: Pennsylvania State University Press, 1999), 142n53.

97 Berry, "The Second Crusade," 479.

98 Allen and Amt, *The Crusades: A Reader*, 135; Hiestand, "The Papacy and the Second Crusade," 41.

99 Hiestand, "The Papacy and the Second Crusade," 41.

100 Ibid., 39.

101 Ibid., 42.

102 Bredero, *Bernard of Clairvaux*, 147; Anderson, "Reconsidering," 146.

103 Evans, *Mind of St. Bernard*, xiv.

104 Bredero, *Bernard of Clairvaux*, 147; Anderson, "Reconsidering," 146.

105 Edgington, "Albert of Aachen, St Bernard," 60; Berry, "The Second Crusade," 482.

Lisbon in October 1147.[106] Other historians argue that this outcome was expected and part of Bernard's original intention.[107] Still other authors affirm the viewpoint that these crusaders were sidetracked.[108] Bernard does indicate having cognizance of this military effort as expressed in a letter (possibly spurious) sent to King Alfonso I of Portugal, where Bernard refers to having received and responded to a previous communication from the king delivered by means of Pedro, the king's brother.[109] This document, assuming its veracity, attests to Bernard's openness to expanding the crusade beyond a focus on the Latin East, consistent with the letter ascribed to him pertaining to the Wends.

The Outcome of the Second Crusade

After the siege of Lisbon, Eugene III spent November 1147 to February 1148 in Trier.[110] Silvas maintains that a council was held at this location to implement the promulgations of the ecumenical Council of Lateran (1139).[111] According to Hildegard's biographers in the *Vita Sanctae Hildegardis*, Bernard was present at Trier at this time when Pope Eugene III read aloud from Hildegard's writings that had previously been acquired from her at Disibodenberg by papal emissaries.[112] Bernard, according to the biographer, persuaded the pope to accept and encourage the dissemination of her writings.[113]

106 Berry, "The Second Crusade," 482. See also Giles Constable, "A Note on the Route of the Anglo-Flemish Crusaders of 1147," *Speculum* 28, no. 3 (1953): 525–26, citing Osbernus (Osbert of Bawdsey), *De expugnatione Lyxbonensi: The Conquest of Lisbon*, trans. Charles W. David (New York: Columbia University Press, 1936).

107 See Jonathan Phillips, "St Bernard of Clairvaux, the Low Countries, and the Lisbon Letter of the Second Crusade," *The Journal of Ecclesiastical History* 48, no. 3 (1997): 485–97. Regarding this Letter, see Susan B. Edgington, "The Lisbon Letter of the Second Crusade," *Historical Research* 69, no. 170 (1996): 328–39; Edgington, "Albert of Aachen, St Bernard," 61–67.

108 Alan Forey, "The Siege of Lisbon and the Second Crusade," *Portuguese Studies* 20 (2004): 1–13, at 1.

109 Ep 397 (James, *Letters*, 469; Ep 308 in *SW* 3:496; *SBO* 8:228). That the letter might be apocryphal, see James, *Letters*, 549.

110 Hiestand, "The Papacy and the Second Crusade," 42; Silvas, *Jutta and Hildegard*, 142n53.

111 Silvas, *Jutta and Hildegard*, 142n53. Silvas must have in mind Lateran II, convened April 4, 1139. See Norman P. Tanner, *Decrees of the Ecumenical Councils* (Washington, DC: Georgetown University Press, 1990), 1:93–203; Heinrich Denzinger, *Enchiridion symbolorum*, 43rd ed., ed. Peter Hunermann (San Francisco, Ignatius Press, 2012), §715–§718 (240–42).

112 *The Life of Hildegard* I.4, in Silvas, *Jutta and Hildegard*, 118–210, at 143. See also Gottfried and Theodoric, *The Life of the Holy Hildegard* (Collegeville, MN: Liturgical Press, 1995).

113 *The Life of Hildegard* I.4, in Silvas, *Jutta and Hildegard*, 144.

From Trier, Eugene III next moved his party to Reims where he was again joined by Bernard (accompanied by Peter Lombard and Robert of Melun) for the purpose of evaluating the Trinitarian doctrine of Bishop Gilbert of Poitiers.[114] Regarding the Council of Reims, convened March 21 through April 7, 1148,[115] Geoffrey writes: "In the council in the city of Reims, which Pope Eugene attended, there was a conflict between Bernard, that notable wrestler, and Gilbert de la Porée for the holy church. After Bernard clearly revealed all the mockery that obscured the errors, he then with indisputable logic and the testimony of the holy fathers demolished them in a disputation that went on for two days."[116] Bernard reports that Gilbert's remarks on the Trinity found in Gilbert's commentary on Boethius's *De Trinitate* were condemned by the pope and bishops at the council.[117] However, according to Häring, "No official records of the trial were written down and, as far as the successor of St. Peter was concerned, the case was closed."[118] Bredero asserts that Bernard's campaign against Gilbert was controversial and resulted in "tension between [Bernard] and some members of the Curia."[119]

After the Council of Reims, Bernard remained with the pope and they again spent some time together.[120] During this occasion, Bernard would have observed more of the pope's affairs and responsibilities. In the summer of 1148, just prior to the passing of Bernard's friend William of St. Thierry in September,[121] the pope returned to Italy, taking up residence again at Viterbo, where he enacted the excommunication of Arnold of Brescia.[122] During this

114 R. W. Southern, *Scholastic Humanism and the Unification of Europe, Volume II, The Heroic Age* (Malden, MA: Blackwell, 2001), 128–30. See also Dinzelbacher, "Bernhards Leben," 41; Merton, "Blessed Eugenius III," 179.

115 Silvas, *Jutta and Hildegard*, 142n53.

116 Geoffrey of Auxerre, *VP*, III, 15 (CF 76:161).

117 Bernard of Clairvaux, "Sermon 80," 4.8, in *On the Song of Songs Vol. IV, Sermons 67–86* (hereafter *SCC*), trans. Irene Edmonds (Kalamazoo, MI: Cistercian, 1980), 153–54 (hereafter CF 40). For a Latin edition, see Bernhard von Clairvaux, *Sämtliche Werke, lateinisch/deutsch*, Bd. VI (hereafter *SW* 6) (Innsbruck: Tyrolia, 1994), 568–81, at 578. *SW* 6 contains *SCC*, 39–86, and reprints the Latin from Bernardus Claraevallensis, *Sancti Bernardi Opera*, vol. 2 (hereafter *SBO* 2), ed. J. Leclercq, C. H. Talbot, and H.-M. Rochais (Rome: Editiones Cistercienses, 1958), 277–83, at 282. Also see Jean Leclercq, "Introduction to Saint Bernard's Doctrine in the Sermons on the Song of Songs," *CSQ* 43, no. 3 (2008): 309–25.

118 *The Commentaries on Boethius by Gilbert of Poitiers*, ed. Nikolaus M. Häring (Toronto: Pontifical Institute of Mediaeval Studies, 1966), 3. See also Nikolaus M. Häring, "The Case of Gilbert de la Porrée, Bishop of Poitiers (1142–1154)," *Mediaeval Studies* 13 (1951): 1–40.

119 Bredero, *Bernard of Clairvaux*, 147.

120 McGuire, "Bernard's Life," 57; Evans, *Mind of St. Bernard*, xv.

121 CS 105:69.

122 Evans, *Bernard of Clairvaux*, 18; Merton, "Blessed Eugenius III," 178.

time (1148–49), Eugene III began to develop an interest in returning to Rome, moving closer in order to reside in Tusculum.[123] He may have been considering a military plan to reenter Rome with the assistance of Roger II of Sicily.[124]

In contrast with Anderson's proposal mentioned above (namely, that Bernard began to write *De consideratione* in mid-1145 in response to a request from Eugene III), Bredero maintains that it was at this time (1148) that Bernard was moved to write Book I of *De consideratione* as a result of the time he spent with the pope after the Council of Reims.[125] It is possible that during this interaction, Bernard learned firsthand of Eugene III's ambitions to engage Rome in a military campaign. Yet Anderson notes that Bernard's style in this first book is without urgency,[126] whereas in Book II the rhetorical style becomes more insistent.[127] As a further opinion, an anonymous translator of *De consideratione* observes that Nicholas of Montiéramey, in a letter to Peter Venerable in 1149, wrote that Bernard had just completed Book I.[128] Whatever the case may be, it is clear that Bernard's authorship of Book I of *De consideratione* predates the summer of 1149 because Bernard makes no reference in Book I to the outcome of the second crusade (whereas Bernard calls specific attention to this outcome at the beginning of Book II).[129]

In 1148–49, the military efforts of the crusaders in the Latin East met defeat.[130] As recounted by William of Tyre, King Baldwin III of Jerusalem (1143–63) and his mother Melisende convened a council at Acre on June 24, 1148, with the crusaders, on the coast north of Jerusalem, where an agreement was reached to attack Damascus.[131] Yet the siege of Damascus was a

123 Kennan, "Bernard of Clairvaux and the Papacy," 109.

124 Elizabeth Kennan, "Antithesis and Argument in the *De Consideratione*," in *Bernard of Clairvaux: Studies Presented to Dom Jean Leclercq*, 91–109, at 102. See also Kennan, "Bernard of Clairvaux and the Papacy," 86 and 111; *The Oxford History of Medieval Europe*, ed. George Holmes (Oxford: Oxford University Press, 1988), 199.

125 Bredero, *Bernard of Clairvaux*, 147.

126 Anderson, "Reconsidering," 145.

127 See Bernard Jacqueline, "Le Pape et les Romains d'après le *De consideratione ad Eugenium papam* de saint Bernard de Clairvaux," *L'Année Canonique* 17 (1973): 603–14.

128 See *St. Bernard's Treatise on Consideration*, trans. A Priest of Mount Melleray (Dublin: Browne and Nolan, 1921), xi; CF 37:184.

129 Kennan, "Introduction," 13; *Csi*, II, 1.1–4 (CF 37:47–52; *SW* 1:660–66; *SBO* 3:410–13). See also Evans, *Bernard of Clairvaux*, 17.

130 W. R. Taylor, "A New Syriac Fragment Dealing with Incidents in the Second Crusade," *The Annual of the American Schools of Oriental Research* 11 (1929–30): 120–30, at 121.

131 Runciman, *A History of the Crusades*, 280; Berry, "The Second Crusade," 506. See also William of Tyre, *History of Deeds Done*, Book XVI (Babcock and Krey, 1:184–86).

failure.[132] Some historians maintain that the crusader army at that point was too small to be effective, reduced in size by battles en route.[133] After the failure at Damascus, the party of Louis VII remained in Jerusalem while Conrad III's party left Acre on September 8, proceeding first to the Byzantine court in Constantinople, then embarking on the journey back to Germany in February 1149.[134] According to Berry, Louis VII was moved to remain in Jerusalem out of concern for the Church in the Latin East.[135] Abbot Suger was unable to exhort Louis VII via letters to return in haste.[136] It may have been during this period that Bernard wrote to Suger to support him in his regency.[137] It is more certain that Bernard wrote to Suger in the early part of the year to express disapproval of the behavior of some of the French nobility who had returned from the crusade before Louis VII.[138] Conrad III's party arrived home in May 1149[139] and Louis VII was back in France by November.[140]

Learning of the outcome of the crusade to the Latin East seems to have motivated Bernard's continuation in writing *De consideratione*.[141] McGuire thus locates the authorship of Book II to 1149 and the next three books between 1150 and 1153.[142] From the first pages of Book II, it is evident that Bernard judged that he had to speak to the reality of the failed crusade although he continued to describe it as a campaign ordained by God: "We rushed into this, not aimlessly but at your command, or rather, through you at God's command. Why, therefore, did we fast and he fail to notice; why did we humble our souls and he ignore us?"[143] This passage supports Constable's

132 Allen and Amt, *The Crusades: A Reader*, 135.

133 Ibid.

134 Runciman, *A History of the Crusades*, 285.

135 Berry, "The Second Crusade," 511.

136 Runciman, *A History of the Crusades*, 285.

137 See Ep 403 and 404 (James, *Letters*, 475–76; Ep 370 and Ep 377 in *SW* 3:684 and 706–8; *SBO* 8:329 and 340–41). James dates these letters to Autumn 1148 and Spring 1149 respectively. See James, *Letters*, 550.

138 Ep 405 (James, *Letters*, 476–77; Ep 376 in *SW* 3:704–6; *SBO* 8:339–40).

139 Timothy Reuter, "The 'non-crusade' of 1149–50," in *The Second Crusade: Scope and Consequences*, 150–63, at 153.

140 Reuter, "The 'non-crusade' of 1149–50," 155.

141 McGuire, "Bernard's Life," 58; Anderson, "Reconsidering," 146.

142 McGuire, "Bernard's Life," 58. See also Evans, *Mind of St. Bernard*, 205.

143 *Csi*, II, 1.1 (CF 37:48; *SW* 1:662; *SBO* 3:411). See also Ferzoco, "Origin of the Second Crusade," 97.

impression that Bernard was "deeply troubled" by the failure of the crusade.[144] The more limited military success of the Spanish crusade in Catalonia does not seem to factor into his thinking.[145]

Despite the defeat in the Latin East, there was interest in resuming the military attempt: according to Berry, Louis VII proposed a renewal of the crusade to Pope Eugene III upon his return to France.[146] The prospect of a renewed military attempt was discussed at two and perhaps three meetings in France; on May 7, 1150, Bernard himself was nominated at Chartres to lead the effort.[147] Writing to Eugene III, Bernard states: "I expect you must have heard by now how the assembly at Chartres, by a most surprising decision, chose me as the leader and chief of the expedition . . . who am I to arrange armies in battle order, to lead forth armed men?"[148] Despite his own reluctance, in the same letter Bernard exhorted the pope to utilize his two swords and rebuild an army, even if God's will had been otherwise with respect to the outcome of the initial campaign: "I believe that the time has come for both swords to be drawn in defence of the Eastern Church . . . Because God does what he wishes, it is no reason why we should not do our duty . . . If you love Christ as you should . . . you will make no reservations, you will leave nothing undone while his bride is in such great danger."[149] One might infer that at this time Bernard was writing Book IV of *De consideratione* where he also exhorts the pope to govern with two swords, spiritual and temporal.[150]

Bernard attempted to involve Peter the Venerable in the effort to renew the crusade (the abbot of Cluny had been absent at Chartres in May 1150); Bernard, with a particular focus on Jerusalem, wrote that the civil princes were ignoring the call to renew the crusading effort and he requested that Peter attend a new meeting at Compiègne on July 15.[151] Bernard's plan to

144 Constable, "Report of a Lost Sermon," 51, in critique of Delaruelle who maintained that Bernard was not disconcerted by the outcome. For Delaruelle, see Étienne Delaruelle, "L'idée de croisade chez saint Bernard," *Mélanges Saint Bernard*, XXIVe Congrès de l'Association bourguignonne des Sociétes savantes 1953 (Dijon: Association des Amis de Saint Bernard, 1954), 53–67, at 59.

145 Berry, "The Second Crusade," 483.

146 Ibid., 511.

147 Reuter, "The 'non-crusade' of 1149–50," 157. See also Bredero, *Bernard of Clairvaux*, 286; McGuire, "Bernard's Life," 58.

148 Ep 399 (James, *Letters*, 470–72, at 472; Ep 256 in *SW* 3:366–70; *SBO* 8:163–65). See also Sommerfeldt, *Spirituality of Relationship*, 116–17; Evans, *Mind of St. Bernard*, 198–99; Reuter, "The 'non-crusade' of 1149–50," 157.

149 Ep 399 (James, *Letters*, 470–72, at 471; Ep 256 in *SW* 3:366–70; *SBO* 8:163–65).

150 *Csi*, IV, 3.7 (CF 37:118; *SW* 1:748; *SBO* 3:454).

151 Ep 400 (James, *Letters*, 472–73; Ep 521 in *SW* 3:984–86; *SBO* 8:483–84).

resume the failed crusade was never realized.[152] According to Silvas, Eugene III would not entertain the proposal to renew the military effort.[153] Further, the pope was forced to relinquish his plans to reenter Rome that year due to political resistance; papal control would not return to the city during his pontificate.[154]

In 1152, Bernard authored one of his final works, the biography *Vita sancti Malachiae*.[155] After Conrad III passed that year,[156] Pope Eugene III allied with Conrad's successor Frederick Barbarossa,[157] who was elected king of Germany on March 4.[158] This alliance, however, did not bring an end to the Roman commune; Eugene III then died in July of the following year.[159] He was followed by Bernard of Clairvaux on August 20.[160] Geoffrey of Auxerre records that Bernard was bedridden prior to his death but continued "to dictate sacred matters" and write letters.[161] It is thus possible that Bernard may not have finished *De consideratione* until this last year of his life (1153).[162] If the treatise was not sent to Eugene III until its completion, the pope would not seem to have had a significant opportunity to implement the meditative practices that Bernard prescribed.

152 McGuire, "Bernard's Life," 59; Reuter, "The 'non-crusade' of 1149–50," 157.

153 Silvas, *Jutta and Hildegard*, 142n52.

154 Kennan, "Bernard of Clairvaux and the Papacy," 79. See also Freed, *Frederick Barbarossa*, 111.

155 Bernard of Clairvaux, *The Life and Death of Saint Malachy the Irishman* (Kalamazoo, MI: Cistercian Press, 1978). For the Latin, see *SW* 1:453–597; *SBO* 3:307–78. For dating, see McGinn, "Bernard and Eschatology," 170.

156 Odo of Deuil, *De profectione Ludovici VII* (Allen and Amt, 142); Reuter, "The 'non-crusade' of 1149–50," 153.

157 Merton, "Blessed Eugenius III," 178; Kennan, "Introduction," 7.

158 Freed, *Frederick Barbarossa*, 114; Silvas, *Jutta and Hildegard*, 142n54.

159 Merton, "Blessed Eugenius III," 180.

160 James, *Letters*, 524. See also McGuire, "Bernard's Life," 18 and 60.

161 Geoffrey of Auxerre, *VP*, V, 1 (CF 76:234). See also CF 37:184.

162 P. Dinzelbacher, "Bernhards Leben in chronologischer Übersicht," in *SW* 1:38–41, at 41; Bruno Michel, "La considération et l'« *unitas spiritus* »," in *Saint Bernard et la Philosophie*, ed. Rémi Brague (Paris: Presses Universitaires de France, 1993), 109–27, at 110. Bredero dates the treatise to 1147–52 or 1147–53. See Bredero, *Bernard of Clairvaux*, 38 and 286.

2

Purpose and Literary Genre

In the previous chapter, I explored Bernard's authorship of *De consideratione* in relation a chronology of the events that shaped his immediate historical context. I turn now to examine more closely his purpose for writing the treatise and how in light of that purpose the treatise might be understood in terms of its literary genre.

Bernard's Purpose for Writing

Describing the process of Bernard when writing *De consideratione*, an author of his biography, the *Vita prima*, states: "The man of God dictated these things and sometimes wrote them on writing tablets, giving sweetness to the wax and indeed more grace to the tablets."[1] I mentioned Anderson's opinion above that Bernard may have initiated authorship on the work in response to Eugene III's request that he elaborate on the content found in a short letter sent in 1145.[2] Whether or not this is true, it is evident that Bernard's purpose in writing *De consideratione* involves the intention to communicate guidance to the pope. Kennan maintains that in writing the treatise Bernard had two goals: (1) to offer a political theology and ecclesiology in order to contextualize the current events with which the pope was contending, and (2) to offer the pope spiritual direction.[3]

1 Arnold of Bonneval, *VP*, II, 51 (CF 76:137). I refer to "the author" here because Bredero maintains that Arnold is not the author of this section of the *Vita prima*, but rather Gregory of Auxerre who inserted it during a later revision. See Bredero, *Bernard of Clairvaux*, 38.

2 Anderson, "Reconsidering," 145; Anderson, "Paul in Book 5," 137.

3 Kennan, "Introduction," 15. See also Evans, "*De Consideratione* of Bernard," 129. Regarding Bernard's possible goal of authoring a political theology, in addition to Kennan, "St. Bernard and the

White focuses on the first goal, arguing that Bernard aimed to question the emphasis given to the judicial power of the papacy found in the previous reforms of Pope Gregory VII (1073–85).[4] Evans interprets *De consideratione* as more focused on the second goal, stating that Bernard's concern was to help Eugene III reconcile the paradox of his situation of being both a monk and a public political figure.[5] The author who describes *De consideratione* in the second book of the *Vita prima* also points to the challenge that Eugene III encountered in fulfilling his monastic and ecclesial roles simultaneously: "He retained the habit of a monk interiorly, even when he had to put on his pontifical robes and standard of living, having the difficult task of expressing in one person the functions of several persons."[6] Barrow thus seems correct to observe that Bernard's aim was to exhort Eugene III to focus more energy on the practice of monastic exercises and exert less energy on administrative and juridical affairs.[7]

If Bernard's aim in *De consideratione* was to author a treatise on monastic philosophy, as Verbaal claims, his discussion of spiritual exercises would need to be understood specifically as involving pastoral concern for Eugene III.[8] Robert Bellarmine notes Bernard's pastoral concern in this regard when Bellarmine describes *De consideratione* in his work *De ascensione mentis* (1614):

> Saint Bernard earnestly warned Pope Eugenius, his former student, against giving himself over completely to business; rather he should recollect himself daily at a set time and enjoy some holy leisure and heavenly repast. He wrote five books, *On Consideration*, in which he not only urges the Pope to persistent meditation on heavenly subjects, but also teaches him a method

Papacy," see Alice Chapman, *Sacred Authority and Temporal Power in the Writings of Bernard of Clairvaux* (Turnhout: Brepols, 2013); Giles E. M. Gasper, "Bernard of Clairvaux, Material and Spiritual Order, and the Economy of Salvation," *Journal of Medieval History* 45, no. 5 (2019): 580–96; Bredero, Bernard of Clairvaux, 145–59; Evans, *Bernard of Clairvaux*, 150–71.

4 Hayden V. White, "The Gregorian Ideal and Saint Bernard of Clairvaux," *Journal of the History of Ideas* 21, no. 3 (1960): 321–48, at 342. See also John R. Sommerfeldt, "Charismatic and Gregorian Leadership in the Thought of Bernard of Clairvaux," in *Bernard of Clairvaux: Studies Presented to Dom Jean Leclercq*, 73–90, at 74 and 88n44. On Gregory VII, see H. E. J. Cowdrey, *Pope Gregory VII: 1073–1085* (Oxford: Oxford University Press, 1998).

5 Evans, "*De Consideratione* of Bernard," 129.

6 Arnold of Bonneval, *VP*, II.50 (CF 76:136).

7 Julia Barrow, "Religion," in *The Central Middle Ages: Europe 950–1320*, ed. Daniel Power (Oxford: Oxford University Press, 2006), 121–48, at 129.

8 Verbaal, "Bernardus Philosophus," 580.

and way of meditating and by meditation of ascending and by ascension of uniting himself to God in mind and heart.[9]

Bellarmine thus calls attention not only to Bernard's pastoral concern for Eugene III, but also to Bernard's outline of a program of meditation that the pope might implement as a regular spiritual exercise.

What was the nature of Bernard's pastoral concern? Bernard as abbot and preacher maintained a perennial pastoral concern for the spiritual health of others.[10] In the prologue to *De consideratione*, he expresses his pastoral concern by admonishing Eugene III out of love ("*monebo te*").[11] Bernard's expression of a warning indicates his intent to communicate a fraternal correction to the pope.[12] More specifically, Bernard writes to encourage Eugene III and provide advice concerning how the pope might integrate his monastic vocation with his unique ecclesiastical role.[13]

Bernard describes himself also as having had similar difficulties in integrating his own monastic and public roles. Writing to a Carthusian prior while authoring *De consideratione* around 1150, Bernard remarks: "I am a sort of modern chimæra, neither cleric nor layman. I have kept the habit of a monk, but I have long ago abandoned the life."[14] Sommerfeldt proposes that

9 Robert Bellarmine, *The Mind's Ascent to God*, Introduction, in *Spiritual Writings*, trans. John Patrick Donnelly and Roland J. Teske (New York: Paulist Press, 1989), 47–230, at 53.

10 For example, in sermon 32 of his *Sermones super cantica canticorum*, Bernard writes: "When men grow weary of studying spiritual doctrine and become lukewarm, when their spiritual energies are drained away, then they walk in sadness along the ways of the Lord" (*Sunt qui in studiis spiritualibus fatigati, et versi in tepore, atque in defectu quodam spiritus positi, ambulant tristes vias Domini*). For the English translation of this sermon, see Bernard of Clairvaux, "Sermon 32," 2.4, in *On the Song of Songs Vol. II, Sermons 21–46* (hereafter CF 7), trans. Kilian Walsh (Kalamazoo, MI: Cistercian, 1976), 134–43, at 136. For a Latin edition of *SCC* 32, see Bernhard von Clairvaux, *Sämtliche Werke, lateinisch/deutsch*, Bd. V (containing *SCC* 1–38, hereafter *SW* 5) (Innsbruck: Tyrolia, 1994), 500–515, at 504. *SW* 5 contains *SCC* 1–38, and reprints the Latin edition of *SCC* 32 from Bernardus Claraevallensis, *Sancti Bernardi Opera*, vol. 1 (hereafter *SBO* 1), ed. J. Leclercq, C. H. Talbot, and H.-M. Rochais (Rome: Editiones Cistercienses, 1957), 226–33, at 228. Regarding *SCC* 32, see Michael Casey, "Mindfulness of God in the Monastic Tradition," *CSQ* 17, no. 2 (1982): 111–26, at 120n23. See the similar discussion focusing on Cistercian abbot Isaac of Stella in David N. Bell, "Is There Such a Thing as 'Cistercian Spirituality'?," *CSQ* 33, no. 4 (1998): 455–71, at 460–61.

11 *Csi*, preface (CF 37:24; *SW* 1:628; *SBO* 3:394).

12 Regarding the topic of fraternal correction in the Benedictine monastic tradition prior to Bernard, see Smaragdus of Saint-Mihiel, *Diadema monachorum: The Crown of Monks*, trans. David Barry (Kalamazoo, MI: Cistercian Publications, 2013), ch. 41 (101–4).

13 See, e.g., *Csi*, II, 5.8 (CF 37:55; *SW* 1:670–72; *SBO* 3:415–16).

14 Ep 326, §4 (James, *Letters*, 401–2; Ep 250 in *SW* 3:330–34; *SBO* 8:145–47). For dating and brief discussion, see Christopher Holdsworth, "Bernard of Clairvaux: His First and Greatest Miracle Was Himself," in *The Cambridge Companion to the Cistercian Order*, 173–85, at 176.

Bernard may also have experienced a conflict between his role as a preaching abbot and his role as a contemplative monk focused on prayerful quietude.[15] Leclercq likewise notes Bernard's more general inconsistency in promoting a Gospel of peace while supporting a military culture prone to warfare.[16] Bernard may thus have had personal insight into the kind of interior spiritual struggle that he suspected the pope was encountering.

Letter Writing as a Literary Genre

If provision of spiritual direction was Bernard's purpose in writing to Eugene III, then this purpose might shed light on the literary form or genre that Bernard adopted to communicate his intent. In terms of internal textual evidence that would be indicative of such a literary genre, Anderson notes that Bernard perceives his work to be some kind of oration.[17] Leclercq also refers in passing to Bernard's goading of Eugene III as a kind of preaching.[18] However, Bernard indicates that his discourse is not an oration in the sense of a sermon.[19]

The literary genre that Bernard previously employed to communicate pastoral concerns to his acquaintances was the genre of the epistle. Bernard fulfilled the role of spiritual advisor through letter writing with respect to many of his contemporaries.[20] For example, he writes in a similar capacity

15 John R. Sommerfeldt, "Bernard of Clairvaux's Abbot: Both Daniel and Noah," in *Studiosorum Speculum: Studies in Honor of Louis J. Lekai, O.Cist.*, ed. Francis R. Swietek and John R. Sommerfeldt (Kalamazoo, MI: Cistercian Publications, 1993), 355–61, at 360 (CS 141).

16 Jean Leclercq, "General Introduction to the Works of Saint Bernard (I)," *CSQ* 40, no. 1 (2005): 3–25, at 24–25.

17 Anderson, "Paul in Book 5," 137–38. See also *Csi*, preface (CF 37:23; *SW* 1:626; *SBO* 3:393); *Csi*, I, 11.14 (CF 37:46; *SW* 1:660; *SBO* 3:410).

18 Leclercq, "L'Art de la Composition," 119.

19 Bernard states to Eugene III: "It is true that I have been freed of maternal obligation toward you . . . You were once in my womb . . ." *Csi*, preface (CF 37:24; *SW* 1:626; *SBO* 3:393). This statement correlates with Bernard's remark in a sermon in his *Sermones super cantica canticorum* that some spiritual persons are like mothers who bring souls to birth by preaching. A basis for the maternal metaphor is found in the writings of the Apostle Paul (1 Thes 2:7). For another reference by Bernard to preaching and spiritual birth, see *SCC*, 85, 4.13 (CF 40:209–10; *SW* 6:644–45; *SBO* 2:315–16).

20 William O. Paulsell, "Bernard of Clairvaux as Spiritual Director," *CSQ* 23, no. 3 (1988): 223–31. With respect to Hildegard of Bingen, however, Bernard seems to step back from assuming such a role: "How could I presume to teach or advise you who are favoured with hidden knowledge . . . ?" Ep 390, in James, *Letters*, 459–60 (Ep 366 in *SW* 3:672–74; *SBO* 8:323–24). See also John R. Sommerfeldt, "Contemplatives and Visionaries: Four Twelfth-Century Monastics," *CSQ* 54, no. 2 (2019): 171–79, at 173.

in early letters to William of St. Thierry (1125),[21] Bishop Henry of Sens (*De moribus et officio episcoporum*, ca. 1127),[22] and Oger of Mont-Saint-Éloi (ca. 1139).[23] Bernard at times in his letters also requests spiritual advice from others.[24]

De consideratione might primarily be understood as exemplifying the literary genre of a letter. Due to its length, however, it is more akin to a letter-treatise—analogous to Bernard's response to Hugh of St. Victor on the nature of baptism (ca. 1127–28).[25] Leclercq also acknowledges the treatise-like nature of *De consideratione* when observing that, although Bernard writes for a focused audience, his work is not an informal letter, but is rather communicated with serious intent and according to a planned compositional structure.[26] Adopting this interpretation of *De consideratione* as a formal letter-treatise, one might observe that within the letter Bernard engages in a variety of secondary modes of literary expression, some rhetorical and some didactic.

With respect to specific rhetorical devices found in the treatise, Kennan maintains that Bernard employs the technique of antithesis throughout the work in order to promote Eugene III's recognition of a virtuous middle ground between extreme behavioral and emotional responses.[27] The entire treatise, then, might be interpreted as taking place within hortatory by which Bernard aims to guide Eugene III in the process of integrating the activities of his papal role with his monastic vocation.[28] If this is the case, Eugene III's embroilment in Roman political upheaval and the legal matters of the papal court locate him at the opposite extreme of monastic quietude. Bernard's

21 Ep 87 (James, *Letters*, 124–27; Ep 85 in *SW* 2:680–86; *SBO* 7:220–23). See also CS 105:69–86, at 71.

22 Ep 42 (*SW* 2:440–503; *SBO* 7:100–131). For an English translation, see Bernard of Clairvaux, "On the Conduct and Office of Bishops" (hereafter *Mor*), in *On Baptism and the Office of Bishops*, trans. Pauline Matarasso (Kalamazoo, MI: Cistercian Publications, 2004), 37–82 (hereafter CF 67). For dating *Mor*, see CF 67:21. Evans examines this early letter in relation to *De consideratione*. See Evans, "*De Consideratione* of Bernard," 131–34. See also John R. Sommerfeldt, *Bernard of Clairvaux: On the Life of the Mind* (Mahwah, NJ: Newman Press, 2004), 62; Evans, *Mind of St. Bernard*, 206.

23 Ep 90 (James, *Letters*, 129–35; Ep 87 in *SW* 2:688–703; *SBO* 7:224–31). See also CS 105:75.

24 Ep 326 (James, *Letters*, 401–2; Ep 250 in *SW* 3:330–34; *SBO* 8:145–47).

25 Ep 77 (*SW* 2:608–41; *SBO* 7:184–200). For an English translation, see Bernard of Clairvaux, "On Baptism and Other Questions," in CF 67:149–77. For dating this text (Ep 77), see CF 67:93.

26 Leclercq, "L'Art de la Composition," 118.

27 Kennan, "Antithesis and Argument," 91–93. See also Elizabeth T. Kennan, "Rhetoric and Style in the *De Consideratione*," in *Studies in Medieval Cistercian History II*, ed. John R. Sommerfeldt (Kalamazoo, MI: Cistercian Publications, 1976), 40–48, at 47–48; Evans, *Mind of St. Bernard*, 201.

28 Kennan, "Antithesis and Argument," 107.

letter-treatise might thus be understood as a rhetorical exhortation that encourages the pope to take time for reflection.[29] In this regard, *De consideratione* develops the spiritual guidance found in the previous short letter that Bernard had sent to Eugene III as well as the recommendations found in the other previous letters Bernard had sent to prelates and pontiffs concerning how to manage assumed ecclesiastical roles.[30]

The Question of Disputation

What other forms of discourse are apparent in *De consideratione*? Bernard at times indicates that his intention in writing the work is didactic in that he observes that his letter-treatise involves an overall argument (*disputatio*).[31] At the very end of *De consideratione*, he refers to ending his *disputatio* and turning to prayer.[32] Is this kind of disputation informed by the art of logic? Sommerfeldt observes that Bernard employed dialectic in his early *Liber de gratia et libero arbitrio* (ca. 1128).[33] However, Sommerfeldt suggests in a later study that one need not understand Bernard's reference to *disputatio* at the end of *De consideratione* as a 'disputation' in the Scholastic sense of

29 Kennan, "Introduction," 12. According to Evans, the difficulty of finding a balance between the active and contemplative modes of life was a frequent topic of Bernard's theology. See Evans, *Bernard of Clairvaux*, 21.

30 See also Jean Leclercq, "Introduction to the Letters of Saint Bernard (II)," *CSQ* 41, no. 3 (2006): 291–310, at 301; Richard ver Bust, "Papal Ministry: A Source of Theology, Bernard of Clairvaux's Letters," in *Heaven on Earth: Studies in Medieval Cistercian History, IX*, ed. E. Rozanne Elder (Kalamazoo, MI: Cistercian Publications, 1983), 55–61, at 60 (hereafter CS 68).

31 *Csi*, IV, 2.3 (CF 37:112; *SW* 1:740; *SBO* 3:450). *At locus dubius, et scrupulosa incidit disputatio.* See also *Csi*, I, 8.11 (CF 37:42; *SW* 1:654; *SBO* 3:407). *Non mihi hoc loco propositum de virtutibus disputare.* For a critique of the Latin text of *Csi* that appears in the *SBO*, see Denis Farkasfalvy, "Remarks and Suggestions Concerning the Critical Text of Saint Bernard's Treatise 'De Consideratione,'" *Analecta Sacri Ordinis Cisterciensis* (hereafter *ASOC*) 54 (2002): 285–310.

32 *Csi*, V, 14.32 (CF 37:179; *SW* 1:826; *SBO* 3:493). *At orando forte quam disputando dignius quaeritur et invenitur facilius.*

33 Bernard of Clairvaux, *On Grace and Free Choice* (hereafter *Gra*), trans. Daniel O'Donovan (Kalamazoo, MI: Cistercian Publications, 1988) (hereafter CF 19a). For the Latin, see *SW* 1:171–255; *SBO* 3:165–203. For dating this work see CF 19a:4. Regarding Sommerfeldt's observation, see John R. Sommerfeldt, "Epistemology, Education, and Social Theory in the Thought of Bernard of Clairvaux," in *Saint Bernard of Clairvaux: Studies Commemorating the Eighth Centenary of His Canonization*, ed. M. Basil Pennington (Kalamazoo, MI: Cistercian Publications, 1977), 169–79, at 172. Verbaal similarly refers to *Liber de gratia* as a "Scholastic" work that gradually transitions into rhetorical prose. See Verbaal, "Bernardus Philosophus," 572–73.

formulating a logical argument.[34] Sommerfeldt might be rejecting the possibility that Bernard used a specific Scholastic method such as the *quaestio disputata*.[35]

Leclercq also contrasts *disputatio* in the sense of an academic debate with the character of monastic theological discourse.[36] If it is true that Bernard's early education in the trivium at the Church of Saint-Vorles in Châtillon-sur-Seine included only grammar and rhetoric and not logic,[37] then it makes sense that Bernard in *De consideratione* might employ only the kind of persuasive argument that was taught in medieval rhetoric. Further, this expressive style is consistent with what is found in his short letter containing spiritual direction to Oger of Mont-Saint-Éloi, mentioned above.[38]

To understand Bernard's writing style further, it is helpful to differentiate his reference to disputation in terms of rhetorical persuasion from the kind of disputation that employs logical argumentation. Bernard is familiar with legal argumentation, "the disputations of advocates and verbal disputes" (*disputationes advocatorum et pugnas verborum*).[39] Disputation in the sense of a rhetorical persuasive argument was a common literary enterprise in the eleventh-century context of Bernard's education. Novikoff explores the approach to disputation found in the works of eleventh-century thinkers Lanfranc and Guitmund of Aversa, who engaged Berengar of Tours, as well as the approach found in the works of Lanfranc's student Anselm (who in turn influenced early twelfth-century thinkers Eadmer, Gilbert Crispin, and Honorius Augustodunensis).[40]

34 Sommerfeldt, *Life of the Mind*, 74.

35 See, e.g., Brian Lawn, *The Rise and Decline of the Scholastic "Quaestio Disputata": With Special Emphasis on Its Use in the Teaching of Medicine and Science* (Leiden: Brill, 1993), 6–17.

36 Jean Leclercq, "The Renewal of Theology," in *Renaissance and Renewal in the Twelfth Century*, ed. Robert L. Benson and Giles Constable (Cambridge, MA: Harvard University Press, 1982), 68–87, at 83.

37 McGuire, "Bernard's Life," 22 and 24. See also *The Cistercian World* (ed. Matarasso), 15; John R. Sommerfeldt, "Bernard of Clairvaux and the Trivial Arts: A Contemplative's Thoughts on Literature and Philosophy," in *Praise No Less than Charity: Studies in Honor of M. Chrysogonus Waddell, Monk of Gethsemani Abbey*, ed. E. Rozanne Elder (Kalamazoo, MI: Cistercian Publications, 2002), 141–59, at 149 (hereafter CS 193).

38 Bernard writes to Oger: "What is the point of all these arguments of mine? Am I trying to persuade you to take up again the burden of your office . . .?" (*Sed ad quid nitor his ratiocinationibus? Numquid suadeo tibi redire ad onus regiminis . . . ?*). Ep 90, §4 (James, *Letters*, 129–35, at 131; Ep 87 in *SW* 2:688–703, at 692; *SBO* 7:224–31, at 226).

39 *Csi*, I, 10.13 (CF 37:44; *SW* 1:656; *SBO* 3:408).

40 Alex J. Novikoff, "Anselm, Dialogue, and the Rise of Scholastic Disputation," *Speculum* 86, no. 2 (2011): 387–418, esp. 392–94, 397, 400, 404, 408, 413. See also Alex J. Novikoff, *The Medieval*

Disputation in this sense involved an eristic controversy and even rhetorical polemic. But if one understands 'disputation' simply as discursive debate between two alternative viewpoints, then the word signifies more generally the effort to resolve perceived contradictions. Lawn quotes Gerbert of Aurillac (ca. 940–1003), who maintained that the art of dialectic might be employed to resolve apparent contradictions in the writings of the Church Fathers.[41] Smalley also notes the admission by a St. Eucher of some kind of *disputatio* that might occur during the spiritual exercise of *lectio divina* prescribed by the Benedictine Rule; this development, she claims, in turn influenced Paschasius Radbertus and John Scotus Eriugena.[42] Given Bernard's familiarity with the works of Anselm (discussed below), Bernard's description of *De consideratione* as communicating some kind of disputation to Eugene III is not entirely isolated from the general Scholastic meaning of the word (understanding Scholasticism in a broad sense as Latin theology informed by the intellectual tradition of Boethius).

Claustral Theology and Scholastic Theology

To what extent did Bernard understand the rhetorical argument that he communicates to Eugene III in his letter-treatise to involve not only an effort of fraternal correction but also a didactic effort, as expressing theological instruction?[43] This question directly pertains to Leclercq's thesis that Bernard's writings exemplify a unique kind of "monastic theology" that is distinct from Scholastic theology.[44] In an early presentation of this thesis,

Culture of Disputation: Pedagogy, Practice, and Performance (Philadelphia: University of Pennsylvania Press, 2013).

41 Lawn, *Rise and Decline*, 8, citing Gerbert's *De corpore et sanguine Domini*, in Patrologia Latina (hereafter PL) 139:185b.

42 Beryl Smalley, *The Study of the Bible in the Middle Ages* (Notre Dame, Ind.: University of Notre Dame Press, 1964), 38. For reference to *lectio divina*, see chap. 48 of the *Rule* (hereafter *RB*): Justin McCann, trans., *The Rule of Saint Benedict in English and Latin* (Fort Collins, Colo.: Roman Catholic Books, 1951), 110–11. For an alternate translation, see Benedict, *The Rule of St. Benedict*, ed. Timothy Fry (New York: Vintage Books, 1998), 47. See also Duncan Robertson, *Lectio Divina: The Medieval Experience of Reading* (Kalamazoo, MI: Cistercian Publications, 2011) (hereafter CS 238).

43 For a study of the historical development of sacred theology in Bernard's time, see J. de Ghellinck, *Le mouvement théologique du XIIe siècle* (Paris: Lecoffre, 1914).

44 Jean Leclercq, "S. Bernard et la Théologie Monastique du XII^e^Siècle," *ASOC* 9, nos. 3–4 (1953): 7–23; Jean Leclercq, *The Love of Learning and the Desire for God: A Study of Monastic Culture*, trans. Catharine Misrahi (New York: Fordham University Press, 1982), esp. 191–235; Jean Leclercq, "Theology and Prayer: The Education of Seminarians," *Encounter* 24, no. 3 (1963): 349–64, at 353; Leclercq, "Psycho-history," 288; Leclercq, "Renewal of Theology," 71. See also Marcia Colish, "The Sentence Collection and the Education of Professional Theologians in the Twelfth Century," in *The*

Leclercq asserts that monastic theology differs from Scholastic theology in three ways: according to object, method, and sources used.[45] In a later essay, Leclercq expanded this contrast to highlight seven differences, adding audience, subjects treated, pastoral tendencies, and approaches to reform.[46] In order to explore further the question of Bernard's didactic intention and the nature of the kind of literary disputation found in *De consideratione*, I will briefly consider each of these seven contrasts.

With respect to its object, Leclercq maintains that monastic theology is focused on union with God rather than on the clarification and logical explication of dogma.[47] This difference relates to the distinct audiences receiving the theology.[48] He writes: "The monastic masters taught cloistered monks, concerned mostly with the problems of their own spiritual growth; the schoolmasters taught secular clerics and laymen who were expected to maintain or improve their faith and answer questions of daily morality in ordinary society."[49] These different audiences correlate, Leclercq observes, with different pastoral tendencies as well as with maintaining different concerns regarding ecclesial reform.[50]

With respect to its method, Leclercq claims that monastic theology proceeded with greater focus on personal experience, synthetically resolving all things back to God within the context of meditative prayer, whereas Scholastic thought proceeded by way of analysis and attempted to clarify obscure matters by formulating distinctions.[51] In a later essay, Leclercq maintains that both contexts emphasized reading (*lectio*), yet in the monastic setting reading occurred within the context of *lectio divina* that proceeded forward to meditation (*meditatio*) and prayer (*oratio*), whereas in the schools reading proceeded forward to academic debate (*disputatio*).[52] Disputation in this sense thus contrasts with meditation, the subject of *De consideratione*.

Intellectual Climate of the Early University: Essays in Honor of Otto Gründler, ed. Nancy van Deusen (Kalamazoo, MI: Medieval Institute Publications, 1997), 1–26, at 2 and 21n3.

45 Leclercq, "Théologie monastique," 10.

46 Leclercq, "Renewal of Theology," 80–84.

47 Leclercq, "Théologie monastique," 13; Leclercq, *Love of Learning*, 217.

48 Leclercq, *Love of Learning*, 191.

49 Leclercq, "Renewal of Theology," 81.

50 Ibid., 81–82.

51 Leclercq, "Théologie monastique," 14; Leclercq, *Love of Learning*, 199–202 and 223.

52 Leclercq, "Renewal of Theology," 82–83, citing Jean Leclercq, "La récréation et le colloque dans la tradition monastique," *Revue d'ascétique et de mystique* 43 (1967): 3–20.

Lectio divina in general might be understood, Leclercq notes elsewhere, as occurring within the context of contemplative prayer.[53] While some twelfth-century monastic authors were like Scholastics in that they were systematic in their thinking (Leclercq cites Rupert of Deutz and William of St. Thierry),[54] Leclercq also claims that Scholastic authors generally speaking were systematic in a "more encyclopedic" manner, as expressed first in the Scholastic literary genre of the *sententiae* and later in the genre of the *summae*; in contrast, he argues, "for the monks, it was rather a matter of synthesis, which always included a personal, subjective element that served as a point of departure for reflection."[55] Leclercq emphasizes that in their general approach to writing theology, monastic authors associated their discourse with a life of prayer in pursuit of contemplation; as a result, the character of that discourse was primarily practical and the doctrine communicated was to be lived and experienced.[56] One might therefore characterize the approach of monastic theological reflection as proceeding as a kind of *contemplative praxis* distinct from the procedures of a Scholastic science. In this respect, monastic theology as a praxis would understandably be associated with the spiritual exercises prescribed by a monastic philosophy.[57]

With respect to its sources, Leclercq argues that monastic theology was focused on scripture and Christian tradition, whereas Scholastic theology also drew on secular philosophers such as Plato, Aristotle, Cicero, and the Stoics.[58] In a later essay, Leclercq again maintains that monastic theology was more so focused on contemplative sources.[59] I will return to the topic of Bernard's specific sources when writing *De consideratione* in the next

53 Jean Leclercq, "Lectio Divina," *Worship* 58, no. 3 (1984): 239–48, at 244.

54 For Rupert, Leclercq may have in mind Book XI of *De divinis officiis* (ca. 1111–12) where, taking occasion when commenting on the office for Trinity Sunday, Rupert employs a "philosophical language" that draws on Boethius and logic in order to critique the Trinitarian theology of Roscellin of Compiègne. See John H. Van Engen, *Rupert of Deutz* (Berkeley: University of California Press, 1983), 74–78, esp. 77. For William of St. Thierry, Leclercq may have in mind the didactic organization of *De natura corporis et animae* (CF 24:101–52). See also Aage Rydstrøm-Poulsen, "William of St. Thierry on the Soul," in *A Companion to William of Saint-Thierry*, ed. F. Tyler Sergent (Leiden: Brill, 2019), 93–108. To these examples, one might also add the "Letter on the Soul" by Isaac of Stella. See Dániel Deme, "The Letter of Isaac of Stella on the Soul," in *The Selected Works of Isaac of Stella* (New York: Routledge, 2007), 143–57; CF 24:155–77.

55 Leclercq, "Renewal of Theology," 77.

56 Leclercq, "Théologie monastique," 15. See also Ulrich Köpf, *Religiöse Erfahrung in der Theologie Bernhards von Clairvaux, Beiträge zur historischen Theologie* 61 (Tübingen: Mohr Siebeck, 1980).

57 See Verbaal, "Bernardus Philosophus," 583.

58 Leclercq, "Théologie monastique," 10; Leclercq, *Love of Learning*, 199 and 223.

59 Leclercq, "Renewal of Theology," 82.

chapter. Here, one might note that the sources consulted in monastic theology also relate to Leclercq's contrast concerning the *subjects treated* in the two approaches to theology: he argues that monastic theology focused on anthropology and an experiential psychology, whereas "in the school, the subjective, personal aspect played a lesser role . . . For those masters who devoted themselves to speculation, the problems of the Trinity were of primary importance."[60]

In an earlier essay, Leclercq locates the origin of this monastic-Scholastic distinction in the physical distinction erected between the interior and exterior schools at monasteries, where the former focused on the education of monks and the latter on the education of clerics and lay persons.[61] Smalley captures the same historical insight in her contrast between monastic schools and cathedral schools.[62] Appropriating a phrase from Benedictine scholar Odom Lottin, Leclercq observes that with the development of the schools into early universities, "clerical theology" gradually grew into what is now commonly called Scholastic theology.[63] In terms of specific usage of the qualification "Scholastic," Leclercq suggests reserving the term to denote thirteenth-century university theology only.[64] It is important to point out that Leclercq qualifies his overall contrast by stating that "this catalogue of differences records shades of difference, nuances rather than oppositions."[65]

What can be said of Leclercq's contrasts? Do these contrasts illuminate Bernard's purpose and choice of literary genre in *De consideratione*? Without

60 Ibid., 81.

61 Leclercq, *Love of Learning*, 194–96. See also Ulrich G. Leinsle, *Introduction to Scholastic Theology*, trans. Michael J. Miller (Washington, DC: The Catholic University of America Press, 2010), 35.

62 Smalley, *Study of the Bible*, 37–82.

63 Leclercq, "Théologie monastique," 8–9, citing Odom Lottin, "Nos. 1–282," *Bulletin de théologie ancienne et médiévale* 6 (1950): 5–88, at 53 (no. 162). There, Lottin is summarizing a work by Dominican medieval scholar Marie-Dominique Chenu. Lottin notes that, according to Chenu, one encounters "two genres" of theology in the twelfth century, one mode of theology where scripture is imparted "to monks by their abbot for their personal sanctification," and another mode of theology where "professors appointed to secular clerics" prepare them to live out their ministerial vocations (53). Lottin adds that the clerical mode of teaching theology derives from Manegold of Lautenbach and Anselm of Laon. Chenu thus suggests that "two kinds of theology coexisted throughout the 12th century: a 'monastic theology' based on Scripture in view of the moral and mystical formation of monks and faithful, and a 'clerical theology' also based on Scripture but enriched with *quaestiones* in view of the professional instruction of clerics and preachers" (53). For Chenu, see M.-D. Chenu, "Évangélisme et théologie au XIIIe siècle," in *Mélanges offerts au R. P. Ferdinand Cavallera, doyen de la faculté de theologie de Toulouse á l'occasion de la quarantiéme année de son professorat á l'institut Catholique* (Toulouse: Bibliothéque de l'Institut Catholique, 1948), 339–46.

64 Leclercq, "Renewal of Theology," 72.

65 Ibid., 83.

rejecting the general category of "monastic theology," Farkasfalvy has called into question some elements of Leclercq's distinctions.[66] First, Farkasfalvy notes that Leclercq's contrast between monastic and Scholastic theologies parallels the self-identified concerns of French *ressourcement* theology vis-à-vis Neo-Scholasticism in Leclercq's time period.[67] There is a risk of anachronism if these respective sets of categories are not further differentiated.[68] Second, Farkasfalvy argues that not all authors who were contemporary with Bernard and who approached theological writing in a similar way were, properly speaking, "monastic" (Farkasfalvy calls special attention to the school of St. Victor).[69] Third, according to Farkasfalvy, the distinction that Leclercq proposes does not comprise a genuine historical contrast if what is primarily meant by the word 'Scholasticism' is, as Leclercq proposed, the university theology authored only in the thirteenth century.[70] Scholasticism in this narrow sense of the word would denote extensive use of the works of Aristotle,[71] as well as the *quaestio disputata* method mentioned above. Were not other twelfth-century authors "Scholastic" in a way that was informed at

66 Denis Farkasfalvy, "Bernard the Theologian: Forty Years of Research," *Communio* 17, no. 4 (1990): 580–94.

67 Farkasfalvy, "Bernard the Theologian," 584.

68 At times, remarks of Leclercq are almost identical with critiques of Neo-Scholasticism advanced by other thinkers of the Vatican II era. For example, contrast Leclercq's juxtaposition of monastic and Scholastic psychology with Bernard Lonergan's distinction between historical and classical mindedness. Leclercq writes: "whereas the monks' psychology started from the analysis of states of the soul and studied their growth, and was in that sense dynamic and 'developmental,' the psychology of the intellectuals strove rather to deduce logical consequences from principles related to the composition of the human being; it was more static and theoretical than dynamic and experiential." Leclercq, "Renewal of Theology," 83. Similarly, Lonergan writes: "I have been contrasting two different apprehensions of man. One can apprehend man abstractly through a definition that applies *omni et soli* and through properties verifiable in every man . . . On the other hand, one can apprehend mankind as a concrete aggregate developing over time, where the locus of development and, so to speak, the synthetic bond is the emergence, expansion, differentiation, dialectic of meaning . . . This component is not fixed, static, immutable, but shifting, developing." Bernard Lonergan, "The Transition from a Classicist World-View to Historical-Mindedness," in *A Second Collection*, ed. William F. J. Ryan and Bernard J. Tyrrell (Toronto: University of Toronto, 1974), 1–9, at 5–6. Yet, whereas Lonergan proposes a transition from one kind of mentality to the other, Leclercq concludes his discussion by stating: "At present one could offer no objective criterion for claiming that one of the two theologies is superior to the other. Each had its own grandeur, its own fruitfulness." Leclercq, "Renewal of Theology," 85.

69 Farkasfalvy, "Bernard the Theologian," 585. On this point, one should note that Leclercq indicates acceptance of the use of the broader category "claustral theology" in Leclercq, "Psycho-history," 288.

70 Farkasfalvy, "Bernard the Theologian," 586.

71 See also Spencer Young, *Scholarly Community at the Early University of Paris: Theologians, Education and Society, 1215–1248* (Cambridge: Cambridge University Press, 2014), 16–17.

least by a method of organizational clarity if not by a use of logic (for example, Robert Pullen, Peter Lombard, or Robert of Melun, discussed below)? Fourth, Farkasfalvy maintains that works of Bernard such as *De consideratione* exhibit a depth of philosophical content; as such, one cannot simply associate philosophy with Scholastic thinkers and not with monastic authors.[72]

Farkasfalvy raises some important observations regarding Leclercq's differentiation of monastic from Scholastic theology. Further, the distinction between these literary genres of theological writing is not simply a contrast between ascetic-mystical literature and doctrinal literature. Bernard does indeed write to Eugene III not only as a pastor but also as a teacher. Leclercq likewise recognizes that monastic theology (generally speaking) was focused on the theological education of monks within the cloister—exemplified, for example, by the Abbey of Bec. It seems, however, in contrast with the Scholastic *sententiae* and *summae*, the literary genres associated with monastic theological education were indeed less organized and more diffuse.

Claustral Education and Judgments of Wisdom

Monastic theological education was carried out in one respect by means of the literary genre of the sermon. This genre, however, is not unique to the monastic setting. While some of Bernard's sermons were occasional and others comprised a planned set—such as his *Sermones super psalmum "Qui habitat"* (ca. 1139)[73] or his *Sermones super cantica canticorum* (1136–53)[74]—at times, a particular sermon stands out as a kind of didactic treatise, such as his *Sermo de conversione ad clericos* (ca. 1139–40).[75] This same kind of literary genre blending also occurs among Bernard's letters: some letters are

72 Farkasfalvy, "Bernard the Theologian," 587.

73 For *Sermo super psalmum Qui habitat* (hereafter *QH*), see Bernard of Clairvaux, *Lenten Sermons on the Psalm 'He Who Dwells'*, in *Sermons on Conversion*, trans. Marie-Bernard Saïd (Kalamazoo, MI: Cistercian Publications, 1981), 80–261. For a Latin edition of *QH*, see Bernhard von Clairvaux, *Sämtliche Werke, lateinisch/deutsch*, Bd. VII (hereafter *SW* 7) (Innsbruck: Tyrolia, 1996), 499–760. *SW* 7 reprints the Latin from Bernardus Claraevallensis, *Sancti Bernardi Opera*, vol. 4 (hereafter *SBO* 4), ed. J. Leclercq, C. H. Talbot, and H.-M. Rochais (Rome: Editiones Cistercienses, 1966), 383–492. For dating *Qui habitat*, see Marie-Bernard Saïd, "Introduction" (CF 25:96). See also McGinn, "Bernard and Eschatology," 184.

74 For dating the *Sermones super cantica canticorum*, see Jean Leclercq, "Introduction" (CF 40:xi–xii).

75 Bernard of Clairvaux, "On Conversion, a Sermon to Clerics" (hereafter *Conv*), in *Sermons on Conversion*, trans. Marie-Bernard Saïd (Kalamazoo, MI: Cistercian Publications, 1981), 29–79 (hereafter CF 25). For a Latin edition, see Bernhard von Clairvaux, *Sämtliche Werke, lateinisch/deutsch*, Bd. IV (hereafter *SW* 4) (Innsbruck: Tyrolia, 1993), 147–246. *SW* 4 reprints the Latin from Bernardus Claraevallensis, *Sancti Bernardi Opera*, vol. 4 (hereafter *SBO* 4), ed. J. Leclercq, C. H.

occasional, but as discussed above at times a longer letter will stand out as a didactic treatise, such as Bernard's *Apologia ad Guillelmum abbatem* (1125),[76] *De moribus et officio episcoporum* (ca. 1127),[77] or *De baptismo* (ca. 1127–28).[78] These works thus cross over in varying degrees into the literary genre of Bernard's more official treatises, such as the *Liber de gradibus humilitatis et superbiae* (1124),[79] the *Liber de diligendo Deo* (ca. 1126–41),[80] the *Liber de gratia et libero arbitrio* (ca. 1128),[81] his treatise on the vocation to knighthood, *In laude novae militiae* (ca. 1130),[82] or the *Liber de praecepto et dispensatione* (1141–44).[83] This last work is noteworthy in that Bernard explicitly states that he initially intended to write a letter, yet after completing the work he added an introduction where he observed that his letter had become a book.[84] The epistolary format that primarily characterizes the literary genre of *De consideratione* arguably exemplifies this same kind of didactic treatise.

If this categorization is accurate, is there some specific didactic approach that Bernard employs that was also customary in the monastic educational setting (in contrast with how theological texts were authored in cleric-lay educational settings)? Such a didactic approach is not found in the monastic literary genre of the *soliloquium* or *meditatio*. Examples of this genre prior to Bernard might be found among the writings of Anselm of Canterbury

Talbot, and H.-M. Rochais (Rome: Editiones Cistercienses, 1966), 69–116. For dating see Bernard of Clairvaux, *Sermons on Conversion*, 12. See also Evans, *Bernard of Clairvaux*, 45.

76 See *Cistercians and Cluniacs: St. Bernard's Apologia to Abbot William*, trans. Michael Casey (Kalamazoo, MI: Cistercian Publications, 1970), 3.

77 For dating *Mor* (Ep 42), see CF 67:21.

78 For dating "On Baptism" (Ep 77), see CF 67:93.

79 Bernard of Clairvaux, *The Steps of Humility and Pride* (hereafter *Hum*), trans. M. Ambrose Conway (Kalamazoo, MI: Cistercian, 1989) (hereafter CF 13a). For a Latin edition of *Liber de gradibus*, see Bernhard von Clairvaux, *Sämtliche Werke, lateinisch/deutsch*, Bd. II (hereafter *SW* 2) (Innsbruck: Tyrolia, 1992), 37–135. *SW* 2 reprints the Latin for *Hum* from *SBO* 3:13–59. For dating, see *SW* 2:30.

80 Bernard of Clairvaux, *On Loving God* (hereafter *Dil*) (Kalamazoo, MI: Cistercian Publications, 1995) (hereafter CF 13b). For the Latin, see *SW* 1:73–151; *SBO* 3:119–54. Stiegman discusses the difficulty of dating this treatise at CF 13b:59.

81 For dating see CF 19a:4.

82 Bernard of Clairvaux, *In Praise of the New Knighthood: A Treatise on the Knights Templar and the Holy Places of Jerusalem*, trans. M. Conrad Greenia (Trappist, Ky.: Cistercian Publications, 2000) (hereafter CF 19b). For the Latin, see *SW* 1:267–321; *SBO* 3:213–39. For dating, see CF 19b:9.

83 Bernard of Clairvaux, *On Precept and Dispensation* (hereafter *Pre*), trans. Conrad Greenia, in *The Works of Bernard of Clairvaux*, vol. 1: *Treatises I*, ed. M. Basil Pennington (Spencer, MA: Cistercian Publications, 1970), 103–50 (hereafter CF 1). For the Latin, see *SW* 1:345–428; *SBO* 3:253–94. For dating, see CF 1:73.

84 *Pre*, 19.61 (CF 1:150; *SW* 1:428; *SBO* 3:294).

(1099–1100),[85] Guigo de Castro (prior of Grande Chartreuse in 1110–37),[86] Hugh of St. Victor (1125–31),[87] William of St. Thierry (1128–32),[88] and Rupert of Deutz (1129).[89] Similar meditative works in this literary genre authored after Bernard include the *Benjamin Minor* and *Major* by canon regular Richard of St. Victor (1153–65)[90] or the *Scala claustralium* authored by Carthusian monk Guigo II (prior of Grande Chartreuse in 1174–80).[91] Could it be that, while Bernard's *De consideratione* is not itself a *meditatio* (it is not a *soliloquium*), it is a didactic work that teaches the spiritual practice of meditation—a teaching that could in turn originate these kinds of writings (*meditationes*)?

In contrast with a monastic *meditatio*, an explicit didactic intention is exemplified in the literary genre of theological *sententiae*. Boschung calls attention to two kinds of sentence collections: (1) an interpretive genre

85 See Anselm of Canterbury, *Meditatio*, in *Complete Philosophical and Theological Treatises of Anselm of Canterbury*, trans. Jasper Hopkins and Herbert Richardson (Minneapolis, MN: Arthur J. Banning, 2000), 419–26. For dating this work, see the annotation at Hopkins and Richardson, 419n1.

86 See *Meditations of Guigo, Prior of the Charterhouse*, trans. John J. Jolin (Milwaukee, Wis.: Marquette University Press, 1976). This work translates Dom André Wilmart, *Le Recueil des pensées du B. Guigue* (Paris: Librairie Philosophie J. Vrin, 1936). For the dates above, see Jolin, "Introduction," 4.

87 See, e.g., Hugh of St. Victor, *De arca Noe morali*, in *Selected Spiritual Writings*, trans. A Religious of CSMV (Eugene, Ore.: Wipf and Stock, 1962), 43–153. For the dates above, see Aelred Squire, "Introduction" in the same work (25). See also Hugh of St. Victor, *De arca Noe mystica*, in Conrad Rudolph, *The Mystic Ark: Hugh of St. Victor, Art, and Thought in the Twelfth Century* (Cambridge: Cambridge University Press, 2014), 393–502. See also Hugh of St. Victor, *On Meditation*, trans. Frans van Liere, in *Writings on the Spiritual Life: A Selection of Works of Hugh, Adam, Achard, Richard, Walter, and Godfrey of St. Victor*, ed. Christopher P. Evans (Turnhout: Brepols, 2013), 381–94.

88 See William of St. Thierry, *Meditations*, trans. Penelope Lawson, in *On Contemplating God, Prayer, Meditations* (hereafter CF 3) (Kalamazoo, MI: Cistercian Publications, 1970), 75–190. For dating these meditations, see Hourlier, "Introduction," 86.

89 Rupert was authoring *De meditatione mortis* at the time of his death in 1129. See Van Engen, *Rupert of Deutz*, 239 and 368–69.

90 See Richard of St. Victor, *Selected Writings on Contemplation*, trans. Clare Kirchberger (New York: Harper and Brothers, 1957). For the dates above, see Kirchberger, "Introduction," 22.

91 Robertson calls attention to the possible influence of Bernard's *Sermones super cantica canticorum* on Guigo II. See CS 238:204 and 224. As evidence that Guigo II had access to Bernard's sermons, Robertson observes similar language found in *SCC* 73, and chap. 5 of Guigo II's *Scala* (CS 238:204). For this sermon of Bernard, see *SCC*, 73, 1.2 (CF 40:76; *SW* 6:482; *SBO* 2:234). For dating Bernard's sermons, see CF 40:xi–xii. For Guigo II, see Guigo II, *The Ladder of Monks*, chap. 5, in *Ladder of Monks and Twelve Meditations*, trans. Edmund Colledge and James Walsh (Kalamazoo, MI: Cistercian Publications, 1981), 70 (hereafter CS 48). For dating this work, see Guigo II, *Ladder of Monks*, 3. See also Guigues II le Chartreux, *Lettre sur La Vie Contemplative (L'Echelle des Moines); Douze Méditations* (Paris: Les Éditions du Cerf, 1976).

(where during a *lectio*, an interpreter would proceed from *littera*, to *sensus*, to an interpretational judgment or *sententia*) and (2) a Scholastic genre focused on conciliatory judgments (where a thinker aims at resolving a dialectical *quaestio* that emerges when that thinker encounters perceived contradictions in the written teachings of traditional authorities).[92] The former kind of *sententiae* might be associated with a collection ascribed to the cathedral school of Laon (ca. 1100).[93] Bernard's contemporary, Gilbert of Poitiers, discusses the nature of the latter kind of Scholastic *quaestio* in the introduction to his commentary on Boethius's treatise on the Trinity.[94] In contrast with the Scholastic genre, the ancient origin of *sententiae* more broadly pertains to works of Wisdom literature that collect interpretational judgments or determinations (consider, for example, the Book of Sirach or the Book of Wisdom).

Knobel traces the development of this literary genre from Cicero's ascription of a set of *sententiae* to Epicurus,[95] to a Greek collection of moral *gnomai* ascribed to a Sextus[96] (Origen of Alexandria references this collec-

92 Peter Boschung, "Boethius and the Early Medieval 'Quaestio,'" *Recherches de théologie et philosophie médiévales* 71, no. 2 (2004): 233–59, at 234–35.

93 See F. Bliemetzrieder, "Anselms von Laon Systematische Sentenzen," *Beiträge zur Geschichte der Philosophie des Mittelaters* 18 (1919): 1–167. See also Alexander Andrée, "Laon Revisited: Master Anselm and the Creation of a Theological School in the Twelfth Century," *The Journal of Medieval Latin* 22 (2012): 257–81; Cédric Giraud, *Per verba magistri: Anselme de Laon et son* école *au XIIe siècle* (Turnhout: Brepols, 2010); Smalley, *Study of the Bible*, 49–51; Luscombe, *School of Peter Abelard*, 173–82.

94 Gisleberti Pictauensis, *Expositio in Boecii librum primum de Trinitate*, Cap. 3, §3, in *Commentaries on Boethius*, ed. N. Häring, 53–180, at 63. For an English translation of this section, see Margaret Gibson, "The *Opuscula Sacra* in the Middle Ages," in *Boethius: His Life, Thought and Influence* (Oxford: Basil Blackwell, 1981), 214–34, at 223. For Boethius, see Boethius, *De Trinitate*, preface, in *Tractates, The Consolation of Philosophy*, trans. H. F. Stewart, E. K. Rand, and S. J. Tester (Cambridge, MA: Harvard University Press, 1973), 2–31, at 2–5. Boethius explains the nature of a Scholastic question as a matter involving doubt in his commentary on Cicero's *Topica*. See Eleonore Stump, trans., *Boethius's In Ciceronis Topica*, Book I, 2.6–2.7 (Ithaca, NY: Cornell University Press, 1988), 29; Niels J. Green-Pedersen, *The Tradition of the Topics in the Middle Ages: The Commentaries on Aristotle's and Boethius' "Topics"* (Munich: Philosophia Verlag, 1984). Cicero's work in turn is a treatise intending to explain the book of Aristotle that has the same title. For Cicero, see Cicero, *Topica* II.6–8, in *De inventione, De optimo genere oratorum, Topica*, trans. H. M. Hubbell (Cambridge, MA: Harvard University Press, 1976), 375–459, at 386–87. For Aristotle, see Aristotle, *Topica* I.10.104a8–9, in *Posterior Analytics, Topica*, trans. Hugh Tredennick and E. S. Forster (Cambridge, MA: Harvard University Press, 1960), 263–739, at 294–95.

95 See also Thomas L. Knoebel, "Introduction," in Isidore of Seville, *Sententiae*, trans. Thomas L. Knoebel (New York: Paulist Press, 2018), 8, citing Cicero, *De finibus bonorum et malorum* II.7, §20, in *On Ends*, trans. H. Rackham (Cambridge, MA: Harvard University Press, 1989), 102–3.

96 See *The Sentences of Sextus: A Contribution to the History of Early Christian Ethics*, ed. Henry Chadwick (Cambridge: Cambridge University Press, 1959). See also Walter T. Wilson, *The*

tion of sentences[97] and Rufinus later translates it into Latin around 400),[98] then to Prosper of Aquitaine's collection of *sententiae* (ca. 450) that includes quotations from Augustine,[99] and finally to the writings of Isidore of Seville (archbishop in 600–636)[100] and Isidore's student, Taio of Zaragoza (also Tajon of Saragossa, bishop in 651–64).[101] Knobel maintains that Isidore was familiar with the *sententiae* of Sextus (believing the work to be partially authored by Pope Sixtus); citing Pevarello, Knoebel further observes that Isidore may have received the work of Sextus as an example of early Christian Wisdom literature.[102] Whether or not this is so, Isidore, citing Wisdom 7:15, does describe a *sententia* as an expression of an interior intuition (*sensus*) that, conforming to justice and to God, communicates a judgment of wisdom that is distinct from knowledge (*scientia*).[103] The literary genre of *sententiae* may thus broadly be associated with ancient Wisdom literature.

Is it then that Bernard's *De consideratione* (to the extent that a letter has grown into a didactic treatise) aims to educate the pope in terms of communicating to Eugene III *sententiae* in the sense of judgments of wisdom (as distinct from those *sententiae* that represent a Scholastic effort to reconcile perceived contradictions among authorities)? Bernard's own set of *sententiae*

Sentences of Sextus (Atlanta: Society of Biblical Literature, 2012). The work of Sextus in turn seems to be influenced by Clitarchus and a set of Pythagorean *sententiae*. See Chadwick, *Sentences*, 73–96.

97 See Chadwick, *Sentences*, 107–16; Wilson, *Sentences*, 7–8.

98 See Knoebel, "Introduction," 9–10, also citing Chadwick. Knoebel observes that there is a similar sentence collection found in an anonymous Nicene-era Egyptian text (9). See *The Gnomai of the Council of Nicaea (CC 0021)*, ed. Alistair Stewart (Piscataway, NJ: Gorgias Press, 2015). Generally speaking, one might associate the *sententiae* genre with the entire set of desert father sayings in ancient Christianity. See, e.g., Benedicta Ward and Metropolitan Anthony, *The Sayings of the Desert Fathers: The Alphabetical Collection* (Collegeville, MN: Liturgical Press, 1984); *Give Me a Word: The Alphabetical Sayings of the Desert Fathers*, trans. John Wortley (Crestwood, NY: St. Vladimir's Seminary Press, 2014).

99 See Knoebel, "Introduction," 10. See also Prosperi Aquitani, *Sententiarum ex operibus S. Augustini delibatarum*, in PL 51:427–534.

100 For a translation, see Isidore of Seville, *Sententiae*, cited above. See also Leinsle, *Introduction to Scholastic Theology*, 31–33 and 54; Joseph F. O'Callaghan, *A History of Medieval Spain* (Ithaca, NY: Cornell University Press, 1983), 85–86; Roger Collins, *Visigothic Spain 409–711* (Malden, MA: Wiley-Blackwell, 2006), 162–66; Thomas O'Loughlin, "Isidore of Seville as a Theologian," in *A Companion to Isidore of Seville*, ed. Andrew Fear and Jamie Wood (Leiden: Brill, 2020), 135–52.

101 Taio Cæsaraugust, *Sententiarum libri quinque*, in PL 80:727–989; Taio Cæsaraugustanus, *Liber sententiarum* (Turnhout: Brepols, 2023). Taio was also a student of St. Braulio of Saragossa, a close friend of St. Isidore. See also O'Callaghan, *A History of Medieval Spain*, 87 (noting the influence of Gregory the Great on Taio); Collins, *Visigothic Spain*, 165–66.

102 See Knoebel, "Introduction," 10, citing Daniele Pevarello, *The Sentences of Sextus and the Origins of Christian Asceticism* (Tübingen: Mohr Siebeck, 2013), 33.

103 Isidore, *Sententiae*, II, 29.10–11 (Knoebel, 115–16).

might also represent this format of interpretive judgments, if Sommerfeldt is correct to maintain that Bernard's notes were authored on the basis of his study of scripture;[104] however, Sommerfeldt also observes that Bernard's *sententiae* are likely indicative of his real sermons, in contrast with Bernard's literary sermons that may never have been delivered.[105]

With respect to Boschung's category of the Scholastic *quaestio* format of *sententiae*, one might note that Bernard associated such a book of sentences with Abelard.[106] On this point, James suggests that Bernard may have had in mind Abelard's work *Sic et non* (1122–26), a work that Abelard authored after the condemnation of Abelard's Trinitarian theology at the Council of Soissons (ca. 1121).[107] Toward the end of the prologue of *Sic et non*, Abelard describes the experience of encountering contradictions in the works of traditional authorities and how this experience leads to a question that requires a judgment:

> It is my purpose, according to my original intention, to gather together various sayings of the holy Fathers which have occurred to me as being surrounded by some degree of uncertainty because of their seeming incompatibility. These may encourage inexperienced readers to engage in that most important exercise, enquiry into truth, and as a result of that enquiry give an edge to their critical faculty. For consistent or frequent questioning is defined as the first key to wisdom.[108]

Abelard's work thus entails a significant theological development in that he is focused on the problem of reconciling authorities whose judgments seem (logically speaking) to contradict one another.[109] This text therefore exemplifies an emergence of the Scholastic *quaestio* or conciliatory *sententiae*

104 See Bernard of Clairvaux, *The Parables and The Sentences*, trans. Michael Casey and Francis R. Swietek (Kalamazoo, MI: Cistercian Publications, 2000), 113–14 (hereafter CF 55).

105 CF 55:113–14.

106 Ep 238 (James, *Letters*, 315–17; Ep 188 in *SW* 3:60–64; *SBO* 8:10–12). See also Luscombe, *School of Peter Abelard*, 62 and 109.

107 James, *Letters*, 316n4. See also Lawn, *Rise and Decline*, 10; Luscombe, *School of Peter Abelard*, 57; Betty Radice, "Chronology," in *The Letters of Abelard and Heloise* (New York: Penguin, 1974), x.

108 Peter Abelard, "Prologue to the *Yes and No*," in *Medieval Literary Theory and Criticism c.1100–c.1375: The Commentary Tradition, Revised Edition*, ed. A. J. Minnis and A. B. Scott (Oxford: Oxford University Press, 1988), 87–100, at 99.

109 Peter Abelard, *Sic et non: A Critical Edition*, ed. Blanche B. Boyer and Richard McKeon (Chicago: University of Chicago Press, 1976).

genre (although Abelard leaves the 158 questions he raises unresolved).[110] Theologians of the cleric-lay schools who parallel Abelard in this regard include Bernard's contemporaries Robert Pullen, Peter Lombard, and Robert of Melun. A work of sentences by Robert Pullen appears in *Sententiarum libri VIII* (ca. 1142–43), likely authored in the years before he assumed his role as papal chancellor, during the time that he taught theology at the cathedral school of Paris as successor of Gilbert of Poitiers.[111] Pullen's effort was followed by the more renowned *Libri sententiarum* of Peter Lombard (ca. 1140–58).[112] Like Prosper's *Sententiae*, Lombard's work contains extensive quotations from Augustine. Meanwhile, in the works of Robert of Melun, a teacher of John of Salisbury in Paris,[113] one finds both *sententiae* and *quaestiones* (ca. 1152–60).[114]

Summary

What might be concluded from this discussion? Bernard's *De consideratione* clearly does not exemplify the specific literary genre of Scholastic *sententiae* that involves an explicit effort to conciliate authorities or argumentative viewpoints (i.e., the dialectical *quaestio disputata* that will become standard in the future).[115] I am thus in agreement with Leclercq that Bernard's didac-

110 See Luscombe, *School of Peter Abelard*, 94–95.

111 Roberti Pulli, *Sententiarum libri octo*, in PL 186:639–1010. Around 1142, Robert Pullen succeeded Gilbert of Poitiers as master of theology at the Parisian cathedral school and had John of Salisbury as a student. See F. Courtney, *Cardinal Robert Pullen: An English Theologian of the Twelfth Century, Analecta Gregoriana* (Rome: Pontifical Gregorian University Press, 1954), 64:9. It was most likely during this period that Pullen authored his *Libri sententiarum VIII* (64:23).

112 For Peter Lombard, see Magistri Petri Lombardi, *Sententiae in IV libris distinctae*, 2 vols., Spicilegium Bonaventurianum IV–V (Grottaferrata: Collegii S. Bonaventurae ad Claras Aquas, 1971–81). For an English translation, see Peter Lombard, *The Sentences*, trans. Giulio Silano, 4 vols. (Toronto: Pontifical Institute of Mediaeval Studies, 2007–10). Dating Lombard's *Libri sententiarum* with precision is difficult. See Philipp W. Rosemann, *The Story of a Great Medieval Book: Peter Lombard's "Sentences"* (Toronto: University of Toronto Press, 2013), 24; Giulio Silano, "Introduction," in *The Sentences: Book 1, The Mystery of the Trinity*, xiii. See also Smalley, *Study of the Bible*, 75; Luscombe, *School of Peter Abelard*, 261–80.

113 Lawn, *Rise and Decline*, 12.

114 See *Oeuvres de Robert de Melun*, ed. Raymond M. Martin (Louvain: Spicilegium Sacrum Lovaniense, 1947–52). See also Smalley, *Study of the Bible*, 73–74; Luscombe, *School of Peter Abelard*, 281–98. For dating Robert of Melun, see Nancy Spatz, "Approaches and Attitudes to a New Theology Textbook: The *Sentences* of Peter Lombard," in *The Intellectual Climate of the Early University*, ed. Nancy van Deusen, 27–52, at 29.

115 One might also consider the *Summa sententiarum* once ascribed to Hugh of St. Victor, a collection of *sententiae* associated with Gilbert of Poitiers, and also the collection associated with a Magister Roland (ca. 1150). This last text is controversially ascribed to Roland Bandinelli (Pope

tic emphasis in *De consideratione* is focused primarily on monastic practice, yet his teaching may also be said to presuppose a broader set of enduring ascetic-mystical judgments, *sententiae* of wisdom that impart a monastic philosophy or wisdom tradition. In this regard, Bernard might appropriately be characterized as an ascetic-mystical theologian. With respect to the traditional sources that are informing Bernard's '*sententiae*' in this regard, one might contend that the monastic practice of *meditatio* is more so indebted to the writings of Gregory the Great than to the writings of Boethius. These diverse Latin thinkers (Gregory and Boethius), in my judgment, typify the monastic and Scholastic approaches, broadly construed. With respect to Gregory as an influence on Bernard, it is to the topic of the sources that informed Bernard in his authorship of *De consideratione* that the discussion now turns.

Alexander III). For the *Summa* once associated with Hugh, see, e.g., "*Summa Sententiarum* I.15–19," trans. Joshua Benson, in *Victorine Christology*, ed. Christopher P. Evans (Hyde Park, NY: New City Press, 2019), 183–206. For Gilbert, see Nikolaus M. Häring (ed.), "Die *Sententiae magistri Gisleberti Pictavensis*," Part I, *Archives d'Histoire Doctrinale et Littéraire du Moyen* Âge 45 (1978): 83–180, and Part II, 46 (1979): 45–195. See also Spatz, "Approaches and Attitudes," 44n12. For Magister Roland, see *Die Sentenzen Rolands nachmals Papstes Alexander III*, ed. Ambrosius M. Gietl (Amsterdam: Rodopi, 1969). See also Leinsle, *Introduction to Scholastic Theology*, 64.

3

Sources

In the previous chapter, I examined Bernard's purpose for writing *De consideratione* and how this purpose related to his selection of the literary genre best suited for communicating his intention. In the present chapter, I will now evaluate the sources that Bernard drew upon when writing the treatise.

Scripture

Immediately one might observe that scripture is the foremost source informing Bernard's thinking. Bernard interweaves constant biblical quotations and paraphrases in his prose. Leclercq, for example, calls attention to Bernard's use of the Hebrew Wisdom literature when Bernard first exhorts Eugene III to take up the practice of consideration.[1] The books of scripture that are most regularly cited in *De consideratione* are the Gospels of John and Matthew as well as 1 Corinthians.[2] Anderson explores in detail Bernard's appropriation of the letters of Paul in *De consideratione*, especially in Book V.[3] A reader of Bernard's writings might readily agree with Anderson's assessment that "Bernard of Clairvaux did not simply memorize Scripture but internalized it and made it his own."[4]

Christian Fathers

After scripture, one might begin to survey the influence that the Latin Fathers exerted on Bernard's thinking and writing. When speaking about

1 Leclercq, "L'Art de la Composition," 118–19, citing *Csi*, I, 5.6 (CF 37:33–34; *SW* 1:638–42; *SBO* 3:399–401).

2 CF 37:185.

3 Anderson, "Paul in Book 5," 137–50. See also Verbaal, "Bernardus Philosophus," 584–85.

4 Anderson, "Paul in Book 5," 148–49.

homilies that he had written on the Virgin Mary, Bernard points to his great regard for the Fathers who preceded him by observing that they should not be contradicted in preaching: "as long as what has been said since the Fathers is not contrary to the Fathers, I see no reason why it should displease the Fathers, or anyone else."[5] If an interpreter of Bernard might be allowed to generalize this statement, one might discern an enduring effort throughout Bernard's writings to preserve the tradition he received. It is not unreasonable then to question whether his teaching on meditation that he transmits to Eugene III is a teaching that Bernard has encountered elsewhere in some sense during his own Christian and monastic formation. Yet which specific patristic thinkers have influenced Bernard in this regard? Among the ancient Christian fathers, Leclercq refers specifically to the influence on Bernard of Origen, Augustine, and Gregory the Great.[6] Gilson also calls attention to the influence of the *Ambigua ad Iohannem* by Maximus the Confessor, mediated to Bernard in a Latin translation of John Scotus Eriugena.[7]

Augustine

Regarding Augustine, Leclercq observes that the works of Augustine were available at Clairvaux.[8] Cvetković argues that despite an absence of texts where Bernard directly quotes Augustine, Bernard's thought remains "deeply inspired" by Augustine.[9] Déchanet agrees that, generally speaking, Bernard appears to be very familiar with a number of Augustinian topics.[10] More specifically, there is explicit textual evidence that indicates Augustine's influence on Bernard with respect to the practice of meditation. In Book II of *De consideratione*, Bernard describes four general kinds of consideration that Eugene III might practice: "I think you should consider four things in this

5 Bernard of Clairvaux, "Homily IV," §11, in Marie-Bernard Saïd, trans., *Homilies in Praise of the Blessed Virgin Mary* (Kalamazoo, MI: Cistercian Publications, 1993), 58 (hereafter CF 18a).

6 CS 7:252. On the influence of Origen, See also CF 24:26n112, citing Jean Leclercq, "Origène au XIIe siècle," *Irenikon* 24 (1951): 425–39.

7 Etienne Gilson, *The Mystical Theology of St. Bernard* (Kalamazoo, MI: Cistercian, 1990), 26–27 and 132n195 (hereafter CS 120). See also CF 24:26n112.

8 Leclercq, "Renewal of Theology," 76, citing Jean Leclercq, "Les manuscrits de l'abbaye de Liessies," *Scriptorium* 6 (1952): 51–62.

9 Carmen Angela Cvetković, *Seeking the Face of God: The Reception of Augustine in the Mystical Thought of Bernard of Clairvaux and William of St. Thierry* (Turnhout: Brepols, 2012), 117.

10 See Jean-Marie Déchanet, "Aux Sources de la Pensée Philosophique de S. Bernard," *ASOC* 9, nos. 3–4 (1953): 59–66, at 63n3.

order: yourself, what is below you, around you and above you."[11] Leclercq maintains that it was Augustine who inspired Bernard with respect to these four modes of reflection.[12] Leclercq points to a specific passage in Augustine's *De doctrina Christiana* where Augustine refers to four kinds of things that might be loved.[13]

In this section of *De doctrina Christiana*, Augustine is discussing how one might focus on created things, one's self, and God, as well as the importance of a person's self-examination in relation to God: "if he loves himself on his own account, he does not relate himself to God, but turns to himself and not to something unchangeable."[14] Augustine in this remark is elaborating on his distinction between use (*uti*) and enjoyment (*frui*).[15] He emphasizes that one should convert one's attention to God as to that which is primarily to be enjoyed and not focus on oneself.[16] Augustine then describes four areas to which one might direct one's love:

> There are four things that are to be loved—one, that which is above us; two, that which we are; three, that which is close to us; four, that which is beneath us [*quattuor sint diligenda, unum quod supra nos est, alterum quod nos sumus, tertium quod iuxta nos est, quartum quod infra nos est*]. No commandments needed to be given about the second and fourth of these. For however much a man may lapse from the truth, he retains a love of his own body. The mind [*animus*] which shuns the unchangeable light which

11 *Csi*, II, 3.6 (CF 37:52; *SW* 1:668–70; *SBO* 3:414–15). "Quatuor, ut occurrunt, tibi consideranda reor: te, quae sub te, quae circa te, quae supra te sunt." See also Evans, *Mind of St. Bernard*, 205.

12 Jean Leclercq, *Bernard of Clairvaux and the Cistercian Spirit*, trans. Claire Lavoie (Kalamazoo, MI: Cistercian Publications, 1976), 151 (hereafter CS 16).

13 Leclercq, "L'Art de la Composition," 130, citing Augustine, *De doctrina Christiana* I.22. See also Anderson, "Reconsidering," 157. The specific passage that Leclercq has in mind is Augustine, *De doctrina Christiana* I.23.22.

14 Augustine, *On Christian Teaching*, trans. R. P. H. Green (Oxford: Oxford University Press, 1999), I.22.21 (17). For the Latin, see Aurelii Augustini, *De doctrina Christiana* I.22.21, ed. Joseph Martin, Corpus Christianorum Series Latina (hereafter CCSL) 32 (Turnhout: Brepols, 1996), 17. "Si autem se propter se diligit, non se refert ad deum, sed ad se ipsum conversus non ad incommutabile aliquid convertitur . . ."

15 For his introduction of this distinction, see Augustine, *De doctrina Christiana* I.4.4 (Green, 9; Martin, 8).

16 For studies concerning Augustine's distinction between use and enjoyment, see K.-Y. Burchill-Limb, "The Actuality of Augustine's Distinction between *Uti* and *Frui*," *Augustiniana* 56, nos. 1–2 (2006): 183–97; Joachim Küpper, "*Uti* and *Frui* in Augustine and the Problem of Aesthetic Pleasure in the Western Tradition (Cervantes, Kant, Marx, Freud)," *MLN (Modern Language Notes)* 127, no. 5 (2012): 126–55.

> is sovereign over all aims to exercise sovereignty over itself and its body, and so cannot fail to love both itself and its body.[17]

One might note that Augustine in this passage indicates that there is a certain hierarchy to the realities that are loved: some are above the mind and some are below. Further, Augustine implies in this passage that the self of his reader (*quod nos sumus*) is the mind (*animus*), whereas the *body* of his reader is beneath the self (*quod infra nos est*). I will return to this observation later when exploring Book III of *De consideratione*. At present, I want to observe that because Augustine's focus in this passage is on love and not intellectual reflection, one cannot say that Bernard is prescribing to Eugene III a specific course of Augustinian meditation. Further, Leclercq observes that Bernard resequences Augustine's teaching when communicating a general course of reflection to the pope.[18]

Regardless, the general influence of Augustine on Bernard seems highly probable. As mentioned above, Leclercq elsewhere notes that the works of Augustine were found in eight volumes at the abbey of Clairvaux.[19] Leclercq also observes that this fourfold Augustinian teaching was absorbed into the Latin monastic tradition. On this point, Leclercq cites first the book *De clericorum institutione* (819) of Benedictine author Hrabanus Maurus (also spelled Rabanus or Rhabanus), an abbot of Fulda,[20] as well as the treatise *De fide, spe et caritate* ascribed to Benedictine author Paschasius Radbertus, an abbot of Corbie (d. ca. 865).[21]

Benedict

Prior to reflecting on Bernard's reception of the Benedictine intellectual tradition as expressed in the Carolingian era, it would be helpful to examine

17 Augustine, *De doctrina Christiana* I.23.22 (Green, 18; Martin, 18).

18 Leclercq, "L'Art de la Composition," 133.

19 Leclercq, "Renewal of Theology," 76, citing Jean Leclercq, "Les manuscrits de l'abbaye de Liessies," as cited above.

20 Leclercq, "L'Art de la Composition," 130–31, citing Rabani Mauri, *De clericorum institutione ad Haistulphum libri tres*, III, 4, in PL 107:293–418, at 381b. Regarding Hrabanus, see Roman Büttner, *Hrabanus Maurus und sein Wirken im Kloster Fulda* (Norderstedt: GRIN, 2006). For the date, see CF 37:185.

21 Leclercq, "L'Art de la Composition," 131, citing Paschasii Radberti, *De fide, spe et charitate*, III, 5, in PL 120:1387–1488, at 1467d. Regarding Paschasius, see George E. McCracken, "Paschasius Radbertus of Corbie: The Lord's Body and Blood (Selections)," in *Early Medieval Theology* (Louisville, Ky.: Westminster John Knox, 1957), 90–108, at 90–93. For the date, see CF 37:186.

the influence of the Benedictine Rule (ca. 530) on Bernard.[22] A first point to note in the Rule pertains to Benedict's own references to consideration or at least to the practice of reflective discretion. With respect to the qualities of a candidate being considered to occupy the role of abbot, Benedict states that the candidate should not be easily excited or anxious but "he must show forethought and consideration in his orders" (*in ipsis imperiis suis providus et consideratus*).[23] The candidate must be "discerning and moderate" and, learning from biblical accounts that serve as "examples of discretion, the mother of virtues," the candidate must exhibit the ability to manage the monastery in a way that is balanced and appropriate for all.[24] Elsewhere, Benedict urges his reader to exercise similar discernment when evaluating the dietary practice of "the old and the young."[25] In that passage, Benedict remarks that "their lack of strength must always be taken into account" and they "should be treated with kindly consideration."[26] Consideration for Benedict, therefore, pertains to the exercise of discretion and prudence when making practical decisions. In contrast with prudential consideration, the word "meditation" in the Rule only appears in relation to monastic reflection on readings.[27]

A second topic to note regarding the influence of the Rule on Bernard is Benedict's metaphorical use of Jacob's ladder (*scala*) mentioned in Genesis 28:12. Using this metaphor, Benedict states: "if we want to reach the highest summit of humility . . . then by our ascending actions we must set up that ladder [*scala*] on which Jacob in a dream saw 'angels descending and ascending.' Without doubt, this descent and ascent can signify only that we descend by exaltation and ascend by humility."[28] The ladder, Benedict indicates, is a spiritual metaphor for human life in the present age.[29] Bernard explic-

22 See, e.g., Bernard's reference at *Mor*, 9.34 (CF 67:78). For dating the Rule, see "Chronology of Christian Monasticism, 150 BC–600 AD," in *The Rule of St. Benedict* (ed. Fry), xxxi–xxxvi, at xxxv. Laistner dates the Rule to ca. 526: M. L. W. Laistner, *Thought and Letters in Western Europe: A.D. 500 to 900*, 2nd ed. (Ithaca, NY: Cornell University Press, 1966), 92.

23 *RB*, chap. 64 (McCann, 146–47; Fry, 63).

24 Ibid.

25 *RB*, chap. 37 (McCann, 92–93; Fry, 39). "Consideretur semper in eis imbecillitas . . ."

26 Ibid. "Sit in eis pia consideratio et praeveniant horas canonicas."

27 *RB*, chap. 8 (McCann, 48–49; Fry, 21). "Those bretheren, who need a better knowledge of them, should devote the time that remains after Matins to the study of the psalms and lessons" (*Quod vero restat post Vigilias, a fratribus qui psalterii vel lectionum aliquid indigent, meditationi inserviatur*).

28 *RB*, chap. 7 (McCann, 38–39; Fry, 16). "Unde, fratres, si summae humilitatis volumus culmen attingere . . . actibus nostris ascendentibus scala illa erigenda est, quae in somno Jacob apparuit, per quam ei descendentes et ascendentes angeli monstrabantur. Non aliud sine dubio descensus ille et ascensus a nobis intelligitur, nisi exaltatione descendere et humilitate ascendere."

29 *RB*, chap. 7 (McCann, 38–39; Fry, 16). "Scala vero ipsa erecta nostra est vita in saeculo . . ."

itly refers to this section of the Rule at the beginning of his early *Liber de gradibus humilitatis et superbiae*.[30] Among Benedict's sources, one might note his explicit references to the *Collationes* and *Instituta* of John Cassian, the *Vitae Patrum*, and the Rule of St. Basil the Great.[31]

Gregory the Great

In addition to Augustine and the Benedictine Rule, Bernard is also influenced by Gregory the Great in a significant way.[32] It is evident that Bernard is familiar with Gregory's work in that Bernard explicitly refers to Gregory "carefully and elegantly" commenting on the book of the prophet Ezekiel (601).[33] Evans observes the similarities between Gregory's *Regula pastoralis* (ca. 590) and Bernard's thought.[34] In the *Regula*, Gregory exhorts ecclesi-

30 *Hum*, 1.1 (CF 13a:29; *SW* 2:44; *SBO* 3, 16).

31 *RB*, chap. 73 (McCann, 160–61; Fry, 69). See also chap. 42 (McCann, 100–101; Fry, 43); John Cassian, *Conferences*, trans. Colm Luibheid (Mahwah, NJ: Paulist Press, 1985); John Cassian, *The Institutes*, trans. Boniface Ramsey (New York: Newman Press, 2000); *The Rule of St. Basil in Latin and English*, trans. Anna M. Silvas (Collegeville, MN: Liturgical Press, 2013); Laistner, *Thought and Letters*, 93.

32 See Jean Leclercq, "Aspects Littéraires de L'Œuvre de S Bernard," in *Recueil D'Études*, 3:13–104, at 72.

33 *Csi*, I, 9.12 (CF 37:43; *SW* 1:654–56; *SBO* 3:407–8). For an English translation of Gregory, see Gregory the Great, *Homilies on the Book of the Prophet Ezekiel* (hereafter *Hiez*), trans. Theodosia Tomkinson (Etna, CA: Center for Traditionalist Studies, 2008). For the Latin of Book II (cited below), see Grégoire le Grand, *Homélies sur* Ézéchiel, Tom. II, trans. Charles Morel, Sources Chrétiennes (hereafter SC) 360 (Paris: Les Éditions du Cerf, 1990). For dating this commentary, see G. R. Evans, *The Thought of Gregory the Great* (Cambridge: Cambridge University Press, 1986), 6. Regarding the general influence of Gregory on the early Cistercians, see Magdalena Aust, "Was uns die Bibliothek von Cîteaux erzählen kann (2): Gregor der Große, Vater der zisterziensischen Mystik," *Cistercienser Chronik* 116 (2009): 17–34. For a study that compares the thought of Gregory the Great with contemporary cognitive psychotherapy, see Roger G. Tweed, "The Psychology of Gregory the Great (A.D. 540–A.D. 604)," *International Journal for the Psychology of Religion* 7, no. 2 (1997): 101–10.

34 See Evans, "*De Consideratione* of Bernard," 130 and 134. See also Basilius Hänsler, "Die 'Pastoralregel' Gregors des Grossen und die Bücher Bernhards 'Über *die Betrachtung*,'" *Cistercienser Chronik* 16 (1904): 147–51. For Gregory, see Gregory the Great, *The Book of Pastoral Rule*, trans. George E. Demacopoulos (Crestwood, NY: St. Vladimir's Seminary Press, 2007). For the Latin, see Gregorii Papae I, *Regulae pastoralis liber, ad Joannem episcopum civitatis Ravennae*, in *Opera Omnia*, in PL 77:13–128; Grégorie le Grand, *La Règle pastorale*, Tom. I, ed. Bruno Judic, Floribert Rommel, Charles Morel, SC 381 (Paris: Les Éditions du Cerf, 1992). For dating the work, see Demacopoulos, "An Introduction for the Reader," 13. Evans maintains that Gregory began preparing the *Regula* when sent to Constantinople by Pope Pelagius II and completed it shortly after succeeding him as Pope in 590. See Evans, *Thought of Gregory*, 5. See also Silke Floryszczak, *Die Regula Pastoralis Gregors des Großen* (Tübingen: Mohr Siebeck, 2005).

astical pastors to engage in exercises that will help them to increase their degree of mental self-regulation. Gregory refers to "some who investigate spiritual precepts with great care" (*spiritalia praecepta perscrutantur*) and who are given to "the study of holy meditation" (*sanctae meditationis studia*), but who contradict their efforts by living an "evil life."[35] He maintains that any person who assumes a clerical role should engage in a "kind of self-examination" (*consideratione*) whereby "he should learn of his own weakness."[36] With respect to such self-consideration, Gregory reiterates at the end of the treatise: "we must turn the eye of our mind to our infirmity" (*ad infirma sua mentis oculus redeat*).[37] In a longer passage, Gregory describes the outflowing dispersion of one's mind (specifically due to loquacity) as a kind of descent that risks vulnerability to sensory temptations. In this text, Gregory explicitly notes the need to regulate the mind within claustral or enclosed limits:

> The human mind behaves like water in that, when it is enclosed, it rises to higher levels because it seeks again the height from which it first descended. But when it is released, it disperses uselessly among the lower things. [By analogy] the meaningless words that are wasted when the censorship of silence is relaxed are like many streams that flow from themselves. The mind is not able to return its thoughts to internal things [*redire interius ad sui cognitionem non sufficit*], because by scattering itself through unprofitable speech, it excludes itself from the mystery of internal considerations [*a secreto se intimae considerationis excludit*]. And it leaves itself completely exposed to the enemy who lies in wait, because it does not surround itself with a barrier of watchfulness [*nulla munitione custodiae circumcludit*].[38]

For Gregory, watchfulness, vigilance, or taking custody of thoughts is required in order to retain one's mind within certain boundaries or limits (later I will explore a variation of this teaching that reappears in Bernard's suggestions to Pope Eugene III).

Gregory makes another reference to the ascent of interior consideration in Book XV of his *Moralia in Job* (ca. 595). There, Benedict's reference to Jacob's ladder is reformulated as a ladder of consideration (*scala*

35 Gregory, *Book of Pastoral Rule*, I, 2 (Demacopoulos, 31; PL 77:13b–15d).

36 Gregory, *Book of Pastoral Rule*, I, "Letter to Bishop John," (Demacopoulos, 27; PL 77:13b).

37 Gregory, *Book of Pastoral Rule*, IV (Demacopoulos, 211; PL 77:126d).

38 Gregory, *Book of Pastoral Rule*, III, 14 (Demacopoulos, 123; PL 77:73b).

considerationis) that one might ascend in thought.[39] It may be that Gregory appropriated the metaphor of the *scala* from the Rule of Benedict: Gregory exhibits familiarity with the Rule when he describes the Rule in a general way in the *De vita Benedicti* section of his *Dialogi* (ca. 593) as "excellent for discretion and also eloquent for the style."[40]

With respect to the metaphor of the *scala*, could Gregory also have been influenced by some party other than Benedict? For example, Demacopoulos maintains that Gregory may have corresponded with the Syrian monk John Climacus, who authored a work entitled *Scala paradisi* while abbot of Mt. Sinai (ca. 600–650).[41] John also uses the metaphor of the ladder to represent personal development in the Christian virtues.[42] I will return to this topic of growth in virtues below when exploring Bernard's use of the metaphor of Jacob's ladder in Book V of *De consideratione*.[43]

Carolingian Commentators on the Rule of Benedict

Did Bernard encounter the Gregorian *scala considerationis* directly in Gregory's *Moralia*, or in a collection of *florilegium* (an anthology of textual extracts), or as mediated by some other author? With respect to the third option, the monastic practice of consideration that Gregory mentions is in fact described and developed within commentaries on the Benedictine

39 Gregory the Great, *Moral Reflections on the Book of Job* (hereafter *Mo*), XV.46.52, trans. Brian Kerns (Collegeville, MN: Cistercian Publications, 2016), 242 (hereafter CS 258), as cited in Carole Straw, *Gregory the Great: Perfection in Imperfection* (Los Angeles: University of California Press, 1988), 33. For the Latin, see Gregorii Papae I, *Moralium libri sive expositio in librum B. Iob* XV.46, §52, in *Opera Omnia*, in PL 75:1107c. Evans maintains that Gregory began preparing this work when in Constantinople, dating its completion to around 595. See Evans, *Thought of Gregory*, 5; Carole Straw, "Gregory I," in *Augustine through the Ages: An Encyclopedia*, ed. Allan D. Fitzgerald (Grand Rapids, MI: Eerdmans, 1999), 402–5, at 404.

40 Gregory the Great, *Dialogues* II.36, ed. Edmund Garratt Gardner (London: Philip Lee Warner, 1911), 99. For dating the *Dialogues*, see Evans, *Thought of Gregory*, 6.

41 Demacopoulos, "An Introduction," 10. For Climacus, see John Climacus, *The Ladder of Divine Ascent*, trans. Colm Luibheid and Norman Russell (Mahwah, NJ: Paulist Press, 1982). Kallistos Ware notes the difficulty of dating John's life and thus the *Scala paradisi*, although he contends that the work was written while John was Abbot of Mt. Sinai near the end of his life. See Ware, "Introduction," *Ladder of Divine Ascent*, 1–70, at 3 and 5. If this is so, authorship of the work might be dated to ca. 640 with the result that John is an unlikely influence upon Gregory.

42 "The holy virtues are like the ladder of Jacob and the unholy vices are like the chains that fell off the chief apostle Peter. The virtues lead from one to another and carry heavenward the man who chooses them. Vices on the other hand beget and stifle one another." John of Climacus, *Ladder of Divine Ascent*, step 9, in Luibheid and Russell, 152.

43 *Csi*, V, 1.1 (CF 37:140; *SW* 1:774; *SBO* 3:467).

Rule. These observations return the discussion to the Benedictine intellectual tradition expressed in the Carolingian era just after Hrabanus Maurus and Paschasius Radbertus.

First, I will focus on an early *Expositio* of the Rule authored by Smaragdus of Saint-Mihiel (817).[44] Smaragdus also uses the word 'consideration' with the same practical emphasis as Benedict. For example, when Benedict states that the candidate who fulfills the role of the monastery cellarer should be "temperate" (*sobrius*),[45] Smaragdus comments that such sobriety entails being "careful and considerate."[46] Smaragdus associates the exercise of consideration with the virtue of prudence when he states that Benedict himself exhibited the virtue of prudence in his recommendations for monastic attire: "Being a considerate man, he very prudently said this."[47] As distinct from prudence, however, Smaragdus also suggests a connection between the practice of consideration that Benedict recommends and a more contemplative kind of meditation. When Benedict in the Rule cautions monks to "prefer moderation in speech,"[48] Smaragdus in his comment quotes Gregory the Great who contrasts immoderate speech with the exercise of a kind of contemplative meditation.[49] I will return to this particular passage of Gregory below. At present, I want to observe Smaragdus's extensive engagement with the thought of Gregory the Great, not only in Smaragdus's *Expositio*, but also in his *Diadema monachorum* that provides a detailed summary of various monastic practices.[50] Barry maintains that Smaragdus likely encountered the

44 For Smaragdus, see *Smaragdi abbatis expositio in regulam S. Benedicti*, ed. Alfred Spannagel and Pius Engelbert, in *Corpus consuetudinum monasticarum* VIII (Siegburg: Franz Schmitt, 1974). For an English translation, see Smaragdus of Saint-Mihiel, *Commentary on the Rule of Saint Benedict*, trans. David Barry (Kalamazoo, MI: Cistercian Publications, 2008). For dating this *expositio*, see Daniel Marcel LaCorte, "The Expositio and Monastic Reform at Cîteaux," in Smaragdus, *Commentary*, 9–24, at 11. See also Terrence G. Kardong, "The Earliest Commentator on *RB*: Smaragdus on Benedict's Prologue," *American Benedictine Review* 55 (2004): 171–93; Matthew Ponesse, "Smaragdus of St. Mihiel and the Carolingian Monastic Reform," *Revue Bénédictine* 116 (2006): 367–92.

45 *RB*, chap. 31 (McCann, 80–81; Fry, 34).

46 Smaragdus, *Commentary*, chap. 31 (Barry, 376).

47 Ibid., chap. 55 (Barry, 457). Benedict proceeds: "This is left to the abbot's discretion" (*Haec ergo consideratio penes abbatem est*). See *RB*, chap. 55 (McCann, 124–25; Fry, 53).

48 *RB*, chap. 4 (McCann, 28–29; Fry, 13). *Multum loqui non amare.*

49 Smaragdus, *Commentary*, chap. 4 (Barry, 224), citing Gregory the Great, *Regulae pastoralis liber* III.14.

50 For an English transition, see Smaragdus of Saint-Mihiel, *Diadema monachorum: The Crown of Monks*, as cited above.

writings of Gregory by means of *florilegium* found in the *Sententiarum libri V* of Taio of Zaragoza.[51]

Is it possible that Gregory influenced Bernard via Smaragdus? It is unclear whether Bernard had access to Smaragdus's works.[52] However, there is an alternative commentator on the Rule that should be considered: Leclercq observes that Bernard may have encountered a different Carolingian era commentary on the Rule authored just after Smaragdus by Hildemar of Corbie-Civate (ca. 845).[53] Hildemar's text with slight omissions also appears in a commentary on the Rule ascribed to a different Carolingian era scholar named Paul the Deacon (ca. 720–ca. 799).[54] It is Hildemar's commentary, according to Leclercq, that is the likely source that informs Bernard's organization of his doctrine of meditation in *De consideratione*.[55] Leclercq states that his attention was drawn to Hildemar by a short soliloquy ascribed to

51 David Barry, "Introduction to Smaragdus's *Crown of Monks*," in Samaragdus, *Crown of Monks*, xiii–xxii, at xvii. See also Vadim Prozorov, "Discipline and Mercy: Moses as a Pattern for Good Rulers in the Works of Pope Gregory the Great," in *The Christian Moses: From Philo to the Qur'ān*, ed. Philip Rousseau and Janet A. Timbie (Washington, DC: The Catholic University of America Press, 2019), 252–63, at 261.

52 La Corte writes: "The book lists for twelfth-century libraries show that the *Diadema* could be found in many Cistercian abbeys, among them Pontigny, Cîteaux, Rievaulx, Meaux, and many other Cistercian and traditional Benedictine houses . . . The founders of Cîteaux found much in the writings of Smaragdus to support their renewal of Benedictine life." Daniel Marcel La Corte, "Smaragdus of Saint-Mihiel: Ninth-Century Sources for Twelfth-Century Reformers," *CSQ* 41, no. 3 (2006): 273–90, at 276 and 290.

53 Jean Leclercq, "Études sur Saint Bernard et le Texte de ses Écrits," *ASOC* 9, nos. 1–2 (1953): 11–201, at 147. For this reference, I am indebted to Anderson, "Reconsidering," 157, and CF 37:185–86. For Hildemar, see Hildemarus, *Expositio regulae ab Hildemaro tradita*, ed. Rupert Mittermüller (Cincinnati: Pustet, 1880). For dating this commentary, see Lynda L. Coon, "Collecting the Desert in the Carolingian West," *Church History and Religious Culture* 86, no. 1–4 (2006): 135–62, at 153. For more information on Hildemar, see Klaus Zelzer, "Überlegungen zu einer Gesamtedition des frühnachkarolingischen Kommentars zur Regula S. Benedicti aus der Tradition des Hildemar von Corbie," *Revue Bénédictine* 91, nos. 3–4 (1981): 373–82; Mayke de Jong, "Growing Up in a Carolingian Monastery: Magister Hildemar and His Oblates," *Journal of Medieval History* 9, no. 2 (1983): 99–128; Klaus Zelzer, "Von Benedikt zu Hildemar: Zu Textgestalt und Textgeschichte der Regula Benedicti auf ihrem Weg zur Alleingeltung," *Frühmittelalterliche Studien* 23, no. 1 (1989): 112–30. According to Hafner, another existing commentary (the *Expositio Basilii Abbatis*) consists of student notes on Hildemar's work. See Wolfgang Hafner, *Der Basiliuskommentar zur Regula S. Benedicti: Ein Beitrag zur Autorenfrage karolingischer Regelkommentare* (Münster: Aschendorff, 1959).

54 For Paul the Deacon, see Pauli Warnefridi, *In sanctam regulam commentarium* (Montecassino: Abbot of Montecassino, 1880). See also Leclercq, "Études sur Saint Bernard," 147n2. For discussion of Paul the Deacon, see Mary Garrison, "The Emergence of Carolingian Latin Literature and the Court of Charlemagne (780–814)," in *Carolingian Culture: Emulation and Innovation*, ed. Rosamond McKitterick (Cambridge: Cambridge University Press, 1994), 111–40, at 117–21.

55 Leclercq, "L'Art de la Composition," 133. See also CF 37:186.

Bernard that is found in several ancient Parisian manuscripts.[56] Leclercq provides an edition of this short soliloquy and seems to accept Bernard's authorship of it.[57] He observes that the soliloquy looks something like a rough draft of the plan for meditation that Bernard will rewrite for Eugene III in *De consideratione* Book II. It is Hildemar, Leclercq maintains, who seems to have inspired the specific content in Bernard's soliloquy.[58]

When Hildemar treats the fourth chapter of Benedict's Rule ("the tools for good works"), he prescribes a course of monastic meditation in his comment on section 46 ("yearn for everlasting life with holy desire").[59] In his comment, Hildemar describes three kinds of meditation: "Eternal life which is good and is to be desired, although it is able to be considered in many ways, nonetheless has three grades which are able to be considered."[60] Hildemar states that the first grade of consideration will focus on one's own soul.[61] Regarding the soul, he writes, "consider from where it comes and to where it goes."[62] Yet he realizes in the exercise of meditation that one may not be content to limit oneself to such introspection: "for because in consideration one is not able to remain in oneself for long, one wills to go outside of oneself, that one might possess that which one does not have."[63] As such, one's meditation might proceed to a second grade: at this point, the mind's "attention [*acies*] is directed toward the consideration of the angels and the blessed spirits."[64] From there, the course of meditation proceeds further:

56 Leclercq, "Études sur Saint Bernard," 147, citing Mss Paris B. N. lat. 14517 (XIIe s., Saint-Victor), f. 167; Paris B. N. lat. 2938 (XIIe s., Mortemer, O. Cist.), f. 52^v; Paris, Mazarine 735 (XIIe s.).

57 Leclercq, "Études sur Saint Bernard," 148. The beginning of the soliloquy is reprinted in Leclercq, "L'Art de la Composition," 134.

58 Leclercq, "L'Art de la Composition," 134. "Or il est un texte mineur de Bernard qui, d'une part, semble inspiré de ces textes d'Hildemar, et, d'autre part, est comme une première ébauche du plan du livre II du De consideratione; il s'agit d'un bref Soliloque . . ."

59 *RB*, chap. 4 (McCann, 28–29; Fry, 12–13). "Vitam aeternam omni concupiscentia spiritali desiderare."

60 Hildemar, *Expositio regulae*, Cap. IV (Mittermüller, 168); Warnefridi, *In . . . regulam commentarium* (108–9). "Vita autem aeterna quam bona et concupiscibilis sit, quamvis multis modis possit considerari, tamen tres sunt maxime gradus, quibus considerari potest." See also Leclercq, "L'Art de la Composition," 134.

61 Hildemar, *Expositio regulae*, Cap. IV (Mittermüller, 168); Warnefridi, *In . . . regulam commentarium* (109). "Primus gradus est consideratio animae; debes enim animam tuam considerare."

62 Ibid., 169 (109). "Considera iterum, unde venit, aut quo vadit . . ."

63 Ibid. "Nam quia in consideratione sui non potest diutius commorari, vult exire foras, eo quod non habet, quid teneat . . ." Notably, most of this passage is missing from the commentary ascribed to Paul the Deacon.

64 Ibid. "Ideo necesse est, ut ejus acies ad considerationem angelorum et beatorum spirituum dirigatur." Hildemar's language in this passage is evocative of the phrase *acies mentis* (the focused attention

"After consideration of the soul and angelic creatures, one should transition to the consideration of the Creator."[65] When considering God, Hildemar warns that one should not picture any figure or image of the one who is omnipotent, invisible, and uncircumscribed.[66]

It is helpful to note the overall context of the fourth chapter of the Rule in which Hildemar's instruction on meditation is found. Benedict closes this chapter by stating that his discussion has been focused on "the tools of the spiritual craft" (*instrumenta artis spiritalis*).[67] The workshop where such tools are to be utilized is the monastic enclosure or cloister.[68] The task of meditation (consideration) for Hildemar, therefore, might be interpreted as the exercise of one such monastic tool.

Platonic Philosophy

As a further source for Bernard when writing *De consideratione*, one might question whether and to what extent Bernard's teaching has been influenced by philosophy.[69] In relation to philosophy, Michel characterizes the practice of meditation for Bernard as involving the pure reflection of thought.[70] Michel proceeds further to describe thought in this way as "present to itself alone."[71] Michel here might have in mind the remark of the Platonic philos-

of the mind) that Bernard also employs and which will be discussed further below. For Bernard, see *Csi*, V, 13.27 (CF 37:174; *SW* 1:820; *SBO* 3:490).

65 Hildemar, *Expositio regulae*, Cap. IV (Mittermüller, 169); Warnefridi, *In . . . regulam commentarium* (109). "Post considerationem animae sive angelicae creaturae debet transire in considerationem creatoris . . ."

66 Ibid. "Verumtamen prius debet anima castigari, ne aliquam figuram aut imaginem fingat in Deo, sed credat, illum esse omnipotentem, invisibilem, incircumscriptum."

67 Ibid., 181 (117). See also *RB*, chap. 4 (McCann, 30–31; Fry, 14). "Ecce haec sunt instrumenta artis spiritalis."

68 Hildemar, *Expositio regulae*, Cap. IV (Mittermüller, 182); Warnefridi, *In . . . regulam commentarium* (117). See also *RB*, chap. 4 (McCann, 32–33; Fry, 14). "Officina vero, ubi haec omnia diligenter operemur, claustra sunt monasterii et stabilitas in congregatione."

69 R. E. Houser, for example, when describing the influence of Bernard's *De consideratione* on thirteenth-century thinker Philip the Chancellor and his doctrine of the virtues, states that the word "consideration" that Bernard employs has a Stoic character. See R. E. Houser, *The Cardinal Virtues: Aquinas, Albert, and Philip the Chancellor* (Toronto: Pontifical Institute of Mediaeval Studies, 2004), 218.

70 Michel, "La considération," 115. "En d'autres termes, la considération est ce moment purement réflexif où la pensée, en un territoire inconnu, recherche et attend le signe qui lui permettrait de vérifier si la voie qu'elle emprunte est celle qu'elle doit suivre pour arriver."

71 Ibid. "Ce moment refléxif, critique est pour Bernard essentiel, parce que le mouvement même de la pensée est ici présent « seul » en un état presque pur, saisi entre une adhésion qu'elle suspend et une certitude qu'elle recherche."

opher Plotinus who described the contemplative life as involving "the flight of the alone to the Alone" or as an "escape in solitude to the solitary" (*phugē monou pros monon*).[72]

What is Bernard's relationship with Platonic and Neo-Platonic philosophy? Citing the views of Dalloz, Déchanet argues that there are Platonic influences on Bernard's philosophical thinking in *De consideratione*.[73] Déchanet provides eight contrasts between Bernard and Plato.[74] Despite recognizing that Bernard draws on texts of Gregory, Déchanet suggests that Bernard's thought is primarily Platonic and that Bernard utilizes Gregorian expressions with a Platonic meaning.[75] Déchanet's view is echoed by Luscombe.[76] However, some of Déchanet's claims require further evaluation. For example, is it true that one should associate Bernard's metaphor of a four-horse chariot—as found in his appropriation of Paul's reference to the "length, width, height, and depth" of God (Eph 3:18)[77]—with Plato's two-horse chariot that serves as a metaphor for the soul's contradictory impulses?[78] In contrast with Déchanet, Leclercq argues that Bernard's metaphor of a chariot is not adopted from Plato, but rather from some other medieval author such as Paschasius Radbertus.[79] Similarly, in response to Déchanet, should one identify Bernard's understanding of theological meditation—which in exercise is primarily inspired by faith in scripture—with Platonic contemplation?[80] And is it true that Bernard's reference to *repatriation* in *De consideratione* Book V is "heavy with Platonic meaning"?[81]

72 See Plotinus, *Enneads* VI.9, in *Enneads, VI.6–9*, trans. A. H. Armstrong (Cambridge, MA: Harvard University Press, 1988), 345. The French rendering of this passage is *fuir seul vers lui seul*. See É. Bréhier, *Plotin: Ennéades* (Paris: Société d'Édition « Les Belles Lettres », 1924–28), 7:187. For this reference, I am indebted to Kevin Corrigan, "'Solitary' Mysticism in Plotinus, Proclus, Gregory of Nyssa, and Pseudo-Dionysius," *The Journal of Religion* 76, no. 1 (1996): 28–42, at 42.

73 Déchanet, "Aux Sources," 60; CF 37:186–87.

74 Déchanet, "Aux Sources," 61–66.

75 Ibid., 63n3.

76 Luscombe, *School of Peter Abelard*, 43.

77 See Anderson, "Paul in Book 5," 146.

78 Déchanet, "Aux Sources," 63. For Bernard on this point, see *Csi*, V, 13.27 (CF 37:174–75; *SW* 1:818–22; *SBO* 3:489–91). For Plato's image of a chariot, see Plato, *Phaedrus* 246b–248b, in *Euthyphro, Apology, Crito, Phaedo, Phaedrus*, trans. Harold North-Fowler (Cambridge, MA: Harvard University Press, 2001), 405–579, at 470–77.

79 CS 16:151. See also CF 37:186, and 207en10 citing: Paschasii Radberti, *De vita s. Adalhardi*, in PL 120:1507–56, at 1517A.

80 Déchanet, "Aux Sources," 63.

81 Ibid., 66. For Bernard's reference to repatriation, see *Csi*, V, 1.2 (CF 37:141; *SW* 1:776; *SBO* 3:468).

At the other extreme from Déchanet, Sommerfeldt proposes that there is an absence of Platonic influence on Bernard.[82] McGinn acknowledges at least an absence of the Platonism of Pseudo-Dionysius on Bernard: "Bernard's debt to Pseudo-Dionysius does not appear to be large."[83] Gilson agrees that there is an absence of the influence of a Neo-Platonic writing style on Bernard (exemplified by Pseudo-Dionysius).[84] The influence of Pseudo-Dionysius upon Gregory the Great is also questionable.[85] On the other hand, Straw claims Gregory the Great "thoroughly absorbed the Neoplatonism of Ambrose."[86] One might also consider, as McGinn suggests, whether Origen or Augustine (or Gregory) may have mediated elements of Platonic philosophy to Bernard.[87] For example, referring to the seven liberal arts in the medieval era (the trivium and the quadrivium), Marenbon contends that customarily in the early medieval era such arts were understood as hierarchically organized according to "Neoplatonic speculation about knowledge, first and most fully expounded in Augustine's *De ordine*"[88] (there is an important connection between Augustine's *De ordine* and Book V of Bernard's *De consideratione* that I will explore below when examining Bernard's teaching on self-recollection).

82 Sommerfeldt, *Life of the Mind*, 72.

83 CF 24:26n112, citing E. Boissard, "S. Bernard et le Pseudo-Aréopagite," *Recherches de Théologie Ancienne et Médiévale* 26 (1959): 214–63.

84 CS 120:25.

85 See Joan M. Petersen, "'Homo omnino Latinus'? The Theological and Cultural Background of Pope Gregory the Great," *Speculum* 62, no. 3 (1987): 529–51, at 530–42.

86 Straw, *Gregory the Great: Perfection in Imperfection*, 13–14. Regarding the presence of Neo-Platonic philosophy in the theology of Ambrose, Conyngham (citing Courcelle and Madec) notes Ambrose's "extensive use of the *Enneads* of Plotinus" in three particular sermons, two of which Courcelle argues may have been heard by Augustine in 386. See Andrew Lennox Conyngham, "Ambrose and Philosophy," in *Christian Faith and Greek Philosophy in Late Antiquity: Essays in Tribute to Christopher George Stead*, ed. Lionel R. Wickham and Caroline P. Bammel (Leiden: Brill, 1993), 112–28, at 114–15. For Courcelle, see Pierre Courcelle, "Aspects varies du platonisme ambrosien," in *Recherches sur les Confessions de saint Augustin*, new ed. (Paris: E. de Boccard, 1968), Appendix IV, 138n2. See also Pierre Courcelle, "Plotin et saint Ambroise," *Revue de philologie, de littérature et d'histoire anciennes* 24 (1950): 29–56; Marcia L. Colish, "Classicism and Catechesis in the Patriarch Treatises of Ambrose of Milan," *Rivista di Storia della Filosofia* 61, no. 1 (2006): 9–42, esp. 11n6. For Madec, see Goulven Madec, *Saint Ambroise et la Philosophie* (Paris: Études Augustiniennes, 1974). For a response to Madec, see Hervé Savon, "Saint Ambroise et la philosophie à propos d'une étude récente," *Revue de l'histoire des religions* 191, no. 2 (1977): 173–96.

87 CF 24:79.

88 John Marenbon, "Carolingian Thought," in *Carolingian Culture: Emulation and Innovation*, ed. Rosamond McKitterick (Cambridge: Cambridge University Press, 1994), 171–92, at 172. For the text by Augustine, see *Divine Providence and the Problem of Evil: A Translation of St. Augustine's "De Ordine,"* trans. Robert P. Russell (New York: Cosmopolitan Science and Art Service, 1942).

Further, what relationship does the biblical metaphor of the ladder have with the Platonic doctrine of the ascent of the mind to the divine?[89] With respect to the metaphor of the ladder, Augustine also ascends in thought according to a hierarchy of meditation—see, for example, Augustine's description of a meditative ascent with his mother Monica at Ostia just prior to her death in the *Confessions*.[90] McMahon observes that the closing structure of *Confessions* X–XIII progresses through an ascent from memory to attention to the human will to God's will.[91] One might consider also Augustine's description of an ontological hierarchy in *De civitate Dei* VIII.6, which proceeds intellectually from considering vegetative life to animal, then to human, angelic, and divine life.[92] A similar hierarchical structure involving intellectual ascent to God may be discerned in the book *De natura corporis et animae* (ca. 1140) authored by Bernard's friend and Cistercian contemporary, William of St. Thierry.[93] An editorial annotation in an English edition of this text observes that William's hierarchical teaching in this regard borrows from Augustine in the work *De quantitate animae* (ca. 387–88).[94] Evans observes that the overall structure of *De consideratione* is also intentionally

89 Regarding the spiritual exercise of Platonic ascent in the works of Plotinus, see Mateusz Stróżyński, "The Ascent of the Soul as Spiritual Exercise in Plotinus' *Enneads*," *Mnemosyne: A Journal of Classical Studies* 74, no. 3 (2021): 448–77, at 457, citing Plotinus, *Enneads* V.3.9. See also Mateusz Stróżyński, "Spiritual Exercise in Plotinus: The Deictic Method," *Classical Philology* 117, no. 3 (2022): 495–517, at 497.

90 Augustine, *Confessions* IX.10, in *Confessions, Books IX–XIII*, trans. William Watts (Cambridge, MA: Harvard University Press, 2000), 46–53.

91 Robert McMahon, *Understanding the Medieval Meditative Ascent: Augustine, Anselm, Boethius, and Dante* (Washington, DC: The Catholic University of America Press, 2006), 72–73.

92 Augustine writes: "The Platonist philosophers . . . who . . . are not undeservedly raised above the rest in fame and glory, saw that God is not a body, and therefore passed beyond all bodies in their search for God . . . They saw that, in every changeable thing whatsoever . . . the form that makes it what it is can have no existence except from Him Who truly is because He is immutable. So it is, then, that, whether we consider the whole body of the world . . . and the elements . . . or all life . . . as in the case of trees; or that which, in addition to this, also has sensation, as with the beasts; or that which has all these things and intelligence besides, as in the case of men; or that which conserves itself . . . without needing to be sustained by food, as with the angels: none of these can have existence other than through Him Who simply is . . . To Him, to exist is to live, to understand and to be blessed." Augustine, *The City of God against the Pagans*, ed. R. W. Dyson (New York: Cambridge University Press, 1998), VIII.6 (320–21). For the Latin, see Augustinus, *De civitate Dei*, Libri I-X, ed. B. Dombart and A. Kalb, CCSL 47 (Turnhout: Brepols, 1955).

93 See William of St. Thierry, *Nature of the Body and the Soul*, Book II, §14 (CF 24:147–50). For dating, see CF 24:28.

94 CF 24:147n38. For an English translation, see Augustine, *The Magnitude of the Soul*, trans. John J. McMahon, chap. 33, §70–§76, in *The Immortality of the Soul, The Magnitude of the Soul, On Music, The Advantage of Believing, On Faith in Things Unseen*, ed. Hermigild Dressler (Washington, DC: The Catholic University of America Press, 1947), 49–149, at 136–44.

hierarchical, in that Bernard guides the pope from what is below him to what is above him, ontologically or existentially speaking.[95]

Could it be that this Augustinian structure of hierarchical ascent (informed by Platonic philosophy) influences the Cistercian authors directly—and also indirectly as mediated through the works of Gregory? The influence of Augustine on Gregory is evident.[96] According to Straw, "Gregory is one of the chief links between Augustine and the Middle Ages," yet at the same time "Gregory is preeminently a moral and ascetical theologian, lacking Augustine's theoretical and speculative side."[97] It is not unreasonable to maintain that what partially characterizes the monastic philosophy that Bernard communicates is—alongside the structure of moral hierarchy that he employs to discuss humility (derived from Benedict who represents it with the biblical metaphor of the ladder)—a structure of cosmological (or at least psychological) hierarchy that is resonant of Platonic philosophy, arguably as mediated by Augustine, Gregory, and Hildemar.[98]

I will explore this topic of hierarchical ascent in Bernard's thought below, particularly in the interpretation proposed for Book V of *De consideratione*. Here, I want to note that while the hierarchy as found in Augustine's *De civitate Dei* VIII.6 is ontological and cosmological, in the present study of Bernard's *De consideratione* I will limit my discussion to focus on a hierarchy of psychological activities—this might be referred to simply as an implicit and general Platonic psychology in Bernard's thought that has been mediated by Augustine, Gregory, and Hildemar.[99] To reiterate, I am not stating that

95 Evans, *Bernard of Clairvaux*, 51.

96 R. A. Markus, *Gregory the Great and His World* (Cambridge: Cambridge University Press, 1997), 40.

97 Straw, "Gregory I," in *Augustine through the Ages*, 402.

98 Leclercq, "Théologie monastique," 7–23; Leclercq, *Love of Learning*, 191–235.

99 Plato refers to various hierarchies of psychological activities in the *Republic*. For example, he states via Socrates that the spirited part (*thumoeides*) mediates between the rational part (*logistikon*) and the appetitive part (*epithumētikon*) in the soul (*psuchē*), just as the social class of helper (*epikourētikon*) mediates between the social class of counselor (*bouleutikon*) and the social class of merchant (*chrēmatistikon*) in the city-state. See Plato, *The Republic, Books I–V*, trans. Paul Shorey (Cambridge, MA: Harvard University Press, 2000), IV.15.440e–441a (402–5). See also F. A. Wilford, "The Status of Reason in Plato's Psychology," *Phronesis* 4, no. 1 (1959): 54–58; George Klosko, "The 'Rule' of Reason in Plato's Psychology," *History of Philosophy Quarterly* 5, no. 4 (1988): 341–56. Another hierarchy is found in Plato's teaching on the four segments of the divided line (509d–511e) just prior to his discussion of the allegory of the cave (514a–517a): Plato describes one ascending in cognition from an image (*eikasia*), to faith (*pistis*), to thinking (*dianoia*), to understanding (*noesis*). See Plato, *The Republic, Books VI–X*, trans. Paul Shorey (Cambridge, MA: Harvard University Press, 2000), VI.21.511e (117). See also John Malcolm, "The Line and the Cave," *Phronesis* 7, no. 1 (1962): 38–45; Kenneth Dorter, "The Divided Line and the Structure of Plato's *Republic*," *History*

Bernard studied Plato directly (as did Bernard's contemporary William of Conches, ca. 1090–ca. 1155), but rather I am noting that Bernard's emphasis on hierarchy has a basis in ancient Platonic thought and that Bernard arguably encountered this topic through the mediation of patristic authors such as Augustine, Gregory, and Hildemar.[100]

of Philosophy Quarterly 21, no. 1 (2004): 1–20; T. M. Robinson, *Plato's Psychology*, 2nd ed. (Toronto: University of Toronto Press, 1995).

100 For the commentary of William of Conches on Plato's *Timaeus*, see Guillelmi de Conchis, *Glosae super Platonem*, ed. Édouard Jeauneau, CCSM 203 (Turnhout: Brepols, 2006).

PART 2

Interpreting the Content of the Treatise

4

Book I

An Introduction to Meditation

Having completed a historical evaluation of Bernard's *De considerati-one* in the first part of this study (where I examined his authorship, context, purpose, selection of a literary genre, and sources), I now proceed with presenting an interpretation of the content of the treatise. In this chapter, I examine the content of Book I before proceeding through each of the remaining books that Bernard may have written at a later time.[1] Book I of *De consideratione* provides an introduction to the practice of meditation. My interpretation of Book I is organized around specific topics that arise in the course of Bernard's text. For example, in order to practice meditation, one must seek quietude. Such an exercise may be understood to have meaning within the context of what might be called a claustral psychology. Further, the practice of meditation may be understood as an act of religious piety oriented toward the Holy Spirit that can facilitate growth in humility and the Christian virtues.

Quietude

In Book I of *De consideratione*, Bernard observes that in the monastery Pope Eugene III once enjoyed the "delights of solitude" (*dulcis quietis*).[2] It was from the enjoyment of such monastic quietude—the "leisure" (*otium*) of the contemplative life—that Bernard perceives Eugene III to have been snatched

1 Anderson, "Reconsidering De consideratione," 149.

2 *Csi*, I, 1.1 (CF 37:25; *SW* 1:628; *SBO* 3:394). See also David A. Clairmont, "Medieval Consideration and Moral Pace: Thomas Aquinas and Bernard of Clairvaux on the Temporal Aspects of Virtue," *Journal of Religious Ethics* 41, no. 1 (2013): 79–111, at 91.

due to his papal election.[3] Bernard states that the pope must again dedicate time to this "pious and beneficial leisure" (*pio tamque utili otio*).[4] Bernard understands leisure in this sense not as time spent in idleness, but rather as time spent in pursuit of wisdom, religious devotion, and development in self-knowledge: according to Leclercq, *otium* refers to a period of "contemplative time" allocated to the praxis of "spiritual activities" such as "ascesis and prayer" in orientation to God.[5]

Bernard may not have been familiar with Aristotle's remarks that attaining the state of well-spiritedness (*eudaimonia*) requires quietude or leisure (*scholē*).[6] However, in sermon 85 of his *Sermones super cantica canticorum*, Bernard quotes Sirach 38:25 which in the Greek version employs the same word (*scholē*). Bernard writes:

> "The wisdom of a scribe comes by leisure," says Solomon. Therefore the leisure of wisdom is exertion, and the more leisure wisdom has, the harder it works in its own fashion. But the more virtue is exercised in its own sphere, the more illustrious it is, and the more ready it is to serve, the more approval it wins. If anyone defines wisdom as the love of virtue, I think you are not far from the truth.[7]

3 Ep 315 (James, *Letters*, 386; Ep 237 in *SW* 3:266–70; *SBO* 8:113–15). For a contemporary use of the term "leisure" in the sense of "contemplative meditation," see Josef Pieper, *Leisure: The Basis of Culture*, trans. Gerald Malsbary (South Bend, IN: St. Augustine's, 1998), 31: "Leisure is a form of that quietness that is the necessary preparation for accepting reality; only the person who is still can hear, and whoever is not still, cannot hear . . . Leisure is the disposition of receptive understanding, of contemplative beholding, and immersion—in the real."

4 *Csi*, I, 8.11 (CF 37:42; *SW* 1:654; *SBO* 3:407).

5 Jean Leclercq, "Experience and Interpretation of Time in the Early Middle Ages," in *Studies in Medieval Culture V*, ed. John R. Sommerfeldt, Larry Syndergaard, and E. Rozanne Elder (Kalamazoo, MI: Western Michigan University Press, 1975), 9–19, at 17.

6 Aristotle, *Nicomachean Ethics*, trans. H. Rackham (Cambridge, MA: Harvard University Press, 2003), X.7.1177b4–5 (614–15). "Dokei te ē eudaimonia en tē scholē einai."

7 *SCC*, 85, 3.8 (CF 40:203–4; *SW* 6:638; *SBO* 2:312). "Sapientiam scribae in otio, ait Sapiens. Ergo sapientiae otia negotia sunt; et quo otiosor sapientia, eo exercitior in genere suo. E regione virtus exercitata clarior est, eoque probatior quo officiosior. Et si quis sapientiam virtutis amorem diffinierit, non mihi a vero deviare videtur." For discussion of this text, see Brian Stock, "Experience, Praxis, Work and Planning in Bernard of Clairvaux: Observations on the *Sermones in Cantica*," in *The Cultural Context of Medieval Learning: Proceedings of the First International Colloquium on Philosophy, Science, and Theology in the Middle Ages – September 1973*, ed. John Emery Murdoch and Edith Dudley Sylla (Boston: D. Reidel Publishing, 1975), 219–61, at 246–47. In contrast with the Latin for Sir 38:25 that Bernard provides, a modern critical edition of the Vulgate has *sapientiam scribe in tempore vacuitatis*. See *Biblia Sacra Iuxta Vulgatam Versionem*, ed. Robert Weber and Roger Gryson, 5th ed. (Stuttgart: Deutsche Bibelgesellschaft, 2007), 1077.

Later in Book III of *De consideratione*, Bernard will reiterate that the pope's unnecessary involvement in the papal courts is limiting his ability to make time for such quietude: "How often has this restless and disquieting evil caused your holy, beneficial leisure to be ended prematurely?"[8]

Although Eugene III may be obliged to give his attention to many ecclesiastical duties, Bernard points to the example of Gregory the Great as a pope who also recognized the need to make time for leisure.[9] In order for Eugene III to make time for quietude, he must exercise discernment in the delegation of ecclesial duties.[10] On this point, Bellarmine comments: "Nor does [Bernard] allow [Eugene III] the excuse, which he could have offered and which many people today do offer, that the vast business of the papal office does not allow enough leisure for a churchman to devote himself to meditation on spiritual subjects."[11] At the same time, it is not the case that Bernard desires that persons who fill ecclesiastical roles ignore their duties in preference of the contemplative life. For example, writing to Thurstan, Archbishop of York around 1139, Bernard states: "I praise your desire for quiet [*quietem*] and your wish to rest peacefully in the Lord. But the reasons you give do not seem to me in themselves sufficient for abandoning your pastoral care . . . It seems best to me . . . that you should stay where you are and exhibit in a bishop the dress and holy life of a monk."[12] Bernard's pastoral concern for Eugene III's well-being thus likely does not involve a desire for the pope's abdication, but rather a desire to communicate a proposal for how the pope might integrate monastic practices into his papal role. Generalizing this perspective, would Bernard likewise have recommended to others the possibility of integrating monastic practices into their own professional and vocational roles?

8 *Csi*, III, 1.5 (CF 37:85; *SW* 1:708; *SBO* 3:434). *Quoties sancta ac fecunda tua abortiri otia fecit inquietum et inquietans malum?*

9 *Csi*, I, 9.12 (CF 37:43; *SW* 1:654; *SBO* 3:407). See also Anderson, "Reconsidering," 153.

10 *Csi*, I, 11.14 (CF 37:46; *SW* 1:660; *SBO* 3:410). See also *Csi*, I, 7.8 (CF 37:37; *SW* 1:646; *SBO* 3:403).

11 Bellarmine, *The Mind's Ascent to God*, Introduction (Donnelly and Teske, 53).

12 Ep 175 (James, *Letters*, 244–45; Ep 319 in *SW* 3:530–31; *SBO* 8:252). In a similar way, Bernard wrote to his friend Oger, a Canon Regular, around 1139 after Oger resigned from his post as superior of Saint-Nicolas-des-Prés in the parish of St. Médard in Tournai: "you have preferred your own will to the designs of God, choosing quiet for yourself [*eligens tibi quiescere*] rather than the work for which he selected you." Ep 90, §5 (James, *Letters*, 129–35, at 131–32; Ep 87 in *SW* 2:688–703, at 694; *SBO* 7:224–31, at 227). For these references, I am indebted to John R. Sommerfeldt, "The Social Theory of Bernard of Clairvaux," in CS 13:35–48, at 40–42.

Spiritual Exercises

Bernard writes to Eugene III: "If you apply all your experiences and knowledge to activity and have nothing for consideration, do I praise you? I do not."[13] The implication is that Bernard is chiding the pope for not continuing to recognize the value of the contemplative life.[14] Bernard, however, observes to Eugene III that not everyone approves of his being devoted to "this philosophy."[15] What kind of philosophy is it that practices meditation in quietude? If Bernard's teaching is intended to guide Eugene III in the search for some kind of wisdom, it is a wisdom that Eugene III must put into *practice* in order to benefit from it.[16] Evans seems correct therefore to describe Bernard's instruction on the exercise of meditation as "applied philosophising."[17] Déchanet argues that *De consideratione* best expresses Bernard's philosophy because the treatise clearly models the practical dimension of his teaching.[18] In a similar way, Sommerfeldt also describes meditation as an ascetic discipline; it comprises a "monastic exercise," yet one that is not exclusive to the monastic way of life.[19]

How is meditative practice to be understood as a spiritual exercise? Michel observes that Bernard had already discussed the practice of consideration in his early *Liber de gradibus humilitatis et superbiae* (1124).[20] In that text, writing to his relative Godfrey of Langres (who at the time may have been the Cistercian abbot at Fontenay),[21] Bernard exhorts: "pay attention

13 *Csi*, I, 5.6 (CF 37:33–34; *SW* 1:638; *SBO* 3:399). *Si quod vivis et sapis, totum das actioni, considerationi nihil, laudo te? In hoc non laudo.* See also Leclercq, "L'Art de la Composition," 118–19.

14 Leclercq, "L'Art de la Composition," 119. For the distinction between the contemplative life and the active life, see Julianus Pomerius, *De vita contemplativa* I.12, trans. Sr. Mary Josephine Suelzer (New York: Newman Press, 1947), 31–33; Thomas Aquinas, *Summa theologiae*, in *Summa Theologica*, 5 vols., trans. Fathers of the English Dominican Province (New York: Benzinger Brothers, 1948), II-II, q. 179.

15 *Csi*, I, 9.12 (CF 37:42; *SW* 1:654; *SBO* 3:407). "Si te philosophiae huic totum repente devoveris, praedecessores tui non ita consueverunt: eris molestus quam pluribus . . ." See also Sommerfeldt, *Life of the Mind*, 101; Verbaal, "Bernardus Philosophus," 580.

16 For a contemporary discussion of Cistercian monastic practices, see Charles Cummings, *Monastic Practices*, rev. ed. (Collegeville, MN: Liturgical Press, 2015).

17 Evans, *Bernard of Clairvaux*, 50.

18 Déchanet, "Aux Sources," 60.

19 Sommerfeldt, "Charismatic and Gregorian Leadership," 76.

20 Michel, "La considération," 109. See also, for dating *Hum*, *SW* 2:30. According to Pennington, Bernard authored this treatise for Godfrey of Langres after serving as abbot of Clairvaux for about ten years (Pennington, "Introduction," 7). Bernard became abbot of Clairvaux in 1115. See Evans, *Bernard of Clairvaux*, 9; Bredero, *Bernard of Clairvaux*, 282.

21 *Hum*, preface (CF 13a:28 and n1; *SW* 2:44; *SBO* 3:16).

to what you are, because you are truly full of misery."[22] Shortly thereafter, Bernard quotes the Apostle Paul who, when writing to the Galatians about correcting the faults of others, encourages the Galatians to maintain a spirit of humility: "consider yourself lest you also should be tempted" (*considerans te ipsum ne et tu tenteris*).[23] Michel thus sees *De consideratione* as developing Bernard's teaching that was briefly touched on in this earlier treatise.[24] Michel interprets Bernard as describing a meditative "office" (where one takes up a role that involves an "orientation" toward the exercise of "reflection"); for Michel, one's application of focused effort in this role might help one bring about a kind of psychological unity and continuity in the course of one's thought.[25] Bernard also discusses assuming roles or "offices," although he does not frequently speak of the exercise of meditation in this specific way.[26]

One finds spiritual exercises associated with the meditative office described in a variety of ways by authors after Bernard. For example, in the Benedictine tradition, Abbot Peter of Celle (writing to the Cistercian general chapter) described himself as an *alumnus* of the school of Bernard.[27] The influence of Bernard on Peter is evident in several ways and is explicit

22 *Hum*, 4.13 (CF 13a:41; *SW* 2:64; *SBO*3, 26). "Attendas quod es, quia vere miser es . . ." See also *Conv*, 11.23 (CF 25:57–58; *SW* 4:202; *SBO* 4:96). There, referring to "the man who has turned away from evil," Bernard states: "Let him consider that within himself he will find no rest for himself, because he is full of misery and desolation. Let him consider that there is no good in his flesh and that the present evil age contains nothing but vanity and affliction of spirit. Let him consider, I repeat, that he will find no comfort—not *within* nor *under* nor *around* himself, until he at last learns to seek it from *above* and to hope that it will come down from above" (*Consideret nullam sibi inveniri requiem in seipso, sed omnia plena miseriae et desolationis. Consideret non esse bonum in carne sua, sed et in saeculo nequam nihil nisi vanitatem et afflictionem spiritus contineri. Consideret, inquam, nec intus, nec subtus, nec circa se sibi occurrere consolationem, ut vel tandem aliquando discat quaerendam sursum, et desursum esse sperandam*). I added emphasis in the English translation just above in order to note that Bernard in this passage already alludes to the same four stages of meditation that he will later explore in greater depth in *De consideratione*. See also *Csi*, II, 3.6 (CF 37:52; *SW* 1:668–70; *SBO* 3:414–15): "quatuor, ut occurrunt, tibi consideranda reor: te, quae sub te, quae circa te, quae supra te sunt."

23 *Hum*, 4.13 (CF 13a:41; *SW* 2:64; *SBO* 3:26), citing Gal 6:1. For an alternate rendering of Paul in the Latin, see *Biblia sacra iuxta Vulgatam versionem*, 1808. The Greek verb Paul uses is *skopeō* which can mean: look at, regard, consider.

24 Michel, "La considération," 109–10.

25 Ibid., 111.

26 For example, in Bernard's letter to Bishop Henry of Sens (*De moribus et officio episcoporum*, ca. 1127), Bernard focuses on "the office of bishops." See Ep 42 or *Mor* (CF 67:37–82; *SW* 2:440–503; *SBO* 7:100–131).

27 Peter of Celle, Epistle 147, in *The Letters of Peter of Celle*, ed. Julian Haseldine (Oxford: Oxford University Press, 2001), 541. On Peter, also see Jean Leclercq, *La spiritualité de Pierre de Celle (1115–1183)* (Paris: Librairie Philosophique J. Vrin, 1946).

when Peter employs some of Bernard's own phrasings to describe monastic practices.[28] Yet, in Bernard's own Cistercian tradition, I discern no significant influence of Bernard on the imagination-focused recommendations for meditation proposed by Abbot Stephen of Sawley.[29]

In the Franciscan tradition, Bonaventure frequently quotes Bernard in Bonaventure's *Soliloquium de quattuor mentalibus exercitiis*, describing Bernard's teaching as a course of "mental exercises."[30] Bonaventure's Dominican contemporary Thomas Aquinas explicitly associates Bernard's teaching on consideration with Richard of St. Victor's account of meditation.[31] A few centuries later, one might observe that the practice of the examen prayer as developed within the Ignatian spiritual tradition is similar to Bernard's first general stage of meditation (self-reflection).[32] Ignatius of Loyola was to some extent familiar with the thought of Bernard.[33] Like Aquinas, Ignatius also refers to the act of consideration in a way that is synonymous with meditation.[34] Details in the procedure of self-examination that Ignatius prescribes in his *Spiritual Exercises* (1548) bear many similarities to Bernard's teaching on self-reflection.[35] There are some differences,

28 Consider, for example, Peter's phrasing *quibus passibus abierat in regionem dissimilitudinis, eisdem revertatur ad similitudinem patris*. Pierre de Celle, *L'École du Cloître*, SC 240 (Paris: Les Éditions du Cerf, 1977), 238–40. For an English translation, see Peter of Celle, *The School of the Cloister*, in *Selected Works*, trans. Hugh Feiss, Cistercian Studies 100 (Kalamazoo, MI: Cistercian Publications, 1987), chap. 20, §2 (105). Regarding Bernard's use of the phrase *regio dissimilitudinis*, see Bernard of Clairvaux: *SCC*, 36, 4.5 (CF 7:177–78; *SW* 5:568; *SBO* 2:7). I discuss this passage in the chapter on Book V below.

29 This may be because Stephen is writing to novices in the selection under consideration. See Stephen of Sawley, *A Mirror for Novices*, in *Treatises*, trans. Jeremiah F. O'Sullivan (Kalamazoo, MI: Cistercian Publications, 1984), 83–122. For the Latin, see E. Mikkers, "Un «Speculum Novitii» Inedit D'Etienne De Salley," *Collectanea Ordinis Cisterciensium Reformatorum* 8 (1946): 17–68.

30 Bonaventure, *Soliloquy on the Four Spiritual Exercises*, in *The Works of Bonaventure* III, Opuscula, Second Series, trans. José de Vinck (Paterson, NJ: St. Anthony Guild, 1966), 33–129.

31 Aquinas, *Summa theologiae* II-II, q. 180, a. 3, ad 1. In 4:1926 of the Fathers of the English Dominican Province translation, an editorial note cites Richard, *De gratia contemplationis* I.3–4. For this text, see Richard of St. Victor, *Benjamin Major* I.3–4, in Richard of Saint-Victor, *Selected Writings on Contemplation*, 136–39. For discussion of Bernard's influence on Aquinas's doctrine of the contemplative life (including reference to this question in the *Summa*), see Mark D. Jordan, "Thomas Aquinas on Bernard and the Life of Contemplation," in *Bernardus Magister*, ed. John R. Sommerfeldt (Kalamazoo, MI: Cistercian Publications, 1992), 449–60, at 455 (hereafter CS 135).

32 See Gallagher, *The Examen Prayer*, as cited earlier.

33 See *The Spiritual Exercises of St. Ignatius*, trans. Louis J. Puhl (New York: Vintage Books, 2000), §351 (124).

34 Ignatius, *Spiritual Exercises*, §39 (Puhl, 18).

35 Ignatius prescribes a five-step method of self-examination (*Spiritual Exercises*, §43; Puhl, 20); the third step involves examining one's thoughts, words, and deeds (see also *Spiritual Exercises*,

however: Bernard differentiates meditation from ecstatic contemplation, as well as (at its ultimate stage) from use of the imagination; as discussed below, Bernard describes the contemplative stage of theological meditation as turning away from perception and representations produced in one's imagination.[36] Further, one might contend that the Ignatian approach involves a more structured method than what Bernard proposes; Gallagher, however, suggests that the Ignatian examen can be interpreted as a development of monastic self-examination.[37]

For Bernard, the exercise of meditation is not entirely synonymous with contemplation.[38] Commenting on *De consideratione*, Louis Bouyer understands Bernard to teach that the exercise of meditation is a kind of self-disposing or self-preparing for contemplation (yet where the kind of contemplation that Bouyer has in mind can only be realized fully in an eschatological sense after the common resurrection).[39] On the other hand, if Bernard's contemporary John of Salisbury is correct, some of Bernard's earliest readers did understand Bernard to outline in *De consideratione* a set of instructions concerning the pursuit of contemplation in this life (however partial that contemplation may be).[40] Leclercq notes that in Book V Bernard describes the highest form of theological meditation as an exercise that leads one to the threshold of contemplation.[41] I will return to the distinction between meditation and contemplation below when exploring Bernard's remarks at the beginning of Book II.

Bernard's assistant Geoffrey of Auxerre describes how Bernard himself would take up the practice of meditation. Geoffrey writes:

---

§32–§43; Puhl, 17–20). While 1548 is the date of the publication of the *Exercises* (Puhl, xxxviii), Ignatius's first notes describing this approach date from 1522 (Puhl, xxxi).

36 In some passages of the *Exercises*, Ignatius seems to identify meditation and contemplation (§77; Puhl, 29). In contrast with Bernard's account, Ignatius refers to the activity of contemplation as focusing on a spiritual reality that is represented in one's imagination (§114; Puhl, 43). In this respect, his teaching is similar to Stephen of Sawley, mentioned above.

37 Gallagher, *Examen Prayer*, 182n4.

38 *Csi*, II, 2.5 (CF 37:52; *SW* 1:668; *SBO* 3:414). See also Sommerfeldt, "Charismatic and Gregorian Leadership," 75–77; Clairmont, "Medieval Consideration," 92–93; CS 125:66 and 223–24.

39 Louis Bouyer, *The Cistercian Heritage*, trans. Elizabeth A. Livingstone (Westminster, MD: Newman Press, 1958), 58.

40 See John of Salisbury, *Policraticus* V.15, trans. Cary J. Nederman (Cambridge: Cambridge University Press, 1990), 98. See also Joannes Saresberiensis, *Polycraticus*, in PL 199:379–822, at 577d, where John refers to Bernard's treatise as *de contemplatione vel consideratione*.

41 Leclercq writes at the close of his commentary on Book V: *Arrivé au sommet de la considération, devenue elle-même une contemplation dans l'amour, Bernard y reste, il ne redescend pas.* Leclercq, "L'Art de la Composition," 129. See also *Csi*, V, 14.32 (CF 37:178; *SW* 1:826; *SBO* 3:493); Clairmont, "Medieval Consideration," 93.

> As often as he could, he escaped matters of business to pray, read, or write. Sometimes he engaged in teaching for the instruction of the brothers or else gave himself to *holy meditation*. In this spiritual occupation he obtained the singular grace of undergoing no boredom or any difficulty, dwelling freely within himself . . .[42]

Geoffrey observed that Bernard was at times so focused on this spiritual exercise that he would practice it while in busy or crowded settings:

> Every moment given to meditation was too brief; every place was suitable for it . . . Whatever company of people or noisy crowd he was in, as long as the matter did not call for his attention, he recollected his mind with total interior facility and tasted the delights of inward solitude, which he carried around within him, heedless of what was going on around him or what he saw outside of himself.[43]

In light of these remarks, Bernard's exhortation to Eugene III may be understood as encouraging the pope to practice the same spiritual exercises in the midst of his busy affairs. In order to become accustomed to this exercise (especially to the degree that one might practice it in a busy setting), one must set aside time for practice in leisure or quietude. Such practice, in turn, cultivates the interior conditions whereby one's mind might be gathered "with interior facility" (as Geoffrey states just above) into contemplative stillness and be present to God.[44]

The Context of a Claustral Psychology

White proposes that meditation for Bernard involves taking time to care for one's own soul.[45] Regarding how Bernard understood the practice of meditation to benefit the human soul, it is helpful to interpret Bernard's teaching on meditation within the context of his anthropology, or—more specifically—within the context of his psychology. In the introduction, I noted how for Leclercq there is a specific kind of medieval psychology connected with

42 Geoffrey of Auxerre, *VP*, III, 2 (CF 76:148).

43 Ibid. (148–49).

44 Regarding *hêsychia* as meaning (for some desert monastic fathers) both exterior solitude and interior stillness, see John Wortley, "What *hêsychia* Meant to the Desert Fathers," *CSQ* 54, no. 2 (2019): 159–70, at 167.

45 White, "The Gregorian Ideal," 342.

monastic or claustral theological writings (writings authored in a cloistered environment); this psychology is distinct from the kind of medieval psychology associated with Scholastic theological writings (works authored in a school and often in an urban setting).[46] It is the former medieval psychology that I am defining as claustral psychology. Also above, I noted that features in Bernard's psychology are evocative of topics in Platonic psychology as mediated by Augustine and Gregory—at least with respect to the topic of hierarchical structure that I will describe just below. Bernard's psychology in this regard might be understood as distinct from the philosophical psychology of Aristotle, which had just appeared in the Latin West.[47]

Regarding Bernard's psychology as a claustral psychology, Leclercq observes that Bernard's emphasis on the relationship of the soul to God points to the possibility of a person achieving an overarching unity in that person's spirituality and basic psychology.[48] This possibility of psycho-spiritual integration is indicated in a sermon in Bernard's *Sermones super cantica canticorum*, where he states that the soul (*anima*) has both a natural and also a spiritual dimension:

46 Leclercq, "Psycho-history," *CSQ*, 288.

47 The psychology of Aristotle found in the *De anima* was translated into Latin along with some of his other works by James of Venice in ca. 1125–50. See Bernard G. Dod, "Aristoteles latinus," in *The Cambridge History of Later Medieval Philosophy: From the Rediscovery of Aristotle to the Disintegration of Scholasticism 1100–1600*, ed. Norman Kretzmann, Anthony Kenny, and Jan Pinborg (Cambridge: Cambridge University Press, 1982), 45–79, at 76. James of Venice is mentioned along with Burgundio of Pisa in a writing by Bernard's contemporary Anselm of Havelberg. See L. Minio-Paluello, "Iacobus Veneticus Grecus: Canonist and Translator of Aristotle," *Traditio* 8 (1952): 265–304, at 266. See also James A. Weisheipl, "Science in the Thirteenth Century," in *The History of the University of Oxford, Vol. 1: The Early Oxford Schools*, ed. J. I. Catto (Oxford: Oxford University Press, 1984), 435–69, at 436; Charles Burnett, "The Introduction of Aristotle's Natural Philosophy into Great Britain: A Preliminary Survey of the Manuscript Evidence," in *Aristotle in Britain During the Middle Ages*, ed. John Marenbon (Turnhout: Brepols, 1996), 21–50, at 25. In terms of the first development of a Latin Aristotelian psychology, the influence of Aristotle's *De anima* can be discerned in John Blund's treatise on the soul authored at Oxford around 1200. For Blund, see John Blund, *Treatise on the Soul*, 2nd ed. (British Academy, 2012). See also Young, *Scholarly Community*, 98. Blund, along with Aristotle's commentator Avicenna, subsequently influenced the psychology of Alexander Nequam (ca. 1201). For Nequam, see Alexander Nequam, *Speculum speculationum* (British Academy, 1988), xvi. See also R. W. Hunt, *The Schools and the Cloister: The Life and Writings of Alexander Nequam (1157–1217)* (Oxford: Oxford University Press, 1984); R. W. Southern, "From Schools to University," in *Early Oxford Schools*, 1–36, at 24.

48 "What most characterizes this vast, complex, and nuanced anthropology . . . is above all the harmony between the spiritual aspect and the psychological content: the faculties and activities of the human person are in no way divided, but are unified and conciliated by the real presence of God." Leclercq, "General Introduction (III)," 384.

> God is life and the soul is life; it is like him, then, but it is not equal. Moreover, it is like him because it is life, because its life is within itself, because it is not only a living thing but a lifegiving thing, just as God himself is all these things; but it is unlike him as a creature is unlike its creator, and unlike because if it had not been quickened by God it would not live. I say it would not live, but I refer to its spiritual life, not its natural one. It must live immortally on the natural [plane], even if it does not on the spiritual plane.[49]

This distinction between a natural psychology and a spiritual psychology is noteworthy. The soul has both natural life and spiritual life; by nature it is immortal, yet the soul can also be made like God "through the Word of life, or rather through the Word which is life, both living and life-giving."[50]

Bernard's discussion of the natural and spiritual life of the soul relates to a distinction he makes in a sermon in his *De diversis* series between different kinds of goods that come from God: natural (*naturalia*), spiritual (*spiritualia*), and eternal (*in aeterna*).[51] There is a kind of hierarchy of goodness involved in this teaching, one that is ontological (or existential), yet also described by Bernard in axiological terms (i.e., in terms of a value hierarchy): "indeed natural goods are great, spiritual goods are greater, and eternal goods are greatest. In the first we are renewed, in the second we are exercised, and in the third we are increased and blessed."[52] Among natural benefits, Bernard focuses on goods of the body, the heart, and social relationships. With

49 *SCC*, 81, 2.4 (CF 40:160–61; *SW* 6:586; *SBO* 2:286). "Vita Deus, vita et anima est: similis quidem, sed dispar. Porro similis, quod vita, quod seipsa vivens, quod non tantum vivens, sed et vivificans, sicut et ille haec omnia est; dispar vero, quantum a creante creata, dispar quod, ut nisi creata ab illo non esset, sic nisi ab ipso vivificata non viveret. Non viveret dico, sed spirituali vita, non naturali. Nam naturali quidem, etiam quae non spiritualiter vivit, immortaliter vivat necesse est." See also Stepsis, "Fulfillment of Self," 353.

50 *SCC*, 81, 2.4 (CF 40:160–61; *SW* 6:586; *SBO* 2:286). "A qua nimirum vitali quadam morte minime umquam resurgat, nisi per verbum vitae, immo per Verbum vitam, viventem utique et vivificantem."

51 Bernard of Clairvaux, *Monastic Sermons* (*Sermones de diversis*), Sermo 16.1 (hereafter *Div*), trans. Daniel Griggs (Collegeville, MN: Liturgical Press, 2016), 87–94, at 87 (hereafter CF 68). For a Latin edition of *Sermones de diversis*, Sermo XVI, see Bernhard von Clairvaux, *Sämtliche Werke, lateinisch/deutsch*, Bd. IX (hereafter *SW* 9) (Innsbruck: Tyrolia, 1998), 308–19. *SW* 9 reprints the Latin from Bernardus Claraevallensis, *Sancti Bernardi Opera* 6.1 (hereafter *SBO* 6.1), ed. J. Leclercq, C. H. Talbot, and H.-M. Rochais (Rome: Editiones Cistercienses, 1970), 144–49.

52 *Div*, 16.1 (CF 68:87–88; *SW* 9:308; *SBO* 6.1:144). "Et quidem naturalia bona magna, spiritualia maiora, sed maxima sunt aeterna. In primis reparamur, in secundis exercitamur, extendimur et beatificamur in tertiis."

respect to the natural benefit of the body, he writes: "because we consist of both soul and body, according to the voice of the apostle, from the animal part, that is from goods of the body, we begin *not first that which is spiritual but that which is animal*."[53] One benefit of the body is the ability for *sensation* which Bernard defines in his *Liber de gratia* as "a vital movement in the body, alert and outward."[54] With respect to the natural benefits of the soul (or the "heart" as named in the *De diversis* sermon), Bernard writes:

> Moreover, just as health is natural to the body, so purity is natural to the heart. For God shall not be seen with a troubled eye, and the human heart was made for the very purpose of seeing its Creator. If, however, one must provide careful protection for the health of the body, so much more imperatively must one be concerned about purity of heart.[55]

Lastly, Bernard also refers to the natural benefit of social relationships: "And because we are social animals, let us cross over from what is within us to those who are around us, so that if it be possible, as much as is in us, we may have peace with all persons. For this is the law of natural society."[56] In light of all of these remarks, Bernard's natural anthropology might be appropriately characterized as bio-psycho-social.[57]

Bernard adds a further dimension to his account when introducing the topic of the good of grace. Bernard makes an explicit distinction between nature and grace.[58] The goods of grace are also distinct from the goods that

53 *Div*, 16.1 (CF 68:88; *SW* 9:310; *SBO* 6.1:145). "Et quia nos ex anima et corpore consistimus, iuxta vocem Apostoli, ab animali parte, id est a bonis corporis, incipiamus, ut 'Non sit prius quod spirituale est, sed quod animale.'"

54 *Gra*, 2.3 (CF 19a:57; *SW* 1:176; *SBO* 3:167). "Sensus vero, vitalis in corpore motus, vigilans et extrinsecus." See also Sommerfeldt, "Bernard of Clairvaux and the Trivial Arts," CS 193:153.

55 *Div*, 16.2 (CF 68:89; *SW* 9:310; *SBO* 6.1:145). "Sicut autem corporis natura est sanitas, ita cordis natura est puritas, quia turbato oculo non videbitur Deus, et cor humanum ad hoc factum est, ut suum videat Creatorem. Si vero sanitati corporis sollicita est providenda custodia, puritati cordis tanto est sollicitior impendenda . . ."

56 *Div*, 16.3 (CF 68:89; *SW* 9:312; *SBO* 6.1:146). "Et quia sociale animal sumus, ex his quae in nobis sunt ad ea quae circa nos sunt transeamus, ut, si fieri potest, quod ex nobis est, pacem habeamus cum omnibus hominibus. Haec enim est lex naturalis societatis . . ."

57 I will discuss this phrase further in chapter 10 in connection with more contemporary authors in philosophical psychiatry such as Adolf Meyer and George Engel. See George L. Engel, "The Clinical Application of the Biopsychosocial Model," *The American Journal of Psychiatry* 137, no. 5 (1980): 535–44.

58 For example, Bernard writes to Thurstan, archbishop of York: "It is one thing to fill the belly of the hungry, and another to have a zeal for poverty. The one is the service of nature, the other the service of grace" (*Aliud est reficere ventrem esurientis, et aliud sanctam zelare paupertatem. Ibi enim*

are eternal: "If you cannot fix your eye of meditation on that height of eternal goods because they are distant and surpass all understanding, then turn your vision to the good things of grace that are in the exercise of virtue."[59] Bernard then differentiates the benefits of grace from natural benefits: "But if these things are exceedingly sublime and pass beyond your weakness, then direct your eyes to the goods of nature, which ought to be as familiar to you as you are familiar to yourself."[60]

Is it that the goods of grace should be identified with the spiritual goods that Bernard states are in between eternity and natural benefits? The answer is yes, but only in part: Bernard indicates in various remarks that grace can be understood in multiple ways. For example, in his early *Liber de gratia et libero arbitrio*, he differentiates creating grace (*gratia creans*) from saving grace (*gratia salvans*).[61] This distinction corresponds to the customary distinction between nature and grace (where the grace of creation is understood as distinct from the grace of redemption and sanctification). When one connects this distinction found in the *Liber de gratia* to what Bernard says in the *De diversis* sermon under consideration (sermon 16), his remarks in the sermon may be understood to refer to salvific grace (redemption and sanctification). Salvific grace may be understood to restore lost natural benefits (restorative grace) as well as to provide additional non-natural spiritual goods (elevating grace). The human need for restorative grace is indicated in the *De diversis* sermon when Bernard explains how the Fall has affected the ability of human beings to benefit fully from creating grace (or original grace):

> Let us not speak of nature's goods as if they were not a grace. But you see, natural goods were instilled and planted together in a certain way for nature itself, before the sin that corrupted not only character but even nature. Since then, the good things at hand do not seem to come to us as

servitur naturae, hic gratiae). Ep 170 (James, *Letters*, 240 and 471; Ep 95 in *SW* 2:728–31, at 730; *SBO* 7:244–45, at 245).

59 *Div*, 16.1 (CF 68:88; *SW* 9:308; *SBO* 6.1:144). "Si non potes oculum meditationis in illam sublimitatem aeternalium bonorum infigere, quia stantia sunt et omnem sensum exsuperant, in bonis gratiae, quae sunt in exercitio virtutum, visum reflecte . . ."

60 *Div*, 16.1 (CF 68:88; *SW* 9:310; *SBO* 6.1:145). "Quod si et haec nimis sublimia sunt et transgredientia infirmitatem tuam, demitte oculos in bona naturae, quae tibi tam familiaria esse debent, quantum tu familiaris es tibi."

61 Bernard writes: "simply to will denotes the subject itself which does either the achieving or the failing. To this subject, however, creating grace gives existence. Saving grace gives it the achievement [*creans gratia fecit; ut proficiat, salvans gratia facit*]." *Gra*, 6.16 (CF 19a:72; *SW* 1:198; *SBO* 3:178).

> graces because of the inflicted wound, even though we sense nature's goods in and around ourselves, as much by our reason as by feelings generally.[62]

In this passage, Bernard remarks that humans have a wounded affective sense of the natural benefits that surround them. In response to how the original provision of creating grace has been affected, he states that salvific grace partially involves the restoration of such natural gifts (restorative grace):

> So then, when we have done that which has been commanded and given to our nature, *We are unprofitable servants; we have done only that which we ought to do*. For scarcely ever, or even never, does one find some command given to human beings that passes beyond the limits and possibilities of nature. In these [natural] goods, however, just as we have said, we are renewed, and in a certain way we are restored to the ancient condition. We revert to the innate sweetness of nature, while indeed to us, and to those around us, we produce the appropriate [due] order of things. So much then for the natural goods.[63]

While Bernard does not explicitly refer to grace in this passage, it is to the good of grace that he implicitly refers when describing the renewal and restoration of human nature, as well as to the recovery of "the due order of things" (a due natural order—a reference to a normative natural anthropology).

In the sermon mentioned above from the *Sermones super canctica canticorum*, I noted how for Bernard the Word of God might spiritually revivify a person's natural soul in this life but—ultimately or eschatologically speaking—the Word can only be expected to revivify that person's natural body in the next life. Regarding the resurrection of the body, Bernard writes in his treatise *De diligendo Deo*:

62 *Div*, 16.1 (CF 68:88; *SW* 9:310; *SBO* 6.1:145). "Nec sic dicimus bona naturae, quasi gratiae non sint, sed ideo quod ipsi naturae quodammodo ingenita et complantata fuerint, antequam fieret peccatum illud quod non solum personam infecit, sed et naturam. Extunc non ita nobis ad manum pervenisse monstrantur propter vulnus inflictum, cum tamen nos illa in nobis et circa nos esse tam rationibus quam affectionibus plerumque sentiamus."

63 *Div*, 16.4 (CF 68:90–91; *SW* 9:314; *SBO* 6.1:147). "Cum haec quae mandata sunt et data naturae fecerimus, 'Servi inutiles sumus: Quae debuimus facere, fecimus.' Aut vix enim, aut numquam invenitur aliquod praeceptum datum hominibus, quod transeat terminos possibilitatemque naturae. In his autem bonis, sicut praediximus, reparamur, et quasi quodammodo restituimur in antiquum, dum ad ingenitam naturae suavitatem revertimur, dum et nobis, et his qui circa nos sunt, et eis qui supra nos sunt, debitum rerum ordinem exhibemus. Et haec quidem pro bonis naturalibus."

> Until death is swallowed up in victory and eternal light . . . takes possession to the extent that heavenly glory shines in their bodies, souls cannot set themselves aside and pass into God. They are still attached to their bodies, if not by life and feeling, certainly by natural affection, so that they do not wish nor are they able to realize their consummation without them. This rapture of the soul which is its most perfect and highest state cannot therefore take place before the resurrection of the bodies.[64]

In referring to the soul's attachment to the body, it should be noted that for Bernard the body is natural and not in and of itself evil, although the body has been affected by the Fall. This wounded state of the body in turn affects one's understanding of spiritual realities. On this point, Bernard writes in his *Sermo de conversione ad clericos*:

> Spiritual insight [*intuitus spiritualis*] is impeded either by the lust of our own flesh or by worldly curiosity and ambition. This we learn as much from our own experience as from Holy Scripture . . . while we are in this body, we wander apart from the Lord, and the fault lies not in the body itself, but in the fact that our flesh is still a body of death, or rather a sinful body . . . It sometimes happens too that the physical eye seems to remain dim for a little while even after the speck has been taken out or blown away. And it is the same with the inner eye [*in interiore oculo*], as the man who walks in the Spirit has often experienced.[65]

One's concern with one's body, Bernard indicates in sermon 16 of the *De diversis* series (where he discusses natural, spiritual, and eternal goods) should be a concern with preserving the health (*sanitas*) of one's body: "All goods of the body are a matter of health, and this is the one and only thing that we owe to the body. Moreover, nothing beyond health should be given or sought for the body. Rather, by this limit [*termino*], the body should be tied

64 *Dil*, 11.30 (CF 13b:32; *SW* 1:124–26; *SBO* 3:144–45). "Donec ergo absorpta sit mors in victoria, et noctis undique terminos lux perennis invadat et occupet usquequaque, quatenus et in corporibus gloria caelestis effulgeat, non possunt ex toto animae seipsas exponere et transire in Deum, nimirum ligatae corporibus etiam tunc, etsi non vita vel sensu, certe affectu naturali, ita ut absque his nec velint, nec valeant consummari. Itaque ante restaurationem corporum non erit ille defectus animorum, qui perfectus et summus est ipsorum status, ne carnis iam sane consortium spiritus non requireret, si absque illa consummaretur." See also Stepsis, "Fulfillment of Self," 358–59.

65 *Conv*, 17.30 (CF 25:67; *SW* 4:222; *SBO* 4:106).

and restrained."[66] Bernard's statement that the praxis or activity of the human body should be brought within certain boundaries (*termini*) that respect the body's health or natural integrity is evocative of Gregory's statement, quoted above, that the praxis or activity of the human mind must be brought within certain boundaries or an enclosure (a psychological cloister, so to speak).[67] One might on this basis refer to Bernard's claustral anthropology as a holistic vision of the "due order" of the human person, body and soul.[68]

Regarding the graced restoration of the natural soul, Bernard's remarks concerning the Word of God revivifying the soul in this life relate to his description of the three comings of Christ mentioned in his *In adventu* sermon series: (1) the historical Advent of Christ's incarnation was in the past, (2) Christ's spiritual Advent can occur in the soul in the present, while (3) Christ's eschatological Advent pertains to his future Parousia.[69] In his first *In vigilia nativitatis Domini* sermon, Bernard refers to Christ's historical incarnation in the past as a miraculous and "supernatural" event.[70] In contrast with Christ's historical incarnation, there is a spiritual character to Christ's second Advent in the soul: Bernard describes Christ as coming not "to humankind" as in his past physical incarnation, but rather "into humankind" in a way that is "spiritual and hidden" (*spiritualis et occultus est*).[71] This spiritual Advent pertains to Christ's work in healing and redeeming the soul,

66 *Div*, 16.2 (CF 68:88; *SW* 9:310; *SBO* 6.1:145). "Sunt autem omnia bona corporis, et quod ei solummodo debeamus, sanitas. Nihil autem ultra ei vel dandum est vel quaerendum est, sed hoc termino ligandum et frenandum est."

67 Gregory, *Book of Pastoral Rule*, III, 14 (Demacopoulos, 123; PL 77:73b).

68 *Div*, 16.4 (CF 68:90–91; *SW* 9:314; *SBO* 6.1:147).

69 Bernard of Clairvaux, *In adventu Domini* (1–7) (hereafter *Adv*). For the English, see Bernard of Clairvaux, *On the Lord's Advent: Sermons 1–7*, in *Bernard of Clairvaux: Sermons for Advent and the Christmas Season*, ed. John Leinenweber (Kalamazoo, MI: Cistercian Publications, 2007), 3–42 (hereafter CF 51). For the Latin, see *SW* 7:58–128; *SBO* 4:161–96. The teaching of the three Advents reappears in the sermons of Guerric of Igny, Bernard's Cistercian contemporary. See Guerric, "The Second Sermon for Advent," in *The Cistercian World* (ed. Matarasso), 129–33. Pousset observes that Bernard also influenced Martin Luther with respect to this teaching of three Advents. See Franz Pousset, "Bernard of Clairvaux as Luther's Source," *Concordia Theological Quarterly* 54, no. 4 (1990): 281–304, at 295. See also Volz, who contends that Luther was also influenced by *Csi* V: Carl Volz, "Martin Luther's Attitude toward Bernard of Clairvaux," in CS 13:186–204, at 190.

70 See Bernard of Clairvaux, *In vigilia nativitatis Domini*, 1.1 (CF 51:44; *SW* 7:132; *SBO* 4:198). "O nativitatis supra naturam, sed pro natura; miraculi excellentia superans, sed reparans virtute mysterii!"

71 *Adv*, 3.4 (CF 51:22; *SW* 7:90; *SBO* 4:177). "Triplicem enim eius adventum novimus: ad homines, in homines, contra homines."

whereas his eschatological Advent will involve his redemption and transformation of the body.[72] Describing this middle Advent, Bernard writes:

> If we want to be found members of Christ, beyond any doubt we must follow our head. So the first thing to be restored in us is concern for the souls for whose sake he has already come, and whose corruption he first set himself to heal. Let us keep care of the body for another time and put it off to that day on which he shall come to transform the body.[73]

Quoting John the Baptist in John 1:29 (that Christ has come to take away the sins of the world), Bernard explains: "He does not say 'diseases of the body' or 'vexations of the flesh,' but 'sin,' which is a disease of the soul and a corruption of the mind."[74] Bernard's references to psychopathology (*morbus animae*) and mental disorder (*corruptio mentis*) denote ailments inconsistent with God's original intention for human beings (these conditions are sins, generally speaking).[75] Regarding a vexation of the body, one might consider Bernard's remark when, quoting Romans 7:24, he contends that the Apostle Paul was aware that "the sin that comes between us and God" originates from "the law of sin that dwells in our members," which Bernard also describes as "that worst of all roots which had been impressed in his flesh."[76] Bernard states that through grace, however, the sins involving lust and evil desire emerging from this root can be regulated, although one is only removed from sin entirely when the soul leaves the body at death.[77]

As distinct from remedying the vexations of the body, Christ's spiritual Advent in the soul can facilitate the healing of some forms of mental corruption (*corruptio mentis*). In expectation of this Advent, Bernard suggests that one "prepare a seat for Christ" in one's heart: "Happy the soul who is the seat

72 *Adv*, 6.1 (CF 51:36; *SW* 7:118; *SBO* 4:191).

73 Ibid. "Deinde si Christi membra volumus inveniri, sequendum nobis est sine dubio caput nostrum, ut videlicet prima nobis reparandum sit sollicitudo animarum, pro quibus ipse iam venit, et quarum prius mederi studuit corruptioni. Corporis vero curam ei magis tempori reservemus et differamus in illum diem, quo reformandi gratia corporis est venturus."

74 *Adv*, 6.1 (CF 51:36–37; *SW* 7:118; *SBO* 4:191). "Non dicit morbos corporis, non molestias carnis, sed peccatum, quod est morbus animae et corruptio mentis."

75 I add "generally speaking" because Bernard might ascribe some conditions of this type to the general woundedness of human nature and not necessarily to the performance of a specific moral sin committed through a person's free choice.

76 *Adv*, 6.2 (CF 51:37; *SW* 7:120; *SBO* 4:192).

77 Ibid. "Ita dico vobis, genus illud peccati, quod toties conturbat nos,—concupiscentias loquor et desideria mala—, reprimi quidem debet et potest per gratiam Dei, ut non regnet in nobis . . . sed non eicitur nisi in morte, quando sic discerpimur, ut anima separetur a corpore."

of Wisdom!"[78] Bernard's remark indicates that the soul in relation to Christ's spiritual Advent is akin to Mary in relation to Christ's historical Advent. With respect to Christ's second Advent (which occurs within the context of faith[79]), Christ brings "rest and consolation" to the soul[80] and "food for the mind" (*cibus mentis*).[81] I will return to discuss this spiritual Advent of Christ in further detail later when examining Bernard's description of theological meditation in Book V. At present, I will focus on his reference to Christ as *cibus mentis*.

What is the relationship between the soul (*anima*) and the mind (*animus* and *mens*)? Bernard indicates in *De diligendo Deo* that the soul in a certain sense *is* the mind—but the mind is distinct from the experience (*experimento*) that one encounters through the bodily senses (*sensu . . . carnali*) as well as distinct from the desires that arise in response to objects of sensation.[82] The mind, Bernard observes in his *Sermo de conversione ad clericos*, "is nothing but reason, memory, and will."[83] This understanding of the mind as comprised of three specific interior capacities is evocative of the psychology of Augustine.[84] Such capacities, Bernard states in a different

78 *Adv*, 3.4 (CF 51:22; *SW* 7:90; *SBO* 4:177). "Beata anima quae sedes est Sapientiae."

79 *Adv*, 7.2 (CF 51:42; *SW* 7:128; *SBO* 4:196). "Atque utinam sic veniat, ut copiosissima dignatione sua, et in nobis per fidem habitans illuminet caecitatem nostram . . ."

80 *Adv*, 5.1 (CF 51:34; *SW* 7:114; *SBO* 4:189).

81 *Adv*, 5.2 (CF 51:34; *SW* 7:114; *SBO* 4:189).

82 *Dil*, 7.20 (CF 13b:23; *SW* 1:108; *SBO* 3:136). See also John R. Sommerfeldt, "Epistemological and Social Hierarchies: A Potential Reconciliation of Some Inconsistencies in Bernard's Thought," *Cîteaux: Commentarii cistercienses* 31, no. 1 (1980): 83–92, at 87. This essay by Sommerfeldt is reprinted in *Jacob's Ladder and the Tree of Life: Concepts of Hierarchy and the Great Chain of Being*, ed. Marion Leathers Kuntz and Paul Grimley Kuntz (New York: Peter Lang, 1987), 141–51. Hankey states that for Augustine, the mind (*animus*) is the highest part of the soul (*anima*). See Wayne J. Hankey, "Mind," in *Augustine through the Ages: An Encyclopedia*, ed. Allan D. Fitzgerald (Grand Rapids, MI: Eerdmans, 1999), 565.

83 *Conv*, 6.11 (CF 25:45; *SW* 4:178; *SBO* 4:84). *Denique tota ipsa nihil est aliud quam ratio, memoria et voluntas.*

84 Augustine describes a "trinity of the mind" (*trinitas mentis*) that involves one not only remembering, understanding, and loving (or valuing) oneself, but also (and primarily) God: "Meminerit itaque dei sui ad cuius imaginem facta est eumque intellegat atque diligat." See Augustine, *The Trinity*, trans. Stephen McKenna (Washington, DC: The Catholic University of America Press, 1963), XIV.12.15 (432). For the Latin edition of this part of the work, see Aurelii Augustini, *De Trinitate libri XV (Libri XIII–XV)*, ed. W. J. Mountain and Fr. Glorie, CCSL 50a (Turnhout: Brepols, 1968), 443. See also CF 24:84. See also Hankey, "Mind," 564, citing Augustine, *The Trinity*, XIV, 8.11. One might note that in the *Confessions*, Augustine identifies himself as the mind in terms of being the subject of the mind's activity of remembering: "it is I myself that remember, I the mind" (*ego sum, qui memini, ego animus*). Augustine, *Confessions* X.16 (Watts, 118–19). See also Nello Cipriani, "Memory," trans. Matthew O'Connell, in *Augustine through the Ages*, 553–55, at 554.

sermon from the *De diversis* series, are a means whereby the soul reflects the uncreated Trinity: "Rational souls bear a certain vestige [*vestigium*] of that highest Trinity in that they consist of memory, reason, and will [*ex memoria, ratione et voluntate consistit*]."[85] Bernard's use of the word "vestige" in this passage may also be indebted to the Augustinian tradition as, according to Cipriani, for Augustine the human mind is the image of God (*imago Dei*) not simply inasmuch as the mind is active, but more so when the mind is active in relation to God.[86]

It is with respect to the mind as a specific domain of the soul that Bernard locates the psychological capacities that are primarily operative during meditation (memory, reason, and will).[87] Déchanet thus appropriately characterizes meditation for Bernard as an exercise of the mind or spirit.[88] Meditation as a spiritual exercise might thus be understood as a means whereby one might train one's mind because, as Bernard observes, one's mind can be prone to distraction: "The restless mind [*vagabundus animus*], running to and fro among the pleasures of this life, is tired out but never satisfied."[89] Bernard states in the same sermon from his *De diversis* series quoted above that the human mind is fallen away from God with respect to the three mental capacities of reason, memory, and will: "There is the creator Trinity, Father and Son and Holy Spirit, from which a created trinity—memory, reason, will—has fallen."[90] The fall of the mind in this respect does not need to be understood as a psychological reduction on Bernard's part of the meaning of the biblical narrative of the Fall, but rather a reference to what Gregory calls the descent of the mind, quoted earlier.[91]

Such a doctrine of a psychological fall is also found in Augustine's *De Trinitate*, where he is careful to note that this approach to the biblical narrative aims to preserve its literal historical meaning.[92] Bernard implies that such

85 *Div*, 45.1 (CF 68:236; *SW* 9:544; *SBO* 6.1:262). For this reference to *Div*, 45.1, I am indebted to Endre von Ivánka, "La Structure de l'Âme selon S. Bernard," *ASOC* 9, no. 3–4 (1953): 202–8, at 203.

86 Cipriani, "Memory," 554. See also Hankey, "Mind," 564, citing Augustine, *The Trinity* XV.12.21.

87 *Csi*, I, 7.8 (CF 37:38; *SW* 1:648; *SBO* 3:404).

88 Déchanet, "Aux Sources," 62.

89 *Dil*, 7.18 (CF 13b:21; *SW* 1:106; *SBO* 3:135).

90 *Div*, 45.6 (CF 68:239; *SW* 9:550; *SBO* 6.1:265). *Est Trinitas creatrix: Pater et Filius et Spiritus Sanctus, ex qua cecidit creata trinitas: memoria, ratio et voluntas.*

91 Gregory, *Book of Pastoral Rule*, III, 14 (Demacopoulos, 123; PL 77:73b).

92 Augustine, *The Trinity*, Book XII, 12.19 (McKenna, 361). For the Latin edition of this part of the work, see Aurelii Augustini, *De Trinitate libri XV (Libri I–XII)*, ed. W. J. Mountain and Fr. Glorie, CCSL 50 (Turnhout: Brepols, 1968), 373. This kind of psychological fall—the descent of the *acies mentis* (the attention of the mind)—should not be misinterpreted as an ontological fall of a pre-existent soul into the body (on this point, see McGinn's discussion at CF 24:7).

a mental fall involves an abuse of volitional freedom: "this created Trinity chose rather to fall by a movement of self-will than to stand firm by the free choice provided by the gift of creation."[93] The three interior capacities of reason, memory, and will have all been wounded due to this fall away from God: "Memory has been made impotent and feeble, reason foolish and dark, the will impure and foul."[94]

Bernard describes each of the three interior capacities as negatively affected in a trifold manner. With the fall of one's reason, one's mind loses the ability "to weigh good and evil, true and false, beneficial and detrimental."[95] Further, "as a result" of the fall of reason, a person stands in need of three sciences, the "trivium of wisdom": ethics, logic, and physics (Bernard also calls these moral science, inspective science, and natural science). It is ethics that weighs good and evil, logic that facilitates recognition of truth and falsity, and physics that facilitates recognition of the beneficial and detrimental.[96] Ethics, Bernard indicates elsewhere, might consider the precepts of the natural moral law.[97] Goods of education might thus be construed as preparatory remedies for the fall of reason.

Due to the fall of one's memory, Bernard states that one's mind might consequently be given over to disordered thinking:

> Memory, which was standing firm contemplating [*stans cogitabat*] the power of simple divinity, fell from that divinity and, as though crashing upon rocks, was shattered and burst into three parts, that is into affectionate, laborious, and idle thoughts [*cogitationes*]. I call those thoughts

93 *Div*, 45.1 (CF 68:236; *SW* 9:544; *SBO* 6.1:262). "Sed haec trinitas creata elegit potius per motum propriae voluntatis cadere quam ex gratia creationis per arbitrium stare."

94 Ibid. "Memoria enim facta est impotens et infirma, ratio imprudens et tenebrosa, voluntas impura et immunda."

95 *Div*, 45.2 (CF 68:237; *SW* 9:546; *SBO* 6.1:263). "Rationis quoque triplex casus est. Eius siquidem est examinare inter bonum et malum, verum et falsum, commodum et incommodum."

96 Ibid. "Unde factum est, ut etiam instrumentum perderet, quo illa administraret, scilicet illud trivium Sapientiam, Ethicam, Logicam, Physicam, quas nos possumus aliis nominibus nuncupare, Moralem, Inspectivam, Naturalem scientiam. Siquidem per Ethicam eligitur bonum, reprobatur malum; per Logicam cognoscitur verum et falsum; per Physicam commodum et incommodum, id est in usum assumendum sit, quid respuendum."

97 "On Baptism" (Ep 77), 1.2 (CF 67:152; *SW* 2:612; *SBO* 7:186). Bernard writes that baptism "is not one of those commands which the law of nature does not allow us to ignore, even where they are not publicly proclaimed . . . This [command for baptism] belongs to positive rather than to natural law" (*Neque enim tale est hoc, quod et absque promulgatione naturalis lex ignorare non sineret . . . Facticium magis quodammodo est, et non naturale mandatum*). See also Sommerfeldt, "Bernard of Clairvaux and the Trivial Arts," CS 193:153.

> affectionate in which one is affected, as in concerned about necessities: of eating, of drinking, and of unnumerable others. Laborious thoughts might be about managing external matters. Idle thoughts are those by which one is neither afflicted nor burdened, but nevertheless through them one is distracted from contemplation of eternal matters, as when one might think about [*cogitet*], for example, a running horse or a flying bird.[98]

One might observe that in this passage Bernard indicates that he understands memory to be more than the cognitive ability to recall past experience. The activity of memory in this passage is inherently bound up with thinking or with giving attention to certain kinds of thoughts; for example, one might attend to thoughts of God or fall away into various other kinds of thoughts involving bodily concerns or fantasies of the imagination. McMahon contends that for Augustine also memory is a mode of attention when one's attention might become focused on the past in contrast with the present or future.[99] Bernard's psychology seems to involve a similar presupposition.

Quoting 1 John 2:15–16, Bernard also describes the fall of one's will, stating that one's mind descends volitionally into the desires of the flesh and eyes, as well as into worldly ambition.[100] The primary remedy for this threefold fall of the mind is also trifold; the restoration (*resurgens*) of the mind is conferred by means of three theological virtues. "There is a trinity through which the fallen trinity is restored: faith, hope, and love."[101] This remark might be associated with the discussion of restorative grace above. Bernard explains that "faith certainly illuminated reason, hope raised memory, love truly cleansed the will."[102] In this respect then, the theological virtues are spiritual goods that in one sense restore the mind's fallen natural capacities.

98 *Div*, 45.1 (CF 68:236–37; *SW* 9:544–46; *SBO* 6.1:262–63). "Porro memoria, quae simplicis divinitatis potentiam stans cogitabat, ab illa cadens et velut super saxa corruens, in tres partes confracta dissiliit, scilicet in cogitationes affectuosas, onerosas, otiosas. Affectuosas voco illas, in quibus ipsa afficitur, ut in curis rerum necessariarum, edendi, bibendi, ceterarumque innumerabilium; onerosas, ut in exterioribus administrationibus; otiosas, quibus nec afficitur nec oneratur, et tamen ab aeternorum contemplatione per illas distenditur, ut si cogitet, verbi gratia, equum currentem aut avem volantem."

99 McMahon, *Understanding the Medieval Meditative Ascent*, 72.

100 *Div*, 45.3 (CF 68:237; *SW* 9:546–48; *SBO* 6.1:263–64). "Sequitur voluntas, cuius ruina similiter tripertita est."

101 *Div*, 45.6 (CF 68:240; *SW* 9:550–51; *SBO* 6.1:265–66). "Est trinitas per quam resurgit, scilicet fides, spes, caritas."

102 *Div*, 45.4 (CF 68:238; *SW* 9:548; *SBO* 6.1:264). "Et fides quidem illuminavit rationem, spes erexit memoriam, caritas vero purgavit voluntatem."

How does elevating grace differ from restorative grace? In a different sermon from the *De diversis* series, Bernard indicates that there is also a kind of spiritual benefit that is different from a natural benefit, namely, the spiritual good of ascetic practice. After describing natural benefits pertaining to the body and the soul as discussed above, Bernard proceeds to state:

> Spiritual goods, in which we are trained so to strive for eternal goods, are the same as natural goods, but different, because they are considered from a different point of view [*alio intuitu*]. Nevertheless, there are also many other spiritual goods which would be too lengthy to list. Some spiritual goods indeed are known to be according to nature [*iuxta naturam*], but these to be above nature [*supra naturam*]. For in spiritual training [*in spirituali exercitio*] we do not owe health to the body, but rather servitude, affliction, and toil according to the voice of that spiritual and supremely spiritual person who said, *I chastise my body and bring it into subjection.*[103]

In this passage, Bernard alludes to two kinds of spiritual goods, natural and supernatural (*supra naturam*).[104]

With respect to restorative grace, Bernard indicates in this *De diversis* sermon that one kind of spiritual benefit involves the restoration of a natural benefit that is being considered from a different point of view (*alio intuitu*)—for example, restoration of the natural purity of the heart. With respect to elevating grace, Bernard also refers in this *De diversis* sermon to another kind of spiritual benefit that transcends the level of natural benefit; such a supernatural endowment for Bernard would seem to be the ability to engage in an ascetic practice or a spiritual exercise (*spirituali exercitio*). Should then one interpret the spiritual exercise of meditation as pertaining to the natural restoration of the fallen human mind, or rather to the supernatural elevation of the human mind? An answer to this question might be found by examining Bernard's description of meditation as occurring within the context of religious piety.

103 *Div*, 16.5 (CF 68:91; *SW* 9:314; *SBO* 6.1:147). "Spiritualia autem bona, in quibus exercemur, ut ad aeterna tendamus, ipsa eadem sunt, sed alia, quia alio intuitu considerata, cum plurimus tamen aliis, quae longum est enumerare. Illa enim iuxta naturam, haec supra naturam esse noscuntur. Nam et in spirituali exercitio non sanitatem debemus corpori, sed servitutem, sed afflictionem, sed laborem, iuxta vocem illius spiritualis et summe spiritualis hominis, qui dicebat: 'Castigo corpus meum et in servitutem redigo.'" He is quoting 1 Cor 9:27.

104 This passage leads me to a different interpretation of Bernard's understanding of saving grace than what is proposed in CF 24:61.

Religious Piety and the Holy Spirit

In Book I of *De consideratione*, Bernard refers to making time for meditation as an exercise of piety (*pietas*).[105] This act, according to Bernard, is not altogether different from making time for divine worship.[106] He maintains that a certain kind of meditation occurs during worship of God, as indicated by Psalm 45:11: "Be still and know that I am God."[107] Yet, in light of Bernard's contrast between meditation and contemplation found in Book II,[108] one might be inclined to associate the practice of maintaining a still and attentive focus on God with contemplation (as discussed below). With respect to meditation as similar to worship, Bernard might be understood to be stating that the religious dimension of meditation derives from its teleological orientation to contemplation of God as its *terminus ad quem*.[109]

Meditation as an exercise of religious piety might be understood as involving a special relation to the Holy Spirit. Returning to the topic of hierarchy, Bernard indicates that within the tripartite mind (reason, memory, will) there is a hierarchical ordering of the psychological capacities insofar as the will occupies a subordinate position vis-à-vis reason (just as reason in turn is subordinate to the Holy Spirit):

> The reason suggests inwardly to the will [*intus suggerit ratio voluntati*] all these and similar things, more insistently as it is perfectly instructed by the light of the Spirit. Happy indeed is the person whose will gives way and follows reason's advice [*consilio rationis*], so that conceiving in fear she may bear heavenly promise and give birth to the spirit of salvation. But it may

105 *Csi*, I, 7.8 (CF 37:37; *SW* 1:646; *SBO* 3:403).

106 Ibid.

107 Ibid. See also Anderson, "Reconsidering," 151.

108 *Csi*, II, 2.5 (CF 37:52; *SW* 1:668; *SBO* 3:414).

109 Farkasfalvy maintains that for Gastaldelli, Bernard might be interpreted as characterizing the monastic spiritual life as proceeding from conversion to contemplation as its goal. See Denis Farkasfalvy, "Bernard's Concept of the Spiritual Life," *ASOC* 53 (1997): 3–14, at 4, citing F. Gastaldelli, "Teologia Monastica, Teologia Scolastica e Lectio Divina," *ASOC* 46 (1990): 25–63. Evans observes that the ancient philosopher Calcidius (who translated Plato's *Timaeus* into Latin) also refers to *consideratio* in connection with theological *contemplatio*. See Evans, *Bernard of Clairvaux*, 52–53, citing Calcidius, *Timaeus, a Calcidio translatus commentarioque instructus*, ed. J. H. Waszink (Leiden: Brill, 1962), 264 and 271. For an English translation that consults this Latin text, see Calcidius, *On Plato's "Timaeus,"* trans. John Magee (Cambridge, MA: Harvard University Press, 2016). This commentary on *Timaeus* was also engaged by Bernard's contemporaries (Bernard of Chartres and William of Conches). See also Anna Somfai, "The Eleventh Century Shift in the Reception of Plato's *Timaeus* and Calcidius's *Commentary*," *Journal of the Warburg and Courtauld Institutes* 65 (2002): 1–21.

> happen that the will is rebellious and recalcitrant . . . Far from being moved by the suggestions made by reason [*mota suggestionibus rationis*], she may be stirred up to even greater fury.[110]

The psychological hierarchy under consideration is *de iure* and normative; *de facto* one's will may or may not abide by the advice and suggestions of reason. In a similar way, one's reason may or may not be developed in instruction by the Holy Spirit.

Bernard urges elsewhere that one grow in awareness of the presence of the Holy Spirit.[111] With respect to the work of the Holy Spirit in the soul, Bernard maintains in his first Pentecost sermon that when imparting the virtue of charity to one's wounded will, the Holy Spirit can also directly influence one's other interior psychological capacities:

> In fact he admonishes, he moves, and he instructs. He admonishes our memory; he instructs our reason; he moves our will. Our whole soul consists in these three [interior mental capacities]. To the memory he suggests good things in holy thoughts [*Memoriae suggerit bona in cogitationibus sanctis*], and in this way he drives away our listlessness and sloth. Therefore as often as you perceive a suggestion of this type of good in your heart [*huiusmodi suggestionem boni senseris in corde tuo*], give glory to God.[112]

110 *Conv*, 11.22 (CF 25:56; *SW* 4:198–200; *SBO* 4:94–95). "Haec igitur et similia intus suggerit ratio voluntati, eo copiosius quo perfectius illustratione spiritus edocetur. Felix sane, cuius voluntas sic cesserit et acquieverit consilio rationis, ut a timore concipiens, promissionibus deinceps caelestibus foveatur, et parturiat spiritum salutis. At forte invenietur rebellis et obstinate voluntas . . . Invenietur forsitan, quae nihil mota suggestionibus rationis, immo et gravi commota furore respondeat."

111 Bernard of Clairvaux, "Sermon 17," 1.1, in *On the Song of Songs, Vol. I, Sermons 1–20* (CF 4), trans. Kilian Walsh (Kalamazoo, MI: Cistercian Publications, 1971), 126 (*SW* 5:244–55, at 244; *SBO* 1:98–103, at 98). See also John R. Sommerfeldt, "Afterword: Looking Back at Bernard," in *A Companion to Bernard of Clairvaux*, 369–74, at 370; Sommerfeldt, *Life of the Mind*, 17–22, esp. 21–22.

112 Bernard of Clairvaux, "Pentecost, Sermon 1, The Holy Spirit: How He Works in Us in Three Ways," §5–§6 (hereafter *Pent*), in *Sermons for the Summer Season*, trans. Beverly Mayne Kienzle (Kalamazoo, MI: Cistercian Publications, 1991), 71–72 (hereafter CF 53). "Profecto monet, et movet, et docet. Monet memoriam, rationem docet, movet voluntatem. In his enim tribus tota consistit anima nostra. Memoriae suggerit bona in cognitionibus sanctis, atque ita ignaviam nostrum torporemque repellit. Propterea quoties huiusmodi suggestionem boni senseris in corde tuo, da honorem Deo." For the Latin edition of this sermon, see Bernhard von Clairvaux, *Sämtliche Werke, lateinisch/deutsch*, Bd. VIII (hereafter *SW* 8) (Innsbruck: Tyrolia, 1997), 390–401, at 396. *SW* 8 reprints the Latin from Bernardus Claraevallensis, *Sancti Bernardi Opera*, vol. 5 (hereafter *SBO* 5), ed. J. Leclercq, C. H. Talbot, and H.-M. Rochais (Rome: Editiones Cistercienses, 1968), 163. See also Ivánka, "La Structure," 204.

In this passage, Bernard refers to one having some kind of cognitive sense or an intuition of a good suggestion. Further, in contrast with memory falling into burdensome and distracting thoughts (as discussed above), Bernard in this text refers to memory as receiving a thought (*cogitatio*) that might be suggested by the Holy Spirit. To remember, Leclercq notes when explaining Bernard's psychology, is to represent or to make something present to oneself.[113]

As indicated by this passage, to remember might also involve the Holy Spirit making something present to one; see also John 14:26. Bernard again implies in *De diligendo Deo* that it may be the Holy Spirit who communicates the suggestion: "without our first receiving divine inspiration, all prayer becomes lukewarm."[114] In order to answer the question then whether meditation as a spiritual exercise for Bernard pertains to the natural restoration of the fallen human mind or rather to the supernatural elevation of the human mind, it may be that for Bernard the practice of meditation as occurring within the context of religious piety involves being attentive to the Holy Spirit in both ways, namely, as being attentive to (1) inspirations bearing upon the restoration of one's mind (a natural benefit), as well as to (2) inspirations bearing upon the supernatural elevation of one's mind through ascetic practices (a supernatural benefit).

Humility, Spiritual Development, and Growth in the Christian Virtues

Bernard emphasizes in Book I of *De consideratione* that when practicing meditation one should also be attentive to oneself.[115] This attention might be referred to as cultivating self-awareness. Apart from ethical or moral self-reflection (being attentive to the kinds of voluntary actions that one might perform), this topic of self-awareness is not significantly developed in Book I, though Bernard will return to this topic in Book II. Bernard does describe in one long paragraph numerous dimensions or aspects of the activity of meditation in general that also touch on the topic of self-awareness:

> Now, of primary importance is the fact that consideration purifies its source, that is, the mind [*mentem*]. Notice also that it controls the emotions, guides action, corrects excesses, improves behavior, confers dignity

113 Leclercq, "General Introduction (III)," 386.

114 *Dil*, 7.22 (CF 13b:25; *SW* 1:112; *SBO* 3:138).

115 *Csi*, I, 5.6 (CF 37:33–34; *SW* 1:638–42; *SBO* 3:399–401).

> and order on life, and even imparts knowledge of divine and human affairs.[116]

How one might approach divine affairs during meditation is the focus of Book V of the treatise. In this same passage, Bernard continues to describe the practice of meditation: "It puts an end to confusion, closes gaps, gathers up what has been scattered, roots out secrets, hunts down truth, scrutinizes what seems to be true, and explores lies and deceit."[117]

In all of these remarks, Bernard is focused on how meditation can contribute to cognitive clarity and integration. He then also observes how meditation can involve a special focus on practical concerns:

> It decides what is to be done and reviews what has been done in order to eliminate from the mind anything deficient or in need of correction. Consideration anticipates adversity when all is going well and when adversity comes, it stands firm. In this it displays both prudence and fortitude.[118]

I will return to the relationship between meditation and specific virtues below. At present, one might note that meditation for Bernard is in one respect simply practical deliberation: "What is as valuable as consideration which benevolently presumes to take part in an action by anticipating and planning what must be done?"[119] The exercise of practical deliberation supports a person in acting in a way that is not haphazard but intentional, in a way that is "thought out and planned in advance" (*praevisa et praemeditata*).[120]

Recall in the passage quoted above that Bernard states that a person in meditation is able to grow in emotional self-regulation (*regit affectus*).[121] In a similar way, Bernard writes that one can also learn how to regulate one's

116 *Csi*, I, 7.8 (CF 37:38; *SW* 1:646–48; *SBO* 3:403–4). "Et primum quidem ipsum fontem suum, id est mentem, de qua oritur, purificat consideratio. Deinde regit affectus, dirigit actus, corrigit excessus, componit mores, vitam honestat et ordinat, postremo divinarum partier et humanarum rerum scientiam confert."

117 *Csi*, I, 7.8 (CF 37:38; *SW* 1:648; *SBO* 3:404). "Haec est quae confusa disterminat, hiantia cogit, sparsa colligit, secreta rimatur, vera vestigat, veri similia examinat, ficta et fucata explorat."

118 Ibid. "Haec est quae agenda praeordinat, recogitat acta, ut nihil in mente resideat aut incorrectum, aut correctione egens. Haec est quae in prosperis adversa praesentit, in adversis quasi non sentit, quorum alterum fortitudinis, alterum prudentiae est."

119 *Csi*, I, 7.8 (CF 37:38; *SW* 1:646; *SBO* 3:403).

120 Ibid.

121 *Csi*, I, 7.8 (CF 37:38; *SW* 1:648; *SBO* 3:404).

will in order not to desire anything excessive, nor to avoid what is due.[122] Ultimately speaking, the religious goal for the development of one's will is to align one's will with God. In a sermon from his *Sermones super cantica canticorum*, Bernard asserts that it is the love of charity that facilitates union between one's will and God's will:

> What is more desirable than charity, by whose operation, O soul . . . you approach the Word with confidence, cling to him with constancy, speak to him as to a familiar friend, and refer to him in every matter with an intellectual grasp proportionate to the boldness of your desire? Truly this is a spiritual contract, a holy marriage. It is more than a contract, it is an embrace: an embrace where identity of will makes of two one spirit.[123]

One's will might be understood in this way to enter a common will (as distinct from one's self-will, isolated from union with Christ).[124]

Bernard explores the distinction between these two kinds of will at length in his *Sermones in resurrectione Domini*.[125] Referring to Mary Magdalene, Mary the mother of James, and Salome bringing spices to the tomb of Jesus in Mark 16:1, Bernard states that one might understand these spices as "spices of the mind" (*aromata mentis*), namely, as the virtues of compassion, zeal for rectitude (justice), and a spirit of discretion.[126] Such qualities of the mind can be developed when one subordinates one's own will to God in order to join with God in a common will of love: "We must buy the three spices for the mind with the money of self-will; by losing it we lose nothing, we gain even more, for we change it for something better so that what was

122 *Csi*, I, 8.10 (CF 37:40; *SW* 1:650; *SBO* 3:405).

123 *SCC*, 83, 1.3 (CF 40:182; *SW* 6:612; *SBO* 2:299). "Quid optabilius caritate, qua fit ut, humano magisterio non contenta, per temet, o anima, fiducialiter accedes ad Verbum, Verbo constanter inhaereas, Verbum familiariter percuncteris consultesque de omni re, quantum intellectu capax, tantum audax desiderio? Vere spiritualis sanctique conubii contractus est iste. Parum dixi, contractus: complexus est. Complexus plane, ubi idem velle, et nolle idem, unum facit spiritum de duobus." See also Stepsis, "Fulfillment of Self," 361.

124 Leclercq, "General Introduction (III)," 389.

125 See Bernard of Clairvaux, "On the Resurrection of the Lord" (hereafter *Res*) 2 and 3, in *Sermons for Lent and the Easter Season* (CF 52), trans. Irene Edmonds (Kalamazoo, MI: Cistercian Publications, 2013), 159–74 (*SW* 8:260–88; *SBO* 5:95–109). See also CS 120:55–57; Stepsis, "Fulfillment of Self," 355.

126 *Res*, 2.3–2.4 (CF 52:160–61; *SW* 8:262–63; *SBO* 5:96–97). Note that in this sermon Bernard refers to discretion as a virtue. Regarding the need for grace in order that one might develop in all three virtues, he states: "The soil of our heart does not make virtues like these sprout up for us, but rather produces thorns and thistles!" (Neque enim talia profert virtutum germina terra cordis nostri, sed magis spinas et tribulos germinat nobis). *Res*, 2.7 (CF 52:162; *SW* 8:266; *SBO* 5:98).

private might be common. The common will is love [*caritas*]."[127] In contrast with the common will of love, Bernard describes self-will further in the next sermon:

> I call self-will the will that is not common to God and humans, but is ours alone. We do what we want, not for the glory of God or to profit our brethren, but for ourselves; not intending to please God or benefit our brethren, but to satisfy our own whims. Love [*caritas*], which God is, is exactly the opposite of this. Self-will engenders hostility toward him and a most cruel war.[128]

Bernard thus contrasts the will united with God in charity (where one wills to proceed in a manner that honors God and benefits others) with self-will (where one wills only to benefit and satisfy oneself). This distinction might also be understood as developing a will centered on others in contrast with a self-centered will.

With respect to the subordination of one's will to the divine will, one might also note Bernard's remarks that self-regulation of one's will facilitates the self-regulation of one's emotions; this ability in turn leads a person to cultivate the moral virtues.[129] Self-reflection in this respect must be united with humility because, as Bernard states at the end of the treatise, "humility is the true and firm foundation of the virtues" (*Virtutum siquidem bonum quoddam ac stabile fundamentum, humilitas*).[130] In humility, one will be honest with oneself during one's self-reflection. With honesty, one might be more genuinely able to discern in what areas of one's psychological activity (thinking, speech, and voluntary bodily actions) one might need to develop in order to obtain stable self-consistency (virtue).[131] Recall that for Bernard (in sermon 16 of the *De diversis* series) one's development in virtue depends upon receiving the good of grace: "If you cannot fix your eye of meditation

127 *Res*, 2.8 (CF 52:163; *SW* 8:266; *SBO* 5:98). "Tria igitur aromata mentis nummo propriae voluntatis emenda sunt, quam quidem dimittentes nihil amittimus, etiam et lucramur plurimum, commutantes illam in melius, ut communis fiat quae propria fuit."

128 *Res*, 3.3 (CF 52:170; *SW* 8:280; *SBO* 5:105). "Voluntatem dico propriam, quae non est communis cum Deo et hominibus, sed nostra tantum, quando quod volumus, non ad honorem Dei, non ad utilitatem fratrum, sed propter nosipsos facimus, non intendentes placere Deo et prodesse fratribus, sed satisfacere propriis motibus animorum. Huic contraria est recta fronte caritas, quae est Deus. Haec enim adversus eum inimicitias exercens est, et guerram crudelissimam."

129 *Csi*, I, 8.11 (CF 37:42; *SW* 1:654; *SBO* 3:407).

130 *Csi*, V, 14.32 (CF 37:179; *SW* 1:826; *SBO* 3:493).

131 See also Sommerfeldt, "Meditation as the Path," 177 and 178.

on that height of eternal goods because they are distant and surpass all understanding, then turn your vision to the good things of grace that are in the exercise of virtue."[132]

With respect to Bernard giving emphasis to the importance of humility in self-reflection for the sake of growth in the virtues, his teaching in *De consideratione* is consistent with reflections found in his *Sermones super cantica canticorum*. For example, in sermon 36 in this series, Bernard argues that growth in self-knowledge is of primary importance because when one is honest with oneself about oneself, this experience will lead one to humility:

> I wish therefore that before everything else a man should know himself, because not only usefulness but right order demand this. Right order, since what we are is our first concern; and usefulness, because this knowledge gives humility rather than self-importance, it provides a basis on which to build [*praeparatio ad aedificandum*]. For unless there is a durable foundation of humility, the spiritual edifice [*spirituale aedificium*] has no hope of standing.[133]

If one is honest in one's self-assessment, meditation will not lead one to self-deception or inflation, but rather to the requisite humility needed for genuine spiritual development (*talis scientia non inflat, sed humiliat*) and spiritual formation (*aedificatio*).[134]

132 *Div*, 16.1 (CF 68:88; *SW* 9:308; *SBO* 6.1:144). "Si non potes oculum meditationis in illam sublimitatem aeternalium bonorum infigere, quia stantia sunt et omnem sensum exsuperant, in bonis gratiae, quae sunt in exercitio virtutum, visum reflecte."

133 *SCC*, 36, 4.5 (CF 7:177; *SW* 5:568; *SBO* 2:7). "Volo proinde animam primo omnium scire seipsam, quod id postulet ratio et utilitatis, et ordinis. Et ordinis quidem, quoniam quod nos sumus primum est nobis; utilitatis vero, quia talis scientia non inflat, sed humiliat, et est quaedam praeparatio ad aedificandum. Nisi enim super humilitatis stabile fundamentum, spirituale aedificium stare minime potest." See also Stepsis, "Fulfillment of Self," 350. Regarding humility as a virtue in *SCC*, see also *SCC*, 27, 2.3 (CF 7:76; *SW* 5:414; *SBO* 1:183), and *SCC*, 46, 2.7 (CF 7:246; *SW* 6:134; *SBO* 2:60). For these references I am indebted to William O. Paulsell, "Virtue in St Bernard's *Sermons on the Song of Songs*," in *Saint Bernard of Clairvaux: Studies* (ed. Pennington), 101–17, at 102–3.

134 In the discussion that follows, I will frequently recall this text on spiritual development (*aedificatio*) from *SCC*, 36, 4.5 (CF 7:177; *SW* 5:568; *SBO* 2:7). Bernard's remarks here in sermon 36 relate to an emphasis found in the work of philosopher Josef Pieper whom I mentioned earlier (as possibly influenced by Bernard regarding the value of quietude—*otium*—see also Pieper, *Leisure*, 31), namely, the topic of self-cultivation (*Bildung*) which Pieper adopts from the tradition of German Romanticism (Pieper, *Leisure*, 23). For *Bildung* in German Romanticism, see W. H. Bruford, *The German Tradition of Self-Cultivation: 'Bildung' from Humboldt to Mann* (Cambridge: Cambridge University Press, 2010); Jennifer A. Herdt, *Forming Humanity: Redeeming the German Bildung Tradition* (Chicago: University of Chicago Press, 2019). See also Christopher W. Gowans, *Self-Cultivation Philosophies in Ancient India, Greece, and China* (Oxford: Oxford University Press,

Bernard reiterates that being honest with oneself is essential to the process that he is describing:

> And there is nothing more effective, more adapted to the acquiring of humility, than to find out the truth about oneself. There must be no dissimulation, no attempt at self-deception, but a facing up to one's real self without flinching and turning aside. When a man thus takes stock of himself in the clear light of truth, he will discover that he lives in a region where likeness to God has been forfeited [*in regione dissimilitudinis*].[135]

If one's self-examination occurs in orientation to the truth, Bernard expects that one will be honest with oneself about how distant one is from reflecting God in one's actions. This presupposes that one has some intuition of God or some understanding of what a human similitude of God might involve.

In this passage, Bernard implies that one's assessment of self-distance from God (in one's thoughts, words, and deeds) can result in several responses. One response might be to turn aside from the truth (or even deny that the criterion of measure that one references is reliable). Bernard indicates in this text that one criterion he references is a "self-intuition in the clear light of truth" (*se intuens clara luce veritatis*).[136] I will return to this text below to explore the topic of a *lux veritatis* in relation to the topic of conscience. Here, it may be said that if one's recognition of one's distance from God does lead one to humility, Bernard indicates that he expects this

---

2021). One might consider whether there is some general connection between Bernard's discussion in sermon 36 on monastic formation (*aedifcatio*) and the German Romantic teaching of cultivation (*Bildung*). The philosopher Hans-Georg Gadamer, for example, does discern such a connection—at least between *Bildung* as discussed by Wilhelm von Humboldt and the formation of the *imago Dei* in the soul as a practice valued by ancient mysticism in general. See Hans-Georg Gadamer, *Wahrheit und Methode*, in *Gesammelte Werke* 1 (Tübingen: Mohr Siebeck, 1990), 16 (hereafter *GW*). For an English translation, see Hans-Georg Gadamer, *Truth and Method*, 2nd ed., trans. Joel Weinsheimer and Donald G. Marshall (New York: Continuum, 2004), 10 (hereafter *TM*). In his study of Bernard's doctrine of spiritual development in light of Maslow's psychology, Stepsis also indirectly brings Bernard's sermon 36 into general connection with the *Bildung* tradition when discussing Goethe on self-development (Goethe was an immediate precursor of the German Romantics). See Stepsis, "Fulfillment of Self," 348, 350, 363. For Goethe as a precursor of the Romantics, see W. H. Bruford, *Culture and Society in Classical Weimar 1775–1806* (Cambridge: Cambridge University Press, 1962).

135 *SCC*, 36, 4.5 (CF 7:177–78; *SW* 5:568; *SBO* 2:7). "Porro ad se humiliandam anima nihil invenire vivacius seu accomodatius potest, quam si se in veritate invenerit: tantum non dissimulet, non sit in spiritu eius dolus, statuat se ante faciem suam, nec se a se avertere abducatur. Nonne ita se intuens clara luce veritatis, inveniet se in regione dissimilitudinis."

136 Ibid.

disposition will in turn help prepare one's soul to grow closer to God in an authentic way. Humility thus serves as a foundation for spiritual formation in relationship with God and simultaneously serves as a foundation for genuine growth in the virtues. As quoted above, Bernard explicitly states at the end of Book V: "Humility is the true and firm foundation of the virtues."[137]

It is helpful at this point to discuss Bernard's teaching on specific virtues in relation to his understanding of emotions or natural affections. In his early *Liber de gratia et libero arbitrio*, Bernard describes the virtues as arising from grace for the purpose of ordering affections that human persons naturally have by way of creation: "For mere affections live naturally in us, as of us, but those additional acts [of virtue], as of grace. This means only that grace sets in order what creation has given, so that virtues are nothing else than ordered affections."[138] Grace, one might interpret Bernard to say, enables one to cultivate the expression of one's natural emotions in a particular way so to structure this expression according to the Christian virtues.

With respect to such natural affections, Bernard observes in *De diligendo Deo* that "love is one of the four natural passions" (*Amor est affectio naturalis una de quatuor*).[139] Love is an affect that moves one's will with a certain spontaneity: "Love pertains to the will, it is not a transaction; it cannot acquire or be acquired by a pact. Moving us freely, it makes us spontaneous."[140] Natural love, along with the other natural affections of joy, fear, and sadness, can be either ordered with virtue or become disordered:

> These four emotions, moreover, are well known: love and joy, fear and sadness [*amor et laetitia, timor et tristitia*]. Without these the human soul [*anima*] does not exist, but for certain people they bring a crown; for certain other people they bring confusion. For once purified and ordered, they render the soul glorious in a crown of virtues [*gloriosam in virtutum*

137 *Csi*, V, 14.32 (CF 37:179). "Virtutum siquidem bonum quoddam ac stabile fundamentum, humilitas."

138 *Gra*, 6.17 (CF 19a:72–73; *SW* 1:198; *SBO* 3:178). "Simplices namque affectiones insunt naturaliter nobis, tamquam ex nobis, additamenta ex gratia. Nec aliud profecto est, nisi quod gratia ordinat, quas donavit creatio, ut nil aliud sint virtutes nisi ordinatae affectiones." See also Emero Stiegman, "Humanism in Bernard of Clairvaux: Beyond Literary Culture," in *The Chimæra of His Age: Studies on Bernard of Clairvaux*, ed. E. Rozanne Elder and John R. Sommerfeldt (Kalamazoo, MI: Cistercian Publications, 1980), 28 (hereafter CS 63).

139 *Dil*, 8.23 (CF 13b:25; *SW* 1:112; *SBO* 3:138). For reference to some of the subsequent texts on natural love, I am indebted to the editorial annotation found in CF 13b:25n220.

140 *Dil*, 7.17 (CF 13b:20; *SW* 1:102–4; *SBO* 3:133–34). "Affectus est, non contractus: nec acquiritur pacto, nec acquirit. Sponte afficit, et spontaneum facit."

> *corona reddunt animam*]. Once disordered through confusion, the soul is disgraced and dejected.[141]

One might note that in the *In quadragesima* sermon series, Bernard also refers to the emotion of delight (*delectatio*) that can be experienced when one abides in a good conscience.[142]

Bernard repeats his doctrine that the natural emotions become ordered by orienting them to God in his second *In quadragesima* sermon:

> Look carefully at the object of your love, your fear, the reason for your joy or your sadness, and you will find a worldly mind under your religious habit . . . All your heart is in these four affects [*Totum enim cor in his quattuor affectionibus est*], and I think it is with reference to them that we should hear what is said about "turning to the Lord with all your heart" [*in toto corde tuo convertaris ad Dominum*]. Let your love be turned, then, so that you love nothing at all except him, or because of him. Next, let your fear too be turned to him, because all the fear that you feel for anything except him, or not because of him, is wrong. Similarly, let both your joy and your sadness be turned to him.[143]

Bernard in this text implies several noteworthy things. First, orienting the four emotions to God is what entails a religious conversion of one's heart to God. Second, spiritual growth through the Christian virtues is inherently relational in that it is based upon a relationship with God. Third, both fear and love can be joined in orientation to God. This integration of affections comprises the complex emotion of monastic compunction (discussed further below in relation to Book V).

With respect to orienting the love, fear, joy, and sadness of one's heart to God, Bernard indicates in sermon 14 of the *Sermones super psalmum "Qui habitat"* that these "four affections" (*affectionibus . . . quattuor*) can either be disordered or ordered depending on whether they are cultivated by means of the four cardinal moral virtues.[144] The pursuit of Christian virtue thus helps

141 *Div*, 50.2 (CF 68:248; *SW* 9:562; *SBO* 6.1:271). "Sunt autem affectiones istae quattuor notissimae: amor et laetitia, timor et tristitia. Absque his non subsistit humana anima, sed quibusdam sunt in coronam, quibusdam in confusionem. Purgatae enim et ordinatae gloriosam in virtutum corona reddunt animam, inordinatae per confusionem deiectam et ignominiosam."

142 Bernard of Clairvaux, "Lent: Sermon Two" (hereafter *Quad*), 5.6 (CF 52:46; *SW* 7:486; *SBO* 4:375).

143 *Quad*, §3 (CF 52:30–35, at 32; *SW* 7:454–65, at 458; *SBO* 4:359–64, at 361).

144 *QH*, 14.9–10 (CF 25:237–38; *SW* 7:682–84; *SBO* 4:474–75).

one orient one's affections to God. With respect to the virtues, the natural affection of love can become ordered through the virtue of prudence or disordered as "greed" (*cupiditas*) and "lust for earthly things" (*concupiscentiam terrenorum*).[145] The natural affection of joy can become ordered through the virtues of justice and humility or disordered as "elation tinged with vanity" (*laetitiae noceat vanitatem*); in humility, one "refuses to appropriate to himself the glory which is God's" (*non ipse sibi accipere gloriam quae Dei est*) and proceeds by "arrogating less to self" (*minus arrogat sibi*).[146] Again, Bernard explicitly refers to the natural affection of fear (*timor*) becoming ordered through the virtue of courage.[147] Lastly, Bernard states that the natural affection of sadness (*tristitia*) might become ordered through the virtues of temperance and modesty whereby one "knows how to suffer want and enjoy abundance."[148]

In a similar discussion in the *Sermones super cantica canticorum*, Bernard again gives emphasis to the dependence of the soul on God in order to develop in virtue. He first cites Psalm 24:3, appropriating the metaphor of ascending the mountain of the Lord as a metaphor for developing in virtue, relating this passage to the bride coming up from the wilderness being supported by the bridegroom in Song of Songs 8:5:

> "Who shall ascend the hill of the Lord [*Quis ascendet in montem Domini*]?" If anyone aspires to climb to the summit of that mountain that is to the perfection of virtue, he will know how hard the climb is, and how the attempt is doomed to failure without the help of the Word [*Verbi adiutorio*]. Happy the soul [*anima*] which causes the angels to look at her with joy and wonder and hears them saying, "Who is this coming up from the wilderness, rich in grace and beauty, leaning upon her beloved [*innixa super dilectum suum*]?" Otherwise, unless it leans on him [*si non innitur*], its struggle is in vain [*frustra nititur*].[149]

Bernard in this passage describes development in virtue as an ascent that will be frustrated unless one takes up a posture of dependence upon God's assistance. Here again, Bernard gives great emphasis to the need for grace in

145 Ibid.

146 Ibid.

147 *QH*, 14.10 (CF 25:238; *SW* 7:682; *SBO* 4:474).

148 *QH*, 14.9–10 (CF 25:237–38; *SW* 7:682–84; *SBO* 4:474–75).

149 *SCC*, 85, 2.5 (CF 40:200–201; *SW* 6:634; *SBO* 2:310).

order to develop in virtue as associated with his understanding of the state of the human condition. He continues:

> But [the soul] will gain force by struggling with itself [*Sane etiam contra se innitens invalescet*] and, becoming stronger, will impel all things toward reason: anger, fear, covetousness, and joy [*coget pro ratione universa: iram, metum, cupiditatem et gaudium*]; like a good charioteer, it will control the chariot of the mind, bringing every carnal affect into captivity, and every sense under the control of reason in accordance with virtue [*veluti quemdam animi currum, bonus auriga reget, et in captivitatem rediget omnem carnalem affectum, et carnis sensum ad nutum rationis in obsequium virtutus*].[150]

In this text, Bernard indicates that to gain spiritual strength (to ascend the mountain of virtue), one's soul (*anima*) will guide one's mind (*animus*) in such a way that one recollects or gathers one's affections under the command of reason (*coget pro ratione . . . ad nutum rationis*) in obedience to virtue (*obsequium virtutis*)—all in dependence upon God's grace. Bernard's emphasis on hierarchy with respect to psychological capacities is implicit in this discussion, as reason is described as mediating between God above the mind and one's emotions below the mind (recall for Bernard that the mind is specifically reason, memory, and will).

At this point, I want to return to Bernard's remark in *De consideratione* that the practice of meditation provides an opportunity to grow in specific virtues such as prudence and fortitude.[151] Bernard writes to Eugene III: "justice seeks; prudence finds. Fortitude lays claim; temperance possesses . . . I have said this much to encourage you to set aside [time] for consideration which leads to the discovery of these virtues and others like them."[152] Meditation thus differs from the exercise of a virtue because meditation leads to the discovery of a virtue and facilitates growth in that virtue. Yet when meditation involves practical deliberation (discussed above), the mental activity of meditation can integrate with the exercise of the virtue of prudence to some extent.[153] According to Bernard, it is prudence that is

150 Ibid.

151 *Csi*, I, 7.8 (CF 37:38; *SW* 1:648; *SBO* 3:404).

152 *Csi*, I, 8.11 (CF 37:42; *SW* 1:654; *SBO* 3:407). "Itaque iustitia quaerit, prudentia invenit, vindicat fortitudo, temperantia possidet. Non mihi hoc loco propositum de virtutibus disputare, sed haec dixerim hortans ad vacandum considerationi, cuius beneficio haec et similia advertuntur."

153 Clairmont also notes the close resemblance of meditation to practical deliberation and prudence: Clairmont, "Medieval Consideration," 82 and 92.

the virtue that subsequently helps one discover the mean (*modum*) in one's actions, a middle way between extremes of excess and defect.[154] In navigating this middle way between "desire and necessity," prudence is "like a judge" who "sets definite boundaries for both."[155] Bernard's remarks indicate that the virtue of prudence might assist a person in expressing a judgment of wisdom (a *sententia*) that proposes boundaries (*termini*) for human activity,[156] evocative of Bernard's statement above concerning the discernment of boundaries of health (*termini sanitatis*) for the body,[157] as well as Gregory's statement above concerning the discernment of boundaries for one's mental activities.[158]

Bernard describes prudence as "the mother of fortitude" and as the virtue that also "forms . . . temperance."[159] Prudence in this respect seems similar to "the light of discretion" which, echoing Benedict,[160] Bernard also refers to as "the mother of the virtues" that helps one "avoid extremes" (*ne quid nimis*).[161] Bernard repeats this maxim (*ne quid nimis*) in *De consideratione*, citing "the Philosopher."[162] Anderson and Kennan maintain that Bernard in this reference may be referring to Aristotle who in the *Rhetoric* ascribes the maxim in turn to Chilon, one of the seven ancient Greek sages.[163] Alternatively, Leinenweber suggests that the Roman playwright Terence is the origin of this maxim.[164]

As an example of avoiding extremes, Bernard suggests in Book II of *De consideratione* that Eugene III explore the moral qualities of zeal and mercy (with respect to the pope's observance "of forgiving and of avenging

154 *Csi*, I, 8.11 (CF 37:42; *SW* 1:654; *SBO* 3:407). See also Emmanuel Martineau, "Prudence et Considération: Un Dessein Philosophique de Saint Bernard de Clairvaux," *Les Études Philosophiques* 1 (1980): 23–45, at 34–35.

155 *Csi*, I, 8.9 (CF 37:39; *SW* 1:648; *SBO* 3:404). "Haec item est, quae inter voluptates et necessitates media, quasi quaedam arbitra, sedens, utrimque certis limitibus disterminat fines."

156 See also Prv 22:28 in the Latin: "ne transgrediaris terminos antiquos quos posuerunt patres tui."

157 *Div*, 16.2 (CF 68:88; *SW* 9:310; *SBO* 6.1:145).

158 Gregory, *Book of Pastoral Rule*, III, 14 (Demacopoulos, 123; PL 77:73b).

159 *Csi*, I, 8.9 (CF 37:38–39; *SW* 1:648; *SBO* 3:404). "Vides fortitudinis matrem esse prudentiam . . . ex alterutro tertiam formans virtutem, quam dicunt temperantiam."

160 *RB*, chap. 64 (McCann, 146–47; Fry, 63). "Discretionis matris virtutum."

161 See Bernard of Clairvaux, *In circumcisione*, 3.11 (CF 51:152; *SW* 7:316; *SBO* 4:290). "Illuminari necesse est lumen discretionis, quae mater virtutum est et consummatio perfectionis. Haec nimirum docet, ne quid nimis." See also Edith Scholl, "The Mother of Virtues: *Discretio*," *CSQ* 36, no. 3 (2001): 389–401, at 397. See also Dominique Bertrand, "Bernardine Discernment: Between the Desert Fathers and Ignatius of Loyola," *CSQ* 36, no. 3 (2001): 325–36, at 329.

162 *Csi*, I, 8.9 (CF 37:39; *SW* 1:650; *SBO* 3:405).

163 See Aristotle, *Rhetoric* II.12.1389b5 (Freese, 251).

164 CF 51:152n5, citing Terence, *Andria* 1.1.34.

injuries").[165] These qualities are indifferent in themselves; but they can become virtues if exercised with discretion in a way that avoids extremes.[166] Bernard states that discretion helps one evaluate "means, place, and time" and supports "the practice of these virtues" (namely, zeal and mercy in the execution of justice).[167]

Toward the end of Book II of *De consideratione*, Bernard indicates that developing in the virtues requires not only grace, but also personal effort: "Indeed, it is not nature but practice [*usus*] which produces virtues of this kind."[168] Conversely, Bernard notes to Eugene III that with wrong practice, "you can make them vices by misusing or confounding them."[169] How might this occur? The answer is found in a failure in the light of discretion which is the mother of the virtues. "The eye of discretion," Bernard observes, "is blinded by two things: anger [*ira*] and extreme softheartedness [*mollis*]."[170] Bernard further explains: "An eye raging in anger sees nothing mercifully and one that filled with a flood of womanly weakness does not see straight."[171] Bernard reiterates in a sermon from his *Sermones super cantica canticorum* that without discretion, any virtue becomes a vice:

> Discretion regulates every virtue, order assigns proportion and beauty, and even permanence . . . Discretion therefore is not so much a virtue as a moderator and guide of the virtues, a director of the affections, a teacher of right living. Take it away and virtue becomes vice, and natural affection itself a force that disturbs and destroys nature.[172]

165 *Csi*, II, 11.20 (CF 37:74–75; *SW* 1:696; *SBO* 3:428).

166 Ibid. "Nam ex se indifferentes esse noscuntur."

167 *Csi*, II, 11.20 (CF 37:74; *SW* 1:696; *SBO* 3:428).

168 Ibid. "Nempe eiusmodi non natura virtutes, sed usus facit."

169 Ibid. "Tuum est . . . abutendo et confundendo, facere vitia."

170 Ibid. "Discretionis oculo . . . Porro calignis duae sunt causae, ira et mollior affectus." I interpret the word *mollis* in this discussion as "affective weakness." See also Shawn M. Krahmer, "The Virile Bride of Bernard of Clairvaux," *Church History* 69, no. 2 (2000): 304–27, at 312; Shawn M. Krahmer, "Adam, Eve, and Original Sin in the Works of Bernard of Clairvaux," *CSQ* 37, no. 1 (2002): 3–12, at 4 and 7.

171 *Csi*, II, 11.20 (CF 37:75; *SW* 1:696; *SBO* 3:428).

172 Bernard of Clairvaux, "Sermon 49," 2.5, in *On the Song of Songs Vol. III, Sermons 47–66* (hereafter CF 31), trans. Kilian Walsh and Irene M. Edmonds (Kalamazoo, MI: Cistercian, 1979), 25 (*SW* 6:166; *SBO* 3:76). "Discretio quippe omni virtuti ponit ordinem, ordo modum tribuit et decorum, etiam et perpetuitatem . . . Est ergo discretio non tam virtus, quam quaedam moderatrix et auriga virtutum, ordinatrixque affectuum, et morum doctrix. Tolle hanc, et virtus vitium erit, ipsaque affectio naturalis in perturbationem magis convertetur exterminiumque naturae." See also Wilhelm Hiss, *Die Anthropologie Bernhards von Clairvaux* (Berlin: Walter de Gruyter, 1964), 116.

Taking these various passages together, Bernard's teaching is that anger and affective weakness can hamper one's discretion, and a lack of discretion in turn disrupts one's discernment of (and growth in) the virtues. In this way, one might observe that just as for Bernard the practice of meditation is distinct from the exercise of prudence (although a meditation may include practical deliberation or help one develop in prudence), so too is the practice of meditation distinct from the exercise of discretion (although in meditation one may reflect on one's discretion as a topic of consideration).[173]

Returning to Book I of *De consideratione*, with respect to the other three cardinal moral virtues, Bernard maintains that a person who meditates is better able to conform to the virtue of justice.[174] Through self-reflection, he states that one should be able to discern the twofold "norm of justice" (*normam iustitiae*), namely, the silver rule: "not to do to another what one would not wish done to himself, nor deny another what one wishes for himself."[175] Regarding fortitude, Bernard contends that exercising this virtue avoids not only acts of cowardice but also acts of "temerity" or rashness that "dare something that prudence has not conceived."[176] Rather, fortitude helps a person "be content" with a "middle way" (*illo medio*) between too much and too little.[177] Regarding temperance, Bernard states that the practice of meditation can help one avoid the excess of indulgence as well as the defect of denying oneself due necessities.[178] This observation indicates some connection between temperance and justice (in terms of discretion helping one discern what is due and undue or just and unjust).

Throughout this discussion, Bernard displays great insight into how the virtues are interconnected: "observe the delightful and harmonious intermingling of the virtues and how one depends on the other."[179] For example, citing Matthew 6:16, Bernard explicitly notes that "justice is necessary for temperance," yet citing Ecclesiastes 7:17 and Romans 12:13, he also observes

173 I base this comment on Bernard's exhortations in *Csi*, II, 11.20 (CF 37:74; *SW* 1:696; *SBO* 3:428).

174 *Csi*, I, 8.10 (CF 37:39; *SW* 1:650; *SBO* 3:405). "Iam de iustitia, quae una ex quatuor est, nonne constat consideratione mentem praeveniri, ut se formet in ea?"

175 *Csi*, I, 8.10 (CF 37:39–40; *SW* 1 650; *SBO* 3:405). "Se enim necesse est prius cogitet, ut ex se normam ducat iustitiae, nec factura utique alteri, quod sibi fieri nolit, nec quod sibi velit fieri negatura."

176 *Csi*, I, 8.9 (CF 37:38; *SW* 1:648; *SBO* 3:404). "Nec fortitudinem, sed temeritatem esse quemlibet ausum, quem non parturivit prudentia."

177 *Csi*, I, 8.10 (CF 37:41; *SW* 1:652; *SBO* 3:406).

178 *Csi*, I, 8.9 (CF 37:39; *SW* 1:648; *SBO* 3:404).

179 Ibid. "Ibi etiam advertere tibi est suavissimum quaedam concentum complexumque virtutum, atque alteram pendere ex altera."

that temperance sets a limit to justice and wisdom respectively.[180] The focus of his discussion at this point in Book I is on the "fittingness" (*convenientia*) or harmony of the four moral virtues.[181] Justice, for example, has a "beautiful connection and coherence" (*pulchram connexionem et cohaerentiam*) with temperance; justice and temperance together relate in a similar fashion to prudence and fortitude.[182] I agree with Stiegman who finds it noteworthy that Bernard introduces the criterion of the beautiful into the domain of the moral at this point, thereby uniting both moral *praxis* and artistic *poiesis* under the broader expanse of the aesthetic.[183]

As a closing point for this chapter, one might note that Bernard's discussion implicitly returns to the interconnection of the virtues with a different emphasis later in Book V when he discusses the self-consistency of moral unity: "There is a moral unity (*unitas potestativa*) by which the man of virtue strives to be free of instability and inconsistency and to be always one with himself."[184] The practice of meditation can thus contribute to personal development in the sense of growth in integrity. It is important to recall that for Bernard this moral unity and beauty are inherently connected with one's relationship with God: "No being can be opposed to God and be in harmony with itself [*sibimet cohaerere*]."[185]

180 *Csi*, I, 8.10 (CF 37:40; *SW* 1:650; *SBO* 3:405).

181 *Csi*, I, 8.10 (CF 37:39; *SW* 1:650; *SBO* 3:405).

182 *Csi*, I, 8.10 (CF 37:40; *SW* 1:650; *SBO* 3:405).

183 Emero Stiegman, "A Tradition of Aesthetics in Saint Bernard," in CS 135:129–47, at 134. See also J. Stephen Russell, "Piety's Dance: The Cardinal Virtues in Bernard's *De consideratione*," *CSQ* 49, no. 1 (2014) 27–42, at 41.

184 *Csi*, V, 8.18 (CF 37:163; *SW* 1:804; *SBO* 3:482). "Est unitas potestativa, qua homo virtutis non instabilis, non dissimilis, sed unus sibimet semper nititur inveniri."

185 *Csi*, V, 12.26 (CF 37:173; *SW* 1:818; *SBO* 3:489). "Non potest Deo esse contrarium quid, et sibimet cohaerere."

5

Book II

Meditative Reflection on Oneself

Having introduced the practice of meditation as discussed in Book I of *De consideratione*, I turn now to examine Book II. In Book II, Bernard is focused on the first stage of meditation, which involves self-reflection or consideration of oneself. The interpretation of Book II that follows is organized around topics that emerge during the course of Bernard's text, namely, how meditation differs from contemplation, how the practice of meditation is exercised within a context that is primarily oriented toward one's religious salvation, and how meditation can facilitate growth in self-knowledge. Such growth requires philosophical reflection on one's human nature, personhood, and life roles, as well as reflection on the formation of one's conscience and moral character.

Differentiating Meditation and Contemplation

At the beginning of Book II of *De consideratione*, Bernard remarks on the failure of the second crusade.[1] Leclercq notes that this is a digression from Bernard's plan of exhorting the pope to take up the practice of meditation.[2] Leclercq's observation lends credence to the historical hypothesis that the news of the crusade's failure had just reached Bernard at this point in his writing. Mayr-Harting, for example, maintains that Bernard shifts his focus in this discussion in order to defend himself from critics.[3] If this is true, Bernard's explicit intent is that the pope also publicly acknowledge the

1 *Csi*, II, 1.1–4 (CF 37:47–52; *SW* 1:660–66; *SBO* 3:410–13).

2 Leclercq, "L'Art de la Composition," 119.

3 Henry Mayr-Harting, "Two Abbots in Politics: Wala of Corbie and Bernard of Clairvaux," *Transactions of the Royal Historical Society* 40 (1990): 217–37, at 228.

situation: "I have intimated that something should be done to console the Church and close the mouths of those who speak evil."[4] McGinn interprets Bernard as locating the cause of the campaign's failure in the lack of unanimity among the military leadership.[5]

After discussing the failed crusade, Bernard returns to the topic of the practice of meditation. At this point, he explicitly contrasts meditation with contemplation.[6] Customarily, Bernard observes, the words "contemplation" and "consideration" might be employed as synonyms.[7] However, Bernard maintains that contemplation engages what is known, whereas meditation explores the unknown.[8] Contemplation involves "the true and sure intuition of the mind of something" and "the apprehension of truth without doubt," whereas meditation involves "thought searching for truth," a "searching of [the] mind to discover truth."[9] Contemplation involves an abiding state of activity (akin to intuition or apprehension), whereas meditation can involve a kind of investigation that is in motion and proceeding toward a destination.[10] However, it could be that a moment of contemplation (as a kind of pause during the course of one's meditation) provides one with the "self-intuition in the clear light of truth" (*se intuens clara luce veritatis*) that Bernard mentions can inform one's self-assessment.[11]

In light of Bernard's juxtaposition of these two kinds of cognitive activities in this passage, Michel describes meditation for Bernard as "a purely reflective state of thought" where (if one pauses during the exercise) the cognitions involved lack the "objective certainty offered by the contemplative grasp of an intelligible reality."[12] When developing his interpretation, Michel

4 *Csi*, II, 1.4 (CF 37:51; *SW* 1:666; *SBO* 3:413).

5 McGinn, "Bernard and Eschatology," 183.

6 *Csi*, II, 2.5 (CF 37:52; *SW* 1:668; *SBO* 3:414). See also John R. Sommerfeldt, "Bernard as Contemplative," in CS 135:73–84, 77; Clairmont, "Medieval Consideration," 92–93.

7 *Csi*, II, 2.5 (CF 37:52; *SW* 1:668; *SBO* 3:414).

8 Ibid.

9 Ibid. "Non enim id per omnia quod contemplationem intelligi volo, quod haec ad rerum certitudinem, illa ad inquisitionem magis se habeat. Iuxta quem sensum potest contemplatio quidem diffiniri verus certusque intuitus animi de quacumque re, sive apprehensio veri non dubia, consideratio autem intensa ad vestigandum cogitatio, vel intensio animi vestigantis verum." See also Sommerfeldt, *Life of the Mind*, 23. Verbaal maintains that Bernard's language in this section is evocative of the Prologue of Abelard's *Sic et non*. See Verbaal, "Bernardus Philosophus," 579.

10 See also Hiss, *Die Anthropologie*, 4.

11 *SCC*, 36, 4.5 (CF 7:177–78; *SW* 5:568; *SBO* 2:7).

12 Michel, "La considération," 114. "Ce que Bernard cherche à isoler, par la notion de considération, c'est un état purement réfléchissant de la pensée, tel qu'il consiste sans doute en une pause de son engagement dans l'action (cette action que, selon le livre I, la considération doit précéder), mais tel,

further characterizes the course of meditation as a search in *terra incognita*, where one's mind seeks evidence to confirm that one is following a true path among various possibilities.[13] It does seem to be the case that meditation for Bernard is a cognitive activity that stands in relation to contemplation in the same way that an unfulfilled mental state relates to a fulfilled state, or in the same way that the mind in an imperfect state relates to the mind as perfected with understanding. Contemplation is thus a *terminus ad quem* of meditation.[14]

An Emphasis on Religious Salvation

Bernard indicates that there is a kind of meta-cognition (a cognition that involves reflective awareness of one's cognitive activity) that enables one to recognize that one has become unfocused or distracted, given over to reverie or a daydream. For example, Bernard states that when the pope's mind begins to wander during meditation, Eugene III must call his mind back to itself: "Whenever [your mind] wanders, call it back to yourself for the sake of your salvation."[15] I will explore the activity of self-recollection during meditation in more detail later when discussing Bernard's teachings in Book V. Here, I want to note Bernard's remark that meditation has an orientation toward religious salvation. He suggests that the pope should think of nothing contrary to his salvation.[16] This statement indicates that for Bernard what characterizes a course of meditation as religious is that the reflection has an overarching orientation toward the goal or purpose of salvation. The practice for Bernard thus seems to involve an inherent religious teleology. In other words, Bernard implies that the primary purpose of the practice of meditation is located within a religious soteriology (a religious understanding of salvation).

également, que cette pause ne se résout pas immédiatement en cette certitude objective qu'offrirait, la saisie, contemplative d'une réalité intelligible."

13 Michel, "La considération," 115. "En d'autres termes, la considération est ce moment purement réflexif où la pensée, en un territoire inconnu, recherche et attend le signe qui lui permettrait de vérifier si la voie qu'elle emprunte est celle qu'elle doit suivre pour arriver."

14 Leclercq, "L'Art de la Composition," 129.

15 *Csi*, II, 3.6 (CF 37:53; *SW* 1:668; *SBO* 3:414). "Quocumque evagetur, ad te revocaveris eam cum salutis fructu."

16 *Csi*, II, 3.6 (CF 37:53; *SW* 1:670; *SBO* 3:415). "Contra salutem propriam cogites nihil."

Self-Knowledge

It is at this point in Book II of *De consideratione* that Bernard outlines the fourfold course of meditation that Eugene III should follow. Bernard writes: "I think you should consider four things in this order: yourself, what is below you, around you and above you."[17] As noted above with respect to Bernard's sources, the hierarchical structure that Bernard prescribes here for the pope's course of meditation is indebted to Augustine.[18] Bernard references a similar structure when addressing monks within the cloister in an Advent sermon, exhorting the monks to be obedient to superiors above them, to be a model for brothers around them, and to be responsible in order to protect and correct any persons over whom they exercise care.[19] This structure reappears again in the soliloquy edited by Leclercq, mentioned above.[20] In his *Soliloquium de quattuor mentalibus exercitiis*, Bonaventure proposes the same four general stages as Bernard in terms of four mental exercises: "the devout soul must consider things within and without, below and above itself."[21] There are differences from Bernard, however: Bonaventure reverses steps two and three, and with respect to meditation on matters below oneself, Bonaventure focuses on death, judgment, and hell.[22]

When describing this order of proceeding, Bernard indicates that the practice of meditation should begin with self-reflection. In some sense, to turn from considering other matters to considering oneself involves a kind of self-remembering. For example, in his letter to the Carthusian prior of Portes, Bernard brings his musings about recent news to an abrupt close: "It is time for me to remember myself . . ."[23] Bernard may have derived this starting point for meditation from Hildemar who also maintains that the course of reflection should begin and end with oneself.[24] The ultimate goal of

17 *Csi*, II, 3.6 (CF 37:52; *SW* 1:668; *SBO* 3:414). "Iam quod ad considerationis attinet fructum, quatuor, ut occurrunt, tibi consideranda reor: te, quae sub te, quae circa te, quae supra te sunt." See also Evans, *Mind of St. Bernard*, 205.

18 Augustine, *De doctrina Christiana* I.23.22 (Green, 18; Martin, 18).

19 *Adv*, 3.5–6 (CF 51:22–23; *SW* 7:92–94; *SBO* 4:178–79).

20 Leclercq, "L'Art de la Composition," 134.

21 Bonaventure, *Soliloquy on the Four Spiritual Exercises*, Prologue, §2 (de Vinck, 36).

22 Ibid. (37).

23 Ep 326 (James, *Letters*, 401–2; Ep 250.4 in *SW* 3:330–34; *SBO* 8:145–47). "Tempus est ut non obliviscar mei."

24 *Csi*, II, 3.6 (CF 37:53; *SW* 1:668; *SBO* 3:414). "A te proinde incipiat tua consideratio; non solum autem, et in te finiatur." See also Anderson, "Reconsidering," 159. For discussion of the long tradition of authors discussing the importance of growth in self-knowledge including Bernard and his contemporaries, see Jack Arthur Walter Bennett, "*Nosce te ipsum*: Some Medieval and Modern

meditation, however, is not self-knowledge. The return to oneself is a return to one's fundamental posture involving a soteriological orientation: "You must reject anything which presents itself for your consideration that does not pertain in some way to your salvation."[25]

Leclercq argues that in prescribing a hierarchical course of meditation to Eugene III, Bernard is exhorting the pope to practice what Bernard himself practices as inspired by Hildemar.[26] Leclercq's basis for this claim is found in the content of the short soliloquy discussed above ("A Soliloquy of His: On a Fourfold Consideration of His Own Condition").[27] As mentioned earlier, Leclercq provides an edited version of this soliloquy.[28] Assuming the authenticity of the work, Bernard introduces the soliloquy by stating that he sometimes is given to a course of meditation where he focuses on three aspects of himself.[29] He reflects on who he is, namely, that he is a human being, as well as his roles as monk and abbot; he considers that he is a human being by nature, a monk by repentance, and an abbot by obedience; as a further meditation, he considers that he is also a Christian by grace.[30] When reiterating the point that this last dimension of his life is due to grace,[31] Bernard observes that meditation on these four aspects of who he is requires a kind

Interpretations," in *The Humane Medievalist and Other Essays in English Literature and Learning from Chaucer to Eliot*, ed. Piero Boitani (Rome: Edizioni di Storia e Letteratura, 1982), 135–72. See also "Introduction," in Franz Posset, *The Two-Fold Knowledge: Readings on the Knowledge of Self and the Knowledge of God Selected and Translated from the Works of Saint Bernard of Clairvaux* (Eugene, OR: Wipf and Stock, 2004), 17–42.

25 *Csi*, II, 3.6 (CF 37:53; *SW* 1:670; *SBO* 3:415). "Si qua adhuc praesens consideranda requirit locus, tractabuntur infra, et forte utilius ex partium collatione." Farkasfalvy also observes that for Bernard self-reflection is a path toward understanding God's work in Christ (Christology): "Bernard's theology is knowing the self for knowing Christ" (Farkasfalvy, "Bernard's Concept," 12).

26 Leclercq, "L'Art de la Composition," 134. "D'abord Bernard, ici comme ailleurs, enseigne en moine: il applique à un pape ce qu'Hildemar avait écrit du moine, ce que lui-même avait dit de sa condition d'abbé."

27 Ibid. "Solliloquium ipsius (Domni Bernardi Abbatis) de consideratione quadripertita propriae conditionis.""

28 Leclercq, "Études sur Saint Bernard," 148. As noted above, the beginning of this soliloquy is reprinted at Leclercq, "L'Art de la Composition," 134.

29 Leclercq, "L'Art de la Composition," 134. "Quando exoccupari queo quandoque quasi quoddam soliloquium facio mihi et meipsum considero, idem tria in meipso considero, tria inquam satis aperta, satis ad manum."

30 Ibid. "Considero quod homo sum, quod monachus, quod abbas; quod homo naturae, quod monachus paenitentiae, quod abbas oboedientiae; adhuc addo et quartum quod est gratiae, videlicet quod homo et christianus."

31 Ibid. "Gratiae inquam et non naturae. Si enim esset naturae, non esset paganus, non esset iudaeus."

of self-recollection.[32] Bernard repeats this teaching in a sermon found in his *De diversis* series when discussing Psalm 45:11: "'be still and see that it is God himself.' In order for you to be truly capable of this, you must first look to yourself in order to see what you are . . . May all your free time be given to this double [consideration]" (*duplici considerationi*) of self and God.[33]

Bernard in the remainder of Book II of *De consideratione* recommends that Eugene III follow a similar path of meditation. Bernard subdivides the exercise of self-reflection in three ways: "You should consider what you are [*quid*], who you are [*quis*], and what sort of man you are [*qualis*]: what you are in nature, who you are in person, and what sort of man you are in [*morals*]."[34] These three reflections, Leclercq observes, concern three dimensions or aspects of Eugene III's personhood: his nature, his person, and his quality. These three aspects could perhaps be understood as his humanity, his temperament and roles, and his moral character.[35] These three aspects of a person arguably correlate with the bio-psycho-social dimensions of Bernard's natural anthropology, as discussed above (the moral character of a person for Bernard would also depend on receiving grace in some respect due to the fallen state of human nature). Bernard is thus prescribing what might be understood as a kind of self-research, an attempt to understand oneself better, where such knowledge is not an end in itself but rather ordered to salvation and relationship with God.[36]

Human Nature and Philosophy

With respect to the first aspect of self-reflection (meditating on one's human nature, *quid*), Bernard states that although the consideration of oneself according to nature is more of a philosophical concern than an apostolic one, it comprises an area of meditation that the pope might wish to explore that can benefit his development toward salvation:

32 Ibid. "Haec quattuor in me recolo quae naturae, quae gratiae, quae paenitentiae, quae oboedientiae: quod homo naturae, quod christianus gratiae, quod monachus paenitentiae, quod abbas oboedientiae."

33 *Div*, 2.1 (CF 68:12; *SW* 9:180; *SBO* 6.1:80). "Vacate, itaque, dilectissimi, et videte quoniam ipse est Deus. Verum ut hoc quandoque possitis, curandum vobis prius, ut videatis quid estis vos . . . Huic duplici considerationi tota haec vestra vacatio tribuatur."

34 *Csi*, II, 4.7 (CF 37:54; *SW* 1:670; *SBO* 3:415). "Et haec tui consideratio in tria quaedam dividitur, si consideres quid, quis et qualis sis: quid in natura, quis in persona, qualis in moribus."

35 See also Leclercq, "L'Art de la Composition," 121–22.

36 Ibid., 122.

> Although the investigation of the first division belongs more to the philosopher than to the apostle, nevertheless, there is in the definition of man, whom they call a rational animal, the notion that he is mortal. And this you may look into more carefully, if you please. For there is nothing inherent in such an investigation which might stand in the way of your calling, or oppose your dignity. On the contrary, it can benefit your salvation.[37]

One might note that Bernard uses the word "philosophy" in a particular manner in this passage, differentiating philosophy in this sense from the pope's apostolic vocation. The content of Bernard's remarks (focusing on a philosophy that defines a human being as a mortal rational animal) is indicative of the Christian philosophy of Boethius.[38] Importantly, Bernard's remark indicates that he does not judge that the study of philosophy (or at least Christian philosophy) need detract from one's ability to follow the way of the apostles. Rather, he indicates that it can be beneficial and can be included within the spiritual exercise of meditation. In this passage, Bernard also calls attention to two particular focal points when investigating one's human nature: human rationality and mortality.[39] He indicates that Eugene III's purpose in investigating his human nature is to grow in self-knowledge and thus to advance in wisdom. Growth in wisdom—seemingly also that human kind of wisdom found in philosophy as distinct from apostolic tradition—also can contribute to one's progress along the path toward ultimate salvation.[40] Bernard teaches something similar in a sermon in his *Sermones super cantica canticorum*:

37 *Csi*, II, 4.7 (CF 37:54; *SW* 1:670; *SBO* 3:415). "Quamquam primum illud philosophicum sit magis quam apostolicum vestigare, attamen est in diffinitione hominis, quem dicunt animal rationale, mortale. Quod diligentius intueri si libet, licet. Non est quod tuae in eo aut professioni obviet, aut dignitati; est vero quod saluti afferre queat." See also Sommerfeldt, *Life of the Mind*, 49.

38 See Boethius, *Contra Eutychen*, chap. 3, in *Tractates, The Consolation of Philosophy*, 72–129, at 85. See also Jenny Teichman, "The Definition of Person," *Philosophy* 60, no. 232 (1985): 175–85.

39 *Csi*, II, 4.7 (CF 37:54; *SW* 1:670; *SBO* 3:415).

40 My statement here should not be interpreted as indicating a Pelagian or semi-Pelagian reading of Bernard, who clearly affirms that restorative grace is needed for one to will what is truly good. For example, recall the passage quoted above from the *Liber de gratia et libero arbitrio*: "simply to will denotes the subject itself which does either the achieving or the failing. To this subject, however, creating grace gives existence. Saving grace gives it the achievement" (*creans gratia fecit; ut proficiat, salvans gratia facit*). *Gra*, 6.16 (CF 19a:72; *SW* 1:198; *SBO* 3:178). Leclercq also warns against a Pelagian misinterpretation of monastic exercises. See CS 7:335; Leclercq, "The Role of Monastic Spirituality," 589.

> You remember that you have agreed with me that no one is saved without self-knowledge [*sui cognitione*], since it is the source of that humility on which salvation depends, and of the fear of the Lord that is as much the beginning of salvation as of wisdom. No one, I repeat, is saved without that knowledge, provided he is old enough and [has the cognitive ability] to possess it . . . Know yourself and you will have a wholesome fear of God; know him and you will also love him. In the first, wisdom has its beginning, in the second its crown.[41]

This passage is noteworthy in that it refers to humility not only as the foundation for spiritual development (*aedificatio*),[42] but also as the foundation for growth toward salvation. Further, this passage also refers to some kind of cognitive ability (*facultatem cognoscendi*) that one must possess prior to spiritual development.

Bernard emphasizes that self-knowledge is more important than other forms of human knowledge, although he does not contend that other forms of knowledge have no value.[43] He writes:

> I am far from saying, however, that knowledge of literature [*scientiarum litterarum*] is to be despised, for it provides culture and skill [*ornat animam et erudit*], and enables a man to instruct others. But knowledge of God and of self are basic and must come first, for as I have already shown, they are essential for salvation.[44]

Growth in self-knowledge and growth in knowledge of God are the primary and fundamental tasks of monastic learning in contrast with learning literary sciences. Bernard's distinction between these two areas of learning

41 *SCC*, 37, 1.1 (CF 7:181; *SW* 5:572; *SBO* 2:9). "Ergo tenetis memoria quod teneam assensum vestrum, neminem absque sui cognitione salvari, de qua nimirum mater salutis humilitas oritur, et timor Domini, qui et ipse sicut initium sapientiae, ita est et salutis. Nemo, dico, absque illa cognitione salvatur, qui tamen aetatem habeat ac facultatem cognoscendi . . . Noveris proinde te, ut Deum timeas; noveris ipsum, ut aeque ipsum diligas. In altero initiaris ad sapientiam, in altero et consummaris."

42 *SCC*, 36, 4.5 (CF 7:177–78; *SW* 5:568; *SBO* 2:7).

43 *SCC*, 36, 1.1–2.3 (CF 7:173–76; *SW* 5:560–64; *SBO* 2:3–5). See also Jean Châtillon, "L'Influence de S. Bernard sur la Pensée Scolastique au XIIe et au XIIIe Siècle," *ASOC* 9, nos. 3–4 (1953): 268–88, at 272 and 285.

44 *SCC*, 37, 1.2 (CF 7:182; *SW* 5:572; *SBO* 2:9). "Non tamen dico contemnendam scientiam litterarum, quae ornat animam et erudit eam, et facit ut possit etiam alios erudire. Sed duo illa oportet et expedit ut praecedant, in quibus summam salutis constitui superior ratio declaravit."

is evocative of a similar distinction that Augustine makes within the mind itself[45]—namely, a distinction between a "higher reason"[46] that regulates a lower "reason to which the administering of temporal things has been delegated."[47] This lower mode of reason would seem to be exercised when learning the literary sciences, as Bernard states.[48] Bernard also explicitly mentions a *ratio superior* in this passage of the sermon (although this reference is missing from the English translation); he remarks that it is this higher mental activity that "declared that the highest point of salvation is established" by means of one's development in self-knowledge and knowledge of God.[49]

In the same sermon, Bernard next quotes the prophet Hosea to describe how learning other forms of knowledge might occur within the context of monastic practice:

> This was the viewpoint of the Prophet, this was the order of precedence he inculcated when he said: "Sow for yourselves righteousness, and reap the hope of life." and then: "Set alight for yourselves the light of knowledge." He puts [science] in the last place, [*ultimam posuit scientiam*] because, like a picture that cannot stand on the air, it requires that the solid structure of the other two precede and support it [namely, self-knowledge and knowledge of God]. I may safely pursue studies if my hope of eternal life has first been rendered secure.[50]

Self-knowledge and knowledge of God is a primary and solid [*solidum*] basis from which one may then proceed to embark upon additional studies in other sciences. Bernard goes on to state that honest self-knowledge can lead one to humility, fear of God, remorse, asceticism, and prayer.[51]

45 Augustine, *The Trinity* XII.8.13 (McKenna, 355).

46 Ibid., XII.2.2 (McKenna, 344). See also the general study of Robert W. Mulligan, "*Ratio Superior* and *Ratio Inferior*: The Historical Background," *The New Scholasticism* 29, no. 1 (1955): 1–32.

47 Augustine, *The Trinity* XII.8.13 (McKenna, 355).

48 *SCC*, 37, 1.2 (CF 7:182; *SW* 5:572; *SBO* 2:9).

49 Ibid.

50 *SCC*, 37, 1.2 (CF 7:182; *SW* 5:574; *SBO* 2:10). "Et vide si non intuebatur, et si non docebat hunc ordinem qui dicebat: Seminate vobis ad iustitiam, et metite spem vitae, et tunc demum Illuminate vobis, ait, Lumen scientiae. Ultimam posuit scientiam, tamquam picturam quae statum habere nequeat super inane, et illa duo praemisit et subiecit illi, tamquam si solidum aliquid picturae substerneret." See also Michel, "La considération," 112.

51 *SCC*, 37, 1.2 (CF 7:182; *SW* 5:574; *SBO* 2:10). Regarding the fear of God in the *Sermones super Cantica Canticorum*, see Catherine Rose Cavadini, "Lips of Fear Kissed by Mercy: Expositions of

The content of this sermon is consistent with Bernard's teaching to Eugene III in *De consideratione.* There, Bernard insists that authentic spiritual development (*aedificatio*) proceeds on the basis of immediate self-knowledge and not on the basis of some other form of knowledge: "If you do not know yourself, you are like a building without a foundation; you raise not a structure but ruins. Whatever you construct outside yourself will be but a pile of dust blown by the wind."[52] Considering these remarks as a whole, Bernard points to the possibility that the monastic life need not be understood as mutually exclusive from a life of study, or exclusive from engaging works of philosophy as long as these pursuits are soteriologically ordered (that is, teleologically oriented toward one's salvation).[53]

The Question of Personality and Meditation on Relationship Roles

With respect to the next aspect of self-reflection (meditation on one's personhood, *quis*), Bernard states to Eugene III that "we must turn our attention to who you are now [*quis*] and who you were before [*de quo*] you were made pope."[54] Stepsis contends that Bernard's writings exemplify the need for theology to be grounded in "a theory of personality or selfhood" (for Stepsis, this seems to be the psychological theory of Maslow).[55] However, Bernard's primary focus in this section of *De consideratione* is not on "who" (*quis*) Eugene III is in terms of the pope's core self or even the pope's temperament, but rather with the pope's self-understanding of who he is in relation to his roles as monk and pope.[56] Bernard's discussion thus hops over the possibility of considering temperament and proceeds directly to focus on Eugene III's vocations or "offices."

Timor Dei in Cistercian Commentary on the Song of Songs," in *Saving Fear in Christian Spirituality*, ed. Ann W. Astell (Notre Dame, IN: University of Notre Dame Press, 2020), 105–24.

52 *Csi*, II, 3.6 (CF 37:53; *SW* 1:668; *SBO* 3:414). "Si te nescieris, eris similis aedificanti sine fundamento, ruinam, non structuram faciens. Quidquid exstruxeris extra te, erit instar congesti pulveris, ventis obnoxium."

53 For an alternative understanding of Bernard, see Philippe Delhaye, "L'Organisation Scolaire au XIIe Siècle," *Traditio* 5 (1947): 211–68, at 226–27.

54 *Csi*, II, 5.8 (CF 37:54; *SW* 1:670; *SBO* 3:415). "Nunc quis sis et de quo sis factus, advertendum."

55 Stepsis, "Fulfillment of Self," 349.

56 *Csi*, II, 6.11 (CF 37:59; *SW* 1:676; *SBO* 3:418). See also Bernard Jacqueline, "Le Pape d'après le Livre II du *De consideratione ad Eugenium papam* de Saint Bernard de Clairvaux," *Studia Gratiana* 14 (1967): 221–39.

What does Bernard mean by a person's assumed office? Writing around 1125, Bernard explains in a letter that it is not Bernard's place (*officium*) to provide requested information to Oger of Mont-Saint-Éloi:

> It is not only that I have not the time, it is also that the sort of work you want me to do is not suited either to my profession or ability. Not teaching, but lamenting is the duty [*officium*] of the monk I am supposed to be and of the sinner that I am. There could not be anything more silly than for an untaught man such as I confess I am, to presume to teach what he knows nothing about.[57]

In this passage, Bernard indicates that he associates one's vocation, office, or role with one's assumption of certain tasks or duties. Whether performing a task is due or undue depends on the nature of the role that one has assumed. In order to help Eugene III clarify his self-understanding of the due tasks associated with his role as pope, Bernard contrasts the papal office with the office of a temporal political sovereign.[58] Unlike a temporal political sovereign, Eugene III has received not dominion, but a ministry.[59] He has received not a throne, but a watchtower.[60] He is not a lord, but a steward.[61]

At this point, Bernard exhorts the pope to integrate his role as monk with his role as pope: "You have not forgotten your first profession; what is out of reach is not out of mind or at least has not left your heart. Your commands, your judgments and your teachings will benefit if you do not lose sight of that [monastic] profession."[62] These remarks point to one of Bernard's primary purposes in writing *De consideratione*, as discussed earlier; out of pastoral concern, Bernard is eager that the pope retain a spiritually healthy perspective on his ecclesiastical vocation. If Eugene III will understand his papacy less in connection with temporal sovereignty and more in

57 Ep 92 (James, *Letters*, 137–38, at 138; Ep 89 in *SW* 2:710–14, at 712; *SBO* 7:235–37, at 236). "Quamquam non solum temporis, sed nec meae professionis est, huic rei operam dare quam postulas, nec possibilitatis adimplere quod optas. Siquidem vel monachi quod esse videor, vel peccatoris quod sum, officium non est docere, sed lugere. Indoctus quoque, quod et vere me fateor esse, si praesumat docere quod nescit, nihil indoctius agit."

58 *Csi*, II, 6.10 (CF 37:57; *SW* 1:674; *SBO* 3:417). "Superintendis, sonans tibi episcopi nomine non dominium, sed officium."

59 *Csi*, II, 6.9 (CF 37:56; *SW* 1:672; *SBO* 3:416). "Impositum senserimus ministerium, non dominium datum."

60 *Csi*, II, 6.10 (CF 37:57; *SW* 1:674; *SBO* 3:417). "Blanditur cathedra? Specula est."

61 *Csi*, II, 6.12 (CF 37:60; *SW* 1:678; *SBO* 3:419). "Exi in illum, non tamquam dominus, sed tamquam villicus."

62 *Csi*, II, 5.8 (CF 37:55; *SW* 1:670; *SBO* 3:415). "Non es oblitus primae professionis."

connection with his enduring monastic vocation, then the pope might avoid suffering spiritual disorder. In a way, the pope in receiving this guidance from Bernard can be understood as a kind of placeholder for any person who can benefit from meditating on how to navigate various life roles and likewise discern one's primary role or "first profession" (to use the language of Bernard). In the letter written to the Carthusian prior of Portes (1150) that I quoted above, Bernard indicates a similar concern with the spiritual risk that can be present when one assumes varied and even contradictory roles:

> I am a sort of modern chimæra, neither cleric nor layman. I have kept the habit of a monk, but I have long ago abandoned the life. I do not wish to tell you what I dare say you have heard from others: what I am doing, what are my purposes, through what dangers I pass in the world, or rather down what precipices I am hurled.[63]

Bernard again touches on the topic of diverse roles and offices within the Church when he refers to "three orders of the Church" symbolized by Noah, Daniel, and Job: Noah crosses the sea of life in the ark, Daniel by a bridge, and Job by locating a shallow place or ford.[64] In a different sermon (his first *Sermo in nativitate Domini*), Bernard again refers to Noah, Daniel, and Job, stating that they respectively symbolize "prelates, celibates, and couples."[65] The office of prelate is symbolized by the ark, the celibate by the bridge, and the married lay couple by the ford. Sommerfeldt remarks that these distinctions concern Bernard's "theory of the states of life," "different paths to salvation" where each is "able to produce heroes of the faith."[66] In light of this discussion, it would seem that Bernard is guiding Eugene III in how to integrate the paths of Noah's ark and Daniel's bridge.

63 Ep 326 (James, *Letters*, 401–2; Ep 250 in *SW* 3:330–34; *SBO* 8:145–47). See also CS 16:68.

64 *Div*, 35, which is *Sermo ad abbates*. For the English, see Bernard of Clairvaux, "A Sermon to the Abbots, How Noah, Daniel, and Job Crossed the Sea, Each in His Own Way: On a Ship, By a Bridge, By the Shallows," in *Sermons for the Autumn Season*, trans. Irene Edmonds (Collegeville, MN: Liturgical Press, 2016) (hereafter CF 54), 85–90, at 85 (*SW* 8:646–57, at 646–48; *SBO* 5:288–93, at 288–89). See also CF 68:196. For this reference, I am indebted to Sommerfeldt, "Social Theory of Bernard," in CS 13:39.

65 Bernard of Clairvaux, *In nativitate Domini*, 1.7 (hereafter *Nat*) (CF 51:99–106, at 105; *SW* 7:234; *SBO* 4:249). For this reference, I am also indebted to Sommerfeldt, "Social Theory of Bernard," in CS 13:39.

66 CS 13:38–39.

Conscience and Moral Character

Bernard next turns to discuss the third aspect of self-reflection (reflection on what sort of person one should be)—a topic that he notes later that he may be introducing prematurely.[67] Regarding Eugene III's exercise of meditation in pursuit of self-knowledge, Bernard exhorts him as follows: "Go out into the field of your Lord [*Exi in agrum Domini tui*] and consider how even today it abounds in thorns and thistles in fulfillment of the ancient curse. Go out, I say, into the world, for the field is the world and it is entrusted to you."[68] Bernard proceeds to explain his reference to a field of meditation by citing a passage in the Book of Genesis that describes Isaac going forth into a field "to meditate" (*ad meditandum*) (24:63 Vulg.).[69] After this citation, Bernard then chides Eugene III for not meditating prior to acting: "You should have meditated already; the time for action is at hand."[70] Toward the end of the discussion, Bernard exclaims, "What a wide field [*latus campus*] for this kind of consideration lies open before you!"[71]

In traversing the field of meditation or plain of thought in order to reflect on one's personal characteristics, Bernard observes that it will be the pope's conscience that will indicate what is displeasing. Bernard wites: "I want you to glory in the testimony of your conscience [*testimonio conscientiae*], but I also want you to be humbled by it."[72] In this respect, meditation for Bernard also can involve an activity akin to what the Ignatian tradition calls the examination of conscience.[73] During such self-examination, Bernard suggests that one expose and not conceal one's bad qualities; such honesty will lead to

67 *Csi*, II, 7.14 (CF 37:63; *SW* 1:682; *SBO* 3:421). "Stilus excurrerit, describere inchoans qualem te oporteat esse, cum necdum quis sis plenius expressisset."

68 *Csi*, II, 6.12 (CF 37:60; *SW* 1:678; *SBO* 3:419).

69 For an alternative rendering of the Hebrew in this verse, see Gary A. Rendsburg, "*Lāśûaḥ* in Genesis XXIV 63," *Vetus Testamentum* 45, no. 4 (1995): 558–60.

70 *Csi*, II, 6.13 (CF 37:61; *SW* 1:680; *SBO* 3:420). "Tibi iam praecessisse meditatio debet: tempus faciendi prae manibus." See also Anderson, "Reconsidering," 158.

71 *Csi*, II, 11.20 (CF 37:74; *SW* 1:696; *SBO* 3:428). "Quam latus tibi patet campus in hoc genere considerandi!"

72 *Csi*, II, 7.14 (CF 37:64; *SW* 1:684; *SBO* 3:422). "Volo glorieris testimonio conscientiae, sed non minus ut eodem ipso humilieris."

73 See also Philippe Delhaye, *Le Problème de la Conscience Morale chez S. Bernard: Étudié dans ses Œuvres et dans ses Sources* (Namur: Éditions Godenne, 1957). For a comparison of Bernard and Abelard on conscience, see Laurence Mellerin, "*Oculus Simplex*: Discernment Spirituel et Progrès Éthique chez Saint Bernard," *Cîteaux: Commentarii Cistercienses* 63 (2012): 147–63. For Ignatius on the examination of conscience, see, e.g., Ignatius, *Spiritual Exercises*, §24–§43 (Puhl, 15–20). See also Timothy M. Gallagher, *The Examen Prayer: Ignatian Wisdom for Our Lives Today* (New York: Crossroad, 2006), 25.

genuine self-knowledge.[74] It seems to me that the "testimony of conscience" (*testimonio conscientiae*)[75] to which Bernard refers in the passage quoted just above is an interior experience that is connected with the "self-intuition in the clear light of truth" (*se intuens clara luce veritatis*) discussed earlier; this interior experience can lead one to take up a foundation in humility as a stable support for further spiritual development (*aedificatio*).[76]

For Eugene III to consider what sort of person he is, he must to some extent exclude from his self-understanding who he is in connection with his office (role) as pope: "if you scatter all these things and blow them away from the face of your consideration [*a facie considerationis tuae*]," then "[you will see] a naked man who is poor, wretched, and miserable."[77] At this point, Bernard refers to another kind of psychological enclosure in association with his claustral perspective. He writes that a meditation that proceeds in honesty might involve one instituting boundaries with respect to one's self-understanding (or core identity) in order to avoid vanity and unrealistic self-expectations: "This consideration will keep you within yourself; it will not permit you to fly from yourself, or walk among great things which are wonderful and beyond your reach."[78] Here again, Bernard is interested in preserving a proper sense of self in humility—a self-understanding that avoids self-deception and inflation. Such an enclosure or boundaries help one avoid, Bernard indicates, a kind of self-exile that is an exile from an authentic self-understanding.[79]

In contrast with a state of false consciousness associated with self-deception and inflation, an honest self-understanding will involve a kind of mean akin to a virtue, a kind of balanced self-understanding where one avoids taking up an alien dwelling place (*mansio*) outside of a true or authentic state:

> Stand firm in yourself. Do not fall lower, do not rise higher. Do not proceed to greater length; do not stretch out to greater width. Hold to the middle if you do not want to lose the mean. The middle ground is safe. The

74 *Csi*, II, 7.14 (CF 37:64; *SW* 1:684; *SBO* 3:422).

75 Ibid.

76 *SCC*, 36, 4.5 (CF 7:177–78; *SW* 5:568; *SBO* 2:7).

77 *Csi*, II, 9.18 (CF 37:70; *SW* 1:692; *SBO* 3:426).

78 *Csi*, II, 10.19 (CF 37:71; *SW* 1:692; *SBO* 3:426). "Haec te sane consideratio tenet in te, nec a te avolare sinit, non ambulare in magnis, neque in mirabilibus super te."

79 There is a different kind of exile (exile from God) that will be considered below.

> middle is the seat of the mean, and the mean is virtue. Every dwelling place beyond the mean is counted an exile by the wise man.[80]

Generally speaking, Bernard seems to be referring to a state of psychological equanimity, a balanced self-understanding that avoids self-deception at two extremes, either thinking too little or too much of oneself. It is humility that facilitates withdrawal from the latter extreme.

Bernard indicates that by residing in this balanced state of self-understanding, one might experience purity of conscience. In sermon 16 of the *De diversis* series, Bernard maintains that one who meditates on "the good things of grace" such as "the exercise of virtue" might come to understand this state of the soul and consequently model it for others:

> That way you will see how a pure conscience and an unburdened brow may be turned and converted in chastity and charity, in patience and humility and the rest of the virtues that render a person [amiable] to God. And thus to other human beings one becomes conciliatory and worthy of imitation.[81]

Bernard indicates in Book II of *De consideratione* that the process of the examination of conscience requires not only honesty and docility before one's conscience, but also caution and fairness (prudence and justice).[82] Perhaps the observance of just fairness during self-examination will lead one to observe that one should not judge oneself too harshly (in this regard, Bernard remarked earlier in Book II to Eugene III that "a completely valid excuse for anyone is the testimony of his own conscience"[83]). Conversely, the observance of a just fairness in self-examination might also incline one

80 *Csi*, II, 10.19 (CF 37:72; *SW* 1:692; *SBO* 3:426). "In te consistito. Non infra deici, non attolli supra, non evadere in longius, non extendi in latius. Tene medium, si non vis perdere modum. Locus medius tutus est. Medium sedes modi, et modus virtus. Omnem extra modum mansionem, sapiens exsilium reputat."

81 *Div*, 16.1 (CF 68:88; *SW* 9:309–10; *SBO* 6.1:144–45). "Videas quam purae conscientiae, quam liberae frontis sit versari et conversari in castitate et caritate, in patientia et humilitate ceterisque virtutibus, quae amabilem Deo, placabilem et imitabilem hominibus reddunt."

82 *Csi*, II, Ch. 11.20 (CF 37:73; *SW* 1:694; *SBO* 3:427). "Tu ergo in hac consideratione tui caute ambules, et tota aequitate verseris, ut nec plus vero tibi tribuas, nec plus iusto parcas."

83 *Csi*, II, Ch. 1.4 (CF 37:51; *SW* 1:666; *SBO* 3:413). "Perfecta et absoluta cuique excusatio, testimonium conscientiae suae." See also Stephan Ernst, *Ethische Vernunft und christlicher Glaube: Der Prozeß ihrer wechselseitigen Freisetzung in der Zeit von Anselm von Canterbury bis Wilhelm von Auxerre* (Münster: Aschendorff, 1996), 162.

away from moral indifference. A middle ground might be located between scrupulosity or severity on one hand and laxity on the other.

In order to recall oneself from self-exile to the balanced dwelling place of the virtuous mean (equanimity), Bernard indicates that Eugene III should evaluate how the pope is using his imagination with respect to visualizing his life and affairs. To be overly preoccupied with visualization of the future (such as concern for living a long life) can lead one to live in exile from the present. This preoccupation can also result in what Bernard refers to as a kind of exile of self-forgetfulness. He writes:

> Does not the man who measures a long lifespan for himself truly set out on the path of exile, passing beyond the boundaries of life with his prolonged concern? Thus it is that men in the present are exiles from themselves through forgetfulness and pass into another time through inane concern, a time which is not profitable, indeed not even possible.[84]

Here again, Bernard is referring to the observance of an enclosure or boundaries with respect to one's psychological activities—this time with respect to the exercise of the imagination in terms of visualizing the future (the same insight might be advised in terms of avoiding an excessive preoccupation with images of the past).

To take up a dwelling in one's imagination outside the present moment can lead to concerns about life possibilities, even anxiety: "A mind stretched in many directions must be torn by many cares. For immoderate stretching causes weakness and excessive weakness causes a break."[85] In this passage, Bernard points to some kind of progressive mental decline that can result from anxiety, with the mind first being stretched (*extensio*), then stretched to a state of diminution (being thinned to a breaking point, *extenuatio*), then being split or separated (*scissio*). To reduce anxiety, Bernard implies that one might regulate the use of one's imagination when having concerns about future possibilities: "the [modest] man will restrain his concerns and abstain from superfluous cares, although he will not ignore those [concerns] that

84 *Csi*, II, Ch. 10.19 (CF 37:72; *SW* 1:694; *SBO* 3:427). "Qui igitur longa sibi metitur tempora, nonne vere ingreditur iter exterminii, transiens vitae terminos productiori sollicitudine? Inde est quod homines in praesenti a sese exsules per oblivionem, in alia per inanem sollicitudinem migrant saecula, non profutura, immo nec futura."

85 *Csi*, II, Ch. 10.19 (CF 37:73; *SW* 1:694; *SBO* 3:427). "Similiter animus distentus in multa, multis laceretur curis necesse est. Nempe immoderata extensio extenuationem, et extenuatio nimia scissionem facit."

are necessary."[86] Bernard's comment implies that discernment is required to distinguish between due concerns and immoderate or undue concerns—in other words, one needs a criterion of balance in order to evaluate whether one's thinking is due or undue, just or unjust.

Bernard recommends that to avoid self-deception, when Eugene III considers what sort of person he is (*qualis*), he should differentiate what it is in him that derives from his own efforts of self-cultivation (*ex te*) and what it is in him that derives from God's grace (*munere Dei*).[87] In either respect, the question of what sort (*qualis*) of person a person is involves, Leclercq observes, reflection on one's personal qualities or characteristics that have been added to one's human nature.[88] For Bernard, good characteristics that might be associated with God's grace include wisdom, understanding, patience, gentleness, humility, affability (i.e., geniality, warmth, and friendliness), flexibility, magnanimity, earnestness (sincerity), and a proper self-confidence.[89] It is at this point in Book II that, as mentioned in the previous chapter, Bernard exhorts Eugene III to "reflect on your zeal, your mercy, and also your discretion . . . Reflect on your manner of forgiving."[90] All of these aspects of Eugene III are "matters to become known" (*innotescere*), to be brought forth into awareness through meditation, and clarified. It is also in this passage toward the end of Book II that Bernard indicates in order to grow in such characteristics, a person must perform acts that instantiate or reinforce them: "It is not nature but practice [*usus*] which produces virtues of this kind."[91] Bernard's implication is that if such qualities are to be primarily ascribed to God's grace, at the same time they will not become developed in a person without the contribution of that person's exercise (*usus*).

86 Ibid. "Modestus moderabitur curas, temperabit a superfluis, non deerit necessariis."

87 *Csi*, II, Ch. 11.20 (CF 37:73; *SW* 1:696; *SBO* 3:428). "Vigilanter discerne qualis ex te et qualis sis munere Dei, et non sit in spiritu tuo dolus."

88 Leclercq, "L'Art de la Composition," 122.

89 *Csi*, II, Ch. 11.20 (CF 37:74; *SW* 1:696; *SBO* 3:428).

90 Ibid. "Oportet innotescat tibi zelus tuus, clementia tua, discretio quoque moderatrix earumdem virtutum."

91 Ibid. "Nempe eiusmodi non natura virtutes, sed usus facit."

6

Book III

Meditative Reflection on What Is Below One

After discussing the practice of meditation in order to grow in self-knowledge, Bernard then proceeds in Book III to discuss meditation on relationships in which one exercises responsibility (or, as he calls it drawing on the phrasing of Augustine,[1] meditation on "what is below one"). My interpretation of Book III is again organized around topics that emerge in the course of Bernard's text, namely, reflection on the exercise of responsibility in terms of stewardship and how stewardship differs from domination. I also further explore the nature of Christian philosophy based on remarks of Bernard found in this book.

Stewardship and Domination

In contrast with self-reflection, it is a different kind of consideration to meditate on realities that are "below one."[2] Bernard begins describing this stage of meditation in a concrete way by focusing on Eugene III's supervision of persons who occupy subordinate ministerial offices in the Church.[3] The author who provides an overview of *De consideratione* in the *Vita prima* describes Book III in this way: "The things below [the pope] and concerning him are those about the customs in society, the equality of nature, the diversity of offices, the distinction of merits, the discerning of the very subtle judgments having to do with promotion to high offices, and the recognition given to all persons in their state of life."[4]

1 Augustine, *De doctrina Christiana* I.23.22 (Green, 18; Martin, 18).

2 *Csi*, II, 14.23 (CF 37:78; *SW* 1:700; *SBO* 3:430).

3 Kennan, "Introduction," 14.

4 Arnold of Bonneval, *Vita prima* II.51 (CF 76:137).

A comment of Leclercq suggests that Bernard's focus at this point might occur with a general assessment of the pope's relationality (*rapport*) with others.[5] Given that Eugene III occupies an office that—institutionally speaking—entails jurisdiction over others, his exercise of the responsibilities of his office must be differentiated from the question of whether he has a personal desire to subordinate others. Regarding such a possible desire, Bernard introduces a distinction between stewardship and dominion, care and possession. Alluding to Psalm 24:1, Bernard writes:

> It seems to me that you have been entrusted with stewardship [*dispensatio*] over the world, not given possession [*possessio*] of it. If you proceed to usurp possession of it, he contradicts you who says, "The world and its fullness are mine" . . . Leave possession and rule to him; you take care of it. This is your portion; beyond it do not stretch your hand.[6]

Bernard warns Eugene III that a "passion to rule" (*libidinem dominandi*) is a poison; the pope should construe his role rather as one akin to an estate manager (*vilicus*), a steward.[7] The topic of the *libido dominandi* is Augustinian, denoting a desire for political power based on self-interest.[8]

In the initial sections of Book III, Bernard describes areas of Eugene III's responsibility in association with his papal office, that is, with his duties of facilitating the religious conversion of others, curbing the ambition of the converted, and correcting heresy and schism: "you must take great care and consider most vigilantly how those who are foolish may become wise, and how those who are wise may not become foolish, and how those who have lost wisdom may recover it."[9] Bernard is particularly concerned with "the voices of ambition" belonging to persons who seek to manipulate the appeal process within the papal court.[10] Not only does ambition drive the expenditure of much of the pope's energy in "learning of the laws and canons," but the demands associated with such procedures inhibit the pope's practice of

5 Leclercq, "L'Art de la Composition," 120.

6 *Csi*, III, 1.1 (CF 37:80; *SW* 1:702; *SBO* 3:431).

7 *Csi*, III, 1.2 (CF 37:81; *SW* 1:704; *SBO* 3:432). "Addo tamen et hoc, nam nullum tibi venenum, nullum gladium plus formido, quam libidinem dominandi." See also Kennan, "Antithesis and Argument," 96; Anderson, "Reconsidering," 158.

8 For Augustine on the "desire of domination," see Augustine, *City of God* I, preface, and XIV.15 (Dyson, 3 and 614).

9 *Csi*, III, 1.2 (CF 37:81; *SW* 1:704–6; *SBO* 3:432–33).

10 *Csi*, III, 1.5 (CF 37:84; *SW* 1:708; *SBO* 3:434). See also Leclercq, "L'Art de la Composition," 123.

meditation: "How often has this [disquiet] and disquieting evil caused your holy, beneficial leisure to be ended prematurely?"[11]

Bernard exhorts Eugene III to reform the appeals process and bring it into order: "How long will you sleep? How long will your consideration fail to keep watch over the confusion and abuse of appeals? Appeals are made beyond what is just and right, contrary to custom and order."[12] Bernard continues at length on this issue, urging the pope prudently to delegate the majority of these tasks to others.[13] Bernard then proceeds to discuss further instances of avarice within the Church and also question whether due order is being preserved in the distribution of jurisdictional authority.[14] As Leclercq observes, Bernard's overall intention is to exhort the pope to implement an ecclesiastical reform.[15] Bernard writes:

> It remains for your consideration to be vigilant over the whole state of the universal Church to see whether the people are humbly obedient to the clerics as they should be; whether the clerics are [obedient] to the priests; whether the priests are [obedient] to God; whether in monasteries and religious houses order is maintained and discipline observed; whether evil deeds and false doctrines are vigorously censured by the Church . . . whether your apostolic decrees and regulations concerning them are observed with fitting diligence so there is nothing in the field of the Lord which is uncultivated out of neglect [*ne quid in agro Domini tui aut neglect incultum*].[16]

At the risk of imposing more modern categories upon these remarks, it is evident that Bernard interprets the pope's role not simply as an agent responsible for ecclesiastical government, but also as an agent responsible for ecclesiastical culture.[17] One sees, in a way, an exhortation on Bernard's part that

11 *Csi*, III, 1.5 (CF 37:85; *SW* 1:708; *SBO* 3:434). "Quoties sancta ac fecunda tua abortiri otia fecit inquietum et inquietans malum?"

12 *Csi*, III, 2.7 (CF 37:87; *SW* 1:712; *SBO* 3:436). "Quousque dormitas? Quousque non evigilat consideratio tua ad tantam appellationum confusionem atque abusionem? Praeter ius et fas, praeter morem et ordinem fiunt."

13 *Csi*, III, 2.9–2.12 (CF 37:89–93; *SW* 1:714–18; *SBO* 3:437–39); Leclercq, "L'Art de la Composition," 123.

14 *Csi*, III, 3.13–4.18 (CF 37:93–103; *SW* 1:718–32; *SBO* 3:439–46); Leclercq, "L'Art de la Composition," 124.

15 Leclercq, "L'Art de la Composition," 124.

16 *Csi*, III, 5.19 (CF 37:104; *SW* 1:732; *SBO* 3:446).

17 For another reference to the pope's responsibility to cultivate the "field of the Lord," see *Csi*, II, 6.12 (CF 37:60; *SW* 1:678; *SBO* 3:419).

through Eugene III's vigilance the entire Church might develop in monastic virtues. For example, in this passage, Bernard refers to humility, obedience, discipline, and diligence. Does Bernard construe ecclesiastical culture to be a kind of extension of monastic culture?

An Excursus on Christian Philosophy

During the course of discussing needed ecclesiastical reforms in Book III, Bernard cites 1 Corinthians 2:15 in order to observe to the pope that when the Apostle Paul refers to the spiritual man who judges all things, such a judgment might be carried out according to a threefold reflection, namely, by asking: Is it lawful (*an liceat*)? Is it suitable (*an deceat*)? Is it advantageous (*an expediat*)?[18] In his comments to Eugene III in this section, Bernard indicates that these three questions might be asked in this particular order—at least "in Christian philosophy" (*christiana philosophia*). Bernard then explains that whatever is advantageous will also be suitable and lawful, and whatever is suitable will also be lawful.[19]

What does Bernard mean by this reference to Christian philosophy? Recall above the discussion of Christian philosophy in relation to Bernard's suggestion that Eugene III consider human nature (Bernard implicitly referred to the anthropology of Boethius).[20] In that passage, Bernard differentiated that kind of philosophical consideration from apostolic teaching. Is it again Boethius that Bernard has in mind when he refers to a Christian philosophy in this passage in Book III?

Bernard is also aware of non-Christian forms of philosophy. This is apparent not only in Book I where Bernard refers to a non-Christian Greek sage as "the Philosopher,"[21] but also in a sermon elsewhere where Bernard clearly differentiates Christian teaching from specific Greek philosophers. There, Bernard writes: "What then have the holy Apostles taught us, or rather do they teach us? Not the fisherman's skill, nor the tent-maker's, nor any other of this kind; not to read Plato, not to interpret Aristotle's subtleties, not to be always learning and never come to knowledge of the truth.

18 *Csi*, III, 4.15 (CF 37:98; *SW* 1:724; *SBO* 3:442). This distinction between liceity and expediency seems to originate from later passages in 1 Cor 6:12 and 10:22. Bernard also quotes these biblical texts in his apology to William of St. Thierry. See Apo, 4.7 (Casey, 42; *SW* 2:158; *SBO* 3:87). See also Sommerfeldt, "Epistemological and Social Hierarchies," 84.

19 *Csi*, III, 4.15 (CF 37:98; *SW* 1:724; *SBO* 3:442).

20 *Csi*, II, 4.7 (CF 37:54; *SW* 1:670; *SBO* 3:415).

21 *Csi*, I, 8.9 (CF 37:39; *SW* 1:650; *SBO* 3:405).

[The apostles] have taught me to live."[22] In this remark, Bernard associates the study of non-Christian philosophy with learning skills and differentiates both kinds of learning from Apostolic teaching. In a similar way, Bernard remarks elsewhere that "the wordy utterances [*verbositate*] of the philosophers" cannot separate the church from the love of God found in Christ.[23]

On the other hand, Bernard also at times refers to biblical teachings as a kind of philosophy. For example, he says a Hebrew proverb represents the "true philosophy."[24] In a different sermon, Bernard contrasts "the philosophy of Paul" (the apostle) with non-Christian philosophy.[25] Bernard refers in a similar way to Pope Clement of Rome: "he was considered the foremost philosopher of his time."[26] In yet another sense of the word philosophy, recall that Bernard in *De consideratione* Book I refers to the practice of meditation as a "philosophy."[27] In this regard, later in Book V, Bernard will explore how during meditation one might employ philosophy to assist one in directing one's mind toward spiritual realities.[28] On the basis of these various remarks, Déchanet seems correct to describe Bernard also as a kind of philosopher.[29]

Should then one emphasize Bernard's teaching more so as a monastic philosophy in lieu of referring to it as a monastic theology?[30] Or should Bernard primarily be understood as a theologian?[31] With respect to the second question, Châtillon answers affirmatively that Bernard was perceived

22 Bernard of Clairvaux, "The Solemn Feast of the Apostles Peter and Paul," I, §3, in *Sermons for the Summer Season* (CF 53:100–103, at 101; *SW* 8:446–53, at 448–50; *SBO* 5:188–91, at 189–90). See also Evans, *Bernard of Clairvaux*, 48.

23 *SCC*, 79, 2.4 (CF 40:140; *SW* 6:562; *SBO* 2:274). See also Verbaal, "Bernardus Philosophus," 586.

24 *QH*, 7.12 (CF 25:162; *SW* 7:576; *SBO* 4:421), citing Prv 4:23. For this reference, I am indebted to Martineau, "Prudence et Considération," 44.

25 *Div* 7, §1 (CF 68:44; *SW* 9:236; *SBO* 6.1:108). See also Evans, *Bernard of Clairvaux*, 48.

26 Bernard of Clairvaux, "On the Feast of Saint Clement, Of the Three Waters," §1, in *Sermons for the Autumn Season* (CF 54:229–34, at 230). For the Latin, see *SW* 8:894–905, at 896; *SBO* 5:412–17, at 413. See also Evans, *Bernard of Clairvaux*, 48.

27 *Csi*, I, 9.12 (CF 37:42; *SW* 1:654; *SBO* 3:407).

28 *Csi*, V, 2.3 (CF 37:142; *SW* 1:776; *SBO* 3:468). "Nec ille minor, qui hunc sibi gradum ad illa invisibilia philosophando constituit."

29 Leclercq, "Théologie monastique," 7–23; Leclercq, *Love of Learning*, 191–235.

30 Leclercq, *Love of Learning*, 101. See also Franklin T. Harkins, "*Lectio exhortatio debet esse*: Reading as a Way of Life at the Twelfth-Century Abbey of St. Victor," in *From Knowledge to Beatitude: St. Victor, Twelfth-Century Scholars, and Beyond, Essays in Honor of Grover A Zinn, Jr.*, ed. E. Ann Matter and Lesley Smith (Notre Dame, IN: University of Notre Dame Press, 2013), 103–30, at 109.

31 Déchanet, "Aux Sources," 57. See also Hiss, *Die Anthropologie*, 6.

to be the *grand théologien* of his age.[32] Due to his sense of reverence for the mysteries of faith, Bernard was sought out for "theological consultations" by contemporaries such as Guy de Trois-Fontaines and Hugh of St. Victor; he maintained an ecclesially accepted role at synods evaluating theological controversies.[33] On the other hand, Evans maintains that when Bernard refers to the discipline of theology, he does so in a pejorative way in reference to the works of Abelard.[34] However, Bernard cannot be said to exhibit disdain for the theology of his contemporaries, namely, the *Sententiae* authors Robert Pullen, Peter Lombard, and Robert of Melun. Regarding Robert Pullen, Bernard exhorts Ascelin, bishop of Rochester, to permit Robert to live in Paris "for the sake of the sound doctrine which is known to be taught there."[35] Regarding Peter Lombard, Bernard writes to Gilduin, abbot of St. Victor in Paris, to care for Peter who is visiting France "for the sake of study"[36] (Bernard states that he had made the same request of the bishop of Lucca when Peter was in Reims).[37] Leclercq remarks that Bernard was Peter's "protector and friend."[38] And, as noted above, Bernard seems to have been acquainted also with Robert of Melun who according to Southern supported Bernard at the Synod of Reims.[39] These authors were, Châtillon maintains, theological allies yet focused on the education of clerics.[40]

In light of this discussion, Verbaal seems correct to note that Bernard's thought lacks a clarified distinction between philosophy and theology.[41] It is worth pondering Verbaal's conjecture that Bernard wanted to promote a "philosophy of the monastic school" involving a monastic praxis that would be perceived as an alternative to the logic-focused philosophy of Abelard; if this is true, such an effort would account for the "philosophical

32 Châtillon, "L'Influence de S. Bernard," 277.

33 Ibid., 276–77. For Guy, see Ep 72 (James, *Letters*, 99–101; Ep 69 in *SW* 2:578–83; *SBO* 7:169–71). For Hugh, see "On Baptism" (Ep 77) (CF 67:149–77; *SW* 2:608–41; *SBO* 7:184–200).

34 Evans, *Bernard of Clairvaux*, 48.

35 Ep 271 (James, *Letters*, 344–45; Ep 205 in *SW* 3:168; *SBO* 8:64). "Si monui magistrum Robertum Pullum aliquantum tempus facere Parisius, ob sanam doctrinam quae apud illum esse dignoscitur." See also *The Metalogicon of John of Salisbury*, trans. Daniel D. McGarry (Gloucester, MA: Peter Smith, 1971), 23n83; Sommerfeldt, "Bernard of Clairvaux and the Trivial Arts," CS 193:148.

36 Ep 442 (James, *Letters*, 508; Ep 410 in *SW* 3:808; *SBO* 8:391).

37 Ibid.

38 Leclercq, "Théologie monastique," 9.

39 Southern, *Scholastic Humanism*, 129; Dinzelbacher, "Bernhards Leben," 41; Merton, "Blessed Eugenius III," 179.

40 Jean Châtillon, "L'Influence de S. Bernard," 277.

41 Verbaal, "Bernardus Philosophus," 583.

self-understanding" that Bernard aimed to cultivate in the minds of his monks in order to preserve their monastic vocations and inculcate a sense of communal identity.[42] Leclercq agrees that in a certain way to be a monk is to be a philosopher.[43]

42 Ibid., 570–71. See also Wim Verbaal, "The Preaching of Community: Bernard of Clairvaux's Sermons and the School of Experience," *Medieval Sermon Studies* 48 (2004): 75–90, at 77–78. Regarding Bernard's general response to Abelard, see John R. Sommerfeldt, "Abelard and Bernard of Clairvaux," *Papers of the Michigan Academy of Science, Arts, and Letters* 46 (1961): 493–501.

43 Leclercq, "Theology and Prayer," 354.

7

Book IV

Meditative Reflection on What Is Around One

After discussing meditation on relationships in which one exercises responsibility, Bernard then proceeds in Book IV to discuss meditation on other relationships in one's context, especially those that have some kind of impact on personal well-being. The interpretation of Book IV presented here is based on two topics that Bernard touches upon in this discussion: (1) bringing stability to relationships in one's context and also (2) how to prepare for relational difficulties by developing specific psychological characteristics that are distinct from the moral characteristics associated with the virtues. I explore Bernard's treatment of these psychological characteristics in detail, as this discussion directly relates to what might be understood as positive mental health in the contemporary context (see chapter 10, below).

Bringing Stability to Relationships

Having discussed the need for Eugene III to bring reform to the appeals process in the papal courts and to meditate on his exercise of jurisdictional authority throughout the Church ("what is below him"), Bernard proceeds to call the pope's attention to "the things which are around him."[1] In a way, this is a continuation of Book III. At the beginning of Book IV, Bernard states, "we must now include those things which are around you. These are really below you, but inasmuch as they are closer, they are more troublesome to you."[2] The "things which are around" Eugene III are his primary relationships with others. As discussed in chapter 4 above, in sermon 16 of

1 *Csi*, III, 5.20 (CF 37:107; *SW* 1:736; *SBO* 3:448).

2 *Csi*, IV, 1.1 (CF 37:109; *SW* 1:736; *SBO* 3:448).

the *De diversis* series, Bernard affirms the natural benefit of peaceful social relationships: "And because we are social animals, let us cross over from what is within us to those who are around us, so that if it be possible, as much as is in us, we may have peace with all persons. For this is the law of natural society."[3] Later in the same sermon, Bernard extends this exhortation to seek social peace even further: "We say also not only that we should show peace to brothers in this life but that we should even be peaceable with those who hate peace, to carry all and to be carried by no one."[4]

The relationships around the pope exert "daily pressure" that Bernard perceives the pope to feel "from the City, from the Curia" and from his own "household."[5] By the "City," Bernard is referring not only to the clergy of the pope's bishopric, but also to "the Roman people."[6] For the Dominican historian Marie-Dominique Chenu, Bernard is expressing a moral regard for the pope's well-being because Bernard perceives the pope to be immersing himself in political affairs and "trying to maneuver between the senate and the emperor."[7] Kennan observes that it is Eugene III's embroilment with Arnold of Brescia that Bernard frequently has in mind when he is exhorting the pope.[8] Bernard's concern might especially be focused on the possibility that Eugene III is interested in resolving the political conflict by means of a military campaign.[9]

The presence of such political conflicts and difficulties in the pope's relationships indicate that he would benefit from meditation in order to reduce tension: "if careful and timely consideration does not intervene, you will continually be occupied and your trouble will be without limit and your anxiety without end. You will have no leisure; your heart will not be free.

3 *Div*, 16.3 (CF 68:89; *SW* 9:312; *SBO* 6.1:146). "Et quia sociale animal sumus, ex his quae in nobis sunt ad ea quae circa nos sunt transeamus, ut, si fieri potest, quod ex nobis est, pacem habeamus cum omnibus hominibus. Haec enim est lex naturalis societatis."

4 *Div*, 16.5 (CF 68:91; *SW* 9:314; *SBO* 6.1:147). "Pacem quoque non solum fratribus exhibendam dicimus in via ista; sed cum his qui oderunt pacem esse pacificum, portare omnes et a nemine velle portari."

5 *Csi*, IV, 1.1 (CF 37:110; *SW* 1:738; *SBO* 3:449). "Dico autem instantia illa tua quotidiana, ab Urbe, a curia, a domestica ecclesia tua." The word "pressure" translates the "insistence" (*instantia*) or relational demands that Bernard must perceive some parties as bringing to the pope. See also Leclercq, "L'Art de la Composition," 124.

6 *Csi*, IV, 2.2 (CF 37:111; *SW* 1:738; *SBO* 3:449).

7 M.-D. Chenu, *Nature, Man, and Society in the Twelfth Century*, trans. Jerome Taylor and Lester K. Little (Chicago: University of Chicago Press, 1968), 267n48.

8 Kennan, "Antithesis and Argument," 99.

9 Kennan, "Bernard of Clairvaux and the Papacy," 89.

You will labor more and accomplish less."[10] Kennan contends that Bernard is exhorting Eugene III to give priority to spiritual pursuits in lieu of exercising temporal political power.[11] However, Bernard is concerned that some persons with whom the pope is interacting might attempt to discourage his interest in meditation: Bernard calls the pope's attention to courtiers who have disdain for anyone "who loves quiet and who sometimes gives himself leisure" (*amatorem quietis, et sibi interdum vacantem*).[12] Recall that in Book I, Bernard observed that not everyone approves of the pope being devoted to "this philosophy."[13] Perhaps Bernard has particular persons in mind: recall that according to Bredero, part of Bernard's concern in writing Book IV was due to Bernard being at odds with some members of the Curia after the Synod of Reims in 1148.[14] Further, according to Kennan, business at the Curia at this time was predominated by civil juridical claims which suffered corruption due to the practice of bribery.[15] It is clear that Bernard held the legal proceedings of the ecclesiastical courts in disdain. He had already written in Book I: "Let cases be tried, but in a suitable manner. The way which is frequently followed now is completely detestable. It would hardly suit civil courts, let alone ecclesiastical. I am astonished that you, a man of piety, can bear to listen to lawyers dispute and argue in a way which tends more to subvert the truth than to reveal it."[16]

With respect to the need to bring order to the relationships surrounding his pontificate, Bernard states that Eugene III must make time for meditative practice in order to organize these affairs: "It is not a useless consideration by which you endeavor to order your house and provide for those who are close to your heart."[17] If Bernard is concerned that the pope is too immersed in the

10 *Csi*, IV, 1.1 (CF 37:110; *SW* 1:738; *SBO* 3:449). "Alioquin, si non cauta opportunaque interveniat consideratio, occupatio continuabitur, et vexationis non erit modus, et sollicitudinis non erit finis. Non tempus vacuum, non liberum cor: plus laboris, et minus utilitatis."

11 Kennan, "Bernard of Clairvaux and the Papacy," 86, citing *Csi*, IV, Ch. 3 (CF 37:119); Kennan, "Antithesis and Argument," 102.

12 *Csi*, IV, 2.5 (CF 37:116; *SW* 1:746; *SBO* 3:453).

13 *Csi*, I, 9.12 (CF 37:42; *SW* 1:654; *SBO* 3:407). See also Sommerfeldt, *Life of the Mind*, 101.

14 Bredero, *Bernard of Clairvaux*, 147.

15 Kennan, "Rhetoric and Style," 47.

16 *Csi*, I, 10.13 (CF 37:44; *SW* 1:656; *SBO* 3:408). "Agitentur causae, sed sicut oportet. Nam is modus, qui frequentatur, exsecrabilis plane, et qui, non dico Ecclesiam, sed nec forum deceret. Miror namque quemadmodum religiosae aures tuae audire sustinent huiusmodi disputationes advocatorum et pugnas verborum, quae magis ad subversionem quam ad inventionem proficiunt veritatis." See also Leclercq, "L'Art de la Composition," 119; James A. Brundage, "St. Bernard and the Jurists," in *The Second Crusade and the Cistercians*, 25–34.

17 *Csi*, IV, 6.17 (CF 37:130; *SW* 1:762; *SBO* 3:461).

affairs of litigation,[18] then the practice of meditation can enable Eugene III to determine how he might delegate some of his responsibilities.[19] In this discussion, Bernard is repeating advice that he had already expressed to Eugene III in Book I.[20] One might discern a further example of Bernard proposing such a delegation in Book IV when Bernard describes the papacy to Eugene III as having two swords, "the material and the spiritual," yet where the material sword should be drawn by the civil authority at the Church's request.[21] As stated previously in chapter 1, it is possible that these remarks relate to Bernard's interest in Eugene III renewing the effort of the second crusade and that Bernard is writing this part of Book IV to the pope during the summer of 1150.[22]

As a further point of counsel in Book IV, Bernard recommends that the pope should evaluate the character of the persons with whom he associates: "be very careful to bring in men whose presence you will not later regret."[23] To assist with the task of discerning candidates, Bernard outlines the qualities and character strengths of persons that he believes are important for persons who might fill ecclesiastical roles supporting the pope (e.g., Bernard states that Eugene III should avoid persons who are over-zealous to assume an ecclesiastical position).[24] Bernard further implies that Eugene III should evaluate the secular accretions incorporated into the papal office that did not originate from the apostolic line of Peter but rather from papal imitations of temporal power: "In this finery, you are the successor not of Peter, but of Constantine."[25] As a closing observation regarding ecclesiastical reform, one might note that in the course of expressing numerous accolades upon

18 See the remark in G. R. Evans, *Alan of Lille: The Frontiers of Theology in the Later Twelfth Century* (Cambridge: Cambridge University Press, 1983), 140–41.

19 *Csi*, IV, 6.18 (CF 37:131; *SW* 1:764; *SBO* 3:462).

20 "You will save a great deal of time for consideration if you refuse to deal with some business and assign some to others." *Csi*, I, 11.14 (CF 37:46; *SW* 1:660; *SBO* 3:410).

21 *Csi*, IV, 3.7 (CF 37:118; *SW* 1:748; *SBO* 3:454). See also Karl F. Morrison, "Hermeneutics and Enigma: Bernard of Clairvaux's *De consideratione*," *Viator* 19 (1988): 129–52, at 129; Leclercq, *Bernard and the Cistercian Spirit*, 54. On Bernard's teaching of the "two swords" (sacred and secular), as well as his affirmation of the pope's "fullness of power" (*plenitudo potestatis*) at least within the Church, see Bredero, *Bernard of Clairvaux*, 149–59.

22 Ep 399 (James, *Letters*, 470–72, at 471; Ep 256 in *SW* 3:366–70; *SBO* 8:163–65).

23 *Csi*, IV, 4.11 (CF 37:122; *SW* 1:754; *SBO* 3:457).

24 *Csi*, IV, 4.12 (CF 37:123; *SW* 1:754; *SBO* 3:457). See also Sommerfeldt, *Spirituality of Relationship*, 48–49.

25 *Csi*, IV, 3.6 (CF 37:117; *SW* 1:746; *SBO* 3:453).

Eugene's III's pontifical office,[26] Bernard also remarks that "you are not the lord of bishops, but one of them."[27] Here again, Bernard indirectly reiterates his emphases on humility and stewardship in contrast with dominion, even while describing the pontifical office in high laudatory style.

The Character of an Undivided Mind

Bernard indicates that by exercising vigilance, the pope can cultivate his mind to become more focused and thus also become more effective in carrying out the tasks associated with his papal role.[28] In order to bring reform to the papal court, Bernard states that Eugene III will need to develop his mind (*animus*) to exhibit nine particular characteristics, including vigilance. Based on a remark that Bernard makes after enumerating these qualities, one might refer to such characteristics as marks of an "undivided mind" (*animus individuus*).[29] That such a mind is "whole" as undivided has a relation to mental health (*sanitas*) if one understands health in terms of wholeness.[30] Bernard's description of the human mind in this regard might be considered in relation to his remark in a sermon from his *De diversis* series that there is a kind of "virtual unity" that one might experience when one is focused on a single goal.[31] I will discuss this point again below when examining Bernard's teachings on the divine unity and also the spiritual unity that can develop between one's soul and God.

With respect to the first five mental qualities that Bernard enumerates, he writes that the pope's mind "ought to be without worry of minor, insignificant concerns. It should be free so no business can forcibly make a claim on its attention. It should be upright so no unworthy attachment can drag it down. It should be righteous so no evil intention can turn it aside. It should

26 Doran states this section of *De consideratione* expresses "the most exalted description of the papal office of the twelfth century." See John Doran, "Innocent III and the Uses of Spiritual Marriage," in *Pope, Church, and City: Essays in Honor of Brenda M. Bolton*, ed. Frances Andrews, Christoph Egger, and Constance M. Rousseau (Leiden: Brill, 2004), 101–14, at 107–8.

27 *Csi*, IV, 7.23 (CF 37:137; *SW* 1:772; *SBO* 3:466). "Te vero non dominum episcoporum, sed unum ex ipsis."

28 See, e.g., *Csi*, III, 5.19 (CF 37:104; *SW* 1:732; *SBO* 3:446), as quoted above: "It remains for your consideration to be vigilant over the whole state of the Church" (Superest ut generaliter super universum Ecclesiae statum vigilet consideratio tua).

29 The Latin in the text above is an interpolation based on Bernard's remark, discussed more below: *Csi*, IV, 6.18 (CF 37:131; *SW* 1:764; *SBO* 3:462). "His te non dubites et bonis privandum, et feriendum malis, si animum dividens, et Dei rebus, et tuis pariter reculis volueris impertiri."

30 See Harald Brüssow, "What Is Health?," *Microbial Biotechnology* 6, no. 4 (2013): 341–48, at 342.

31 *Div*, 80.1 (CF 68:313; *SW* 9:660; *SBO* 6.1:320).

be cautious so no suspicion can furtively enter it."[32] The first two qualities seem related: a mind that is devoid (*vacuus*) of minor concerns is also a mind free from (*liber*) or unrestricted by distractions.[33] A mind that is upright or noble (*ingenuus*) with respect to the affairs to which it attends would also seem to have the ability to preserve its psychological freedom.

Regarding this third quality, Bernard indicates that the mind's nobility is a benefit of nature that should be valued and preserved. Speaking of the mind of "every soul" (*omnem animam*), he writes:

> Why should it not venture with confidence into the presence of him by whose image it sees itself honored [*cuius se insignem cernit imagine*] and in whose likeness it knows itself made glorious [*illustrem similitudine novit*]? All it has to do is take care to preserve its natural purity [*naturae ingenuitatem*] by innocence of life, or rather to study to beautify and adorn with the brightness of its actions and dispositions the glorious beauty which is its birthright. Why then does it not set to work? There is a great natural gift within us [*Grande profecto in nobis donum naturae ipsa est*], and if it is not allowed full play the rest of our nature will go to ruin [*turpabitur*], as though it were being eaten away by the rust of decay . . . This is why God, its Creator, desires the divine glory and nobility [*divinae insigne generositatis*] to be always preserved in the soul, so that it may have within itself that by which it may be admonished by the Word, either to stay with him or to return to him if it has strayed.[34]

32 *Csi*, IV, 6.17 (CF 37:131; *SW* 1:764; *SBO* 462). "Vacuum prorsus a sollicitudine rerum minorum et vilium oportet esse animum, tam magnis et tam multis intentum rebus. Oportet liberum, quem nulla sibi vindicet violenta occupatio. Oportet ingenuum, quem nulla deorsum trahat indigna affectio. Oportet rectum, quem nulla seorsum avertat sinistra intentio. Oportet cautum, quem nulla subeat furtiva suspicio."

33 I interpret the mental quality of *vacuus* that Bernard mentions as referring to activity that is not distracted or preoccupied, not necessarily as involving a mental state of emptiness (śūnyatā) as understood in the Buddhist monastic tradition. Regarding śūnyatā, see William Theodore de Bary (ed.), *The Buddhist Tradition in India, China and Japan* (New York: Random House, 1969), 77–78 and 95.

34 *SCC*, 83, 1.1–1.2 (CF 40:181–82; *SW* 6:611–12; *SBO* 2:298–99). "Quid enim non tute audeat apud eum, cuius se insignem cernit imagine, illustrem similitudine novit . . .? Tantum est ut curet naturae ingenuitatem vitae honestate servare; immo caeleste decus, quod sibi originaliter inest, dignis quibusdam studeat morum affectuumque venustare et decorare coloribus. Ut quid enim dormitet industria? Grande profecto in nobis donum naturae ipsa est, quae si minus suas exsequatur partes, nonne quod reliquum habet natura in nobis turpabitur, totum quasi quadam vetustatis operietur rubigine . . .? Et utique ad hoc auctor ipse Deus divinae insigne generositatis perpetuo

According to the gift of its natural nobility (*ingenuitas*), one's mind is marked as an image of God and distinguished as a likeness of God.[35] Because nobility is a natural gift of the mind, the exercise of meditation for the cultivation of this quality might be understood as an effort motivated by restorative grace to help recover a natural benefit—a benefit perhaps as understood from a different point of view (*alio intuitu*).[36]

The nobility of the mind is a mark of divine generosity that one must work to preserve so to avoid its disfigurement (*turpitudo*). Bernard indicates that this disfigurement can occur when one does not regulate one's natural affections with discretion (without discretion "natural affection itself [becomes] a force that disturbs and destroys nature").[37] With respect to the disfigurement of the soul, Bernard states that such can also result from straying from the Word of God (although the soul's nature cannot be totally destroyed):

> It strays—as is the nature of a spiritual substance, in its affections, or rather its defections, and it degenerates and becomes unlike itself when it becomes unlike him in its depravity of life and manners [*cum se sibi vitae et morum pravitate dissimilem facit*]; but this unlikeness is not the destruction of its nature but a [vice] [*dissimilitudo, non naturae abolitio, sed vitium est*], for natural goodness is increased as much by comparison with itself as it is spoiled [*foedans*] by communication with evil. So the soul returns and is converted to the Word to be reformed by him and conformed to him.[38]

The good nature of the soul, a created gift from God, cannot be abolished, but its nobility can become disfigured (*foeda*).

---

voluit in anima conservari, ut semper haec in sese ex Verbo habeat, quo admoneatur semper, aut stare cum Verbo, aut redire, si mota fuerit." See also Stepsis, "Fulfillment of Self," 353–54.

35 See also CF 24:78, citing M. Standaert, "La Doctrine de l'Image chez S. Bernard," *Ephemerides Theologicae Lovanienses* 23 (1947): 70–129.

36 *Div*, 16.5 (CF 68:91; *SW* 9:314; *SBO* 6.1:147).

37 *SCC*, 49, 2.5 (CF 31:25; *SW* 6:166; *SBO* 3:76). "Tolle hanc, et virtus vitium erit, ipsaque affectio naturalis in perturbationem magis convertetur exterminiumque naturae."

38 *SCC*, 83, 1.2 (CF 40:181–82; *SW* 6:612; *SBO* 2:299). "Mota, sicut substantiae utique spirituali moveri est, cum suis affectibus, immo defectibus, a se quodammodo in peius vadit, cum se sibi vitae et morum pravitate dissimilem facit, reddit degenerem: quae tamen dissimilitudo, non naturae abolitio, sed vitium est, bonum ipsum naturae quantum sui comparatione attollens, tantum foedans coniunctione. Iam vero animae reditus, conversio eius ad Verbum, reformandae per ipsum, conformandae ipsi."

Could this mental quality of nobility also be understood as the mind's dignity? If so, Bernard indicates that the dignity of the mind also involves a moral dimension, not only with respect to the rectitude of one's thinking—one's mind exhibits rectitude (*rectus*) when it is not diverted by an evil intention (*intentio*)—but also with respect to whether one takes care (*cautus*) when focusing on some concern. Maintaining a right intention might be associated with staying focused on developing in the virtues for the purpose of pleasing God.[39] On this point, Bernard writes in one of the sermons in his *In Quadragesima* series that because some "are disturbed by temptations," they therefore

> strive more energetically to obtain the virtues . . . for the sake of the virtues themselves, and to please God alone, with all their concentration [*tota intentione*] if not with all their feeling. No doubt a person of this kind fulfills completely the prophet's admonition to "delight in the Lord" (Psalm 37:4), since he is not speaking of a feeling but of a practice [*exercitio*]. The feeling is of happiness, but the practice is of virtue.[40]

Development in the virtues, this passage indicates, requires focused exercise (*exercitium*), and focused exercise requires one's entire intention (*tota intentione*). This remark thus seems to elaborate on the mental quality of the focused rectitude of the mind that Bernard proposes to Eugene III.

Bernard then describes four additional desirable mental qualities: the pope's mind "should be vigilant so no curious, wandering thought can distract it. It should be firm so no sudden disturbance can shake it. It should be invincible so no tribulation, even if it be continuous, can exhaust it. It should be expansive so no temporal loss can constrain it."[41] The mind's quality of vigilance (*vigil*) is a significant feature of mental self-regulation for Bernard, namely, taking care not to be distracted by wandering thoughts as well as to inhibit inclinations toward disordered states of thinking. In Book V, Bernard

39 On God being pleased, see, e.g., Mt 3:17. That a virtue is delightful (*amabilis*) to God, see *Div*, 16.1 (CF 68:88; *SW* 9:309–10; *SBO* 6.1:144–45).

40 *Quad*, 5.7 (CF 52:46–47; *SW* 7:486; *SBO* 4:375). "Quia tentationibus . . . exercentur, multoque virilius agunt, si virtutes ipsas . . . pro virtutibus ipsis et pro solo beneplacito Dei tota intentione, etsi non tota affectione, sectantur. Nec dubium quin optime compleat, qui eiusmodi est, Prophetae admonitionem, qui dicit: Delectare in Domino; quoniam non de affectu loquitur, sed de exercitio. Affectus enim ille beatitudinis est, exercitium vero virtutis."

41 *Csi*, IV, 6.17 (CF 37:131; *SW* 1:764; *SBO* 3:462). "Oportet vigilem, quem nulla ab sese abducat peregrine et curiosa cogitatio. Oportet firmum, quem nulla concutiat repentina turbatio. Oportet invictum, quem nulla fatiget vel continua tribulatio. Oportet amplum, quem nulla coarctet rei temporalis amissio."

will describe one who thinks in this disordered manner as proceeding along a wandering journey (*peregrinatio*) that leads to a kind of self-exile.[42] One might interpret the mental quality of vigilance as arising not only due to the practice of mental self-regulation, but also as involving a special form of attentiveness involving cognitive self-awareness (mindfulness). When a person is self-aware of that person's own mental activity, then that person might proceed to practice what later monastic authors refer to as "taking custody of thoughts."[43] Taking custody of one's own mental activity in this respect might also be understood as self-appropriation. This kind of self-appropriation requires a meta-cognition; a cognition that knows one's cognitions and evaluates them as ordered or disordered.

Bernard alludes to the practice of taking custody of one's thoughts in a sermon from his *De diversis* series: "Above all else indeed let us take care to decline from evil as much as we can, not only evil actions, but also evil thought, even if we lack the power to avoid sin thoroughly on account of human frailty."[44] Bernard states in a sermon just prior to this one that it is thought that is the origin of the decline of the soul resulting in the increasing commitment of one's will to pursue an immoral suggestion. At a first stage of this pursuit, Bernard states that sin can be suggested by thought to one's memory, yet such a suggestion can occur without the will's consent.[45] In this remark, Bernard is consistent with his statement elsewhere (as discussed above) that memory is not only a psychological capacity that enables one

42 *Csi*, V, 1.2 (CF 37:141; *SW* 1:776; *SBO* 3:468).

43 In terms of Bernard's influence on subsequent spiritual authors, his concern with the self-regulation of one's thinking is repeated by the monk Denis the Carthusian who in his treatise *De meditatione* (1469) refers to the practice as taking custody of one's intellect: "If we are to make any progress, if we are to save our soul, we must hold fast to custody of the intellect. We must not allow our mind to wander; we must keep sleepless vigil over it, with virtuous love." See Denis the Carthusian, *Meditation*, prologue, in *The Spiritual Writings of Denis the Carthusian*, trans. Íde M. Ní Riain (Dublin: Four Courts, 2005), 273–98, at 275. "Ad omnem igitur profectum ac salute animarum nostrarum necesse est custodiae intellectus insistere, evagationibus mentis resistere, ac per hoc virtuosis invigilare affectibus." For the Latin, see Doctoris ecstatici D. Dionysii Cartusiani, *De meditatione*, Prooemium, in *Opera omnia*, Tom. XLI, *Opera minora*, IX, ed. Monachorum sacri ordinis Cartusiensis (Tornaci: Typis Cartusiae Sanctæ Mariæ de Pratis, Ex Editionibus Coloniae, 1912), 71.

44 *Div*, 33.5 (CF 68:184; *SW* 9:470; *SBO* 6.1:225). "Ante omnia quidem solliciti, etsi penitus cavere pro humana fragilitate non praevalemus, quantum tamen declinare a malo possumus, non modo actionis, sed et cogitationis."

45 *Div*, 32.3 (CF 68:178; *SW* 9:460; *SBO* 6.1:220). "Eodem modo in anima, si peccatum suggeritur memoriae per cogitationem, nullum tamen praebuerit aut voluntas affectum, aut deliberatio ipsa consensum, fateor quidem deformitas est, nec audire interim anima illa meretur: 'Tota pulchra es, amica mea.' Ceterum etsi naevus est, sed non morbus."

to recall a past experience, but it also involves one's attention and focus.[46] At a second stage when pursuing an immoral suggestion, one's will might experience pleasure in response to the suggestion (although one still resists it through the exercise of reason).[47] At a third stage, one's reason also acquiesces to the suggestion by means of intention (in contrast with maintaining a right intention, as mentioned above).[48] According to these stages, the emergence of sin causes the soul to advance from having a mark or blemish (*naevus*) to a state of sickness (*morbus*) and weakness (*infirmitas*), eventually reaching a state of spiritual death (*mors*). Bernard describes this progress as one where sin moves ever more deeply into the interior dwelling of the mind, first through the gate of memory, then through the gate of the will, then through the gate of reason.[49]

The advance of this spiritual debilitation can be avoided, Bernard argues, if one cultivates the practice of recollection. Recollection serves as a kind of guardian of one's thinking such that, as soon as one is aware of the immoral suggestion, the thought can be blocked:

> Therefore, lest a numerous crowd of intruding thoughts expel God from one's memory, thoughts that usually flow forth like a common mob in a palace hall, a porter is placed at memory's gate whose name is "recollection of one's own profession." So when the mind senses that it is weighed down by shameful thoughts, it rebukes itself and says to itself, "Should you think about these things, you who are a priest, you who are a cleric, you who are a monk? Should one who cherishes justice allow any thoughts of this nature within oneself? Is it proper for a servant of Christ, lover of God, to consider any such thing even for a moment?" By saying these things, one's mind shuts out the flow of illicit thought through recollection of own's own profession.[50]

46 See *Div*, 45.1 (CF 68:236–37; *SW* 9:544–46; *SBO* 6.1:262–63).

47 *Div*, 32.3 (CF 68:179; *SW* 9:460; *SBO* 6.1:220). "Quod si voluntas quoque ipsa iam sensu delectationis afficitur, resistit tamen adhuc deliberatio rationis, infirmatur quidem, sed necdum moritur anima." See also Hiss, *Die Anthropologie*, 115–16.

48 *Div*, 32.3 (CF 68:179; *SW* 9:460; *SBO* 6.1:220). "Tunc enim mori dicitur, quando et ipsa ratio ad peccatum per intentionem curvatur."

49 *Div*, 32.4 (CF 68:179–80; *SW* 9:462; *SBO* 6.1:221).

50 Ibid. "Ne ergo a memoria expellat Deum irruens turba plurimarum cogitationum, quae solent effluere tamquam vilis plebs in atrium, ponatur ad eius portam ianitor, cuius nomen est recordatio propriae professionis, ut, cum turpibus sese cogitationibus senserit animus praegravari, increpet se et dicat sibi: "Tune haec debes cogitare, qui sacerdos es, qui clericus es, qui monachus es? Cultor iustitiae debet in se huiusmodi quidquam admittere? Decet servum Christi, amatorem Dei, tale

In this discussion, Bernard describes the suggestion of immoral thoughts as akin to the flow of an intruding mob overwhelming the dwelling of the mind. When one senses or perceives (*sentire*) this cognitive intrusion—seemingly again by way of some kind of higher cognition or meta-cognition by means of which one passes judgment on the harmfulness of the thought "flow" (*fluxum*)—one might interrupt this flow of cognitive activity by the exercise of a focused recollection (*recordatio*).[51]

Bernard proposes having recourse to a similar practice if the flow of disruptive thinking moves past one's memory and begins to overtake one's will. Quoting Revelation 3:20, he next states that, just as a recollection is placed at the gate of memory, so too does a recollection serve as a guard at the gate of one's will:

> Similarly at the gate of the will, in which carnal desires are accustomed to lurk, a doorkeeper is placed like a domestic servant in one's home, a doorkeeper who is called "recollection of one's heavenly homeland." For he is able to expel immoral desire, as wedge drives out wedge. This doorkeeper can accept without hesitation him who says, *Behold, I stand at the gate and knock*.[52]

Bernard again suggests that a recollection serve as a guard at the gate of reason:

> Now, however, so excellent and so fierce a guardian must be employed at the bedroom of reason, a guardian who spares no one. Rather, should any enemy dare to enter secretly or openly, the guardian keeps it at a distance. And this guardian is "recollection of Gehenna."[53]

---

aliquid vel ad modicum meditari?" Haec dicendo, excludet fluxum illicitae cogitationis per recordationem propriae professionis."

51 While there are some similarities, it seems to me that this recollection differs from Freud's dream censor which works to separate consciousness from unconsciousness to the extent that what Bernard is describing is a conscious practice that one intentionally cultivates and not a defense process of which one is largely unaware. See, e.g., Sigmund Freud, *A General Introduction to Psychoanalysis* (New York: Horace Liveright, 1920), 113.

52 *Div*, 32.4 (CF 68:179–80; *SW* 9:462; *SBO* 6.1:221). "Similiter ad portam voluntatis, in qua solent manere carnalia desideria, tamquam in domo domestica familia, statuatur ostiarius, qui vocatur recordatio caelestis patriae. Hic enim potest pravum desiderium, quasi cuneus cuneum, expellere, et ipsum qui ait: 'Ecce sto ad ostium et pulso,' sine cunctatione recipere."

53 *Div*, 32.4 (CF 68:180; *SW* 9:462; *SBO* 6.1:221). "Iam vero ad thalamum rationis talis et tam ferox adhibendus est custos, qui nemini parcat, sed quicumque hostis, sive clam, sive palam ingredi praesumpserit, procul eum arceat; et hic sit recordatio gehennae."

The intruding flow of illicit and shameful thoughts that can overtake reason is, for Bernard, the most grievous concern:

> Among the first two, that is, memory and will, it is not so intolerable if at some time either the memory accepts a stray thought or the will accepts an impure affection. But this is most serious and utterly harmful: if ever the reason should lose uprightness of intention.[54]

Here again, Bernard emphasizes the importance of preserving the mental quality of rectitude (right intention) and he indicates that the mental quality of vigilance protects it. One might observe in this discussion that Bernard contrasts thought (*cogitatio*) and reason *(ratio*). He also refers to reason being invaded by defiling thoughts. The discussion indicates a differentiation of reason from thinking (just as Bernard differentiates memory from thinking). It would seem therefore that it is reason that enables the meta-cognition that would interrupt the flow of intrusive thinking.

In summary, at each gate of the mind, Bernard suggests placing a recollection (*recordatio*) to prevent an illicit thought from intruding more deeply: the recollection of one's profession or role as a servant of Christ stands at the gate of memory, the recollection of one's search for heaven stands at the gate of the will, and the recollection of one's desire to avoid hell stands at the gate of reason, this last recollection serving as a "fierce watchman" (*ferox custos*) over one's deepest interior domain and spiritual well-being. In a sense, in light of Bernard's description of corrupting thoughts as "rushing in" (*irruens*) and "flowing" (*effluere*), it follows that one's "positioning" of each recollection in this way serves as a kind of dam that blocks or arrests the disturbing stream of thought. One might infer then that these three recollections of the mind correlate with three degrees of vigilance, the last recollection protecting reason itself in order to avoid the mind becoming entirely overcome.

Elsewhere in a sermon in the *Sermones super cantica canticorum*, Bernard again briefly touches on vigilance as a quality of an undivided mind. Referring to the soul (*anima*), he states:

> By virtue of the single-minded devotion of watchfulness, the care and attention, the diligence and zeal with which she has ceaselessly and ardently studied to please God, she recognizes these attributes in him also

54 Ibid. "In ceteris siquidem, id est memoria et voluntate, non ita est intolerabile, si vel memoria recipiat quandoque vagam cogitationem, vel voluntas impuram affectionem: hoc vero gravissimum est et omnino damnosum, si umquam ratio perdiderit intentionis rectitudinem."

> . . . recalling his promise "with what measure you measure it shall be measured out to you in return."[55]

In this passage, Bernard describes the quality of vigilance with a variety of synonyms such as maintaining a singular intention and exercising concern, care, making an effort, being attentive and interested. Bernard also notes that when one has a religious experience of the divine Word, as discussed in Book V below, one will also recognize these same traits in Christ as well.

A further noteworthy passage on mental vigilance can be found in a sermon from Bernard's *De diversis* series. In sermon 16, he writes:

> Would that we had both more eager zeal and more vigilant care for our thoughts my brothers. For by our thoughts, I say, we regularly attend to the material of such holy meditation. You see, night and day, we read and sing for our edification the words of the prophets, the evangelists, and the apostles . . . So how do such vain, such harmful, such obscene thoughts come to us? Sometimes dirty and vainglorious thoughts, sometimes pride, ambition, and the rest of the passions agitate us so that we can scarcely ever take a rest in the serenity of holy thoughts. For good reason it is said that the souls who suffer in places of purification run through foul and muddy places because in this life they did not fear to inhabitat such places by their thoughts.[56]

What is noteworthy in this passage is not only Bernard's reiteration of the importance of taking custody of one's thoughts (self-appropriation), but also his metaphorical description of how one's thinking can occupy unhealthy states ("foul and muddy places"). In contrast, meditation on scripture ("the prophets, the evangelists, and the apostles") removes one's thinking from such "mental locations" and transitions one to a mental place where thought

55 *SCC*, 69, 3.7 (CF 40:34; *SW* 6:426; *SBO* 2:206). "De sua singulari intentione, sollicitudine, cura, opera, diligentia studioque, quo incessanter et ardenter invigilat, quemadmodum placeat Deo, aeque haec omnia in ipso indubitanter agnoscit, recordans promissionis eius: In qua mensura mensi fueritis, remetietur vobis."

56 *Div*, 16.1 (CF 68:87; *SW* 9:308; *SBO* 6.1:144). "Et propensius stadium, et cura vigilantior nostris esset cogitationibus adhibenda, fratres mei: nostris, inquam, quibus tam sanctarum meditationum assidue materia ministratur. Nocte enim et die nobis propheticae et evangelicae, sed et apostolicae voces canuntur et leguntur . . . Unde ergo nobis tam vanae, tam noxiae, tam obscenae cogitationes, quae nunc immunditia et elatione, nunc superbia et ambitione ceterisque passionibus contorquent nos, ut vix aliquando in serenitatem sanctarum cogitatuum respiremus? Non immerito animae illae, quae in locis purgatoriis patiuntur, per loca caenosa et lutosa dicuntur discurrere, quandoquidem nunc eadem loca suis cogitationibus inhabitare non metuunt."

abides in serenity (*in serenitatem*). Bernard's comments indicate that this transition involves a certain process of purification that one undergoes in the afterlife if not in this life.

With respect to the remaining mental qualities that Bernard discusses in Book IV of *De consideratione* (being firm, unconquered, and broad), it would not be unreasonable to associate what Bernard means by the mental quality of firmness (*firmus*) with the emphasis given to stability found in the Benedictine Rule: when a new novice is received into the monastic community, he is kept apart for a time where, after making an initial promise of "perseverance in his stability,"[57] he later "comes before the whole community in the oratory and promises stability, fidelity to the monastic life, and obedience."[58] The topic of stability reappears in Bernard's work *Liber de praecepto et dispensatione*: there, he describes some precepts of the Rule as having stability even if admitting of occasional exceptions according to the needs of charity; in contrast, there are other exceptionless precepts from which only God can grant a dispensation (such as the precepts of the Decalogue), as well as other absolutely incommutable precepts from which there is no dispensation (such as seeking growth in charity and humility).[59] Stability in this sense thus pertains to the enduring character of a teaching or precept, depending on its level.[60] It is not unreasonable to interpret Bernard as suggesting that the mental quality of firmness has a similar nature.

Regarding the remaining mental qualities that Bernard mentions, he also indicates that it is desirable for the pope's mind to remain unconquered or undefeated (*invictus*). This might be interpreted in the sense of one's mind not being overwhelmed by adversity, abiding in an attitude of hope or optimism. Or it might mean that Eugene III is not subjected to anything that would compromise his mind's freedom and nobility—that he would be able to maintain self-appropriation and self-regulation. If so, the mental quality of remaining unconquered would connect with the final mental quality that involves not becoming overwhelmed by adversity: Bernard states that Eugene III's mind must be broad (*amplus*) so to withstand loss. Recall Bernard's statement quoted above that "a mind stretched in many directions must be

57 *RB*, chap. 58 (McCann, 130–31; Fry, 56). "Si promiserit de stabilitate sua perseverantiam, post duorum mensium circulum legatur ei haec regula per ordinem." The translation above is by Fry.

58 Ibid. "Suscipiendus autem in oratorio coram omnibus promittat de stabilitate sua et conversatione morum suorum, et obedientiam." The translation above is by Fry.

59 *Pre*, 2.4–2.5 (CF 1:108–9; *SW* 1:352–54; *SBO* 3:256–57).

60 Bernard proceeds to describe how an abbot who can dispense from the Rule is not thereby to be understood as above the Rule and that obedience to human authority has limitations. See *Pre*, 4.9–5.11 (CF 1:111–13; *SW* 1:358–62; *SBO* 3:259–61).

torn by many cares."[61] In light of this remark, one might interpret the ninth mental quality of broadness (*amplus*) as describing a mind that is flexible, elastic, or exhibiting resilience.

At the close of this passage on mental qualities, Bernard remarks to Eugene III: "Do not doubt that you must be deprived of all these goods and afflicted with evils if you divide your attention and wish to devote it equally to the things of God and to your trivial affairs."[62] In other words, if the pope's mind is divided (*animum dividens*) by attempting to focus equally on divine matters (*Dei rebus*) and on his household affairs (*tuis reculis*), then the pope's mind will subsequently lack these desirable traits and be stricken with evils (*feriendum malis*). Such mental qualities thus might be described as the characteristics of an undivided mind (*animus individuus*). To summarize the nine qualities of an undivided mind, Bernard states that through the practice of meditation one might develop one's mind to be empty of minor concerns, free from impositions and coercions, noble in its attachment, right in intention, cautious when doubting, vigilant in custody of thoughts, firm (stable), unconquered (hopeful), and broad (resilient). If focusing on divine matters facilitates one's mind in developing these mental characteristics, then the implication is that such qualities might emerge through the practice of theological meditation. It is to this topic that the discussion now turns.

61 *Csi*, II, Ch. 10.19 (CF 37:73; *SW* 1:694; *SBO* 3:427). "Similiter animus distentus in multa, multis laceretur curis necesse est. Nempe immoderata extensio extenuationem, et extenuatio nimia scissionem facit."

62 *Csi*, IV, 6.18 (CF 37:131; *SW* 1:764; *SBO* 3:462). "His te non dubites et bonis privandum, et feriendum malis, si animum dividens, et Dei rebus, et tuis pariter reculis volueris impertiri."

8

Book V

Meditative Reflection on What Is Above One

Bernard has described several stages of suggested meditation in the previous books of *De consideratione* (meditation on self, meditation on relationships below one and around one) and now arrives at the final stage of reflection, meditation on relationship with God. Bernard provides an overview of this final and most complex stage of meditation in Book V. In what follows, I focus on topics of interest as they arise in Bernard's text. These topics include an exploration of the nature of theological meditation and how it may be characterized as an ascent of the mind that can be represented by the biblical symbol of Jacob's ladder. Bernard describes this ascent as involving three steps: practical theological meditation, investigative theological meditation, and contemplative theological meditation. Bernard recommends that an act of self-recollection and an evaluation of one's theological beliefs precede this last and highest meditation. Contemplative theological meditation is so named because it serves to transition a person to contemplation as such, where one becomes focused not on beliefs but attentive to God's presence, focusing on personal experience involving spiritual affect and prayer.

Theological Meditation in General

At the beginning of Book V, Bernard observes that the previous books described not meditation as such, but rather meditation as ordered to action; now he states that he will focus on a kind of meditation that proceeds by way of inspection (*inspectio*) alone.[1] More specifically, one's reflection at this

1 *Csi*, V, 1.1 (CF 37:139; *SW* 1:774; *SBO* 3:467). "Quae enim supra sunt,—id quidem instat—, actu non indigent, sed inspectu."

point becomes inherently spiritual—oriented toward the self apart from bodily sensation and then oriented toward angels and God.[2] One's meditation on spiritual realities does not involve exterior action: "There is no way in which you can act upon those things which always exist in the same way and which will be the same for all eternity (some of these have even been the same from all eternity)."[3] William of St. Thierry describes Bernard's personal practice of theological meditation in this regard: "He was totally absorbed in the spirit; his thoughts were often completely directed toward God, as were his spiritual meditations, and his mind was totally occupied with God."[4] The author of a selection in Book II of the *Vita prima* also describes Bernard's teaching in Book V of *De consideratione*: "In those things that are above human thoughts, [Bernard] gave attention to heavenly matters, not in the way that the angels contemplate, those who always adhere to God, but in the way that a man with a pure heart and mind may conform the temporal priesthood to the celestial hierarchy."[5]

Meditative Ascent (Jacob's Ladder)

Regarding spiritual meditation, Bernard writes: "To consider in this way is to return to one's homeland,"[6] that is, to seek the Jerusalem that is above (Gal 4:26).[7] The return to one's homeland, Bernard observes, typically will proceed by way of a meditative ascent: "Clearly, exiles, not citizens, need this ladder [*scala*]."[8] Here, Bernard returns to the metaphor of Jacob's ladder, the *scala* discussed above with respect to Benedict (the ladder of humility),[9]

2 See also Alberich Martin Altermatt, "Bernhard von Clairvaux: Sein Gottesbild im 5. Buch des Traktates '*De consideratione,*'" *Cistercienser Chronik* 77 (1970): 101–23.

3 *Csi*, V, 1.1 (CF 37:139; *SW* 1:774; *SBO* 3:467). "Non est quod is eis actites, quae uno modo semper sunt, et in aeternum; porro aliqua et ab aeterno."

4 William of St. Thierry, *VP*, I, 20 (CF 76:23). Casey urges that Bernard's preoccupation should not be interpreted to indicate his lack of awareness of his physical surroundings. See Michael Casey, "Bernard the Observer," in *Goad and Nail: Studies in Medieval Cistercian History X,* ed. E. Rozanne Elder (Kalamazoo, MI: Cistercian Publications, 1985), 1–20, at 8.

5 See Arnold of Bonneval, *VP*, II, 51 (CF 76:137). The reference here to a celestial hierarchy is evocative of the work of the same title by Pseudo-Dionysius. See Pseudo-Dionysius, *The Celestial Hierarchy*, in *The Complete Works*, trans. Colm Luibheid (New York: Paulist Press, 1987), 143–91.

6 *Csi*, V, 1.1 (CF 37:139–40; *SW* 1:774; *SBO* 3:467). "Sic considerare, repatriare est."

7 *Csi*, V, 4.7 (CF 37:146; *SW* 1:782; *SBO* 3:471). "Age iam dirigatur consideratio in eam quae sursum est Ierusalem, mater nostra."

8 *Csi*, V, 1.1 (CF 37:140; *SW* 1:774; *SBO* 3:467). "Sane hac scala cives non egent, sed exsules."

9 *RB*, chap. 7 (McCann, 38–39; Fry, 16).

Gregory the Great (*scala considerationis*),[10] as well as John Climacus (the ladder of virtue).[11]

With respect to the nature of this ladder, Bernard indicates that philosophy has a role in helping one discern the steps that one might ascend:

> He is great who is satisfied to use the senses as if they were the wealth of those citizens and to employ them for his own salvation and that of others. And he is no less great who uses philosophy to establish the senses as a step [*gradum*] toward invisible things. The latter is more pleasant, the former more beneficial; the latter more delightful, the former more courageous.[12]

In this passage, Bernard contrasts use of the senses with use of philosophy. By using philosophy, one is able to re-envision the experience of sensation as belonging to a series of steps whereby one might ascend toward spiritual (invisible) realities. Bernard used similar language in his *Liber de gradibus humilitatis et superbiae* to describe growth in humility as ascent according to steps (adopting Benedict's teaching of the grades of humility found in the Rule, mentioned above).[13] While it may be self-evident, Bernard takes time to point out in *De consideratione* that to ascend spiritually in meditation does not entail a physical ascent that proceeds by moving toward the heavenly bodies (although, considered in relation to God, the beauty of the cosmos might serve as a topic for spiritual meditation).[14]

What kind of ascent might occur during meditation? Bellarmine comments on this topic. Citing Ephesians 3:18 (where the Apostle Paul refers to the dimensions of breadth, length, height, and depth), Bellarmine writes:

> Certainly that outstanding contemplative, Saint Bernard, made himself a ladder for understanding God from these dimensions in the book *On Consideration*, which he wrote for Pope Eugenius. He was not the inventor of

10 *Mo*, XV, 46.52 (CS 258:242; PL 75:1107c).

11 John of Climacus, *Ladder of Divine Ascent*, step 9, in Luibheid and Russell, 152.

12 *Csi*, V, 2.3 (CF 37:142; *SW* 1:776; *SBO* 3:468). "Magnus ille, qui usum sensuum, quasdam veluti civium opes, expendere satagit, dispensando in suam et multorum salutem. Nec ille minor, qui hunc sibi gradum ad illa invisibilia philosophando constituit." See also Sommerfeldt, *Life of the Mind*, 73 and 101.

13 *RB*, chap. 7 (McCann, 48–49; Fry, 20). Citing 1 Jn 4:18, Benedict writes: "Now, therefore, after ascending all these steps of humility, the monk will quickly arrive at that *perfect love* of God which *casts out fear*" (*Ergo his omnibus humilitatis gradibus ascensis, monachus mox ad caritatem Dei perveniet illam quae "perfecta foris mittit timorem")*.

14 *Csi*, V, 3.5 (CF 37:144; *SW* 1:780; *SBO* 3:470).

> this kind of ladder, but rather learned this way of ascent from the Apostle, who penetrated to the third heaven and to paradise.[15]

In his theological meditations in Book V, Bernard employs the thematic structure of these four dimensions from Ephesians 3:18 that Bellarmine describes.[16] However, for Bernard, Paul exemplifies someone who is able to bypass the ladder of meditation altogether. Bernard writes:

> But he is greatest of all, who, scorning the use of sensible objects insofar as is possible to human frailty, has accustomed himself occasionally to soar in contemplation to the sublime, not by gradual steps [*non ascensoriis gradibus*] but by sudden ecstasies [*excessibus*].[17]

Citing 2 Corinthians 5:13 and 12:2 in relation to this comment, Bernard shortly thereafter states more explicitly that the Apostle Paul is someone who proceeded by "ecstasies, not ascents [*excessus, non ascensus*]."[18] According to Gilson, Bernard's Latin phrasing for "ecstasy of the mind" (*excessus*) as exemplified in this passage derives from his reception of Eriugena's Latin translation of an *Ambiguum* of Maximus the Confessor.[19]

The experience of contemplative ecstasy, Bernard states in his early *Liber de gradibus humilitatis et superbiae* (1124), is advanced; it pertains to an experience of truth after humble self-evaluation and growth in compassion.[20] As such, the "self-intuition in the clear light of truth" (*se intuens clara luce veritatis*) that might lead one to a foundation of humility is an intuition that likely would occur prior to the experience of contemplative ecstasy.[21] In fact, Bernard observes a few years later in his *Liber de gratia et libero arbitrio* (ca. 1128) that the kind of ecstatic experience under consideration is rare:

15 Bellarmine, *The Mind's Ascent to God* 10.1 (Donnelly and Teske, 154).

16 See also Leclercq, "L'Art de la Composition," 128–29.

17 *Csi*, V, 2.3 (CF 37:142; *SW* 1:776–77; *SBO* 3:468–69). "At omnium maximus, qui, spreto ipso usu rerum et sensuum, quantum quidem humanae fragilitate fas est, non ascensoriis gradibus, sed inopinatis excessibus, avolare interdum contemplando ad illa sublimia consuevit."

18 *Csi*, V, 2.3 (CF 37:142; *SW* 1:778; *SBO* 3:469).

19 CS 120:26. For Maximus, see the second ambiguum to John: Maximos the Confessor, Ambiguum 7, in *On Difficulties in the Church Fathers, The Ambigua, Vol. 1*, trans. Nicholas Constas (Cambridge, MA: Harvard University Press, 2014), 75–141, at 86–87. If an intellectual being "loves, it certainly suffers an ecstasy toward [what it loves] as an object of love." See also Evans, *Bernard of Clairvaux*, 54–55.

20 *Hum*, 6.19 (CF 13a:47, *SW* 2:74; *SBO* 3:31).

21 *SCC*, 36, 4.5 (CF 7:177–78; *SW* 5:568; *SBO* 2:7).

> But what of those who, at times, being caught up in the Spirit through [the ecstasy] of contemplation [*per excessum contemplationis*], become capable of savoring something of the sweetness of heavenly bliss? Do these attain to freedom from sorrow as often as this happens to them? Yes, indeed. Even in this present life, those who with Mary have chosen the better part . . . enjoy freedom of pleasure; rarely, however, and fleetingly . . . on this earth, contemplatives alone can in some way enjoy freedom of pleasure, though only in part, in very small part, and on the rarest of occasions.[22]

Despite the perceived rarity of contemplative ecstasy, Bernard indicates in his *Sermones super cantica canticorum* that he personally seeks such an experience of rapture:

> But, if I may say so, let me die the death of angels that, transcending the memory of things present, I may cast off not only the desire for [things that] are corporeal and inferior but even their images, that I may enjoy pure conversation [*pura . . . conversatio*] with those who bear the likeness of purity. This kind of ecstasy, in my opinion, is alone or principally called contemplation [*Talis, ut opinor, excessus, aut tantum, aut maxime, contemplatio dicitur*].[23]

Sommerfeldt seems correct to emphasize that for Bernard the experience of contemplative ecstasy in this regard is understood as a kind of special gift from God.[24] Bernard discloses in this same sermon series that he has at times experienced this rare gift:

> There is a place where God is seen in tranquil rest, where he is neither Judge nor Teacher but Bridegroom. To me—for I do not speak for others—this is

22 *Gra*, 5.15 (CF 19a:71; *SW* 1:196; *SBO* 3:177). "An tamen fatendum est eos, qui per excessum contemplationis rapti quandoque in Spiritu, quantulumcumque de supernae felicitatis dulcedine degustare sufficiunt, toties esse liberos a miseria, quoties sic excedunt? Hi plane, quod negandum non est, etiam in hac carne, raro licet raptimque, complaciti libertate fruuntur, qui cum Maria optimam partem elegerunt . . . in hac vita soli contemplativi possunt utcumque frui libertate complaciti, et hoc ex parte, et parte satis modica, viceque rarissima." Regarding the rarity of ecstatic contemplation in Bernard, also see Gastaldelli, "Teologia Monastica," 62; Farkasfalvy, "Bernard's Concept," 5n6; Sommerfeldt, *Life of the Mind*, 73; Sommerfeldt, "Bernard as Contemplative," 76; CS 7:262; Leclercq, "General Introduction (III)," 384.

23 *SCC*, 52, 2.5–3.5 (CF 31:53; *SW* 6:198–200; *SBO* 3:92–93). See also CS 120:240–41n213.

24 Sommerfeldt, *Life of the Mind*, 26.

> truly the bedroom to which I have sometimes gained happy entrance. Alas! how rare the time, and how short the stay![25]

Later, in a different section of this sermon series, Bernard elaborates more on his personal experiences of the divine Word stating that while these experiences are rare, they have also been many:

> I want to tell you of my own experience, as I promised . . . I admit that the Word has also come to me—and has come many times. But although he has come to me, I have never been conscious of the moment of his coming. I perceive his presence, I remembered afterwards that he had been with me; sometimes I had a presentiment that he would come, but I was never conscious of his coming or his going. And where he comes from when he visits my soul, and where he goes, and by what means he enters and goes out, I admit that I do not know even now.[26]

Bernard proceeds to describe the nature of these experiences at length and in intimate detail.[27] Later in the same sermon series, Bernard again states that such experiences are rare:

> But notice that in spiritual marriage there are two kinds of birth, and thus kinds of offspring, though not opposite. For spiritual persons, like holy mothers, may bring souls to birth by preaching, or may give birth to spiritual insights by meditation [*meditando, intelligentias pariunt spirituales*]. In this latter kind of birth the soul leaves even its bodily senses and is separated from them, so that in her awareness of the Word she is not aware of herself. This happens when the mind is enraptured [*mens . . . rapitur*] by the unutterable sweetness of the Word, so that it withdraws, or rather is transported, and escapes from itself to enjoy the Word . . . But when does

25 *SCC*, 23, 6.15 (CF 7:38; *SW* 5:344; *SBO* 1:148). "Sed est locus ubi vere quiescens et quietus cernitur Deus: locus omnino, non iudicis, non magistri, sed sponsi, et qui mihi quidem,—nam de aliis nescio—, plane cubiculum sit, si quando in illum contigerit introduci. Sed, heu! rara hora et parva mora!"

26 *SCC*, 74, 2.5 (CF 40:89–90; *SW* 6:498; *SBO* 2:242). "Volo dicere, nam et hoc pactus sum, quomodo mecum agitur in eiusmodi . . . Fateor et mihi adventasse Verbum,—in insipientia dico—, et pluries. Cumque saepius intraverit ad me, non sensi aliquoties cum intravit. Adesse sensi, affuisse recordor; interdum et praesentire potui introitum eius, sentire numquam, sed ne exitum quidem. Nam unde in animam meam venerit, quove abierit denuo eam dimittens, sed et qua introierit vel exierit, etiam nunc ignorare me fateor."

27 *SCC*, 74, 2.6 (CF 40:91–92; *SW* 6:500; *SBO* 2:243).

> this happen, and for how long? It is sweet intercourse, but lasts a short time and is experienced rarely![28]

While in this passage Bernard does not explicitly refer to experience of the divine Word as a kind of ecstatic contemplation (*excessus*)—he refers to it instead as emerging out of the context of meditation—he does state that one's mind (*mens*) can become withdrawn from the bodily senses (*seceditur . . . a corporeis sensibus*) in such a way that entails a kind of ecstasy. This is evident in his reference to the mind's experience of being seized (*raptus*) or in a state of rapture, as well as in his reference to the mind sensing and being focused entirely upon the Word rather than upon itself (*sese non sentiat quae Verbum sentit*).[29] The *sensus Verbum* so described thus seems equivalent to a kind of contemplative ecstasy (*excessus*). This kind of union of the mind with the Word subsequently generates a spiritual insight or understanding (*intelligentias pariunt spirituales*). In this respect, analogous to a preacher, a contemplative is like a holy mother (*sancta matre*).

Overall, despite the one passage referring to frequent encounters with the divine Word, the majority of Bernard's texts refer to the experience of contemplative ecstasy as rare. And all the texts indicate the experience entails brevity. Further, due to the transitory nature of the ecstatic contemplative experience, one must differentiate it from the soul's eschatological fulfillment, namely, receipt of the beatific vision (the blessedness of knowing God in a manner that is not transitory but that endures). With respect to this vision, Bernard writes in *De diligendo Deo*: "The vision of God which makes us resemble him [*Dei et deifica visio*], and its incalculable delight are rightly figured by the right hand [of God]."[30] The resemblance that Bernard

28 *SCC*, 85, 4.13 (CF 40:209–10; *SW* 6:644–45; *SBO* 2:315–16). "Sed attende in spirituali matrimonio duo esse genera pariendi, et ex hoc etiam diversas soboles, sed non adversas, cum sanctae matres aut praedicando, animas, aut meditando, intelligentias pariunt spirituales. In hoc ultimo genere interdum exceditur et seceditur etiam a corporeis sensibus, ut sese non sentiat quae Verbum sentit. Hoc fit, cum mens ineffabili Verbi illecta dulcedine, quodammodo se sibi furatur, immo rapitur atque elabitur a seipsa, ut Verbo fruatur . . . At quando hoc, aut quamdiu hoc? Dulce commercium, sed breve momentum et experimentum rarum!"

29 Because the mind in sensing and knowing the divine Word consequently gives birth to "understandings" (*intelligentias*), Bernard's spirituality arguably cannot be described as *voluntarist*. See also Leclercq, "General Introduction (III)," 381. However, as clear above in Bernard's discussion of a person joining with God in a common will of love (and also below in relation to his teaching on compunction), Bernard's spirituality clearly involves the integration of affect, as well as striving to experience a divine peace that transcends all understanding.

30 *Dil*, 4.12 (CF 13b:15; *SW* 1:94; *SBO* 3:129). "Merito illa Dei et deifica visio, illa divinae praesentiae inaestimabilis delectatio in dextera deputatur." See Sommerfeldt, "Bernard as Contemplative," 76 and 82.

mentions in this remark involves, as he states elsewhere in a sermon from his *Sermones super cantica canticorum*, the culmination of a process where the soul that beholds God is a soul that in some sense has fully transformed into an image of God: "when the soul can once perceive the glory of God without a veil, it is compelled by some affinity of nature to be conformed to it, and be transformed to its very image."[31] In this sense, the beatific vision constitutes the goal of the soul's contemplation to which meditation, supported by God's grace and led by the Holy Spirit, ultimately leads. Receipt of this vision requires that one recover and preserve the natural purity of the human heart (see also Mt 5:8).[32]

These various observations concerning contemplative ecstasy, mystical experience of the divine Word, and the vision of God, all provide a context for interpreting how the "consideration of what is above one" in meditation might involve the "use of philosophy." Intellectual ascent in meditation typically proceeds in a way that is in between sensuality (use of the senses in orientation to salvation) and ecstatic contemplation. However, Bernard also indicates that there might be an approach to meditation that integrates (1) use of the senses, (2) use of philosophy, and (3) seeking ecstatic contemplation as a divine gift. On this point, he writes:

> Moreover, these three occur together when consideration, even in the place of its exile, is strengthened by the efforts of virtue and the assistance of grace and either restrains sensuality so it does not grow haughty, or constrains it so it does not stray, or flees it so it cannot corrupt.[33]

Oriented toward contemplative ecstasy, the course of meditation can be described as proceeding by way of metaphorical steps. Déchanet points to a correlation here between Bernard and the ascent of Platonic dialectic toward philosophical contemplation (*theōria*).[34] Dresser also describes Bernard's hierarchical thought as that of "a metaphysician in the platonic tradition,"

31 *SCC*, 69, 3.7 (CF 40:34; *SW* 6:426; *SBO* 2:206). "Nescio enim qua vicinitate naturae, cum semel revelata facie gloriam Dei speculari anima poterit, mox illi se conformari necesse est, atque in eamdem imaginem transformari." See also Stepsis, "Fulfillment of Self," 359–60.

32 *Div*, 16.2 (CF 68:89; *SW* 9:310; *SBO* 6.1:145). "Sicut autem corporis natura est sanitas, ita cordis natura est puritas, quia turbato oculo non videbitur Deus, et cor humanum ad hoc factum est, ut suum videat Creatorem. Si vero sanitati corporis sollicita est providenda custodia, puritati cordis tanto est sollicitior impendenda."

33 *Csi*, V, 2.3 (CF 37:142; *SW* 1:778; *SBO* 3:469). "Porro haec tria ita contingunt, cum consideratio, etsi in loco peregrinationis suae, virtutis studio et adiutorio gratiae facta superior, sensualitatem aut premit ne insolescat, aut cogit ne evagetur, aut fugit ne inquinet."

34 Déchanet, "Aux Sources," 62.

yet not in the sense that Bernard is a "crypto-pantheist or emanationist."[35] Sommerfeldt, however, is more reserve in his interpretation of Bernard as a hierarchical thinker.[36]

What more can be said about the general hierarchical nature of Bernard's account of meditation at this point? As mentioned earlier, a possible proximate influence on Bernard in this respect is Hildemar's description of three grades of consideration (where Hildemar encourages a monk to ascend in meditation from reflection on his soul to reflection on angels and then God).[37] Meditative ascent for Hildemar may be associated with reference to a cosmological and ontological hierarchy also found, as noted above, in the work of Augustine,[38] as well as in works by Gregory the Great—such as the *Moralibus*[39] and his homilies on Ezekiel.[40]

For all of these thinkers, God as Creator transcends the entire hierarchy of creatures; God, as Bernard notes when quoting Romans 11:36 in a sermon in his *Sermones super cantica canticorum*, is causally above and beyond the being (*esse*) of all created things:

35 Robert M. Dresser, "Gradation: Rhetoric and Substance in Saint Bernard," in *Goad and Nail*, 71–85, at 76.

36 Sommerfeldt rejects interpreting Bernard to affirm a social hierarchy (lay, cleric, and monk) associated with an epistemological hierarchy (Sommerfeldt, *Life of the Mind*, 72–74). In these remarks, Sommerfeldt is critiquing his own interpretation of Bernard as found in an earlier essay (Sommerfeldt, "Epistemological and Social Hierarchies," 83–92). In that earlier essay, Sommerfeldt described a hierarchy of epistemological orientations as particular "methods appropriate to the various states of life: contemplation for the monk, reason for the cleric, and a sort of common-sense training and method for the lay man" (Sommerfeldt, "Epistemological and Social Hierarchies," 85). What Sommerfeldt seems to be rejecting therefore is that Bernard affirms a hierarchy of methods of knowledge associated with a hierarchy of social positions. This does not affect my interpretation that Bernard teaches that a monk might proceed in meditation by way of a hierarchy—that is, by ascending psychological steps (*ascensoriis gradibus*) that philosophy helps one posit in between one's use of the senses and the rare experience of contemplative ecstasy. Sommerfeldt also recognizes a kind of hierarchy of knowledge for Bernard in relation to faith, special charisms, and ecstatic contemplation. See Sommerfeldt, "Afterword: Looking Back at Bernard," 370, citing *Life of the Mind*, 12–17, 17–22, 22–29, for each respective category of knowledge.

37 Hildemar, *Expositio regulae*, Cap. IV (Mittermüller, 168–69); Warnefridi, *In regulam commentarium* (108–9).

38 See Augustine, *City of God* VIII.6 (Dyson, 320–21), quoted above.

39 *Mo*, V.31.54 and 34.62, trans. Brian Kerns (Collegeville, MN: Cistercian Publications, 2014), 353–54 and 360–61 (hereafter CS 249), as cited in Bernard McGinn, "Contemplation in Gregory the Great," in *Gregory the Great: A Symposium*, ed. John C. Cavadini (Notre Dame, IN: University of Notre Dame Press, 1995), 146–67, at 149.

40 See especially *Hiez*, II, 5.8–5.9 (Tomkinson, 339–40; SC 360:240–44).

> For what is more intimate to anything than its own being [*esse*]? And yet, what is more incomprehensible to any of us than the being of all things [*esse omnium*]? Of course when I say God is the being of all things, I do not wish it to be understood in the sense that he and they are identical, but rather in the sense of the words of Scripture: "All that exists comes from him, all is by him and in him." He is the creator, the efficient cause, not the material of every creature.[41]

One might note in relation to this passage that Bernard infrequently describes God in terms of ontological causation using language that is evocative of Aristotle (e.g., "God is the reason for loving God . . . he is the efficient and final cause of our love"[42]). Bernard's language when describing ascent to God is customarily more biblical, while also exhorting one to leave behind sensation and imagination.

Bernard describes the process of ascent as repatriation, returning to one's homeland. He writes:

> This will be a returning home [*repatriasse*]: to have left the land of the body for the region of the spirit, which is our God, the Supreme Spirit, the most sublime dwelling [*mansio*] of blessed spirits. Let the bodily sense, the imagination, not usurp for itself anything here, for here is Truth, here is Wisdom, Virtue, Eternity, the Supreme Good. For the time being we are absent from this place and where we are is a valley, a valley of tears, in which sensuality rules and consideration is in exile.[43]

41 *SCC*, 4, 3.4 (CF 4:21–24, at 24; *SW* 5:84–91, at 88; *SBO* 1:18–21, at 20). "Quid nempe cuique rei praesentius quam esse suum? Quid cuique tamen incomprehensibilius quam esse omnium? Sane esse Deum omnium dixerim, non quia illa sunt quod est ille, sed quia Ex Ipso Et Per Ipsum Et In Ipso Sunt Omnia. Esse est ergo omnium quae facta sunt, ipse factor eorum, sed causale, non materiale." See also Sommerfeldt, *Life of the Mind*, 102.

42 *Dil*, 7.22 (CF 13b:24; *SW* 1:110; *SBO* 3:137). "Causa diligendi Deum, Deus est. Verum dixi, nam et efficiens, et finalis."

43 *Csi*, V, 1.2 (CF 37:141; *SW* 1:776; *SBO* 3:468). "Repatriasse erit hoc, exisse de patria corporum in regionem spirituum. Ipsa est Deus noster, maximus spiritus, maxima mansio spirituum beatorum, et, ne quid hic sibi usurpet carnis sensus seu imaginatio, veritas est, sapientia est, virtus, aeternitas, summum bonum. Unde interim absumus, et ubi sumus, vallis est, et vallis lacrimarum, in qua sensualitas regnat et consideratio exsulat."

Bernard's reference to returning to one's homeland (*patria*) correlates with his description elsewhere of one's soul existing in a state that is distant from God, in a region of dissimilitude.[44]

Can one's soul in exile be understood as having undergone a kind of diaspora, becoming dispersed among a multiplicity of sensations, imaginations, and desires? Could this dispersion of one's attention be understood as a fall or descent? Bernard indicates that when one's mind wanders away from God in this way, one will give primary attention to visible things as sources of knowledge and focus on practical affairs; but if one turns one's mind back to God, then one's mind "does not go into exile."[45] Bernard's account is evocative of a psychological interpretation of the Fall as found in the works of Athanasius and Augustine as mentioned previously (the latter carefully warning that such a spiritual interpretation should not be taken to replace the literal historical sense of the biblical narrative).[46]

The First Two Steps of the Ladder: Practical and Investigative Theology

What are the steps of meditation whereby one might return from exile and set out on an ascent toward God? Proceeding forward with the discussion of Book V, Bernard describes three degrees of spiritual meditation: practical, investigative, and speculative.[47] Ivánka makes the interesting proposal that these three degrees might relate in some way to the tripartite capacities of the soul (will, memory, and reason).[48] Hierarchical ascent understood in this way is not primarily cosmological and ontological, but rather psychological (ascent involves focusing on different psychological capacities being exercised): one moves beyond sensation and imagination,[49] focusing first on the exercise of the will with respect to practical pursuits, then on memory

44 *SCC*, 36, 4.5 (CF 7:177–78; *SW* 5:568; *SBO* 2:7), as quoted earlier.

45 *Csi*, V, 1.1 (CF 37:139; *SW* 1:774; *SBO* 3:467). See also *Div*, 12.2 (CF 68:71–72; *SW* 9:276; *SBO* 6.1:128).

46 For Athansius, see Athanasius, *Contra gentes* 3–4, in *"Contra Gentes" and "De Incarnatione,"* trans. Robert W. Thomson (Oxford: Oxford University Press, 1971), 8–13. For Augustine, see his *The Trinity* XII.8.13–12.19 (McKenna, 355–61).

47 *Csi*, V, 2.4 (CF 37:142; *SW* 1:778; *SBO* 3:469). "Dicamus, si placet, primam dispensativam, secundum aestimativam, tertiam speculativam." See also Evans, *Bernard of Clairvaux*, 54; Leclercq, "L'Art de la Composition," 126.

48 Ivánka, "La structure," 205.

49 See *Csi*, V, 1.2 (CF 37:141; *SW* 1:776; *SBO* 3:468), quoted just above.

with respect to theological investigation, and lastly on reason with respect to theological contemplation.

According to Bernard, one's meditation is practical (*dispensativam*) when one discerns how to use the bodily senses and objects of sensation "in an orderly and unified manner to win God's favor."[50] This kind of meditation seems to be practiced by one who, as quoted above, "is satisfied to use the senses . . . and to employ them for his own salvation and that of others."[51] As Michel observes, Bernard's focus here is on the use of material goods.[52] This step of meditation particularly concerns evaluating one's use of created things in relation to God. Additionally, recall Bernard's statement that "it is not nature but practice [*usus*] which produces virtues."[53] Insofar as meditation at this degree is focused on use or exercise, such a meditation might arguably return to a focus on one's use of virtues in relation to God. If this is so, it seems noteworthy that in a sermon from the *De diversis* series (quoted above) Bernard indicates that for some persons, meditation will remain at this step: "If you cannot fix your eye of meditation on that height of eternal goods because they are distant and surpass all understanding, then turn your vision to the good things of grace that are in the exercise of virtue."[54]

With respect to the next step of theological meditation (the investigative step), recall Bernard's statement that theological meditation might employ philosophy: "And he is no less great who uses philosophy to establish the senses as a step [*gradum*] toward invisible things."[55] The use of philosophy in meditation, Bernard teaches, is investigative (*aestimativam*) when, using prudence and diligence, one "scrutinizes and ponders everything to discover God" (*quaeque scrutans et ponderans ad vestigandum Deum*).[56] Bernard

50 *Csi*, V, 2.4 (CF 37:142–43; *SW* 1:778; *SBO* 3:469). "Dispensativa est consideratio sensibus sensibilibusque rebus ordinate et socialiter utens ad promerendum Deum." See also Déchanet, "Aux Sources," 63.

51 *Csi*, V, 2.3 (CF 37:141–42; *SW* 1:776; *SBO* 3:468). "Magnus ille, qui usum sensuum, quasdam veluti civium opes, expendere satagit, dispensando in suam et multorum salutem." See also Sommerfeldt, *Life of the Mind*, 73 and 101.

52 Michel, "La considération," 116.

53 *Csi*, II, 11.20 (CF 37:74; *SW* 1:696; *SBO* 3:428). "Nempe eiusmodi non natura virtutes, sed usus facit."

54 *Div*, 16.1 (CF 68:88; *SW* 9:308; *SBO* 6.1:144). "Si non potes oculum meditationis in illam sublimitatem aeternalium bonorum infigere, quia stantia sunt et omnem sensum exsuperant, in bonis gratiae, quae sunt in exercitio virtutum, visum reflecte."

55 *Csi*, V, 2.3 (CF 37:142; *SW* 1:776; *SBO* 3:468). "Nec ille minor, qui hunc sibi gradum ad illa invisibilia philosophando constituit." See also Sommerfeldt, *Life of the Mind*, 73 and 101.

56 *Csi*, V, 2.4 (CF 37:143; *SW* 1:778; *SBO* 3:469). "Aestimativa est consideratio prudenter ac diligenter quaeque scrutans et ponderans ad vestigandum Deum." See also Déchanet, "Aux Sources," 63.

writes in *De diligendo Deo* that generally speaking, in the exercise of one's estimation, one might come to desire some benefit that one discerns in a matter being investigated: "Every rational being naturally desires always what satisfies more its mind and will [*aestimatione atque intentione*]. It is never satisfied with something which lacks the qualities it thinks it should have."[57] Because this investigation into created benefits occurs within the context of a theological meditation, one might, following the suggestion of scripture, associate the desirable qualities that one observes in created things in some way with God.[58]

Emphasis should be given to the theological orientation of an investigative consideration. Bernard calls attention to the spiritual disorder that arises when a person seeks knowledge for its own sake, through inquisitiveness or curiosity.[59] He hints at this concern also at the beginning of Book V when he observes that preoccupation with visible things solely for their practical application (*usus*) or for the knowledge (*notitia*) that they might provide risks embarking upon a wandering journey (*peregrinatio*) into exile if one does not orient such sensual interests back toward spiritual realities:

> I would wish, most wise Eugene, that you be intelligent enough to realize that your consideration wanders whenever it turns from these [spiritual] things to lesser, visible things, whether they be regarded as a source of knowledge, or sought for practical application, or administered and employed officially.[60]

In this remark, one sees Bernard again make an indirect reference to the need to develop the mental quality of vigilance in order that one's mind not

57 *Dil*, 7.18 (CF 13b:21; *SW* 1:104; *SBO* 3:134). "Inest omni utenti ratione naturaliter pro sua semper aestimatione atque intentione appetere potiora, et nulla re esse contentum, cui quod deest, iudicet praeferendum."

58 Wis 13:5 and Rom 1:20.

59 See, e.g., discussion of "the perverse man"—"He used to watch over his own conduct; now all his watchfulness is for others" (*dum a sui circumpectione torpescit incuria sui, curiosam in alios facit*). *Hum*, 10.28 (CF 13a:57; *SW* 2:88; *SBO* 3:38). This passage is also cited by St. Bonaventure as describing "the primary vice" of "inquisitiveness": Bonaventure, *Collations on the Six Days*, Collation 19, §4, trans. José de Vinck, in *The Works of Bonaventure* (Paterson, NJ: St. Anthony Guild, 1970), 5:285. Regarding inquisitiveness as curiosity in contrast with the virtue of studiousness, see Aquinas, *Summa theologiae* II-II, qq. 166–67.

60 *Csi*, V, 1.1 (CF 37:139; *SW* 1:774; *SBO* 3:467). "Et hoc velim sollerter advertas, vir sagacissime Eugeni, quia toties peregrinatur consideratio tua, quoties ab illis rebus ad ista deflectitur inferiora et visibilia, sive intuenda ad notitiam, sive appetenda ad usum, sive pro officio disponenda vel actitanda."

fall into exile by way of unnecessary sensual distractions.[61] Châtillon is thus correct to observe that for Bernard investigative meditation in this sense is not an end in and of itself; rather, the acquisition of knowledge (*notitia*) is further ordered toward enriching one's relationship with God.[62] In a similar way, Leclercq remarks: "We must . . . distinguish, but not separate, 'theology as science' and 'theology as prayer.'"[63] Déchanet likewise describes investigative theological meditation, along with practical theological meditation, as a "necessary preparation" for the highest form of theological meditation (namely, speculative or contemplative theology).[64]

The Third Step: Contemplative Theology and Self-Recollection

Bernard refers to the last and highest kind of theological meditation as speculative (*speculativam*).[65] Because the English word "speculative" today might mean "conjectural" (or alternatively "speculative" might be associated with unverifiable ideational abstractions[66]), I suggest that this highest form of meditation be understood as contemplative meditation—keeping with the qualification that this activity of the mind differs from and is inferior to ecstatic contemplation (but meditation at this step is contemplative as oriented toward that higher kind of contemplation). Bernard writes: "Consideration is speculative when it recollects itself and, insofar as it is aided by God, frees itself for contemplation of God."[67] Contemplative meditation requires two reorientations of one's mental attention. First, there is a reorientation to oneself (introspection or interiority) away from practical and investigative concerns. Next, there is a reorientation to God (superspection or self-transcendence) away from oneself. By reorientation, I mean directing one's attention (first toward oneself and then toward God), what Bernard at the end of Book V refers to as the focused attention of the

61 *Csi*, IV, 6.17 (CF 37:131; *SW* 1:764; *SBO* 462). "Oportet vigilem, quem nulla ab sese abducat peregrine et curiosa cogitatio."

62 Châtillon, "L'Influence de S. Bernard," 274.

63 Leclercq, "Theology and Prayer," 360.

64 Déchanet, "Aux Sources," 63.

65 *Csi*, V, 2.4 (CF 37:143; *SW* 1:778; *SBO* 3:469).

66 Leclercq, for example, at times associates speculation with abstraction in this particular way. See Leclercq, "Théologie monastique," 14; Leclercq, *Love of Learning*, 218 and 223–24.

67 *Csi*, V, 2.4 (CF 37:143; *SW* 1:778; *SBO* 3:469). "Speculativa est consideratio se in se colligens et, quantum divinitus adiuvatur, rebus humanis eximens ad contemplandum Deum." See also Déchanet, "Aux Sources," 63.

mind (*acies mentis*).[68] With respect to the importance of contemplative meditation, Bernard reiterates his caveat that the lower practical theological meditation must be ordered to this higher kind of theological reflection: "The first kind of consideration, without an awareness of the last, sows much and reaps nothing."[69] This same insight also applies to the second level of scientific theological meditation: unless investigative consideration "directs itself toward the third" (*ad istam se dirigat*), it moves but does not advance.[70]

I want to explore in a special way Bernard's description of how one's mind at the outset of contemplative meditation becomes interiorly reoriented by recollecting itself or by "gathering itself into itself" (*se in se colligens*).[71] The verb 'to gather' or 'to collect' (*colligere*) signifies a mental activity that is arguably similar to the exercise of vigilance, discussed above. Yet self-gathering as discussed here is different in that it involves recalling one's attention rather than inhibiting its outward wandering (*peregrinatio*). Déchanet describes self-gathering in this respect as withdrawing one's attention from everyday human realities—not unlike a religious retreat.[72] Déchanet observes that the subsequent movement of the mind toward God on this basis (as distinct from receiving the grace of ecstatic contemplation) involves acquiring some degree of self-knowledge.[73] The acquisition of self-knowledge is not an end in and of itself,[74] but rather involves a *preparation* of one's mind for the contemplation of God. If God is Spirit[75] and God cannot be located by the mind among sensual realities, then God similarly will not be found in one's memories of sensual realities, nor in imaginative fantasies constructed

68 *Csi*, V, 13.27 (CF 37:174; *SW* 1:820; *SBO* 3:490). The phrase *acies mentis* (and its counterpart *oculus mentis*) has a long history, originating from Plato as mediated to Augustine by Plotinus. See Frederick van Fleteren, "Acies mentis," in *Augustine through the Ages*, 5–6, who describes it as a concentrated effort at intellectual intuition. Hankey agrees that for Augustine the *acies* is the "point" of the mind with respect to the intellect or higher reason (*ratio superior*) oriented toward the divine as simple and immutable. See Wayne J. Hankey, "*Ratio*, Reason, Rationalism," in *Augustine through the Ages*, 696–702, at 700.

69 *Csi*, V, 2.4 (CF 37:143; *SW* 1:778; *SBO* 3:469).

70 Ibid. Hankey contends that for Augustine, the *scientia* of reason involves knowledge oriented toward corporeal things that are encountered via the bodily senses, whereas the *sapientia* of reason involves a reorientation toward the divine above the mind. See Hankey, "Mind," 565, citing Augustine, *The Trinity* XII.

71 *Csi*, V, 2.4 (CF 37:143; *SW* 1:778; *SBO* 3:469).

72 Déchanet, "Aux Sources," 63.

73 Ibid., 63n3.

74 Ibid. "L'âme se recueille . . . non pour se voir, s'étudier, se connaître, mais pour pouvoir, toutes ses forces regroupées, reductis affectibus, s'élancer librement vers Dieu, les ailes de la pureté et de l'agilité assurant son vol."

75 Jn 4:24.

out of such memories. It is helpful to remember that for Bernard this practice of self-gathering is not carried out simply in accordance with one's own effort—rather, Bernard states that self-recollection serves as a preparation for contemplation insofar as the mind "is aided by God" (*quantum divinitus adiuvatur*).[76]

Bernard's reference to self-recollection is evocative of the teaching of Gregory the Great who, as discussed above, was a source for Bernard's teaching on meditation. Déchanet recognizes that Bernard's reference to self-recollection in this text echoes a similar passage of Gregory the Great found in a homily on Ezekiel.[77] This passage by Gregory in turn may have a basis in a statement by Augustine found at the beginning of *De ordine* where Augustine is discussing the importance of self-knowledge. There, Augustine writes: "for acquiring this self-knowledge, he needs a constant habit of withdrawing from things of the senses and of concentrating his thought within himself and holding it there" (*habet consuetudine recedendi a sensibus et animum in seipsum colligendi atque in seipso retinendi*).[78] Augustine's use of the verb *retinere* might imply that the activity of one's mind is to be brought within certain structural boundaries or an enclosure (that is, a claustral psychology).

Augustine's teaching that one should condition oneself in the practice of mental self-gathering (*consuetudine . . . animum in seipsum colligendi*) is taken up by Gregory in a homily on Ezekiel.[79] Referring to the goal of receiving the beatific vision, Gregory starts by discussing how a course of meditation might be understood as a procession through metaphorical doors where "through the entrance of faith is opened the entrance of the vision of God."[80] However, Gregory immediately recognizes the difficulty of reaching this goal, in that one can be distracted by a multiplicity of corporeal images. Speaking of contemplative meditation, Gregory writes:

> We often wish to ponder [*considerare*] the invisible nature of Almighty God but by no means avail, and the soul [*anima*], wearied by the very difficulties, withdraws into herself and makes for herself and from herself the

76 *Csi*, V, 2.4 (CF 37:143; *SW* 1:778; *SBO* 3:469).

77 Déchanet, "Aux Sources," 63n3.

78 Augustine, *De ordine* I.1, §3, in Russell, 10–11. Van Bavel interprets this remark by Augustine as attesting to his early disvaluation of the body and sensation. See Tarcisius van Bavel, "'No One Ever Hated His Own Flesh': Eph. 5:29 in Augustine," *Augustiniana* 45, nos. 1–2 (1995): 45–93, at 51. The context of Augustine's remark is focused on growth in self-knowledge as an embodied spiritual being.

79 *Hiez*, II, 5.8.

80 Ibid. (Tomkinson, 339; SC 360:240). "Per aditum fidei aperitur aditus visionis Dei."

> steps of her ascent [*ad semetipsam recedit, sibique de seipsa gradus ascensionis facit*], so that she first considers herself, if she can [*primum semetipsam, si valet, consideret*], and then examines [*investiget*] insofar as she can the nature which is above her. But our mind [*mens*], if spread out [*sparsa*] in carnal images, by no means suffices to consider itself or the nature of the soul because it is led by as many thoughts [*cogitationes*] as it is, so to speak, to be blinded by obstacles.[81]

Recall above that Bernard also describes one's mind as able to fall into (or be dispersed among) various distracting thoughts (specifically this involves the fall of memory, when memory is understood as a mode of attention, as discussed above).[82] Thoughts can impose themselves between one's attention and God—recall also Bernard's metaphor discussed above in his sermon in the *De diversis* series where he described intrusive thoughts as invading the bedroom of reason.[83]

In Gregory's passage considered just above, one might also discern a core doctrine of meditation (common also to Hildemar and ascribed to Paul the Deacon), namely, that when one ascends toward contemplation, this ascent first involves withdrawal from sensual realities and images. Gregory also refers to one ascending a ladder of reflection (*scala considerationis*) in Book XV of his *Moralia in Iob*. There, he writes: "all carnal beings ought to judge from their own makeup that invisible entities are superior to visible ones and through this ladder of reflection, so to speak, mount toward God, since he remains there where he is invisible, and he remains there in the highest place, where he can never be grasped [*quo comprehendi nequaquam potest*]."[84] In his homily on Ezekiel, Gregory describes three grades on the *scala* that one might ascend during contemplative meditation:

> The first step is to compose oneself [*primus ergo gradus est ut se ad se colligat*], the second to see the like of this composure [*secundus ut videat qualis est collecta*], the third to rise above oneself [*tertius ut super semetipsam surgat*] and by intention submit to the contemplation of the invisible Creator. But one by no means composes himself [*se ad se . . . colligit*] unless he has first learned to curb the apparitions of earthly and heavenly images

81 Ibid.

82 *Div*, 45.1 (CF 68:236–37; *SW* 9:544–46; *SBO* 6.1:262–63).

83 *Div*, 32.4 (CF 68:180; *SW* 9:462; *SBO* 6.1:221).

84 *Mo*, XV, 46.52 (CS 258:242; PL 75:1107c).

> from his mind's eye and cast out and tread down whatever of sight, hearing, smell, touch and taste occurs to his bodily thought [*corporeo cogitationi*], in order that he may inwardly seek such as is free thereof. For when he ponders [*cogitat*] these things he turns, as it were, some bodily shadows inwards.[85]

It is Gregory's reference to self-composition (*se ad se colligit*) in this excerpt that captures Déchanet's attention,[86] in that the phrasing is very close to Bernard's *se in se colligens*[87] (and likewise to Augustine's *in seipsum colligendi*).[88] One might note that in this passage Gregory also suggests that one should evaluate the quality of one's self-recollection before turning to God (I will refer to this suggestion below as a self-assessing the degree of one's self-recollection).

Gregory makes similar remarks regarding meditation in his *Moralia in Iob*. Referring to a "vital quiet" that one might experience "when earthly desires" are calmed, he writes:

> Such is the case obviously when the holy mind represses the disturbance caused by earthly desires and consequently knows the interior world more truly; the more it avoids external excitement, the more eagerly it stands guard over its internal activity. This reality is nicely symbolized by Jacob in his rest along his journey; he put a stone under his head and went to sleep. He saw a ladder reaching from earth to heaven, the Lord leaning against the ladder, and angels ascending and descending on it . . . Seeing angels ascending and descending . . . means the contemplation of the citizens of the heavenly homeland.[89]

The "rest" or "contemplative sleep" signifies turning one's attention away from exterior realities. Gregory's reference to the mind "standing guard over its internal activity" is evocative of Bernard's image of the porter at the gate of reason. Shortly thereafter, in the same part of the *Moralia in Iob*, Gregory makes use of the symbol of the ladder as a representation of the soul: "This is the way the soul presents itself to itself as a kind of ladder by which it may

85 *Hiez*, II, 5.9 (Tomkinson, 339–40; SC 360:242). See also Evans, *Thought of Gregory*, 106.

86 Déchanet, "Aux Sources," 63n3.

87 *Csi*, V, 2.4 (CF 37:143; *SW* 1:778; *SBO* 3:469).

88 Augustine, *De ordine* I.1, §3, in Russell, 10–11.

89 *Mo*, V, 31.54 (CS 249:353–54).

ascend from external reality and transmit itself inside itself, so that it may reach out from itself to the Creator."[90]

In his homily on Ezekiel, Gregory describes the soul's spiritual growth in a similar way as becoming more aware of its ontological position, so to speak, in between God and sensual realities: "all things are to be driven away by the hand of discernment from the mind's eye [*manu discretionis ab oculis mentis*] so that the soul may regard herself as she was created, above the body but below God [*sub Deo super corpus*], so that being quickened by her superior she may quicken the inferior which she administers."[91] Regarding this reorientation of the mind to God after entering a kind of self-enclosure, Gregory writes:

> When the mind, you see, abandons bodily images and comes inside itself, it is no small ascent. Although the soul is not a body, yet it is unified with a body, so it is known by that very quality that is held within the confines of the body. While it forgets what it knows, it learns what it does not know; it remembers what has been consigned to oblivion, it grows happy after sorrow, and after joy there is judgment.[92]

The intellectual reorientation at hand involves for Gregory an act of self-knowing that transcends immersion in somatic sensations and imaginations.[93] But, for Gregory, one does not stop at this point as if reaching a state of pure intellectual self-reflection: "it is a great wonder if the soul casts aside its own bodily form and is even led to knowledge of itself. If it thinks of itself without the aid of a bodily image, by this self-knowledge it prepares a way

90 *Mo*, V, 34.62 (CS 249:360).

91 *Hiez*, II, 5.9 (Tomkinson, 340; SC 360:242).

92 *Mo*, V, 34.62 (CS 249:360–61).

93 In my interpretation of Gregory in this passage, reflective self-knowledge involves self-understanding in the sense of an active self-intuition and self-presence (see also Aristotle's description of the divine, quoted just below in this note). Self-knowledge in this sense is not self-understanding in the sense of knowing a posited self-concept or idea that one represents to oneself in order to model oneself or one's behavior. Rather, the mental activity that pertains to this meditative praxis obtains to a state that is prior to (and above) not only imagination, but also theory in the modern Western sense of ideation (an idea that one mentally conceives). Similarly, with respect to Aristotle, he refers to God as follows: "thought thinks itself by participation in the object of thought"—or perhaps "the intellect understands itself according to a grasp of understanding" (*auton de noei ho nous kata metalēpsin tou noētou*). Aristotle, *Metaphysics* XII.7.1072b20–21, in *Metaphysics Books X–XIV, Oeconomica, Magna Moralia*, trans. Hugh Tredennick and G. Cyril Armstrong (Cambridge, MA: Harvard University Press, 1997), 148–49. However, Gregory's discussion here is not focused on knowing the Creator's mind, but rather on one's own self-reflective mental activity.

for itself to gaze upon the nature of eternity."[94] Gregory refers to this course of meditation as involving a way of negation:

> The mind thinks of this absolute substance, accustomed as it is to bodily reality, and supports the appearances of various images. While the mind puts these images out of sight, away from the focus of its attention, with the hand of discernment, making everything else secondary, then it already to some degree sees that substance. If the mind does not yet perceive that substance as it is, it at least knows what it is not. We find ourselves in unfamiliar territory when we examine God's nature.[95]

I will return below to the topic of reorienting oneself to God's unity above one's mind. At present, it suffices to note Gregory's indication that this reorientation may involve a kind of negative theology (turning one's mind away from what God is not).

Gregory provides a reader of Bernard with a fruitful interpretive context in other ways as well. For example, Sommerfeldt notes that one should not interpret Bernard as identifying theological meditation with ecstatic contemplation, as mentioned previously. Rather, theological meditation should be understood as the highest kind of reflection (what Sommerfeldt refers to as "meditation properly so called"[96]). As discussed above, this meditation culminates in a kind of contemplation, yet this kind of contemplation is distinct from infused or ecstatic contemplation.[97] Bernard also refers to theological meditation (specifically reflection on God's power and charity) as involving certain "kinds of contemplation" (*contemplationis species*).[98] On this point, Gregory agrees that theological meditation "to some extent" (*aliquatenus*) enters through the door of contemplation:

> Then if the quickened life is of such magnitude that it cannot be comprehended, who avails to comprehend with his understanding [*intellectu comprehendere*] how great is the majesty of the Life which quickens? But the very consideration and discernment thereof is already to enter to some extent [*sed hoc ipsum considerare atque discernere iam est aliquatenus*

94 *Mo*, V, 34.61 (CS 249:360).

95 *Mo*, V, 34.62 (CS 249:361).

96 Sommerfeldt, *Spiritual Teachings of Bernard*, 67, citing CS 120:19–37. See also Sommerfeldt, "Charismatic and Gregorian Leadership," 76–77.

97 See also Leclercq, "L'Art de la Composition," 129.

98 *Csi*, V, 14.32 (CF 37:178; *SW* 1:826; *SBO* 3:493).

> *intrare*], because from her appraisement the soul gathers what she perceives of the uncircumscribed Spirit [*ex sua aestimatione anima colligit quid de incircumscripto spiritu sentiat*] which incomprehensibly rules those things which He incomprehensibly created.[99]

In this passage, Gregory refers to one having a sense or intuition (*sensus*) of the Holy Spirit. On this cognitive basis, one arguably would have some kind of means for differentiating God from other created things (as required for a negative theology) and also for assessing one's dissimilitude from God when engaging in honest self-reflection (discussed above).

When philosophy is employed at this stage of meditation to establish an intellectual ladder which one's mind might ascend (*qua ascendatur*),[100] it is not used for focusing on practical pursuits (ethics) or for investigating the exterior world (physics), nor even for organizing one's thought (logic), but rather for establishing one's mind on a cognitive foundation proper for the investigation of divine realities. This foundation (the rung of the ladder on which one stands so to speak) is not at this point entirely clarified in Bernard's teaching. He does state that when one's mind by way of contemplative meditation begins to attend to spiritual realities, use of human language becomes more difficult: "What is above is not taught through words but is revealed through the Spirit."[101] Bernard continues: "Truly, what words do not explain, consideration seeks, prayer aspires to, life merits, purity attains."[102] While Bernard does not altogether avoid technical theological language, Leclercq observes that Bernard's preference at this point in meditation is to express himself using the language of scripture.[103] I turn now to consider Bernard's discussion of scripture and how theological meditation at this point may involve an assessment of one's various beliefs.

Three Kinds of Theological Belief: Faith, Rational Understanding, and Opinion

Bernard proceeds at this point to discuss various kinds of theological thoughts that might arise in one's mind during the course of meditation

99 *Hiez*, II, 5.9 (Tomkinson, 340; SC 360:244).

100 *Csi*, V, 3.5 (CF 37:143; *SW* 1:780; *SBO* 3:470).

101 Ibid. "Ergo quae supra sunt, non verbo docentur, sed Spiritu revelantur."

102 *Csi*, V, 3.5 (CF 37:143–44; *SW* 1:780; *SBO* 3:470). "Verum quod sermo non explicat, consideratio quaerat, oratio expetat, mereatur vita, puritas assequatur."

103 Leclercq, *Love of Learning*, 200, citing *SCC*, 74, 2.

as one's mind becomes reoriented toward God. Referring to God, Bernard writes: "He and the blessed spirits who are with him must be investigated by our consideration in three ways—as if by three avenues of approach—opinion, faith, and understanding."[104] Differentiating these three kinds of theological belief involves differentiating the source of the beliefs. One might contrast a cognition based on faith (*fides*) supported by authority with a cognition based on understanding (*intellectus*) supported by reason, and contrast both of these with an opinion (*opinio*) that may have some degree of verisimilitude (semblance of truth).[105]

"Faith," Bernard states in this section of Book V, "is a kind of voluntary and sure foretaste of truth not evident."[106] His remark is evocative of a statement he makes elsewhere in a sermon from his *Sermones super cantica canticorum*, namely, that faith proceeds as an anticipation of experience: "What they do not know from experience, let them believe, so that one day, by virtue of their faith, they may reap the harvest of experience."[107] In Book V of *De consideratione*, Bernard implies that faith is grounded in one respect on the authority of the teaching found in scripture. When describing various attributes of the angels, he writes: "All this we learn by reading, and we hold by faith."[108] This remark indicates that faith in authority may be subsequent to reading (*lectio*). In other words, *lectio* can precede or accompany *meditatio*.[109] Bernard indicates that biblical interpretation might proceed according to different senses or levels of meaning where allegorical interpretation can support one in faith and moral interpretation can discern teaching for actions in life.[110]

104 *Csi*, V, 3.5 (CF 37:144; *SW* 1:780; *SBO* 3:470). "Is, et qui cum eo sunt beati spiritus, tribus modis, veluti viis totidem, nostra sunt consideratione vestigandi, opinione, fide, intellectu."

105 Ibid. See also Sommerfeldt, *Life of the Mind*, 74–80; Leclercq, "L'Art de la Composition," 127.

106 *Csi*, V, 3.6 (CF 37:145; *SW* 1:782; *SBO* 3:471). "Fides est voluntaria quaedam et certa prelibatio necdum propalatae veritatis." See also Emero Stiegman, "Bernard of Clairvaux, William of St. Thierry, the Victorines," in *The Medieval Theologians: An Introduction to Theology in the Medieval Period*, ed. G. R. Evans (Malden, MA: Blackwell, 2001), 129–55, at 138.

107 *SCC*, 84, 1.7 (CF 40:194; *SW* 6:626; *SBO* 2:306). "Credant quod non experiuntur, ut fructum quandoque experientiae, fidei merito consequantur." See also Kilian McDonnell, "Spirit and Experience in Bernard of Clairvaux," *Theological Studies* 58 (1997): 3–18, at 4.

108 *Csi*, V, 4.7 (CF 37:146; *SW* 1:784; *SBO* 3:472). "Haec omnia legendo comperimus, fide tenemus."

109 See Leclercq, *The Love of Learning*, 72–73.

110 "Let us return now to ourselves, let us examine our paths . . . Now that we have passed through the shadow-land of allegories, it is time to explore the great plains of moral truths. Our faith has been strengthened, let our lives reveal its influence; our intellects have been enlightened, let them prescribe the right behavior." *SCC*, 17, 4.8 (CF 4:132; *SW* 5:252–54; *SBO* 1:102–3). "Sed revertamur ad nos ipsos, scrutemurque vias nostras . . . Transivimus allegoriarum umbras; ventum est ad

Regarding biblical study during meditation, Illich contends that Bernard is referring to meditative reading when he exhorts his monks in a sermon elsewhere to be "clean, cud-chewing animals."[111] Illich explains that the comparison of a "meditating monk" and a "grazing cow" is common metaphor in monastic literature to represent mulling over the meaning of scripture.[112]

Regarding the meditative evaluation of beliefs based on scripture, Geoffrey of Auxerre describes Bernard reading scripture during meditation:

> He used the Scriptures so freely, so relevantly, that instead of following them, he paved the way for them as he liked, taking their author, the Holy Spirit, as his lead . . . As he himself confessed, sometimes when he was meditating and praying, the whole of Sacred Scripture appeared to him as if it were placed open before him.[113]

Geoffrey's remarks indicate that for Bernard reading (*lectio*), meditating (*meditatio*), and praying (*oratio*) might be integrated as a composite monastic exercise (however, at the end of Book V in *De consideratione*, Bernard also notes a distinct transition from meditation to prayer[114]). In his seventh parable, Bernard refers to these three spiritual exercises through the literary character of a figurative monk who, in dialogue with the Lord, refers to "readings, meditations, prayers, contemplations."[115] Whether or not these practices should be understood to occur in terms of a specific sequence, it is clear that for Bernard beliefs of faith based on reading serve as a foundation for theological meditation.

Although Bernard initially stated that God and spiritual realities might be investigated in the three modes of faith, understanding, and opinion,[116]

---

indaganda moralia. Aedificata est fides, instruatur vita; exercitatus est intellectus, dictetur actus." See also CS 63:26.

111 Bernard of Clairvaux, *Sermo in festivitate Omnium Sanctorum*, 1.5. For the English, see Bernard of Clairvaux, *On the Feast of All Saints: Sermons 1–5* in *Sermons for the Autumn Season* (CF 54:133). For the Latin, see *SW* 8:730; *SBO* 5:330. "Vos estote animalia munda et ruminantia." See also Ivan Illich, *In the Vineyard of the Text: A Commentary to Hugh's "Didascalicon"* (Chicago: University of Chicago Press, 1996), 56.

112 Illich, *In the Vineyard*, 56n22.

113 Geoffrey of Auxerre, *VP*, III, 7 (CF 76:153).

114 *Csi*, V, 14.32 (CF 37:179; *SW* 1:826; *SBO* 3:493).

115 Bernard of Clairvaux, "Parable 7, The Story of the Eight Beatitudes," in *Parables and the Sentences* (CF 55:86–100, at 91). *SW* 4 reprints the Latin for parable 7 from Bernardus Claraevallensis, *Sancti Bernardi Opera* 6.2, ed. J. Leclercq, C. H. Talbot, and H.-M. Rochais (Rome: Editiones Cistercienses, 1972), 295–303. See also Sommerfeldt, "Meditation as the Path," 177.

116 *Csi*, V, 3.5 (CF 37:144; *SW* 1:780; *SBO* 3:470).

he also comments that some matters of faith—such as the mystery of the Trinity—elude investigation: "Let it suffice for him to believe this [teaching on the Trinity], not as something evident from reason, nor wavering with opinion, but as something certified by faith. This is a great mystery, to be worshipped, not investigated."[117] Elsewhere, Bernard repeats that the assent of faith should be maintained in orientation to such divine realities that transcend the limits of rational understanding: "I believe the eternal and blessed Trinity, although I do not understand it, and I hold fast by faith what I cannot grasp with my mind."[118] This remark is evocative of the statement of Gregory who also maintained that God "can never be comprehended."[119] Rational understanding differs from faith in this respect in that what is understood by way of reason is not "wrapped in mystery" (*involucrum*)."[120] When reason enters into the mysteries of faith in the search for understanding, Bernard states that in a sense reason is a kind of intruder (*effractor*); citing Proverbs 25:27, he states that reason can become a "searcher of majesty" (*scrutator maiestatis*) when attempting to scrutinize what is beyond scrutiny.[121] He makes similar remarks in the *Sermones super cantica canticorum*, differentiating any attempt at forceful scrutiny from receiving the gift of ecstatic contemplation:

> What other mortal then would presume to involve himself by his own attempts at an awesome scrutiny of the divine majesty, what insolent contemplative would force his way into those dread secrets? The scrutinizers of majesty described as invaders [*irruptores*] are not, I think then, those who are rapt into it, but those who force their way in.[122]

This is not to say that one should refrain from attempting to understand divine mysteries in meditation. What Bernard is arguably focused on in these remarks is that one cultivates an appropriate disposition—that is, one should

117 *Csi*, V, 8.18 (CF 37:163; *SW* 1:804; *SBO* 3:482). "Sufficiat ei tenere sic esse, atque hoc non rationi perspicuum, nec tamen opinioni ambiguum, sed fidei persuasum. Sacramentum hoc magnum est, et quidem venerandum, non scrutandum." See also Sommerfeldt, *Life of the Mind*, 14; Leclercq, "L'Art de la Composition," 128.

118 *SCC*, 76, 3.6 (CF 40:115; *SW* 6:530; *SBO* 2:258). "Aeternam beatamque Trinitatem, quam non intelligo, credo, et fide teneo quam non capio mente." See also Sommerfeldt, "Afterword: Looking Back at Bernard," 370; Sommerfeldt, *Life of the Mind*, 12–17.

119 *Mo*, XV, 46.52 (CS 258:242; PL 75:1107c).

120 *Csi*, V, 3.6 (CF 37:145; *SW* 1:782; *SBO* 3:471).

121 Ibid. "Intellectus, si signata fidei tentet irrumpere, reputatur effractor, scrutator maiestatis." See also Emero Stiegman, "Bernard of Clairvaux," 137; Leclercq, *Love of Learning*, 204.

122 *SCC*, 62, 3.4 (CF 31:155; *SW* 6:330; *SBO* 2:158).

not attempt to ascend to spiritual realities by way of intellectual force, but rather proceed in humility and out of love of God. This is evident when, again alluding to Proverbs 25:27, Bernard elaborates: "nor need one fear the scriptural threat about the scrutinizer of majesty. Just bring to [the divine mystery] an eye that is pure and simple [*purum et simplicem oculum*], and you will not be overwhelmed by glory but led into it—unless you seek your own glory, not God's."[123]

In *De consideratione*, Bernard states that a belief involving rational understanding also differs from an opinion that can be mistaken.[124] Bernard thus implies that there can be a kind of certainty afforded by reason: "true understanding has not only certain truth, but knowledge of the truth."[125] In other words, at times when one genuinely understands, one not only knows something, but one has knowledge (*notitia*) that what one understands is true. While "understanding is a sure and manifest knowledge of something not seen," one may by opinion believe that something is true simply because it is not known to be false.[126] In a statement where he is likely alluding to his concern with the theology of Abelard, Bernard states that beliefs of faith are higher than the uncertainty of opinion; faith is not grounded on opinion.[127] Of these three kinds of theological belief (faith, rational understanding, and opinion), Bernard clearly gives emphasis to the first: "we prefer to know nothing more than that which we already know by faith."[128]

Bernard proceeds next in this discussion to note how in relation to divine realities these three different kinds of belief (faith, rational understanding,

123 *SCC*, 62, 3.4 (CF 31:154; *SW* 6:328; *SBO* 2:157), as cited in Henri de Lubac, *Medieval Exegesis*, vol. 3: *The Four Senses of Scripture*, trans. E. M. Macierowski (Grand Rapids, MI: Eerdmans, 2009), 227.

124 *Csi*, V, 3.6 (CF 37:145; *SW* 1:782; *SBO* 3:471). "Si falli potuit, intellectus non fuit, sed opinio."

125 Ibid. "Verus nempe intellectus certam habet non modo veritatem, sed notitiam veritatis." It is possible that Bernard has in mind (at least in part) the compelling nature of a demonstration, given that elsewhere he remarks that the judgment that piety should be preferred above all else is a conclusion that "irrefutable logic demonstrates" (*prorsus irrefragabilis ratio monstrat*). *Csi*, I, 7.8 (CF 37:37; *SW* 1:646; *SBO* 3:403). See also Evans, *Mind of St. Bernard*, 91.

126 *Csi*, V, 3.6 (CF 37:145; *SW* 1:782; *SBO* 3:471). "Intellectus est rei cuiuscumque invisibilis certa et manifesta notitia; opinio est quasi pro vero habere aliquid, quod falsum esse nescias." See also Sommerfeldt, *Life of the Mind*, 75.

127 *Csi*, V, 3.6 (CF 37:145; *SW* 1:782; *SBO* 3:471). "Fides ambiguum non habet, aut, si habet, fides non est, sed opinio." On Bernard's judgment that Abelard defined faith as opinion, see Bernard of Clairvaux, "Letter CXC," in *Life and Works of Saint Bernard, Abbot of Clairvaux*, trans. Samuel J. Eales (London: Burns and Oates, 1889–96), 2:565–91, at 574–76 (Ep 190 in *SW* 3:74–120; *SBO* 8:17–40). See also Evans, *Mind of St. Bernard*, 212–13.

128 *Csi*, V, 3.6 (CF 37:145; *SW* 1:782; *SBO* 3:471). "Nil autem malumus scire, quam quae fide iam scimus." See also Sommerfeldt, *Life of the Mind*, 90.

and opinion) each contribute to one's theological meditation. He observes that faith follows scripture in affirming the purity and impassibility of angels; reason affirms that angels have intelligence on the basis of making an inference; opinion considers whether or not angels have bodies.[129] Bernard meditates at length in this passage on the nature and characteristics of angels.[130] Further, in his discussion of the hierarchy of nine grades of angelic beings, Bernard indicates familiarity with the angelology of Gregory the Great.[131]

As a final point for this section concerning the various cognitions that might influence one's theological meditation, Bernard observes that while one may ascend to some degree in meditation by way of one's intellect, one's affections might remain attached to some inferior temporal good perceived through the bodily senses. The implication is that a complete self-recollection prior to contemplative meditation would not only be cognitive but also affective. This kind of affective self-recollection might be assessed prior to turning to God (as Gregory suggests).[132] On this point, Bernard writes:

> What if the soul were totally recollected [*se colligat anima*] and with affections recalled from all the places they were held captive by fearing what should not be feared, loving what was unworthy, grieving vainly and more vainly rejoicing, it began to soar with total liberty [*tota libertate*], to drive on under the impulse of the spirit [*pulset in impetus spiritus*] and to glide along in abundance of grace?[133]

129 *Csi*, V, 4.7 (CF 37:146; *SW* 1:782; *SBO* 3:471). See also Sommerfeldt, *Life of the Mind*, 76. In his retraction placed at the beginning of the *Liber de gradibus humilitatis et superbiae*, Bernard is again careful to note that one of his teachings on angels is not based on scripture but his own opinion (CF 13a:25). One might also observe that in the passage of *De consideratione* under consideration (Csi, V, 4.7), Bernard makes a remark that further illuminates his perspective on rational understanding. Referring to the angels, he states: the fact "that they are endowed with understanding we hold not by faith, not by opinion, but by understanding because they cannot be devoid of understanding and at the same time enjoy the possession of God." Bernard's belief in this regard is based on an inference.

130 *Csi*, V, 4.7–5.12 (CF 37:146–54; *SW* 1:782–94; *SBO* 3:471–77). See also Leclercq, "L'Art de la Composition," 127.

131 *Csi*, V, 4.8 (CF 37:147–49; *SW* 1:784–86; *SBO* 3:472–73). For Gregory, see Gregory the Great, "Homily 34," in *Forty Gospel Homilies*, trans. David Hurst (Kalamazoo, MI: Cistercian Publications, 1990), 280–300, esp. 288–89. Bernard's discussion in this passage aligns more with Gregory than with what is found in the angelology of Pseudo-Dionysius. For the latter, see Pseudo-Dionysius, *The Celestial Hierarchy* 6–9 (Luibheid, 160–73). Also see Bonaventure, *Collations on the Six Days*, Collation 21, §25 (de Vinck, 335); Bonaventure, *The Journey of the Mind to God*, 4.4, trans. José de Vinck, in *The Works of Bonaventure*, vol. 1: *Mystical Opuscula* (Quincy, IL: Franciscan, 1997), 39.

132 *Hiez*, II, 5.9 (Tomkinson, 339–40; SC 360:242).

133 *Csi*, V, 4.9 (CF 37:149–50; *SW* 1:786–88; *SBO* 3:473–74). "Quid si totam se colligat anima et, reductis affectibus e cunctis locis, quibus captivi tenentur, timendo quae non oportet, amando quae

Not only is the mind (*animus*) to be recollected at this point in meditation in terms of memory, reason, and will, but the soul (*anima*) is to be recollected in terms of affect also. Perhaps this kind of grace-based self-gathering of various cognitions and affects can be understood as an exercise promoting personality integration or recapitulation. Bernard explicitly refers to the importance of grace in this passage when he indicates that the ascent of the soul toward God is motivated by the impulse of the Holy Spirit—although elsewhere he refers to impulses originating from other kinds of spirits. For example: "If each one is carried away by his own impulse [*impetu*] in accord with the spirit he receives . . . there will clearly be no unity but confusion instead [*non plane unitas erit, sed magis confusio*]."[134] These latter impulses might be associated with emotions (recall the passage quoted previously where Bernard promoted one's emotions becoming ordered according to the unity of the virtues).[135]

Orientation to God's Unity

On the basis of Bernard's discussion thus far, one might observe that the ascent of contemplative meditation involving self-recollection and a reorientation to God pertains to a withdrawal from multiplicity and a turn toward unity, whereas descent down Jacob's ladder results in psychological diversification. Gregory the Great also refers to the soul in a similar manner:

> By its very diversity it proves how far distant it is from the nature of eternal unchangeability. The latter is always the same as it is now: everywhere present, everywhere invisible, everywhere complete, everywhere incomprehensible. The longing mind perceives it without seeing, hears it without doubting, accepts it without moving, touches it without body, and holds it without a physical place.[136]

In addition to these divine attributes that Gregory mentions (God is omnipresent, invisible, fulfilled in himself, incomprehensible), Bernard also emphasizes that meditative ascent toward God is an ascent toward unity:

---

non decet, dolendo vane, gaudendo vanius, cum his ineat tota libertate volatum, pulset in impetu spiritus et in pinguedine gratiae illabatur?"

134 *SCC*, 49, 2.5 (CF 31:26; *SW* 6:166; *SBO* 2:76). See also John R. Sommerfeldt, "Bernard on Charismatic Knowledge: The Truth as Gift," *CSQ* 32, no. 3 (1997): 295–301, at 299.

135 *Div*, 50.2 (CF 68:248; *SW* 9:562; *SBO* 6.1:271).

136 *Mo*, V, 34.62 (CS 249:361).

"he is one to a superlative degree" (*unissimus est*).[137] All of God's various divine attributes (his eternity, goodness, greatness, blessedness) might be understood as unified and integrated: "his being [*esse*] is what all these things are."[138]

What effect does Bernard's emphasis on God's unity have on the course of one's meditation? In his interpretation of Bernard, Michel indicates that one's course of meditation itself can take on an inherent unity.[139] This might occur to the extent that (supported by God) one is able to gather oneself together for the sake of an integrated and focused reflection.[140] But Michel proceeds further to maintain that the entire purpose of contemplative meditation "has no other object" than this goal of achieving a state of unified mental equilibrium.[141] Michel here seems to focus on a secondary effect of theological meditation (self-integration), rather than on Bernard's teaching that the primary purpose of meditation is growing in relationship with God. In contrast with Michel, I read Bernard to indicate that through meditation, one's mind self-integrates to the extent that one's mind remains focused on growth toward God's unity.[142] Contemplative meditation does not for Bernard have the primary purpose of self-unification—although this self-unification can occur as a result of meditation focused on God and as

137 *Csi*, V, 7.17 (CF 37:160; *SW* 1:800; *SBO* 3:480).

138 *Csi*, V, 6.13 (CF 37:155; *SW* 1:794; *SBO* 3:477). "Nempe hoc est ei esse, quod haec omnia esse." See also Sommerfeldt, *Life of the Mind*, 45–47.

139 Michel, "La consideration," 115. "C'est dans se moment « considératif » que la pensée s'éprouve dans son unité, qu'elle parvient à un sentiment d'elle-même—non pas, donc, dans la certitude d'une vision contemplative de l'objet même (qui, en tant que telle, fait défaut), mais au contraire dans ce seul état d'incertitude, saisi pour lui-même."

140 Ibid. "En effet, pour Bernard (accentuant ainsi la réponse qui avait été celle de saint Augustin), c'est en elle-même (consideratio se in se colligens), dans cet état de pure réflexion, qu'elle trouve à s'orienter, et c'est ce que le livre V s'efforce de « montrer »."

141 Michel, "La consideration," 116. "La perception de ce double mouvement (qui, dans son équilibre « contraire », constitue la dimension « spéculative »—il faudrait presque dire spéculaire ou réfléchissante—de la considération) est ce que celle-ci, dans l'usage de sa dispensatio (c'est-à-dire dans son administration des réalités sensibles) et dans l'usage de son aestimatio (c'est-à-dire dans son évaluation, théorique, de ces mêmes réalités), ne doit pas perdre de vue, faute de quoi cette administration et cette évaluation « ne sont plus que l'apparence et non la réalité d'elles-mêmes ». L'argument « théologique » qui conclut le livre V (« quid est Deus? » répète inlassablement Bernard avec cette sorte de provocation rhétorique qui caractérise assez bien sa « manière »), n'a pas d'autre objet que de détailler la nature de cet équilibre contraire qui oriente la pensée dans son exercice."

142 An attempt to self-integrate apart from God would arguably (for Bernard) end in failure. For example, as quoted earlier, Bernard writes in *Ad clericos de conversione*: "Let [the person seeking conversion to God] consider that within himself he will find no rest for himself, because he is full of misery and desolation." *Conv*, 11.23 (CF 25:57; *SW* 4:202; *SBO* 4:96).

initiated by God; indeed, as stated just above, Bernard may be read to teach that the prompting one experiences to undertake meditation (*pulset in impetus spiritus*) arises from the Holy Spirit.[143]

How should God's unity be understood by a person who reaches this point of meditation? Sommerfeldt notes that at this point in Book V, Bernard's writing becomes "precise" and "tightly reasoned," in part because of his concern to respond to perceived Trinitarian errors in the theology of Gilbert of Poitiers.[144] Bernard elsewhere observes that Gilbert's works continue to be copied and studied after the Synod of Reims in 1148.[145] Bernard may feel an obligation at this point in *De consideratione* again to enumerate the errors that he perceives in Gilbert's writings. In corroboration of Sommerfeldt's claim, Kennan also notes that Bernard's style of writing changes when he reaches this point in Book V (in contrast with his previous discussion of angels).[146]

Bernard indicates in this section of Book V that he is familiar with the theology of Anselm of Canterbury in the *Proslogion*.[147] Bernard explicitly echoes Anselm,[148] stating: "What is God? That than which nothing better can be thought."[149] However, when addressing his "contemporaries" (namely, Gilbert of Poiters, whom Bernard believed attempted to cognize a higher form of *deitas* beyond the Trinity), Bernard goes further than Anselm and adds that in reality God is beyond human thought:

> He is his own form, he is his own essence [*essentia*] . . . Must we fear that thought will surpass him? However lofty a height it might attain, he is beyond it. It is absurd to seek the Most High beneath the heights to which

143 *Csi*, V, 4.9 (CF 37:149–50; *SW* 1:786–88; *SBO* 3:473–74).

144 Sommerfeldt, *Life of the Mind*, 108 and 135–36. See in particular: *Csi*, V, 6.13–8.19 (CF 37:155–64). Bernard's contemporary, John of Salisbury, also asserts that Bernard has partially written some of the content in *Csi* V against Gilbert. See *The "Historia Pontificalis" of John of Salisbury*, ed. Marjorie Chibnall (Oxford: Clarendon Press, 1986), chap. 11 (25). See also Leclercq, "Théologie monastique," 18. For a different engagement with Gilbert by Bernard, see *SCC*, 80 (CF 40:145–56; *SW* 6:568–81; *SBO* 2:277–83).

145 *SCC*, 80, 4.9 (CF 40:155; *SW* 6:580; *SBO* 2:283). See also Häring, *Commentaries on Boethius*, 5.

146 Kennan, "Rhetoric and Style," 42–43.

147 See also CF 37:186; Leclercq, "General Introduction (III)," 379.

148 See Anselm of Canterbury, *Proslogion*, chap. 2, in *Complete Philosophical and Theological Treatises*, 88–112, at 93.

149 *Csi*, V, 7.15 (CF 37:158; *SW* 1:798; *SBO* 3:479). See also Leclercq, "L'Art de la Composition," 128.

> man's thoughts can attain; to place God there is impious. He must be sought beyond the limits of our thought and not within them.[150]

Here again, Bernard echoes the teaching of Gregory that God is beyond (*ultra*) the human mind.[151]

The divine unity beyond thought differs from numerous other kinds of unity that one's mind might consider. For example, Bernard refers also to the unity of a collection (such as a pile of stones), the unity of a whole made of parts (such as a house), the unique conjugal unity of spouses, a natural unity (an individual human being), moral unity (integrity), the unity of accord (as when men in a group work toward a common goal), the unity of desire (the bond of a lover to a beloved), and lastly the unique unity that is Christ's hypostatic union (the union of humanity and divinity in Christ's hypostasis or person that occurred historically with the first Advent of the Word).[152] A noteworthy omission from this list is the union of the human soul with God which, according to Leclercq, is a topic with respect to which Bernard makes a significant contribution to Christian thought.[153] This unity would involve sharing in a common will of charity, mentioned previously.[154] Bernard does refer to this kind of spiritual unity in a sermon from his *De diversis* series—along with reference to the divine unity (the "principal unity") and also reference to a distinct kind of unity that he calls virtual unity (where a person becomes self-unified by remaining focused on a goal).[155] This virtual unity would seem to involve some kind of self-consistency that could be reinforced by the practice of meditation. For a person moved by grace to seek union with God, the virtual unity effected by pursuit of this goal would arguably be coextensive with the spiritual unity that involves one's participation in a common will with God.

With respect to these various understandings of unity, I want to explore Bernard's remarks in Book V of *De consideratione* regarding God's unity and

150 *Csi*, V, 7.16 (CF 37:160; *SW* 1:800; *SBO* 3:480). "Ipse sibi forma, ipse sibi essentia est . . . Numquid verendum, ne cogitatio transvolet illum? Quantumcumque in altum proficiat, ultra est. Infra quod homo cogitare possit, altissimum quaerere, ridiculum est; statuere, impium. Ultra, non citra quaerendus est."

151 *Mo*, XV, 46.52 (CS 258:242; PL 75:1107c).

152 *Csi*, V, 8.18 (CF 37:163; *SW* 1:804–6; *SBO* 3:482–83).

153 Leclercq, "Théologie monastique," 21.

154 *Res*, 2.8 (CF 52:163; *SW* 8:266; *SBO* 5:98).

155 *Div*, 80.1 (CF 68:313; *SW* 9:660; *SBO* 6.1:320). "Est unitas naturalis, unitas carnalis, unitas virtualis, unitas moralis, unitas spiritualis, unitas socialis, unitas personalis, unitas principalis . . . Unitas virtualis est, quae hominem sibi ipsi coniungit, ut non per diversa effluat, sed, cum Propheta, unam petat a Domino." Regarding Bernard on natural unity, see Hiss, *Die Anthropologie*, 43.

Christ's hypostatic union in more detail. The hypostatic union, Bernard states, is "a great and powerful expression of unity" (*expressam unionis vim*).[156] In this union, there is on one hand the primary divine unity that is a "supreme" and "unique unity" (*summum . . . unice unum*).[157] The Trinity of three Persons is a unity of divinity; the unity of body and blood, soul, and divinity in Christ (the unity of the hypostatic union) mirrors this primary divine unity. Bernard describes the hypostatic union as a secondary unity of three substances in one Person (*tres substantiae una in Christo persona sunt*).[158] Shortly thereafter, Bernard makes a similar statement:

> It was fitting, indeed, that the mystery which was accomplished on man's behalf should be in close and intimate harmony with the nature of man. It was also fitting that it conform to that supreme unity which is in God and is God, so that just as in God three persons are one essence, so here by a most appropriate turn-about three essences are one person [*tres essentiae sint una persona*].[159]

Do Bernard's references to three substances and essences in Christ indicate that in his anthropology, a human being is comprised of two distinct substances or essences, soul and body? An answer to this question is found when noting that Bernard elsewhere refers to a human being as composed of a "twofold substance" (*substantiam duplicem*), seemingly one substance with two dimensions.[160] Further, with respect to the hypostatic union, Bernard indicates in *De consideratione* that he is speaking of Christ's soul and body as distinct substances or essences in the sense of making a numeric distinction:

> I say that in Christ, the Word, a soul and flesh are one person without confusion of essences [*sine confusione essentiarum*], and that without prejudice

156 *Csi*, V, 9.20 (CF 37:165; *SW* 1:808; *SBO* 3:484).

157 *Csi*, V, 8.19 (CF 37:163; *SW* 1:806; *SBO* 3:483).

158 *Csi*, V, 8.19 (CF 37:164; *SW* 1:806; *SBO* 3:483). "Igitur inter omnia quae recte unum dicuntur, arcem tenet unitas Trinitatis, quae tres personae una substantia sunt. Secundo loco illa praecellit, qua e converso tres substantiae una in Christo persona sunt."

159 *Csi*, V, 9.20 (CF 37:165; *SW* 1:806–8; *SBO* 3:483–84). "Decuit quippe familiarius similiusque cum hominis convenire constitutione, quod pro homine constitutum est sacramentum. Decuit et cum summa, quae in Deo est et Deus est, unitate congruere, ut quomodo ibi tres personae una essentia, ita hic convenientissima quadam contrarietate tres essentiae sint una persona."

160 "But perhaps on account of the twofold substance in which our human condition consists, since each of the two is so miserable, we may not inappropriately call human misery twofold, although it is manifold in each of the two." *Nat*, 5.4 (CF 51:127; *SW* 7:272; *SBO* 4:268). See also Hiss, *Die Anthropologie*, 56.

> to the unity of his person, they remain numerically distinct. And I would not deny that this unity belongs to that kind of unity by which the soul and flesh are one man.[161]

This remark might be interpreted to indicate that body and soul are not two separated substances or natures and the distinction at hand is one to be made according to "numerosity" (*numerositate*).[162]

One might note that at this point in Book V, when discussing the hypostatic union, Bernard connects the topic of Christ's historical incarnation with the topic of salvation—and therefore he also implicitly connects the topic of the incarnation with the topic of the union between the human soul and God.[163] The mystery or sacrament of the hypostatic union was—with respect to the historical incarnation of Christ that occurred during the first Advent of the Word—a work that God "accomplished on man's behalf" (*pro homine constitutum*).[164] With respect to this soteriological dimension of the hypostatic union, Bernard writes:

> Do you see how beautifully between either unit is placed this unity in him who has been appointed mediator of God and man, the man Christ Jesus? It is beautifully appropriate, I say, in that the mystery of salvation corresponds by suitable degree of similarity both to the Savior and to the saved.[165]

Bernard indicates that there is a relationship—a similitude—between the person who is saved in Christ and Christ himself, a relationship involving a certain kind of proportion or fittingness (*convenientia*). His reference to the beauty of this proportion indicates that his appreciation of Christian

161 *Csi*, V, 9.20 (CF 37:164–65; *SW* 1:806; *SBO* 3:483). "Dico in Christo Verbum, animam et carnem, sine confusione essentiarum unam esse personam, et item absque praeiudicio personalis unitatis in sua numerositate manere. Nec negaverim hanc ad illud quoque genus unitatis pertinere, qua anima et caro unus est homo."

162 Ibid. What this means for Bernard, however, is not entirely clear.

163 For this observation, I am indebted to Anderson, "Paul in Book 5," 141 and 148.

164 *Csi*, V, 9.20 (CF 37:165; *SW* 1:806–8; *SBO* 3:483–84).

165 *Csi*, V, 9.20 (CF 37:165; *SW* 1:808; *SBO* 3:484). "Videsne pulchre inter utramque unitatem hanc collocari, in eo utique qui constitutus est mediator Dei hominisque, homo Christus Iesus? Pulcherrima, inquam, convenientia, ut salutare sacramentum congrua quadam similitudine ambobus respondeat, et salvanti videlicet et salvato."

soteriology might arise according to what Hufgard calls a kind of mystical aesthetic.[166]

Personal Experience with Spiritual Affection and Prayer

Near the end of Book V, Bernard describes four particular modes of contemplative meditation that focus respectively on God's power, wisdom, charity, and eternity.[167] Bernard suggests that Eugene III integrate "holy affection" into these specific meditations.[168] He writes: "Holy affection makes a saint" (*Sanctum facit affectio sancta*).[169] It is important to note that Bernard in his recommendations at this point gives more and more emphasis to the role of affect in meditation as well as to prayerful attention to God and less emphasis to the intellectual exploration of specific theological beliefs.

Bernard includes within holy affection the affections of reverence and love in orientation to God. Bernard's remarks arguably refer to the exercise of monastic compunction which he describes in a slightly different way in his *Sermones super cantica canticorum*: "there are two kinds of compunction—the one in sorrow for our deviations, the other in rejoicing for God's gifts."[170] Compunction might be understood in this sense not as a confused and mixed emotion, but rather as a complex group of affections: sorrow or grief (*moeror*) conjoined with humility as well as reverence for God integrate with rejoicing (*exsultatio*), hope, and love. This twofold set of affections, according to Leclercq, relates to the "double experience" of self (sorrow, grief, humility) and God (reverence, joy, hope, love).[171] Recall also, as quoted above, that Bernard refers to compunction in a sermon from the *De diversis* series as

166 According to Hufgard: "Bernard's aesthetics and mystical theology are of one piece." M. Kilian Hufgard, "Saint Bernard of Clairvaux: Friend or Foe of the Arts?," CS 68:62–71, at 64. See also Stiegman, "Tradition of Aesthetics in Saint Bernard," in CS 135:129–47.

167 *Csi*, V, 13.28 (CF 37:175–76; *SW* 1:822; *SBO* 3:491).

168 It would be a mistake in my opinion to read Leclercq as suggesting that for Bernard at this point in the meditative ascent one leaves behind the level of intelligence, solely emphasizing affect: "Sur ce dernier point, saint Bernard a parlé, jusqu'ici, de la considération telle qu'il l'avait définie comme une activité de l'intelligence. Mais il ne peut s'arrêter à ce niveau. Il faut qu'il monte: ascendamus, vient-il de répéter (n. 27). Il finira par un hymne à l'amour." After these remarks, Leclercq then observes that one's intellectual activity continues as meditation transitions into experiential contemplative prayer: "la réflexion intellectuelle se prolonge dans l'adoration." Leclercq, "L'Art de la Composition," 129.

169 *Csi*, V, 14.30 (CF 37:177; *SW* 1:824; *SBO* 3:492).

170 *SCC*, 56, 3.7 (CF 31:93; *SW* 6:250; *SBO* 2:118). "Sint duo genera compunctionis, unum in moerore pro nostris excessibus, alterum in exsultatione pro divinis muneribus."

171 CS 7:252.

involving a "double consideration."[172] A little later in the same *De diversis* sermon series, Bernard writes:

> The whole summit of spiritual conversion [*spiritualis conversationis*] dwells in these two: that when we consider ourselves we are troubled and saddened in a salutary way, and that in the divine [orientation], we enjoy rest and consolation from joy of the Holy Spirit. From considering ourselves comes fear and humility [*hinc timorem et humilitatem*]; from divine consolation we take up true hope and charity.[173]

Bernard's reference here to self-reflection resulting in humility seems topically related to the testimony of conscience (*testimonio conscientiae*)[174] which, as discussed previously, may be understood to involve a kind of contemplative self-intuition in the clear light of truth (*se intuens clara luce veritatis*).[175] I will return to discuss this topic of a light of truth (*lux veritatis*) further below.

Here, as noted by Casey, one might observe that understanding compunction as twofold is a teaching that is also found in the thought of Gregory the Great.[176] In Gregory's *Homiliae in Ezechielem*, which Bernard cites in *De consideratione*, Gregory writes: "Truly there is one compunction which is born of fear, and another which springs from love, since it is one thing to flee from punishment and another to desire rewards."[177] Is it possible to fear and love God simultaneously? Or does one transition from fear to love? Perhaps the answer depends on how one understands the affection of fear under consideration. Referencing the first letter of John ("There is no fear in love. But perfect love casts out fear"[178]), Bernard states:

172 *Div*, 2.1 (CF 68:12; *SW* 9:180; *SBO* 6.1:80). "Vacate, itaque, dilectissimi, et videte quoniam ipse est Deus. Verum ut hoc quandoque possitis, curandum vobis prius, ut videatis quid estis vos . . . Huic duplici considerationi tota haec vestra vacatio tribuatur."

173 *Div*, 5.5 (CF 68:39; *SW* 9:180; *SBO* 6.1:80). "In his enim duobus tota spiritualis conversationis summa versatur, ut in nostra consideratione turbemur et contristemur ad salutem, in divina respiremus et de gaudio Spiritus Sancti habeamus consolationem; et hinc timorem et humilitatem, inde vero spem concipiamus et caritatem."

174 *Csi*, II, 7.14 (CF 37:64; *SW* 1:684; *SBO* 3:422).

175 *SCC*, 36, 4.5 (CF 7:177–78; *SW* 5:568; *SBO* 2:7).

176 See Michael Casey, *Athirst for God: Spiritual Desire in Bernard of Clairvaux* (Kalamazoo, MI: Cistercian Publications, 1987), 122, where Casey quotes Gregory the Great in the *Dialogues* (3.34) at length on the twofold affective dimension of compunction. Casey also cites *Hiez*, II, 10.20–21.

177 *Hiez*, II, 10.20 (Tomkinson, 455–56; SC 360:524).

178 1 Jn 4:18.

> Charity will never be without fear but it will be a chaste fear . . . Piety mixed with fear does not destroy fear; it chastens it. The punishment alone is taken away, without which fear could not exist while servile. But chaste and filial fear [*timor . . . castus et filialis*] remains forever. When one reads: "Perfect charity drives away fear," this must be understood of the punishment which is inseparable from servile fear.[179]

Following Bernard, it seems appropriate to refer to filial fear or reverence in order to differentiate compunction from servile fear. Ultimately, one might understand compunction with Gregory simply as involving the spiritual affection of reverential love for God.

In connection with cultivating affective reverence for God in meditative practice, Bernard states that this affection conjoins with a meditation on God's power and wisdom; meanwhile, the holy affection of love conjoins with meditation on God's charity and eternity.[180] As mentioned earlier, Bernard refers to these four meditations as "four kinds of contemplation" (*contemplationis species quattuor*).[181] Reverence purifies the heart so to admire God's majesty and power; reverence also inspires the search for virtue whereby one might live in accordance with God's wisdom.[182] Love arises from gratitude when one makes time for quietude to remember God's benefits; in this respect, meditation can foster one's appreciation for God's charity.[183]

In his *Sermones super cantica canticorum*, Bernard indicates that the love of God flows from God and returns to God, as a kind of ever-renewing circuit of affectivity between the soul and God: "the love of God gives birth to the love of the soul for God, and his surpassing affection fills the soul with affection, and his concern evokes concern."[184] Bernard explains this circuit more in a sermon later in the same series:

> Love needs no cause beyond itself, nor does it demand fruits; it is its own purpose. I love because I love; I love that I may love. Love is a great reality,

179 *Dil*, 14.38 (CF 13b:40; *SW* 1:140; *SBO* 3:152). "Numquam erit caritas sine timore, sed casto . . . Porro timori permixta devotio ipsum non annullat, sed castificat. Poena tantum tollitur, sine qua esse non potuit, dum fuit servilis; et timor manet in saeculum saeculi castus et filialis. Nam quod legitur: Perfecta caritas foras mittit timorem, poena intelligenda est, quae servili."

180 *Csi*, V, 14.30 (CF 37:177; *SW* 1:824; *SBO* 3:492).

181 *Csi*, V, 14.32 (CF 37:178; *SW* 1:826; *SBO* 3:493).

182 *Csi*, V, 14.32 (CF 37:178–79; *SW* 1:826; *SBO* 3:493).

183 *Csi*, V, 14.32 (CF 37:179; *SW* 1:826; *SBO* 3:493).

184 *SCC*, 69, 3.7 (CF 40:34; *SW* 6:426; *SBO* 2:206). "Ita est: amor Dei amorem animae parit, et illius praecurrens intentio intentam animam facit, sollicitudoque sollicitam."

> and if it returns to its beginning and goes back to its origin, seeking its source again, it will always draw afresh from it, and thereby flow freely . . . when God loves, he desires nothing but to be loved, since he loves us for no other reason than to be loved, for he knows that those who love him are blessed in their very love.[185]

Love also entails affection for the beloved in a way that focuses on the beloved as an end as such—not as a tool to be used or as a means to be employed in order to reach some other goal.[186]

In connection with cultivating *love* for God in meditative practice, one might benefit from studying Bernard's teaching on the four degrees of love described in his treatise *De diligendo Deo*.[187] The first degree of love, according to Bernard, is self-love. The second degree involves loving God on the basis of self-love, where love of God is still grounded in love of self as its root support or foundation. But through study and prayer, one might begin to love God not on the basis of self-love, but rather because God has become one's beloved—God is now loved for himself. Bernard observes that one might reside at this third degree of love for a long time, in that the fourth degree of love involves an uncommon union with God:

> Let those who have had the experience [*qui experti*] make a statement; to me, I confess, it seems impossible . . . In some wondrous way [a person at the fourth degree of love] forgets himself and ceasing to belong to himself, he passes entirely into God and adhering to him, he becomes one with him in spirit.[188]

185 *SCC*, 83, 2.4 (CF 40:184; *SW* 6:614–16; *SBO* 2:300–301). "Amor praeter se non requirit causam, non fructum: fructus eius, usus eius. Amo, quia amo; amo, ut amem. Magna res amor, si tamen ad suum recurrat principium, si suae origini redditus, si refusus suo fonti, semper ex eo sumat unde iugiter fluat . . . Nam cum amat Deus, non aliud vult, quam amari: quippe non ad aliud amat, nisi ut ametur, sciens ipso amore beatos, qui se amaverint." See also Gallagher, *Examen Prayer*, 156.

186 *Dil*, 7.17 (CF 13b:20; *SW* 1:104; *SBO* 3:134). "Whatever you seem to love because of something else, you do not really love; you really love the end pursued and not that by which it is pursued" (*Nam quidquid propter aliud amare videaris, id plane amas, quo amoris finis pertendit, non per quod tendit*).

187 Leclercq indicates that Bernard may have been influenced when writing this work by Cicero's *De amicitia*. See Jean Leclercq, "General Introduction to the Works of Saint Bernard (II)," *CSQ* 40, no. 3 (2005): 243–51, at 244. For Cicero, see Cicero, *Laelius de amicitia*, in *On Old Age, On Friendship, On Divination*, trans. W. A. Falconer (Cambridge, MA: Harvard University Press, 1923), 108–210. See also Stepsis, "Fulfillment of Self," 357–58.

188 *Dil*, 15.39 (CF 13b:40–41; *SW* 1:142; *SBO* 3:153).

The fourth degree of love for Bernard thus involves a kind of self-transcendence and a more complete realization of spiritual unity with God, sharing in a common will of love.

A final path of theological meditation that Bernard proposes to Pope Eugene III is that the pope should at this point forget the past and anticipate the future with God: "This [reflection], since it is the meditation of eternity—for what is promised is eternal—nourishes patience and gives vigor to perseverance."[189] It is worth nothing that the path of meditation that Bernard mentions here with respect to the topic of eternity involves the exercise of memory. One makes time for quietude in order to reflect on (or bring to attention) God's gifts; such remembrance might lead one to thanksgiving and growth in the love of God. Bernard exhorts his readers of sermon 11 from the *Sermones super cantica canticorum* to dwell on (to fix their attention on) the memory of God's gifts with thanksgiving; they should meditate on God's work of redemption by recalling both Christ's self-emptying in the incarnation (the first historical Advent) and his coming interiorly to the soul through the Holy Spirit in order to fill the redeemed (the second spiritual Advent).[190] This second Advent might be associated with the sacrament of Eucharistic communion.

In a different sermon series, Bernard alludes to John 14:26 when observing that it is the Holy Spirit who helps one to remember.[191] The course of one's meditation, therefore, might at this point be understood significantly to involve the exercise of memory in terms of directing one's attention to the Holy Spirit.[192] Is it possible then that when Bernard refers to the testimony of conscience (*testimonio conscientiae*)[193]—which, as discussed several times, can be interpreted to involve a kind of contemplative self-intuition in the

189 *Csi*, V, 14.32 (CF 37:179; *SW* 1:826; *SBO* 3:493). "Quae, cum sit meditatio aeternitatis,—siquidem quae promittuntur, aeterna sunt—, longanimitatem alit et perseverantiae dat vigorem."

190 See *SCC*, 11, 1.2–2.3 (CF 4:69–76, at 70–72; *SW* 5:156–67, at 158–60; *SBO* 1:54–59, at 55–56). See also Daniel K. Griggs, "Augustine's Influence on Bernard of Clairvaux's Teaching on Memory," *CSQ* 32, no. 3 (1997): 475–85, at 484. See also Casey, "Mindfulness of God," 120. I refer to "readers" of Bernard's sermon rather than "hearers" because Bernard's sermons may not have been preached (or not preached in the form in which they are preserved). See Bredero, *Bernard of Clairvaux*, 4; Emero Stiegman, "The Literary Genre of Bernard of Clairvaux's *Sermones super Cantica Canticorum*," in *Simplicity and Ordinariness: Studies in Medieval Cistercian History IV*, ed. John R. Sommerfeldt (Kalamazoo, MI: Cistercian Publications, 1980), 68–93, at 71 (hereafter CS 61); Verbaal, "The Preaching of Community," 84n36.

191 *Pent*, 1.5 (CF 53:71–72). See also Smith, "Bernard's Anthropology," 424. See also the discussion of meditation involving the consolation of memory prior to the experience of contemplation in *Dil*, 3.10–5.15 (CF 13b:12–17; *SW* 1:88–101; *SBO* 3:126–32).

192 See Leclercq's description of monastic reminiscence: Leclercq, *Love of Learning*, 15 and 73–75.

193 *Csi*, II, 7.14 (CF 37:64; *SW* 1:684; *SBO* 3:422).

clear light of truth (*se intuens clara luce veritatis*)—that the light of truth (*lux veritatis*) enabling this self-intuition is in some way related to the Holy Spirit?[194] Is it an inspiration that leads one to respond to this self-intuition by taking up a foundation in humility?[195]

Ultimately, the four paths of theological meditation that Bernard prescribes at the end of *De consideratione* Book V might coalesce so to lead a person to develop an integrated cognitive-affective sense of God's one reality (*una res*).[196] This integrated orientation entails receptivity to a sublime mystery that transcends the finitude of human awareness:

> I seem to have mentioned many things, but they are one. The one God has been described for our understanding, not as he actually is. Divisions exist in our understanding, not in God. There are various names, many paths; but one thing is signified by the names, one [reality] is sought by the paths.[197]

Bernard indicates elsewhere that cognitive-affective self-integration is brought to ultimate completion only when encountering God directly, primordially, and intimately, in what is customary referred to as the beatific vision. Perhaps alluding to Psalm 16:11, Bernard states:

> His right hand portrays the beatific vision [*beatam visionem*] which he promised them and the joy of his majestic presence [*praesentia maiestatis*]. The vision of God [*deifica visio*] which makes us resemble him, and its incalculable delight [*illa divinae praesentiae inaestimabilis delectatio*] are rightly figured by the right hand . . .[198]

Citing 1 Corinthians 13:12, Bernard asserts that upon receiving the grace of the beatific vision, one's mind and soul will become thoroughly integrated, reflecting the integrity of the divine unity:

> We cannot deal with the simplicity of God; while we strive to comprehend him as one, he appears to us as fourfold . . . But when we see him face to

194 *SCC*, 36, 4.5 (CF 7:177–78; *SW* 5:568; *SBO* 2:7).

195 Ibid.

196 *Csi*, V, 13.29 (CF 37:176; *SW* 1:824; *SBO* 3:492).

197 *Csi*, V, 13.27 (CF 37:174). "Visus sum protulisse plura, sed unum est. Unus Deus signatus est pro captu nostro, non pro suo statu. Diversus hic est, non ille. Voces diversae, semitae multae; sed unum per eas significatur, unus quaeritur."

198 *Dil*, 4.12 (CF 13b:15; *SW* 1:94; *SBO* 3:129).

> face we will see him as he is. At that time the fragile gaze of our souls [*acies mentis*], however assiduously applied, will in no way return or break down into its own multiplicity. It will draw more together, unite, and conform itself to God's unity [*Colliget sese magis, adunabit conformabitque unitati illius*], so one will answer the other face to face.[199]

Complete psychological integration, Bernard states, can only be realized as an eschatological or ultimate goal. Conversely, Bernard implies in this passage that in the current embodied life there is always a possibility of psychological disintegration, no matter what degree of self-integration one obtains. The path of meditation that Bernard prescribes might be characterized as a quest for self-integration in imitation of the divine unity, even if such a quest cannot be fulfilled prior to the experience of ultimate beatification.[200] Here, one sees again that the practice of meditation is not an end to itself; rather, this spiritual exercise is a means to the goal of union with God wherein lies one's religious salvation.

Bernard closes Book V by indicating that beyond all discussion and disputation is to be found the more comprehensive knowledge of the saints who followed the path of experience when seeking the reality of God. Referring to experiential knowledge of the divine attributes, he writes:

> We know these things. Do we think, therefore, we have also comprehended them? It is not disputation [*non ea disputatio*] but sanctity that comprehends them, if, however, what is incomprehensible can in any way be comprehended . . . The saints, then, comprehend. Do you ask how? If you are a saint, you have comprehended and you know; if you are not, be one and you will know through your own experience [*tuo experimento scies*].[201]

199 *Csi*, V, 13.27 (CF 37:174; *SW* 1:820; *SBO* 3:490). "Nobis autem, quia non possumus cum Deo simplicitate contendere, dum contendimus apprehendere unum, occurrit veluti quadruplicatum . . . Cum autem videbimus facie ad faciem, videbimus sicuti est. Nec enim iam tunc fragilis acies mentis nostrae, quantumlibet vehementer intendens, aliquatenus resiliet dissilietve in suam pluralitatem. Colliget sese magis, adunabit conformabitque unitati illius, vel potius unitati illi, ut una uni facies respondeat faciei."

200 See Stiegman, "Bernard of Clairvaux, William of St. Thierry, the Victorines," 138.

201 *Csi*, V, 14.30 (CF 37:177; *SW* 1:824; *SBO* 3:492). "Novimus haec. Num ideo et arbitramur nos comprehendisse? Non ea disputatio comprehendit, sed sanctitas, si quo modo tamen comprehendi potest quod incomprehensibile est. At nisi posset, non dixisset Apostolus ut comprehendamus cum omnibus sanctis. Sancti igitur comprehendunt. Quaeris quomodo? Si sanctus est, comprehendisti et nosti; si non, esto, et tuo experimento scies." See also Leclercq, *Love of Learning*, 216.

Bernard thus points to an experiential knowledge beyond theological disputation, a wisdom beyond technical discussion. It is by way of prayer that such experience is to be sought: "He must still be sought who has not yet sufficiently been found and who cannot be sought too much; but he is perhaps more worthily sought and more easily found by prayer than by discussion [*disputando*]."[202] Leclercq observes that in this closing remark, Bernard gives emphasis to a spiritual search for God that includes but transcends an intellectual search.[203] This closing to Book V marks a transition from meditation (which can be written about and communicated) to the experience of the attention of the mind (*acies mentis*) turning toward God in contemplative affection.[204] In this way, Bernard closes his letter-treatise with the suggestion that the search for God continue—not in contemplative meditation, but rather in contemplative prayer. In other words, the *contemplatio* of *meditatio* transitions to the *contemplatio* of *oratio* in a quiet stillness that approximates God's sabbath rest: "Therefore, let this be the end of the book but not the end of the search."[205]

202 *Csi*, V, 14.32 (CF 37:179; *SW* 1:826; *SBO* 3:493). "Quaerendus adhuc fuerat, qui nec satis adhuc inventus est nec quaeri nimis potest; at orando forte quam disputando dignius quaeritur et invenitur facilius." See also Leclercq, "L'Art de la Composition," 129.

203 Leclercq, *Love of Learning*, 211.

204 "Il trouve encore une transition parfaite, qui annonce une suite qui sera, non plus écrite, mais vécue, expérimentée dans la prière: la réflexion intellectuelle se prolonge dans l'adoration, dans le consentement à Dieu déjà trouvé, mais non encore suffisamment." Leclercq, "L'Art de la Composition," 129.

205 *Csi*, V, 14.32 (CF 37:179; *SW* 1:826; *SBO* 3:493). "Proinde is sit finis libri, sed non finis quaerendi."

PART 3

Applications for Personal Spiritual Development

9

A Consolidated Summary

Having completed a historical evaluation of Bernard's treatise in Part 1 and provided an interpretation of its content in Part 2, I proceed now to consider the relationship of Bernard's teaching on meditation to the contemporary time period. In this part of the study, I discuss how his teaching might be appropriated by contemporary persons in a way that is helpful for spiritual growth. Analogous to Stepsis who interpreted Bernard's works in light of a Maslowian personality theory,[1] I present Bernard's teaching on meditation here in light of how it might be practiced by persons today seeking spiritual development.

In the introduction, I referred to this re-presentation of Bernard's teaching in terms of a recontextualization,[2] which is equivalent to what Lonergan in Catholic theology describes as a transposition,[3] or what Gadamer in hermeneutic philosophy refers to as the reintroduction of meaning.[4] I noted earlier that Leclercq questioned whether Bernard maintained any specific

1 Stepsis, "Fulfillment of Self," 348–64.

2 Morse, "'Emerging from the Data,'" 34.

3 Lonergan is drawing on the hermeneutic philosophy of Wilhelm Dilthey. See Bernard Lonergan, "Horizons and Transpositions," in *Philosophical and Theological Papers 1965–1980*, ed. Robert C. Croken and Robert M. Doran (Toronto: University of Toronto Press, 2004), 409–32, at 410. For Dilthey, see, e.g., Wilhelm Dilthey, *The Formation of the Historical World in the Human Sciences* (Princeton, NJ: Princeton University Press, 2002), 234–37. See also Matthew L. Lamb, *History, Method, and Theology: A Dialectical Comparison of Wilhelm Dilthey's Critique of Historical Reason and Bernard Lonergan's Meta-Methodology* (Missoula, Mont.: Scholars Press, 1978).

4 *TM*, 392–95; *GW*, 1:394–97. Gadamer's phrase *Rückverwandlung* (translated as "transformation" or "transformation back") might be misunderstood as stating that any interpretation necessarily involves some kind of semantic development; this phrase can be associated with Gadamer's reference to *Wiederholen* which he explains as a presentation of meaning that is not simply a repetition of the past, but rather a renewal of meaning in the present. I choose the word reintroduction as a translation for *Rückverwandlung*.

theory of human development.[5] At the same time, when describing Bernard's doctrine in Book V of *De consideratione*, Leclercq observed that Bernard's teaching does contain a certain "structure" that is "solid, precise, and artistic."[6] Leclercq also outlined two substructures that he discerned within Book V.[7] During the course of presenting my interpretation of Bernard's teaching in Part 2, I often noted how his discussion suggested that one bring one's psychological activities (thinking, self-understanding, use of imagination) into a certain structure or enclosure as associated with a claustral psychology. These observations indicate that Bernard's teaching involves not only a doctrinal structure as Leclercq observes, but also the presupposition of a psychological structure toward which one might develop.[8] McMahon observes a similar "ascent pattern" or "structural pattern" in Augustine's teaching on meditation in the *Confessions*.[9] The effort to clarify such boundaries might be called a structural hermeneutics.[10]

Following Leclercq, in this chapter I outline the overarching structure of meditation that may be discerned in the whole of *De consideratione* (Books I–V). In the next chapter, I then discuss contemporary recontextualizations of Bernard's teaching. For the sake of summarizing the various kinds of meditations that Bernard describes in *De consideratione*, I condense Bernard's teaching (see the outline below).[11] For example, I combine Bernard's discussion of meditating on "what is below one" (Book III) with meditating on "what is around one" (Book IV).[12] The resulting course of meditation involves three general stages (*gradibus*): (1) self-reflection, (2) reflection on human relationships, and (3) reflection on relationship with God. For the sake of consolidation, I also propose moving some specific topics around within these three general stages of meditation.

5 CS 105:xiv.

6 Leclercq, "L'Art de la Composition," 127. "Il y a certes, dans les quelques pages qui viennent d'être ici résumées, une structure à la fois solide, précise et artistique."

7 Leclercq, "L'Art de la Composition," 126–27 and 129.

8 See also Leclercq's remarks about a structural psychology in Leclercq, *Monks and Love*, 6.

9 McMahon, *Understanding the Medieval Meditative Ascent*, 95.

10 For use of the phrase "structural hermeneutics" in cultural sociology, see Jeffrey Alexander and Philip Smith, "The Strong Program in Cultural Theory: Elements of a Structural Hermeneutics," in *Handbook of Sociological Theory*, ed. Jonathan H. Turner (New York: Kluwer Academic, 2002), 135–50.

11 That condensation occurs as a stage in qualitative research, see Morse, "'Emerging from the Data,'" 32–34.

12 This condensation is warranted because Bernard indicated that Book IV is in a sense a continuation of Book III. See *Csi*, IV, 1.1 (CF 37:109; *SW* 1:736; *SBO* 3:448).

With respect to the first general stage of self-reflection, a person taking up meditation might develop some cognizance of that person's religious context and purpose for meditation; Bernard indicates that for Christian persons, meditation might be understood to occur for the ultimate purpose of salvation[13] and involve an orientation toward the Holy Spirit.[14] As self-reflection for Bernard involves making qualitative judgments concerning one's personal character, it might also be helpful for a person to develop some degree of understanding what it means to conduct an informal self-assessment. Unless judged to be helpful by a civil health care provider, however, this kind of qualitative assessment would not necessarily need to proceed in a technical manner using pre-designed instruments such as inventories or standardized evaluation tools.[15] Rather, conducting a qualitative self-assessment in this way might be understood as developing a general ability for self-discernment as well as clarifying the criteria that one will reference during such self-evaluations.

I suggest relocating consideration of "who one is" to this first general stage of self-reflection because this meditation would also involve cultivating a balanced sense of self (as Bernard suggested to Eugene III).[16] Next, one might reflect on one's human nature (i.e., oneself as an embodied spiritual, mental, and emotional being) then proceed also to reflect on one's character. With respect to meditation on one's character, I propose adding meditations on personality and innate temperament (in contrast, recall that Bernard recommended that Eugene III proceed directly to meditation on relationship roles).[17] One might also relocate to this point in meditation a self-assessment of where one stands in relation to the nine mental qualities that Bernard prescribed to Eugene III (e.g., discerning to what extent one's mind is free from minor concerns, firm, expansive, etc.).[18] Lastly, one might close this first stage of self-reflection by considering the moral dimension of one's characer

13 *SCC*, 37, 1.2 (CF 7:182; *SW* 5:572; *SBO* 2:9). "Non tamen dico contemnendam scientiam litterarum, quae ornat animam et erudit eam, et facit ut possit etiam alios erudire. Sed duo illa oportet et expedit ut praecedant, in quibus summam salutis constitui superior ratio declaravit."

14 See, e.g., *Pent*, 1.5–6 (CF 53:71–72; *SW* 8:396; *SBO* 5:163).

15 For an example of this kind of approach, see Tami Borneman, Betty Ferrell, and Christina M. Puchalski, "Evaluation of the FICA Tool for Spiritual Assessment," *Journal of Pain and Symptom Management* 40, no. 2 (2010): 163–73; Wendy Cadge and Julia Bandini, "The Evolution of Spiritual Assessment Tools in Healthcare," *Society* 52, no. 5 (2015): 430–37; Lance D. Laird, Cara E. Curtis, and Jonathan R. Morgan, "Finding Spirits in Spirituality: What are We Measuring in Spirituality and Health Research?," *Journal of Religion and Health* 56, no. 1 (2017): 1–20.

16 *Csi*, II, 10.19 (CF 37:72; *SW* 1:692; *SBO* 3:426).

17 *Csi*, II, 5.8 (CF 37:54; *SW* 1:670; *SBO* 3:415).

18 *Csi*, IV, 6.17 (CF 37:131; *SW* 1:764; *SBO* 462).

(e.g., one's exercise of the virtues and for Christian persons development in becoming more Christ-like).[19]

With respect to the second general stage of meditation on human relationships, one might reflect on one's relationship roles past and present (e.g., being a mother, a wife, a sister, or a professional) as well as reflect on the persons who modeled for one how to live out such roles. Further, one might consider whether any given relationship involves another person who is distant or close by, what responsibility one has in the relationship (duties and obligations), the stability of the relationship (a Benedictine quality), as well as one's own stability regarding the role that one has assumed in the relationship (e.g., being a father).[20] One might also reflect on the degree of peace that one experiences in relationships with others,[21] or alternatively whether one experiences conflict (e.g., one might discern whether one experiences tension or domination in a certain relationship—Augustine's *libido dominandi*[22]). Lastly, recalling Bernard's self-description as a "modern chimæra,"[23] one might discern whether one experiences any conflict within oneself with respect to one's relationship roles; a person today, for example, might experience conflict between responsibilities in filling the role of a mother and responsibilities in filling a professional role.[24]

With respect to the third general stage of theological reflection, one might interpret this kind of meditation as focused on one's relationship with God. The metaphor of Jacob's ladder might be employed as a way to picture the meditative ascent of one's mind toward God. For Bernard, following Benedict, such an ascent of the mind is also proportionate to growth in humility.[25] At the outset of this third stage of meditation, one might reflect on the importance of grace for assistance in one's development.

One might then proceed to the first step of a practical theological reflection. For example, one might discern what areas God is calling one to grow in. Such growth pertains to one's spiritual development or formation

19 *Csi*, I, 8.10 (CF 37:39; *SW* 1:650; *SBO* 3:405).

20 *RB*, chap. 58 (McCann, 130–31; Fry, 56).

21 *Div*, 16.3 (CF 68:89; *SW* 9:312; *SBO* 6.1:146); *Div*, 16.5 (CF 68:91; *SW* 9:314; *SBO* 6.1:147).

22 Augustine, *City of God* I, preface, and XIV, 15 (Dyson, 3 and 614); *Csi*, III, 1.2 (CF 37:81; *SW* 1:704; *SBO* 3:432).

23 Ep 326, §4 (James, *Letters*, 401–2; Ep 250 in *SW* 3:330–34; *SBO* 8:145–47).

24 This is one area where Bernard's thought offers a significant contribution to civil psychotherapy, as mentioned in the next chapter. Such possible role conflicts are also indicated in Edith Stein, "The Separate Vocations of Man and Woman according to Nature and Grace," in *Essays on Woman*, 2nd ed., trans. Freda Mary Oben (Washington, DC: ICS Publications, 1996), 78–79.

25 *RB*, chap. 7 (McCann, 38–39; Fry, 16); *Csi*, V, 1.1 (CF 37:140; *SW* 1:774; *SBO* 3:467).

(*aedificatio* or *Bildung*).[26] One might then proceed in meditation to the next step of investigative theological reflections (e.g., one might consider God by means of reading scripture or employ philosophy for reflecting on nature). One might also relocate reflection on one's beliefs to this step of theological meditation. In terms of one's beliefs about God, one might also ask: are such theological beliefs derived from scripture or from some other source? In other words, are such beliefs based on authoritative teachings that one has received in faith or are such beliefs conclusions one has drawn by way of rational inference? Are such beliefs matters of opinion? Finally, with respect to contemplative meditation, one might retain all of Bernard's recommendations discussed in Book V: conducting a self-recollection,[27] assessing the degree of this recollection,[28] cultivating attentiveness to God's unity,[29] as well as developing in compunction (reverent love oriented to God).[30] The overall course of one's meditation might then close with a transition to contemplative prayer.[31]

Stage I: Self-Reflection
- 1. The present moment
  - a. Making time for quietude (leisure—*otium*)
  - b. Orientation to the Holy Spirit (piety and worship)
  - c. Focusing on a goal: Salvation in Christ (soteriology and eschatology)
  - d. The nature of qualitative self-assessment
- 2. Who one is
  - a. A balanced sense of self
- 3. What one is: human nature
  - a. One's body
  - b. One's soul (*anima*)
    - i. One's sensations and imagination
    - ii. One's emotions (love, joy, fear, sadness)
    - iii. One's mind (*animus, mens*) (reason, memory, will)

26 *SCC*, 36, 4.5 (CF 7:177; *SW* 5:568; *SBO* 2:7).

27 *Csi*, V, 2.4 (CF 37:143; *SW* 1:778; *SBO* 3:469).

28 See Gregory the Great: *Hiez*, II, 5.9 (Tomkinson, 339–40; SC 360:242).

29 *Csi*, V, 7.17 (CF 37:160; *SW* 1:800; *SBO* 3:480).

30 *SCC*, 56, 3.7 (CF 31:93; *SW* 6:250; *SBO* 2:118).

31 *Csi*, V, 14.32 (CF 37:179; *SW* 1:826; *SBO* 3:493).

4. One's character
    a. Personality (innate personal character, temperament), moods, response patterns
    b. Mental characteristics (undivided mind)
        i. Devoid of minor concerns
        ii. Free from imposition and coercion
        iii. Dignified and noble in attachment
        iv. Right in intention
        v. Cautious when doubting (regulating suspicion)
        vi. Vigilant in custody of thoughts (self-appropriated)
        vii. Firm (stable, self-consistent)
        viii. Unconquered (hopeful)
        ix. Broad (resilient)
    c. Conscience and honesty (self-intuition in the *lux veritatis*)
    d. The foundation of humility
    e. Moral characteristics and virtues (prudence, justice, fortitude, temperance)
    f. Religious characteristics and virtues (faith, hope, charity)

Stage II: Reflection on Relationships

1. Relationship roles (past and present)
2. Distant and proximate relationships
3. Responsibility in relationships (duties and obligations)
4. Stability in relationships and stability in roles (see also: Benedictine Rule)
5. Peace (unity of accord) vs. conflicts or domination (Augustine's *libido dominandi*)
6. Relationship role conflicts (Bernard's chimæra)

Stage III: Theological Reflection

1. Meditative ascent (Jacob's ladder, *scala considerationis*)
    a. The assistance of grace
2. Step A: Practical theological meditation (self-cultivation—*aedifcatio, Bildung*)
    a. Use (*uti*) and enjoyment (*frui*) (Augustine)
3. Step B: Investigative theological meditation (exploring nature; use of philosophy)
    a. Sources of theological belief: faith (for example, scripture), reason, opinion
4. Step C: Contemplative theological meditation
    a. Self-recollection
    b. Assessing one's degree of self-recollection (Gregory the Great)
    c. Self-transcendence
        i. Attentiveness to God's unity (Augustine's *acies mentis*)
        ii. Compunction (reverent love in relation to God)
        iii. Transition to contemplative prayer (spiritual unity)

It is evident from this summary that even an attempted consolidation of Bernard's teachings on meditation involve a spiritual exercise that is complex and multifaceted. It may not be possible to proceed through each of the three stages in one sitting (or it may not be possible to give equal time to every nuanced dimension of each stage). Further, certain aspects might be given more or less emphasis depending on a person's interests and goals or as suggested by a spiritual director or therapist.

10

Spiritual Direction and Spiritually Integrated Civil Psychotherapy

Having provided a consolidated summary of Bernard's teaching on meditation as derived from his treatise *De consideratione*, I will now proceed to conduct a more detailed exploration regarding how the path of meditation that Bernard describes intersects with contemporary Catholic spiritual direction and spiritually-integrated civil psychotherapy. I first differentiate Catholic spiritual direction and spiritually-integrated civil psychotherapy. I then consider each of the three stages of meditation found in Bernard's teaching with respect to these respective professional services. For the sake of review, these three stages are: (1) self-reflection, (2) reflection on human relationships, and (3) reflection on relationship with God.

Differentiating Spiritual Direction and Spiritually Integrated Civil Psychotherapy

When Leclercq referred to Bernard as a "psychotherapist" for others, he immediately qualified this anachronistic ascription by writing:

> If we have any right to consider Bernard as a psychotherapist, it is in the sense that he did spiritual therapy. He was more concerned with intentions, problems of conscience, than with psychological problems. What counted in his eyes were intentions, the faithfulness of each person to himself and to God. It was, so to speak, a committed, and not an impersonal, therapy

> because he was involved . . . He used his talent, duly controlled, as well as his passions in the service of spiritual consultations.[1]

If Bernard's teaching on meditation is interpreted as proposing a kind of spiritual therapy for others,[2] his recommendations for Eugene III might be adapted and serve as a resource for persons interested in spiritual self-cultivation today. Meditative practice can support personal growth whether one is seeking such development informally through self-study, or with the assistance of a spiritual director, or during a course of spiritually-integrated civil psychotherapy.

In order to explore the contemporary relevance of Bernard's teaching, one need not transform Bernard's recommendations into a particular technique, method, or skill-building program (i.e., attempt to develop some kind of technical manual of Cistercian spirituality).[3] As Leclercq maintains, "It is . . . vain and superfluous to seek a method of prayer. Rather the best method is to pray without a method. The Holy Spirit is an incomparable artist in this area, and we need only let Him bear us without looking backwards to find out by what path He is leading us."[4] But to pray and meditate without a method is not to proceed without any structure at all. It was in order to clarify the structure of Bernard's teaching in this regard that in the previous chapter I provided a summative outline of his recommendations for Eugene III.

The three general stages of meditation discussed above are relevant for Catholic-Christian spiritual direction.[5] More broadly speaking, there is significant contemporary interest in meditation exercises in the sense of mindfulness practices.[6] Such mindfulness practices are integrated into a variety

1 CS 105:74–75.

2 Regarding "spiritual therapy," see also John Paul II, *Vita consecrata*, Post-Synodal Apostolic Exhortation, March 25, 1996, §87; available at www.vatican.va.

3 See, e.g., Merton's warning against rigidity in meditation: Thomas Merton, *Spiritual Direction and Meditation* (Collegeville, MN: Liturgical Press, 1960), 77.

4 Jean Leclercq, *Alone with God*, trans. Elizabeth McCabe (New York: Farrar, Straus, and Giroux, 1989), 86.

5 For discussion of meditation exercises within the context of Catholic-Christian spiritual direction, see, e.g., Jean Leclercq, *The Interior Life*, trans. Fergus Murphy (New York: P. J. Kennedy and Sons, 1961), 134–47; Benedict J. Groeschel, *Spiritual Passages: The Psychology of Spiritual Development* (New York: Crossroad, 1987), 141–42; Thomas Dubay, *Seeking Spiritual Direction: How to Grow the Divine Life Within* (Ann Arbor, MI: Servant Publications, 1993), 181–83; Thomas Dubay, *Prayer Primer: Igniting the Fire Within* (Cincinnati: Servant Books, 2002), 65–81.

6 See, e.g., Jon Kabat-Zinn, *Wherever You Go, There You Are: Mindfulness Meditation in Everyday Life* (New York: Hachette Books, 1994); Thich Nhat Hahn, *The Miracle of Mindfulness: An*

of treatment modalities in civil psychotherapy.[7] While psychotherapeutic authors often point to the Buddhist tradition as a source for understanding mindfulness practices,[8] some authors have also attempted to clarify a distinctive Christian perspective.[9] The current study can be associated with this Christian literature.

Introduction to the Practice of Meditation (Boston, MA: Beacon Press, 1996); Bhante Gunaratana, *Mindfulness in Plain English* (Somerville, MA: Wisdom Publications, 2011).

7 Inclusion of mindfulness practices is featured in a large number of therapeutic modalities. For Cognitive Behavioral Therapy (hereafter CBT), see Judith S. Beck, *Cognitive Behavior Therapy: Basics and Beyond*, 2nd ed. (New York: Guilford Press, 2011), 264; David H. Rosmarin, *Spirituality, Religion, and Cognitive-Behavioral Therapy: A Guide for Clinicians* (New York: Guilford Press, 2018), 119–20 and 169–71. For Dialectical Behavior Therapy (hereafter DBT), see Lane D. Pedersen, "Mindfulness," in *Dialectical Behavior Therapy: A Contemporary Guide for Practitioners* (Malden, MA: John Wiley and Sons, 2015), 118–24 and 216–17; Cedar R. Koons, *The Mindfulness Solution for Intense Emotions: Take Control of Borderline Personality Disorder with DBT* (Oakland, CA: New Harbinger Publications, 2016). For Acceptance and Commitment Therapy (hereafter ACT), see Steven C. Hayes, Victoria M. Follette, and Marsha M. Linehan (eds.), *Mindfulness and Acceptance: Expanding the Cognitive-Behavioral Tradition* (New York: Guilford Press, 2004); Kelly G. Wilson, *Mindfulness for Two: An Acceptance and Commitment Therapy Approach to Mindfulness in Psychotherapy* (Oakland, CA: New Harbinger Publications, 2008). For Mindfulness-Based Cognitive Therapy (hereafter MBCT), see William Hathaway and Erica Tan, "Religiously Oriented Mindfulness-Based Cognitive Therapy," *Journal of Clinical Psychology: In Session* 65, no. 2 (2009): 158–71; Zindel V. Segal, J. Mark G. Williams, John D. Teasdale, *Mindfulness-Based Cognitive Therapy for Depression*, 2nd ed. (New York: Guilford Press, 2013), 44–62. For a distinct kind of "detached mindfulness" in Metacognitive Therapy (hereafter MCT), see Peter Fisher and Adrian Wells, *Metacognitive Therapy* (New York: Routledge, 2009), 27–29 and 104–6. See also Adrian Wells, *Emotional Disorders and Metacognition: Innovative Cognitive Therapy* (New York: John Wiley and Sons, 2000), 87–89.

8 Pargament, *Spiritually Integrated Psychotherapy*, 11, citing B. Alan Wallace and Shauna L. Shapiro, "Mental Balance and Well-Being: Building Bridges between Buddhism and Western Psychology," *American Psychologist* 61, no. 7 (2006): 690–701. See also Paul R. Fulton and Ronald D. Siegel, "Buddhist and Western Psychology: Seeking Common Ground," in *Mindfulness and Psychotherapy*, 2nd ed., ed. Christopher K. Germer, Ronald D. Siegel, and Paul R. Fulton (New York: Guilford Press, 2013), 36–58; Tullio Giraldi, *Psychotherapy, Mindfulness, and Buddhist Meditation* (Cham: Palgrave Macmillan, 2019); *Mindfulness and Buddhist-Derived Approaches in Mental Health and Addiction*, ed. Edo Shonin, William van Gordon, and Mark D. Griffiths (New York: Springer, 2016).

9 See, e.g., L. Vandenberghe and F. Costa Prado, "Law and Grace in Saint Augustine: A Fresh Perspective on Mindfulness and Spirituality in Behaviour Therapy," *Mental Health, Religion and Culture* 12, no. 6 (2009): 587–600; Thomas J. Bushlack, "Mindfulness and the Discernment of Passions: Insights from Thomas Aquinas," *Spiritus: A Journal of Christian Spirituality* 14, no. 2 (2014): 141–65; Gregory Bottaro, *The Mindful Catholic: Finding God One Moment at a Time* (North Palm Beach, FL: Beacon Publishing, 2018); Stefan Gillow Reynolds, *Living with the Mind of Christ: Mindfulness in Christian Spirituality* (Minneapolis, MN: Augsburg Books, 2020).

Before proceeding, I want to clarify the distinction between the provision of spiritual direction and the provision of civil psychotherapy.[10] With respect to the general features of Catholic spiritual direction, Barry and Connolly characterize such a service from the perspective of the Jesuit tradition as one Christian person helping another grow in relationship with God; this might occur by cultivating in a directee attentiveness, responsiveness, a sense of intimacy, and faithfulness as exhibited in the directee's manner of life.[11] Nemeck and Coombs, writing from the spiritual perspectives of the Missionary Oblates of Mary Immaculate and the eremetic tradition, respectively, maintain that there is a "contemplative dimension inherent in all spiritual direction," a "contemplative thrust [that is] integral to the universal call to holiness."[12] Spiritual direction thus helps directees develop a "contemplative attitude" that contributes to their reflection on possibilities of personal growth in living out their vocation as followers of Christ.[13]

Bernard's recommendation of meditation exercises to Eugene III corresponds with a variety of approaches in Catholic spiritual direction that aim to facilitate a directee's development in introspective self-awareness.[14] As discussed above, for Bernard, meditation is distinct from but oriented toward contemplation.[15] The practice of meditative reflection can thus be differentiated from both vocal and contemplative prayer.[16] With respect to meditation, various modalities of Catholic spiritual direction today frequently recommend some kind of meditation exercises.[17] Such recommendations may be very general; they might not explore meditation to the depth that Bernard describes it, especially with respect to some of the focused topics

10 The discussion that follows draws on: Benedict M. Ashley, Jean Deblois, and Kevin D. O'Rouke, *Health Care Ethics: A Catholic Theological Analysis,* 5th ed. (Washington, DC: Georgetown University Press, 2006), 143, 152–54, 241–49.

11 William A. Barry and William J. Connolly, *The Practice of Spiritual Direction*, 2nd rev. ed. (New York: HarperCollins, 2009), 8.

12 Francis Kelly Nemeck and Marie Theresa Coombs, *The Way of Spiritual Direction* (Collegeville, MN: Liturgical Press, 1985), 14.

13 Barry and Connolly, *Practice of Spiritual Direction*, 47–66.

14 See *Catechism of the Catholic Church*, §1779 (New York: Image, 1997), 491. See also Thomas Acklin and Boniface Hicks, "Interiority," in *Spiritual Direction: A Guide for Sharing the Father's Love* (Steubenville, OH: Emmaus Road, 2017), 21–48.

15 *Csi*, II, 2.5 (CF 37:52; *SW* 1:668; *SBO* 3:414).

16 *Catechism of the Catholic Church*, §2700–§2724. See also Teresa of Ávila, *The Way of Perfection*, 16.4, trans. Kieran Kavanaugh (Washington, DC: Institute of Carmelite Studies, 2000), 170.

17 See Leclercq, *The Interior Life*, 134–47; Groeschel, *Spiritual Passages*, 141–42; Dubay, *Seeking Spiritual Direction*, 181–83; Dubay, *Prayer Primer*, 65–81; Merton, *Spiritual Direction and Meditation*, 77–102.

that are treated in the chapters above (e.g., conducting a self-assessment with respect to the qualities of an undivided mind, orienting one's mind to God's unity, or cultivating the affections associated with monastic compunction). Yet the recommendation of some kind of theological meditation within the course of spiritual direction gives directees an opportunity to reflect on their theological assumptions, questions, and new insights experienced through prayer and study.[18]

In contrast with Catholic spiritual direction, one might understand the general goal of spiritually-integrated civil psychotherapy as aiming to cultivate a client's holistic development in conjunction with receiving psychological treatment by use of an evidence-based therapeutic modality.[19] There is not a presupposition in civil psychotherapy that a client has a relationship with God; rather, spiritual integration would occur in civil psychotherapy only if a client already exhibits some kind of general orientation to the domain of the sacred and also if the integration at hand is relevant for the provision of psychological services.[20] Because religion can be a significant dimension of a client's life and relevant for presenting therapeutic concerns, mental health providers might utilize customized interventions for religious clients in order to include a client's religion in the therapeutic process.[21]

One approach to clinical spiritual integration is to interact with a client's religion in a way that is extrinsic to the therapeutic modality being employed. In other words, when engaging in treatment planning with a client who is interested in integrating religion and spirituality, the religious beliefs and practices of that client need not be reduced to (or forced to conform to) any particular psychological theory; rather, the psychological activity associated with that client's religious practice might be "translated" into a psychological context for assessment by a provider in a non-reductive way.[22] Such religious

18 On theological inquiry as part of spiritual direction, see Janet K. Ruffing, *Spiritual Direction: Beyond the Beginnings* (Mahwah, NJ: Paulist Press, 2000), 89.

19 Regarding evidence-based treatment, see John Geddes, "Evidence-Based Practice in Mental Health," in *Evidence-Based Practice: A Critical Appraisal*, ed. Liz Trinder with Shirley Reynolds (Malden, MA: Blackwell Science, 2000), 66–88. For an empirical argument supporting the integration of spirituality into evidence-based psychotherapy, see Kenneth I. Pargament, Nichole A. Murray-Swank, and Nalini Tarakeshwar, "An Empirically-Based Rationale for a Spiritually-Integrated Psychotherapy," *Mental Health, Religion and Culture* 8, no. 3 (2005): 155–65.

20 See Pargament, *Spiritually Integrated Psychotherapy*, 32.

21 See L. Rebecca Propst, "Cognitive-Behavioral Therapy and the Religious Person," in *Religion and the Clinical Practice of Psychology*, ed. E. P. Shafranske (Washington, DC: American Psychological Association, 1996), 391–407.

22 After gaining some understanding of a client's worldview, "the therapist may use his or her psychological theory to translate religious thoughts or behaviors as well as various philosophies of

practices may exercise the same psychological capacities under consideration for therapeutic treatment (and likewise a person's religious practice can be affected by any problems associated with such capacities).[23]

This observation aligns with Bernard's insight that spiritual exercises can be "the same as natural goods, but different, because they are considered from a different point of view [*alio intuitu*]" and that "some spiritual goods indeed are known to be according to nature [*iuxta naturam*]."[24] Such an integration of spirituality into clinical practice does not promote a "spiritual bypass" where a client might escape into spirituality in order to avoid dealing with concrete and immediate life problems, but rather involves the clinical attempt to align with a client's existing spiritual practices in order to facilitate working through such problems.[25] At the same time, clinically treating the psychosocial activity of a client is a task that remains distinct from guiding that client with respect to religious teachings or providing spiritual direction.[26]

Alternatively, religious and spiritual practices might be integrated into civil psychotherapy in an intrinsic way such that the practice itself becomes an inherent part of the therapy. This occurs, for example, when religious

life into psychological language (while not reducing that level to the psychological) and to assist the client in dealing with his or her problems." Dominic O. Vachon and Albert A. Agresti, "A Training Proposal to Help Mental Health Professionals Clarify and Manage Implicit Values in the Counseling Process," *Professional Psychology: Research and Practice* 23, no. 6 (1992): 509–14, at 513.

23 "Although a theological level of analysis may not be reduced to a psychological level of analysis, it is certainly the case that one's psychological dynamics influence other levels just as neurophysiological deficiencies may affect one's behavior." Vachon and Agresti, "A Training Proposal," 513.

24 *Div*, 16.5 (CF 68:91; *SW* 9:314; *SBO* 6.1:147).

25 Regarding spiritual bypass, see Craig S. Cashwell, Paige B. Bentley, and J. Preston Yarborough, "The Only Way Out Is Through: The Peril of Spiritual Bypass," *Counselings and Values* 51, no. 2 (2007): 139–48; Gabriela Picciotto, Jesse Fox, and Félix Neto, "A Phenomenology of Spiritual Bypass: Causes, Consequences, and Implications," *Journal of Spirituality in Mental Health* 20, no. 4 (2018): 333–54.

26 Vachon and Agresti, observing that clients of civil psychotherapy may subscribe to various belief systems (such as belief in a Creator, in reincarnation, or in atheistic humanism), write: "No matter what one's beliefs about ultimate reality, it is not the role of psychology to adjudicate the veracity of that level of explanation. The therapist, however, must proceed with recognition that this level of explanation is true for the client even as the therapist operates within a psychological level of analysis." See Vachon and Agresti, "A Training Proposal," 513. Gonsiorek similarly argues that a civil psychotherapist should not presume competence in directing a client with respect to religious beliefs or practices. See John C. Gonsiorek, P. Scott Richards, Kenneth I. Pargament, and Mark R. McMinn, "Ethical Challenges and Opportunities at the Edge: Incorporating Spirituality and Religion into Psychotherapy," *Professional Psychology: Research and Practice* 40, no. 4 (2009): 385–95, at 386.

principles are communicated to a client receiving Taoist Cognitive Therapy.[27] This intrinsic integration approach has been developed to include a number of modalities for persons who practice Buddhism—for example, Buddhist counseling,[28] cognitive therapy,[29] gestalt therapy,[30] or psychoanalysis.[31] Such modalities often emphasize the practice of meditation as a key element of the therapy.[32] Even with the intrinsic integration of specifically Buddhist religious principles, some researchers propose that such therapeutic interventions (insofar as they are also evidence-based) are appropriate for all clients regardless of a client's religious background.[33] A similar intrinsic integration approach has been developed in Christianity with Christian Devotional Meditation[34] or Christian gestalt therapy.[35]

Advocating for the inclusion of Buddhist meditation exercises in psychotherapy, Hwang and Chang contend that meditation helps persons realize specific health benefits such as the ability to self-regulate one's attention, to act less impulsively, and to decrease the activity of the sympathetic nervous system and thus protect "the body from the adverse effects of stress."[36]

27 See Yudan Ding, Li Wang, Jindong Chen, Jingping Zhao, and Wenbin Guo, "Chinese Taoist Cognitive Therapy for Symptoms of Depression and Anxiety in Adults in China: A Systematic Review and Meta-Analysis," *Frontiers in Psychology* 11, no. 769 (2020): 1–12.

28 See Kin Cheung George Lee, *Buddhist Counseling: An Introduction for Mental Health Professionals* (Saarbrücken: Lambert Academic Publishing, 2017).

29 See Dennis Tirch, Laura R. Silberstein, and Russell L. Kolts, *Buddhist Psychology and Cognitive-Behavioral Therapy: A Clinician's Guide* (New York: Guilford Press, 2016).

30 See Eva Gold and Stephen Zahm, *Buddhist Psychology and Gestalt Therapy Integrated: Psychotherapy for the 21st Century* (Portland, OR: Metta Press, 2018).

31 See Jeffrey B. Rubin, *Psychotherapy and Buddhism: Toward an Integration* (New York: Plenum Press, 1996).

32 See, e.g., the discussion of meditation as a Buddhist application in psychotherapy in Roshni Daya, "Buddhist Moments in Psychotherapy," in *Integrating Traditional Healing Practices into Counseling and Psychotherapy*, ed. Roy Moodley and William West (Thousand Oaks, CA: Sage Publications, 2005), 182–93, at 186.

33 See, e.g., S. Kelly Avants, Mark Beitel, and Arthur Margolin, "Making the Shift from 'Addict Self' to 'Spiritual Self': Results from a Stage I Study of Spiritual Self-Schema (3-S) Therapy for the Treatment of Addiction and HIV Risk Behavior," *Mental Health, Religion and Culture* 8, no. 3 (2005): 167–77, at 169; see also 170 and 176. See also Pargament, *Spiritually Integrated Psychotherapy*, 282 and 325.

34 Fernando Garzon, "Christian Devotional Meditation for Anxiety," in *Evidence-Based Practices for Christian Counseling and Psychotherapy*, ed. Everett L. Worthington, Jr., Eric L. Johnson, Joshua N. Hook, and Jamie D. Aten (Downers Grove, IL: IVP Academic, 2013), 59–80.

35 Philip Brownell, *Christianity and Gestalt Therapy: The Presence of God in Human Relationships* (New York: Routledge, 2020).

36 Kwang-Kuo Hwang and Jeffrey Chang, "Self-Cultivation: Culturally Sensitive Psychotherapies in Confucian Societies," *The Counseling Psychologist* 37, no. 7 (2009): 1010–32, at 1024.

Pargament maintains that meditation is therapeutically helpful in that it helps persons develop alternative psychological response processes in lieu of focusing on "cravings" or thinking about "painful emotions and experiences."[37] In an older study focused on the benefit of a kind of philosophical meditation as a supplement for psychotherapy, Carrington and Ephron agree that meditation can lead to a reduction in tension associated with stress, as well as lead to other therapeutic benefits such as greater productivity, lower anxiety, increased self-acceptance, less addictive-prone behaviors, psychological differentiation (the ability to differentiate self from environment), improved mood, and availability of affect.[38]

Regarding such perceived therapeutic benefits, when he was at the Congregation for the Doctrine of the Faith (before he became Pope Benedict XVI), Cardinal Ratzinger similarly observed that some Christians have recourse to "non-Christian forms of meditation" in order to seek "interior peace and psychic balance."[39] Pope Francis later added that regardless of a person's religion, "we all need to meditate, to reflect, to discover ourselves," noting that through such a practice "a barrier" is "raised against the daily stress" and that when meditation is practiced in a Christian context, the exercise takes on a "uniqueness."[40] Is it possible then that—in addition to the role meditation might serve as a religious exercise and a spiritual therapy—Bernard's proposed course of meditation could facilitate psychosocial benefits that would also be of interest to civil psychotherapists?

As discussed above in the second interpretive part of this study, Bernard's teaching on meditation focuses on cultivating awareness of a variety of psychosocial domains. When a therapist judges that the exercises are culturally appropriate (as with Christian clients), they might be recommended by a provider in lieu of other mindfulness exercises.[41] How Bernard's teaching

37 Pargament, *Spiritually Integrated Psychotherapy*, 256–57, also citing *Mindfulness and Psychotherapy*, ed. Christopher Germer, Ronald D. Siegel, and Paul R. Fulton, 2nd ed. (New York: Guilford Press, 2016).

38 Availability of affect involves the ability to recognize and modify psychological defense processes that keep difficult emotions at bay in order that the emotions may be more accessible during in-session therapeutic work. Patricia Carrington and Harmon S. Ephron, "Meditation as an Adjunct to Psychotherapy," in *New Dimensions in Psychiatry: A Worldview*, ed. Silvano Arieti and Gerard Chrzanowski (New York: John Wiley and Sons, 1975), 261–91, at 269–75.

39 Congregation for the Doctrine of the Faith, "Letter to the Bishops of the Catholic Church on Some Aspects of Christian Meditation," October 15, 1989, §2; available at www.vatican.va.

40 Francis, "General Audience: Catechesis on Prayer 31, The Meditation," April 28, 2021; available at www.vatican.va.

41 In a similar way, Knabb proposes Cistercian centering prayer as an alternative to the Buddhist mindfulness exercises contained in the therapeutic modality MBCT. See Knabb, "Centering Prayer as an Alternative," 908–24.

might be integrated into a specific treatment, however, will ultimately depend on the interest of the client and its relevance for the therapeutic goals at hand. I turn now to explore some additional details concerning the relationship that each of the three general stages of meditation that Bernard recommends has to Catholic spiritual direction and spiritually-integrated civil psychotherapy. Recall that in condensed form the three general stages of meditation that Bernard suggests are: (1) self-reflection, (2) reflection on human relationships, and (3) reflection on relationship with God.

Stage 1: Self-Reflection

In the context of practicing self-reflection in order to grow in self-knowledge, a person seeking spiritual direction from a Christian anthropological perspective might reflect on that person's human nature, temperament, and personal character. As Bernard indicates, reflection on one's humanity will benefit from drawing on philosophy (today this suggestion might be expanded to promote drawing on the human sciences as well). In accordance with the Platonic background of Bernard's psychology (mediated by Augustine), one might reflect on one's memory, intellect, and will, as well as on one's natural affections (emotions). One might self-assess the psychological qualities of one's mind as well as one's moral character strengths (virtues) and weaknesses. One might ask: to what extent is one able to regulate one's thinking, one's use of memory and imagination, one's emotions? To what extent does one have a balanced self-understanding and realistic ambition in life?[42] Is one's self-assessment honest? Does one value and practice humility? For Bernard, this virtue provides a foundation for spiritual development (*aedificatio*) and self-cultivation (*Bildung*).[43]

With respect to exercises associated with Catholic spiritual direction, the meditative practice of self-reflection might be conjoined with an examination of conscience (or the Ignatian examen prayer) where one reviews one's thoughts, words, and actions.[44] These reflections can lead one in turn to discern areas of needed growth in relation to virtues (moral character strengths).[45] In this kind of meditation, one might give special attention to

42 *Csi*, II, 10.19 (CF 37:72; *SW* 1:692; *SBO* 3:426).

43 *SCC*, 36, 4.5 (CF 7:177; *SW* 5:568; *SBO* 2:7).

44 See Gallagher, *The Examen Prayer*, 29–41.

45 Benedict Ashley, *Spiritual Direction in the Dominican Tradition* (New York: Integration Books, 1995), 118–19. See also Teresa of Ávila, *Way of Perfection*, 16.3 (Kavanaugh, 170); Dubay, *Seeking Spiritual Direction*, 249.

Christ in the biblical narratives as a model of the Christian virtues.[46] Like Catholic spiritual direction, civil psychotherapy also can give emphasis to growth in self-awareness by means of practicing self-reflection.[47] Growth in self-awareness through the practice of self-reflection might be understood as a kind of psychoeducational approach that can supplement therapy for a variety of psychological concerns.[48]

It is difficult, however, to align Bernard's anthropology with any specific contemporary personality theory.[49] While one can discern numerous similarities between Bernard's thought and elements found in a variety of contemporary theoretical paradigms,[50] it is not my purpose at present to reassemble Bernard's psychology as a kind of contemporary cultural psychology.[51] At present, my purpose is only to note a few correlations between

46 See St. Basil the Great, *On the Holy Spirit*, chap. 15, §35 (Crestwood, NY: St Vladimir's Seminary Press, 1980), 59.

47 Regarding the value of self-reflection exercises for civil psychotherapists and mental health providers, see Mary Ann La Torre, "Self-Reflection: An Important Process for the Therapist," *Perspectives in Psychiatric Care* 41, no. 2 (2005): 85–87; Jessica Rosin, "The Necessity of Counselor Individuation for Fostering Reflective Practice," *Journal of Counseling and Development* 93 (2015): 88–95. Regarding therapist spirituality, see Diane Langberg, "The Spiritual Life of the Therapist: We Become What We Habitually Reflect," *Journal of Psychology and Christianity* 25, no. 3 (2006): 258–66; Marsha I. Wiggins, "Therapist Self-Awareness of Spirituality," in *Spirituality and the Therapeutic Process: A Comprehensive Resource from Intake to Termination*, ed. J. D. Aten and M. M. Leach (Washington, DC: American Psychological Association, 2009), 53–73; Cyrus P. Olsen, "Spirituality and the Health-Care Professional," *The Linacre Quarterly* 78, no. 4 (2011): 437–54.

48 For example, see E. M. Engku Kamarudin, W. S. Wan Sulaiman, N. H. Sarnon, and A. S. Amin, "Data on Self-Awareness, Self-Determination, and Self-Efficacy of Opioid-Dependent Patients Receiving Methadone Treatment Before and After Getting Individual Psycho-educational (i-SEAZ) Intervention," *Data in Brief* 30 (2020): 1–6.

49 See CS 105:xiv.

50 For a Christian evaluation of various contemporary therapeutic modalities, see Stanton L. Jones and Richard E. Butman, *Modern Psychotherapies: A Comprehensive Christian Appraisal* (Downers Grove, IL: IVP Academic, 2011).

51 In terms of my reference to reintroducing a version of Bernard's psychology as a contemporary cultural psychology, see discussion of how indigenous cultural psychologies might draw on the philosophical and theological teachings associated with the history of a cultural tradition in John Berry, "Global, Indigenous, and Regional Perspectives on International Psychology," in *Caribbean Psychology: Indigenous Contributions to a Global Discipline*, ed. J. L. Roopnarine and D. Chadee (Washington, DC: American Psychological Association, 2016), 45–68, at 56. See also the discussion of Yang on how a global psychology might take into account these various religious cultures: Kuo-Shu Yang, "Monocultural and Cross-Cultural Indigenous Approaches: The Royal Road to the Development of a Balanced Global Psychology," *Asian Journal of Social Psychology* 3, no. 3 (2000): 241–63, at 257–59. A religious psychology in this sense (where a religion is understood as a kind of culture and the associated cultural psychology could also be called a religious psychology) is not necessarily to be identified with the "religious psychology" of Fr. Antoine Vergote, who had recourse to a naturalistic method that he described as "a-theistic in principle" (*A-thée en principe*). See Antoine Vergote, *Psychologie Religieuse, Deuxième* édition (Brussels: Charles Dessart, 1966),

Bernard's teaching and topics found in civil psychotherapy. To reiterate, I am not discussing such correlations here for the purpose of suggesting how an integrated psychological model might be developed that unites Bernard's claustral psychology with a particular contemporary paradigm,[52] nor am I presenting cross-cultural comparisons (e.g., aiming to contrast the psychology of medieval monasticism as represented by Bernard with a specific psychological theory).[53] Rather, my purpose in outlining these correlations is to note how certain topics that are central to Bernard's spiritual praxis intersect with the exercise of psychological capacities during psychotherapeutic intervention.[54] If a client practices meditation in order to develop such capacities for a religious purpose, these exercises might align with clinical efforts related to therapeutic interventions.[55]

An initial observation that one might make is that Bernard's anthropology in general correlates with what might be called a bio-psycho-social-spiritual model.[56] His psychology is evocative of contemporary theories

16; Antoine Vergote, *The Religious Man: A Psychological Study of Religious Attitudes* (Dayton, OH: Pflaum Press, 1969), 9. See also Leclercq, *Monks and Love*, 3 and 7n1.

52 For examples of this kind of approach (drawing not on the work of Bernard but instead on Thomas Aquinas), see Thomas Verner Moore, *The Driving Forces of Human Nature and Their Adjustment* (New York: Grune and Stratton, 1950); Benedict Ashley, *Healing for Freedom: A Christian Perspective on Personhood and Psychotherapy* (Washington, DC: The Catholic University of America Press, 2013); Paul C. Vitz, William J. Nordling, and Craig Steven Titus, *A Catholic Christian Meta-Model of the Person: Integration with Psychology and Mental Health Practice* (Sterling, VA: Divine Mercy University Press, 2020). Regarding Moore, see also Robert Kugelmann, "The Theory and Practice of Thomas Verner Moore's Catholic Psychiatry and Psychotherapy," *History of Psychology* 22, no. 2 (2019): 186–204.

53 For an example of this kind of approach, see Alexis Trader, *Ancient Christian Wisdom and Aaron Beck's Cognitive Therapy: A Meeting of Minds* (New York: Peter Lang, 2012). For discussion of some epistemological concerns regarding cross-cultural psychological research, see Fons J. R. van de Vijver and Ype H. Poortinga, "Towards an Integrated Analysis of Bias in Cross-Cultural Assessment," *European Journal of Psychological Assessment* 13, no. 1 (1997): 29–37.

54 Regarding such possible overlap between religious practice and psychotherapeutic intervention, see Rosmarin, *Spirituality, Religion, and Cognitive-Behavioral Therapy*, 3, 51–58, 64.

55 Following Ashley's distinction between spiritual direction and civil psychotherapy (discussed above), one might note that Ashley describes the kind of development that occurs in spiritual direction as primarily involving a person's *apex mentis* and *ratio superior*. See Benedict Ashley, "Spirituality and Counseling," in *The Ashley Reader: Redeeming Reason* (Ave Maria, FL: Sapientia Press, 2006), 291–303, at 299. See also Vachon and Agresti, "A Training Proposal," 513. Regarding the phrase "pinnacle of the mind" (*apex mentis*), see Endre von Ivánka, "*Apex Mentis*. Wanderung und Wandlung eines stoischen Terminus," in *Plato Christianus:* Übernahme *und Umgestaltung des Platonismus durch die Väter* (Einsiedeln: Johannes Verlag, 1990), 315–51.

56 See Len Sperry, "Integrative Spiritually Oriented Psychotherapy," in *Spiritually Oriented Psychotherapy*, ed. Len Sperry and Edward P. Shafranske (Washington, DC: American Psychological Association, 2004), 307–29, at 308–9, citing George L. Engel, "The Need for a New Medical Model: A Challenge to Biomedical Medicine," *Science* 196 (1977): 129–36. See also Len Sperry,

that approach the soul (*anima*) or psyche not as a machine, but rather as an organic structure of interconnected activities, a structure always growing and developing.[57] What is missing from Bernard's teaching is a focus on personality traits or temperament as distinct from moral character traits.[58] I suggested in the previous chapter when outlining Bernard's course of meditation that one might add a reflection on personality—for example, attempting to discern one's particular personality traits such as extroversion[59] or how one may have acquired specific psychological defense processes.[60]

"Integrative Spiritually Oriented Psychotherapy: A Case Study of Spiritual and Psychological Transformation," in *Casebook for a Spiritual Strategy of Counseling and Psychotherapy*, ed. P. Scott Richards and Allen E. Bergin (Washington, DC: American Psychological Association, 2004), 141–52, at 147. A biopsychosocial approach to therapy differs from a biomedical approach. See David Pilgrim, "The Biopsychosocial Model in Anglo-American Psychiatry: Past, Present and Future?," *Journal of Mental Health* 11, no. 6 (2002): 585–94. Some health care authors explicitly refer to a "biopsychosocial spiritual" perspective that (as mentioned previously in chapter 4) generally matches Bernard's anthropology very well. See Rola O. Aamar, Angela L. Lamson, and Doug Smith, "Qualitative Trends in Biopsychosocial-Spiritual Treatment for Underserved Patients with Type 2 Diabetes," *Contemporary Family Therapy* 37, no. 1 (2015): 33–44. This perspective also aligns with Leclercq's own sketch of a contemporary psychological theory that he describes as "physiological," "psycho-sociological," and "spiritual." See Leclercq, *Monks and Love*, 4. Other health care authors refer alternatively to a "biopsychosocial cultural" perspective (where the cultural dimension might include spirituality). See Donald M. Hilty, "Advancing Science, Clinical Care and Education: Shall We Update Engel's Biopsychosocial Model to a Bio-Psycho-Social-Cultural Model?," *Psychology and Cognitive Sciences* 1, no. 1 (2015): 1–6.

57 See Calvin S. Hall and Gardner Lindzey, *Theories of Personality* (New York: John Wiley and Sons, 1957), 296–335, citing the theory of psychobiology proposed by Adolf Meyer and its summary as presented by Thomas Rennie. For Meyer, see *The Commonsense Psychiatry of Dr. Adolf Meyer: Fifty-Two Selected Papers*, ed. Alfred Lief (New York: McGraw-Hill, 1948). For Rennie, see Thomas A. C. Rennie, "Adolf Meyer and Psychobiology: The Man, His Methodology and Its Relation to Therapy," in *Papers from the Second American Congress on General Semantics*, ed. M. Kendig (Chicago: Institute of General Semantics, 1943), 156–65. See also the reference to organicism as a contemporary school of thought in psychology in Anthony Biglan and Steven C. Hayes, "Functional Contextualism and Contextual Behavioral Science," in *The Wiley Handbook of Contextual Behavioral Science*, ed. Robert D. Zettle, Steven C. Hayes, Dermot Barnes-Holmes, and Anthony Biglan (Malden, MA: John Wiley and Sons, 2016), 37–61, at 43–44.

58 On traits of moral character as distinct from traits of personality, see K. S. Kitchener, "There is more to Ethics than Principles," *The Counseling Psychologist* 24, no. 1 (1996): 92–97, at 95, citing William K. Frankena, *Ethics*, 2nd ed. (Englewood Cliffs, NJ: Prentice-Hall, 1973), 63.

59 See, e.g., Lewis R. Goldberg, "An Alternative 'Description of Personality': The Big-Five Factor Structure," *Journal of Personality and Social Psychology* 59, no. 6 (1990): 1216–29; Paulina F. Kernberg, Alan S. Weiner, and Karen K. Bardenstein, "Components of Personality," in *Personality Disorders in Children and Adolescents* (New York: Basic Books, 2000), 15–30, at 15–16; David Watson and Lee Anna Clark, "Personality Traits as an Organizing Framework for Personality Pathology," *Personality and Mental Health* 14 (2020): 51–75.

60 Regarding defense processes, see Anna Freud, *The Ego and the Mechanisms of Defence* (London: Karnac Books, 1993); Nancy McWilliams, *Psychoanalytic Diagnosis: Understanding Personality Structure in the Clinical Process*, 2nd ed. (New York: Guilford Press, 2011).

As evident by Bernard's emphasis on God as the goal of human life (or more generally speaking by his recognition of a kind of virtual unity that can arise when one pursues a goal, as discussed above[61]), Bernard indicates that psychic growth involves teleological (goal-oriented) psychological activity.[62] For some theorists, goal-oriented activity arises as a natural inclination on the part of a person toward holistic or organismic integration.[63] In this respect, some kind of overarching goal might be understood to orient any person's organic growth and integration.[64] Regarding personal development toward such a goal, some recent authors in contemporary positive psychology emphasize not only the benefit of stable or healthy psychosocial activity, but also the value of a developmental outlook oriented toward flourishing (in the sense of experiencing psychosocial well-being).[65] In order to help one's psychological capacities grow and flourish, one must engage in self-exertion: each specific activity associated with a psychological capacity has to be located, differentiated, and reflexively known (self-awareness), possessed and organized (self-appropriation), as well as managed and developmentally directed (self-cultivation through the exercise of self-regulation).[66] Regarding the differentiation of psychological capacities, the hierarchical structure of

61 *Div*, 80.1 (CF 68:313; *SW* 9:660; *SBO* 6.1:320).

62 See Edward L. Deci, *Intrinsic Motivation* (New York: Plenum Press, 1975), 119–21.

63 Kurt Goldstein, *The Organism* (New York: Zone Books, 1995), 323–24. Regarding organismic integration, see Kennon M. Sheldon and Tim Kasser, "Coherence and Congruence: Two Aspects of Personality Integration," *Journal of Personality and Social Psychology* 68, no. 3 (1995): 531–43; Kennon M. Sheldon, Tim Kasser, Kendra Smith, and Tamara Share, "Personal Goals and Psychological Growth: Testing an Intervention to Enhance Goal Attainment and Personality Integration," *Journal of Personality* 70, no. 1 (2002): 5–31. See also Julius Seeman, "Toward a Concept of Personality Integration," *American Psychologist* 14, no. 10 (1959): 633–37.

64 This discussion of the psyche (*anima*) as organic does not need be understood as reductive or as implying anthropological materialism. See, e.g., reference to the "organism of virtues" in Servais Pinckaers, *The Sources of Christian Ethics*, trans. Sr. Mary Thomas Noble (Washington, DC: The Catholic University of America Press, 1995), 178.

65 See Martin E. P. Seligman, *Flourish: A Visionary New Understanding of Happiness and Well-Being* (New York: Atria, 2011); Corey L. M. Keyes, "The Mental Health Continuum: From Languishing to Flourishing in Life," *Journal of Health and Social Research* 43, no. 2 (2002): 207–22; Corey L. M. Keyes, "Promoting and Protecting Mental Health as Flourishing," *American Psychologist* 62, no. 2 (2007): 95–108. As evaluated from a theological point of view, mental health or psychosocial well-being in this sense is distinct from Christian spiritual well-being: "Mental health and spiritual well-being are not synonymous. It is a serious theological error—a Pelagian error, I would suggest—to identify the two." E. F. O'Doherty, *The Priest and Mental Health* (Staten Island, NY: Society of St. Paul, 1963), 7.

66 On self-exertion, see Yung-Jong Shiah and Kwang-Kuo Hwang, "Socialized Reflexivity and Self-Exertion: Mandala Model of Self and Its Role in Mental Health," *Asian Journal of Social Psychology 22*, no. 1 (2019), 47–58, at 48. On self-cultivation, see Hwang and Chang, "Self-Cultivation," 1011.

Bernard's psychology (influenced by Augustine and Gregory) continues to have contemporary relevance in terms of the organization of such psycho-social processes.[67] With respect to locating interior capacities that perform such psychological activities, one might first meditate on the constitution of one's mind (*animus*).[68] It is evident that for Bernard—within the context of his religious perspective oriented toward Christian eschatology—mental activity is not assumed to reduce to neurological or brain activity.[69]

With respect to the capacities of the mind (which for Bernard are reason, memory, and will),[70] I pass over here exploring contemporary literature pertaining to cognition and memory.[71] However, recall Bernard's emphasis on attention—the *acies mentis*, where the dimension of the mind under consideration might also involve the higher intuition of reason (the *ratio superior*) as distinct from reason in the mode of logical argumentation and disputation. Bernard's emphasis on attention is evocative of a distinction between "wise mind" and "rational mind" as proposed by theorists in dialectical behavioral therapy.[72] Regarding one's will as a capacity of one's mind, the topic of volition reappears in some contemporary psychological theories in terms of perceived self-efficacy and agency.[73] One approach to civil psychotherapy, in fact, is focused on the goal of supporting and increasing

67 Writing from the viewpoint of extrinsic spiritual integration into clinical work, Vachon and Agresti allude to a psychosomatic hierarchy involving theology (or activity bearing upon ultimate reality), then psychology, then neurology, where a lower level can influence a higher level. See Vachon and Agresti, "A Training Proposal," 512–13. See also Goldstein, *The Organism*, 364.

68 Goldstein, *The Organism*, 359–60.

69 Vachon and Agresti write: "neurological explanations may be implicated in certain psychological problems, but the psychological level cannot be completely reduced to the lower level of neurology because much explanatory power would be lost. Each level of explanation has legitimacy in its own right." Vachon and Agresti, "A Training Proposal," 512. See also Daniel J. Siegel, *The Developing Mind: How Relationships and the Brain Interact to Shape Who We Are*, 3rd ed. (New York: Guilford Press, 2020).

70 *Conv*, 6.11 (CF 25:45; *SW* 4:178; *SBO* 4:84).

71 In the contemporary milieu, one might encounter reference primarily to Ulrich Niesser as the founder of contemporary cognitive psychology. See Ulrich Niesser, *Cognitive Psychology* (New York: Appleton-Century, 1967). However, also see Thomas Verner Moore, *Cognitive Psychology* (New York: Lippincott, 1939).

72 See, e.g., Pedersen, *Dialectical Behavior Therapy*, 125–30, 165–76, 197. See also Richard S. Sharf, *Theories of Psychotherapy and Counseling: Concepts and Cases*, 6th ed. (Boston, MA: Cengage Learning, 2015), 326.

73 See James E. Maddux, "Self-Efficacy," in *The Encyclopedia of Positive Psychology*, ed. Shane J. Lopez (Malden, MA: John Wiley and Sons, 2009), 874–80. With respect to assessing perceived agency, see Adam Tapal, Ela Oren, Reuven Dar, and Baruch Eitam, "The Sense of Agency Scale: A Measure of Consciously Perceived Control over One's Mind, Body, and the Immediate Environment," *Frontiers in Psychology* 8 (2017): 1–11.

(but not determining) a client's degree of volitional activity.[74] With respect to other non-mental psychological capacities, one might note that in some therapeutic modalities there is a reappearance of Bernard's concern with the distractions or distortions that can emerge from one's imagination.[75]

Turning to the topic of personal character, another distinction that is indicated in Bernard's account is a differentiation between mind and mentality, where the latter word denotes how a person's mind has developed or been cultivated over time.[76] Regarding one's mental character in general, one might note that the self-assessment of one's mental qualities in itself is an exercise of what Bernard referred to as vigilance (or what is later called the custody of thoughts); in terms of the quality of one's mode of thinking, Bernard's teaching gives emphasis to a kind of reflective mindfulness practice that can cultivate meta-cognitive awareness.[77] Also of relevance for civil psychotherapy is the mental quality that Bernard describes as broadness; his reference might be associated with the feature of positive mental health that is referred to today as resilience.[78]

As described by clinical psychologist George A. Bonanno, resilience is the psychological ability to maintain "a stable equilibrium" despite encountering environmental difficulties and challenges.[79] Shiah and Hwang similarly maintain that resilience (understood in relation to self-efficacy and self-exertion and also paired with growth in self-reflection) can help a person

74 See Maarten Vansteenkiste and Kennon M. Sheldon, "There's Nothing More Practical than a Good Theory: Integrating Motivational Interviewing and Self-Determination Theory," *British Journal of Clinical Psychology* 45 (2006): 63–82, at 74. Thomas Verner Moore in his psychotherapeutic practice also exhibited an interest in therapy for a patient's will. See Moore, *Driving Forces*, 388–426.

75 Aaron T. Beck, Gary Emery, and Ruth Greenberg, *Anxiety Disorders and Phobias: A Cognitive Perspective* (Cambridge, MA: Basic Books, 1985), 210–11.

76 With respect to the distinction between mind and mentality, see Peter Graf, Laura L. Carstensen, Franz E. Weinert, and Richard A. Shweder, "Epilogue: Reflections and Future Perspectives," in *Interactive Minds: Life-Span Perspectives on the Social Foundation of Cognition*, ed. Paul B. Baltes and Ursula M. Staudinger (Cambridge: Cambridge University Press, 1996), 430–40, at 433; Richard A. Shweder, "The Psychology of Practice and the Practice of the Three Psychologies," *Asian Journal of Social Psychology* 3 (2000): 207–22, at 210–11.

77 See Wells, *Emotional Disorders and Metacognition*; Fisher and Wells, *Metacognitive Therapy*.

78 On the topic of resilience from a constructionist perspective, see Erica Frydenberg, *Coping and the Challenge of Resilience* (London: Palgrave Macmillan, 2017). See also Craig S. Titus, *Resilience and the Virtue of Fortitude: Aquinas in Dialogue with the Psychosocial Sciences* (Washington, DC: The Catholic University of America Press, 2006).

79 George A. Bonanno, "Loss, Trauma, and Human Resilience: Have We Underestimated the Human Capacity to Thrive after Extremely Adverse Events?," *Psychological Trauma: Theory, Research, Practice, and Policy*, S, no. 1 (2008): 101–13, at 102.

maintain "psychosocial homeostasis" as an indicator of positive mental health.[80] Rutter elaborates further that the ability to exhibit resilience when encountering environmental stress is supported in turn by protective psychosocial processes such as self-esteem, interpersonal ability, and perceived self-efficacy, where such processes are cultivated by positive life experiences involving relational security and success in meeting task demands.[81] I suggested in the interpretive discussion in Part 2 above that Bernard is referring to something like resilience when he warns Eugene III that "a mind stretched in many directions must be torn by many cares."[82]

Regarding one's moral character, it is almost self-evident that Bernard's psychology involves a normative moral psychology (normative in the sense of observing religious precepts and laws as well as valuing specific virtues).[83] Because the mind is partially constituted by the activity of the will, to the extent that the domain of the voluntary is also the domain of morality, for Bernard a complete understanding of mental health will also include moral health—at least in terms of including the natural good that is found in psychosocial activity that is consistent with what Bernard judges to comprise the due order of things (*debitum rerum ordinem*)[84] (namely, observance of a natural law,[85] if not also observance of monastic ascesis).

Bernard's emphasis on development in moral virtue or character strengths in this respect is not foreign to contemporary civil psychotherapy (as exemplified by clinical positive psychology).[86] Existential psychotherapist Adrian van Kaam observed that one's inclination to develop in virtue is

80 Shiah and Hwang, "Socialized Reflexivity," 55.

81 Michael Rutter, "Psychosocial Resilience and Protective Mechanisms," *American Journal of Orthosychiatry* 57, no. 3 (1987): 316–31, at 317 and 327.

82 *Csi*, II, Ch. 10.19 (CF 37:73; *SW* 1:694; *SBO* 3:427). "Similiter animus distentus in multa, multis laceretur curis necesse est. Nempe immoderata extensio extenuationem, et extenuatio nimia scissionem facit."

83 For a contemporary discussion of moral psychology, see J. Haidt, "Moral Psychology for the Twenty-First Century," *Journal of Moral Education* 42, no. 3 (2013): 281–97.

84 *Div*, 16.4 (CF 68:90–91; *SW* 9:314; *SBO* 6.1:147).

85 "On Baptism" (Ep 77), 1.2 (CF 67:152; *SW* 2:612; *SBO* 7:186).

86 Regarding clinical positive psychology, see Alex M. Wood and Nicholas Tarrier, "Positive Clinical Psychology: A New Vision and Strategy for Integrated Research," *Clinical Psychology Review* 30 (2010): 819–29. For a specific focus on virtue, see Len Sperry and Jonathan J. Sperry, "Psychotherapy and Virtue: Positive Psychology and Spiritual Well-Being," in *Religion, Spirituality, and Positive Psychology: Understanding the Fruits of Faith*, ed. Thomas G. Plante (Denver, Colo.: Praeger, 2012), 145–58; Frank J. Moncher and Craig S. Titus, "Foundations for a Psychotherapy of Virtue: An Integrated Catholic Perspective," *Journal of Psychology and Christianity* 28, no. 1 (2009): 22–35. See also Mike W. Martin, *From Morality to Mental Health: Virtue and Vice in a Therapeutic Culture* (Oxford: Oxford University Press, 2006).

realized not simply by exterior behavioral observance, but more so by fulfilling an interior desire that arises from deep within one, from within one's core self.[87] A virtue in this sense might be understood as an intentionally or voluntarily cultivated disposition that differs from preconscious habits and conditioned response patterns (such as acquired cognitive schemas that might incline a person to interpret events in a particular way).[88] Further, Bernard exhibits important insights into how certain virtues order or structure the expression of specific emotions.[89]

Stage 2: Reflection on Relationships

The next general stage of meditation that Bernard suggests concerns reflection on one's relationships. In terms of relationship roles where one has immediate responsibility for others, meditation at this point pertains to reflection on matters that are 'below' one; this might be interpreted in the contemporary context as focusing on relationships in which one has an obligation to care for others (a parent for children, a teacher for students, a priest for a parish, or a supervisor in a workplace). Civil psychotherapy can focus in special way on helping clients understand and remedy relational conflicts.[90] As mentioned, one area where Bernard's thought can make a contribution to civil psychotherapy (in terms of his self-assessment as a "modern chimæra"[91]) pertains to a person's possible need for assistance in navigating role conflicts or the experience of discord when attempting to fulfill two different roles perceived to be incompatible or even contradictory.[92]

87 Adrian van Kaam, *The Art of Existential Counseling* (Wilkes-Barre, PA: Dimension Books, 1966), 69. Regarding a "core self," see Holley S. Hodgins and C. Raymond Knee, "The Integrating Self and Conscious Experience," in *Handbook of Self-Determination Research*, ed. Edward L. Deci and Richard M. Ryan (Rochester, NY: University of Rochester Press, 2002), 87–100, at 87.

88 See Aaron T. Beck. A. John Rush, Brian F. Shaw, and Gary Emery, *Cognitive Therapy of Depression* (New York: Guilford Press, 1979), 12. Thomas Verner Moore also discusses conditioned response patterns that are tacit or preconscious (patterns that might be clarified and modified during the course of therapy). Regarding such a preconscious psychic domain, see Thomas Verner Moore, *The Nature and Treatment of Mental Disorders* (New York: Grune and Stratton, 1944), 35. Regarding response patterns, see Moore, *Driving Forces*, 268–72.

89 *Div*, 50.2 (CF 68:248; *SW* 9:562; *SBO* 6.1:271); *QH*, 14.9–10 (CF 25:237–38; *SW* 7:682–84; *SBO* 4:474–75).

90 See, e.g., Susan M. Heitler, *From Conflict to Resolution: Skills and Strategies for Individual, Couple, and Family Therapy* (New York: Norton, 1990).

91 Ep 326, §4 (James, *Letters*, 401–2; Ep 250 in *SW* 3:330–34; *SBO* 8:145–47).

92 Interpersonal psychotherapy is an existing evidence-based modality that focuses on patient role difficulties in terms of role transitions and role disputes with others, but not necessarily on role

Recall Bernard's reference to a unity of accord that can arise in a relationship where one person cooperates with another in pursuit of a common goal.[93] For example, citizens might cooperate together in promoting the common good of their society.[94] The therapeutic relationship itself might promote such a unity of accord between a therapist and a client.[95] In this respect, a client might engage in meditation in order to assess the relational bond or therapeutic alliance that can be experienced with a health care provider.[96] This effort might be facilitated by reflecting on one's personal style of relational attachment (attachment theory appears in a number of contemporary therapeutic modalities).[97] With respect to Bernard's reference to evaluating one's possible experience of domination in relationships (Augustine's *libido dominandi*), a client might also reflect on the power dynamic perceived within the therapeutic relationship.[98]

Stage 3: Theological Reflection

At the third general stage of meditation, a person receiving spiritual direction might take up a consideration of matters 'above' (psychologically and

conflicts experienced by one person. See John C. Markowtitz and Myrna M. Weissman, "Interpersonal Psychotherapy: Principles and Applications," *World Psychiatry* 3, no. 3 (2004): 136–39.

93 *Csi*, V, 8.18 (CF 37:163; *SW* 1:804–6; *SBO* 3:482–83).

94 See Benestad, *Church, State, and Society*, 81–112.

95 See Charles J. Gelso and Jean A. Carter, "Components of the Psychotherapy Relationship: Their Interaction and Unfolding During Treatment," *Journal of Counseling Psychology* 41, no. 3 (1994): 296–306. See also Charles J. Gelso, *The Real Relationship in Psychotherapy: The Hidden Relationship of Change* (Washington, DC: American Psychological Association, 2010); Clara E. Hill, *Helping Skills: Facilitating Exploration, Insight, and Action*, 4th ed. (Washington, DC: American Psychological Association, 2014), 39–40; Michael Kahn, *Between Therapist and Client: The New Relationship*, rev. ed. (New York: Henry Holt and Company, 1997), 151.

96 See Alastair J. Mackie, "Attachment Theory: Its Relevance to the Therapeutic Alliance," *British Journal of Medical Psychology* 54 (1981): 203–12; Amie E. M. Smith, Rachel M. Msetfi, and Laura Golding, "Client Self-Rated Adult Attachment Patterns and the Therapeutic Alliance: A Systematic Review," *Clinical Psychology Review* 30 (2010): 326–37; Marina Christina Skourteli and Clare Lennie, "The Therapeutic Relationship from an Attachment Theory Perspective," *Counseling Psychology Review* 26, no. 1 (2011): 20–33; Mario Mikulincer, Phillip R. Shaver, and Ety Berant, "An Attachment Perspective on Therapeutic Processes and Outcomes," *Journal of Personality* 81, no. 6 (2013): 606–16.

97 On attachment, see John Bowlby, *The Making and Breaking of Affectional Bonds* (New York: Routledge, 2005). For an example of a contemporary therapeutic modality that draws on attachment theory, see Susan M. Johnson, *Attachment Theory in Practice: Emotionally Focused Therapy (EFT) with Individuals, Couples, and Families* (New York: Guilford Press, 2019).

98 On this topic in civil psychotherapy, see Adolf Guggenbühl-Craig, *Power in the Helping Professions* (Thompson, CT: Spring Publications, 2021).

ontologically speaking—see Col 3:2), that is, engage in a theological reflection, and so begin the intellectual ascent up the ladder of the soul (to employ the metaphor that Bernard adopts from Gregory the Great). While the recommendation of this kind of meditation might be typical in Christian spiritual direction, such a recommendation may not be culturally appropriate for all clients of civil psychotherapy.[99] Further, this kind of meditation may not be relevant for all presenting concerns of Christian clients who want to integrate spirituality in some way into psychotherapeutic treatment.

Following Bernard, theological meditation will be practical to the extent that realities of perception are evaluated in terms of how they might be used in relation to God.[100] One's meditation might explore Augustine's distinction between use (*uti*) and enjoyment (*frui*), discussed above.[101] Theological meditation will be investigative if the focus is on how realities of perception can contribute to one's understanding of God.[102] The study of scripture and theological writings might precede or even be understood to occur in tandem with meditation at this stage. As mentioned in the previous chapter, one might at this point in meditation engage in reflection on one's theological beliefs (faith, reason, opinion) and their origination (scripture, inference, personal association). The clarification of such beliefs often pertains to what is called the exploration of one's "God representation" in psychotherapy today.[103]

Lastly, the theological reflection will be contemplative in terms of facilitating self-recollection, when one's mind and emotions are recalled from sensual attachments and from preoccupation with the imagination.[104] Within Catholic spiritual direction, the exercise of self-recollection might be integrated with the prayer of recollection as described by Teresa of Ávila in the

99 A civil psychotherapist might, however, continue to find stages one and two of Bernard's course of meditation helpful for use with non-religious clients. Plante has developed a similar non-religious version of Ignatian discernment. See Thomas G. Plante, "The 4 Ds: Using Ignatian Spirituality in Secular Psychotherapy and Beyond," *Spirituality in Clinical Practice* 4, no. 1 (2017): 74–79.

100 *Csi*, V, 2.4 (CF 37:142; *SW* 1:778; *SBO* 3:469).

101 Augustine, *De doctrina Christiana* I.4.4 (Green, 9; Martin, 8).

102 *Csi*, V, 2.4 (CF 37:142; *SW* 1:778; *SBO* 3:469).

103 See, e.g., Ana-Maria Rizzuto, "The Psychological Foundations of Belief in God," in *Toward Moral and Religious Maturity* (Glenview, IL: Silver Burdett Company, 1980), 115–35, at 127, where the focus is on an idea of God that one develops throughout one's life. Note that for Bernard, however, contemplative meditation involves not a focus on an idea of God within one's mind or on a product of one's imagination, but rather involves an orientation to God who is present above one's mind (ontologically and psychologically speaking).

104 *Csi*, V, 2.4 (CF 37:142; *SW* 1:778; *SBO* 3:469).

Carmelite spiritual tradition.[105] For Teresa, this approach to prayer precedes other approaches that she describes as the prayer of quiet and the prayer of union[106] (this last prayer—union—could involve infused contemplation and is described in a way that is doctrinally similar to Bernard's discussion of ecstatic contemplation).[107] As described earlier, for Bernard, self-recollection entails a reorientation of the attention of the mind (*acies mentis*)—first toward oneself (self-presence)[108] and then toward God's unity (through an act of self-transcendence).[109] Bernard indicates that such meditative practice can contribute toward one's psychological unity (self-integration), even if this process necessarily remains incomplete short of heavenly beatitude.[110] It is not so much that one practices God's presence in this effort (God's existence does not depend on one's mind), but rather one practices being present—first to oneself and then to God.[111] This final state of "presence to God" locates the *apex mentis* at the top of the ladder (the *scala considerationis*) and thus also at the pinnacle of Bernard's psychology.[112] Entering into this state of contemplation, one's meditation comes to rest, abiding at the summit of prayerful attentiveness to God in stillness: "Be still and know that I am God."[113]

105 See Teresa of Ávila, *Way of Perfection*, chap. 28, §4, and chap. 29 (Kavanaugh, 300 and 317–21). Kavanaugh observes that Teresa writes for persons who have difficulty with more disciplined approaches to meditation. See Teresa of Ávila, *Way of Perfection*, 23.

106 Teresa of Ávila, *Interior Castle* IV.3, trans. E. Allison Peers (New York: Image, 1989), 85.

107 Teresa of Ávila, *Interior Castle* V (Peers, 96–123).

108 Emphasis on the monastic practice of self-presence was one of the perennial teachings of Fr. Matthew Lamb, OCSO (d. 2018) to whom this study is dedicated.

109 *Csi*, V, 13.27 (CF 37:174; *SW* 1:820; *SBO* 3:490).

110 Ibid.

111 See also Beatrice Bruteau, "On Being Observant," *CSQ* 26, no. 1 (1991): 72–85, at 79. The phrase "practicing God's presence" might be misinterpreted to indicate that God's presence is dependent upon one's mind. Reformulating this as "practicing being present to God" avoids this concern. See also Brother Lawrence, *The Practice of the Presence of God* (New Kensington, PA: Whitaker House, 1982).

112 Leclercq, "General Introduction (III)," 378.

113 Ps 45:11.

Appendices

Appendix 1: Cistercian Fathers Series Cited

1 Bernard, *On Precept and Dispensation*

3 William of St. Thierry, *On Contemplating God*

4 Bernard, *Sermons on the Song of Songs, 1–20*

7 Bernard, *Sermons on the Song of Songs, 21–46*

10 Bernard, *The Life and Death of Saint Malachy*

13a Bernard, *The Steps of Humility & Pride*

13b Bernard, *On Loving God*

18a Bernard, *Homilies in Praise of the Blessed Virgin Mary*

19a Bernard, *On Grace and Free Choice*

19b Bernard, *In Praise of the New Knighthood*

24 *Three Treatises on Man: A Cistercian Anthropology* (ed. Bernard McGinn)

25 Bernard, *Lenten Sermons on the Psalm "He Who Dwells"*

31 Bernard, *Sermons on the Song of Songs, 47–66*

37 Bernard, *On Consideration*

40 Bernard, *Sermons on the Song of Songs, 67–86*

51 Bernard, *Sermons for Advent and the Christmas Season*

52 Bernard, *Sermons for the Lent and the Easter Season*

53 Bernard, *Sermons for the Summer Season*

54 Bernard, *Sermons for the Autumn Season*

55 Bernard, *The Parables & the Sentences*

76 *The First Life of Bernard of Clairvaux* (trans. Hilary Costello)

Appendix 2: Cistercian Studies Series Cited

7 Leclercq, *Aspects of Monasticism*

13 *Studies in Medieval Cistercian History: Presented to Jeremiah F. O'Sullivan* (ed. M. Basil Pennington)

16 Leclercq, *Bernard of Clairvaux and the Cistercian Spirit*

24 *Studies in Medieval Cistercian History II* (ed. John R. Sommerfeldt)

48 Guigo II, *The Ladder of Monks*

61 *Simplicity and Ordinariness: Studies in Medieval Cistercian History IV* (ed. John R. Sommerfeldt)

63 *The Chimæra of His Age: Studies on Bernard of Clairvaux* (ed. E. Rozanne Elder and John R. Sommerfeldt)

68 *Heaven on Earth: Studies in Medieval Cistercian History, IX* (ed. E. Rozanne Elder)

84 *Goad and Nail: Studies in Medieval Cistercian History, X* (ed. E. Rozanne Elder)

105 Leclercq, *A Second Look at Saint Bernard*

120 Gilson, *The Mystical Theology of St. Bernard*

125 John R. Sommerfeldt, *The Spiritual Teachings of Bernard of Clairvaux*

135 *Bernardus Magister* (ed. John R. Sommerfeldt)

141 *Studiosorum Speculum: Studies in Honor of Louis J. Lekai, O.Cist.* (ed. Francis R. Swietek and John R. Sommerfeldt)

193 *Praise No Less than Charity: Studies in Honor of M. Chrysogonus Waddell, Monk of Gethsemani Abbey* (ed. E. Rozanne Elder)

238 Duncan Robertson, *Lectio Divina: The Medieval Experience of Reading*

249 Gregory the Great, *Moral Reflections on the Book of Job: Volume 1, Preface and Books 1–5*

258 Gregory the Great, *Moral Reflections on the Book of Job: Volume 3, Books 11–16*

Select Bibliography

Works of Bernard of Clairvaux

Latin Editions of the Works of Bernard of Clairvaux

Bernardus Claraevallensis. *Sancti Bernardi Opera*. 8 vols. Edited by J. Leclercq, C. H. Talbot, and H.-M. Rochais. Rome: Editiones Cistercienses, 1957–77.

Bernhard von Clairvaux. *Sämtliche Werke, lateinisch/deutsch*. 10 vols. Edited by Gerhard B. Winkler, Alberich Altermatt, Denis Farkasfalvy, and Polykarp Zakar. Innsbruck: Tyrolia-Verlag, 1990–99.

English Translations of the Works of Bernard of Clairvaux

Bernard of Clairvaux. *Five Books on Consideration: Advice to a Pope*. Translated by John D. Anderson and Elizabeth T. Kennan. Cistercian Fathers Series 37. Kalamazoo, MI: Cistercian Publications, 1976.

———. *Homilies in Praise of the Blessed Virgin Mary*. Translated by Marie-Bernard Saïd. Cistercian Fathers Series 18a. Kalamazoo, MI: Cistercian Publications, 1993.

———. *In Praise of the New Knighthood: A Treatise on the Knights Templar and the Holy Places of Jerusalem*. Translated by M. Conrad Greenia. Cistercian Fathers Series 19b. Trappist, KY: Cistercian Publications, 2000.

———. *Lenten Sermons on the Psalm 'He Who Dwells.'* In *Sermons on Conversion*, translated by Marie-Bernard Saïd, 80–261. Cistercian Fathers Series 25. Kalamazoo, MI: Cistercian Publications, 1981.

———. *The Letters of Saint Bernard of Clairvaux*. Translated by Bruno Scott James. Kalamazoo, MI: Cistercian, 1998.

———. *The Life and Death of Saint Malachy the Irishman*. Translated by Robert T. Meyer. Cistercian Fathers Series 10. Kalamazoo, MI: Cistercian Press, 1978.

———. *Life and Works of Saint Bernard, Abbot of Clairvaux*. Translated by Samuel J. Eales. London: Burns and Oates, 1889–1896.

———. *Monastic Sermons (Sermones de diversis)*. Translated by Daniel Griggs. Cistercian Fathers Series 68. Collegeville, MN: Liturgical Press, 2016.

———. "On Baptism and Other Questions." In *On Baptism and the Office of Bishops*, translated by Pauline Matarasso, 149–77. Cistercian Fathers Series 67. Kalamazoo, MI: Cistercian Publications, 2004.

———. "On Conversion, a Sermon to Clerics." *In Sermons on Conversion*, translated by Marie-Bernard Saïd, 29–79. Cistercian Fathers Series 25. Kalamazoo, MI: Cistercian Publications, 1981.

———. *On Grace and Free Choice*. Translated by Daniel O'Donovan. Cistercian Fathers Series 19a. Kalamazoo, MI: Cistercian Publications, 1988.

———. *On Loving God*. Cistercian Fathers Series 13b. Kalamazoo, MI: Cistercian Publications, 1995.

———. *On Precept and Dispensation*. Translated by Conrad Greenia. In *The Works of Bernard of Clairvaux, Volume One, Treatises I*, edited by M. Basil Pennington, 103–50. Cistercian Fathers Series 1. Spencer, MA: Cistercian Publications, 1970.

———. "On the Conduct and Office of Bishops." In *On Baptism and the Office of Bishops*, translated by Pauline Matarasso, 37–82. Cistercian Fathers Series 67. Kalamazoo, MI: Cistercian Publications, 2004.

———. *On the Song of Songs, Vol. I, Sermons 1–20*. Translated by Kilian Walsh. Cistercian Fathers Series 4. Kalamazoo, MI: Cistercian Publications, 1971.

———. *On the Song of Songs Vol. II, Sermons 21–46*. Translated by Kilian Walsh. Cistercian Fathers Series 7. Kalamazoo, MI: Cistercian, 1976.

———. *On the Song of Songs Vol. III, Sermons 47–66*. Translated by Kilian Walsh and Irene M. Edmonds. Cistercian Fathers Series 31. Kalamazoo, MI: Cistercian, 1979.

———. *On the Song of Songs Vol. IV, Sermons 67–86*. Translated by Irene Edmonds. Cistercian Fathers Series 40. Kalamazoo, MI: Cistercian, 1980.

———. *The Parables and The Sentences*. Translated by Michael Casey and Francis R. Swietek. Cistercian Fathers Series 55. Kalamazoo, MI: Cistercian Publications, 2000.

———. *Selected Works*. Translated by G. R. Evans. Mahwah, NJ: Paulist Press, 1987.

———. *Sermons for Advent and the Christmas Season*. Edited by John Leinenweber. Cistercian Fathers Series 51. Kalamazoo, MI: Cistercian Publications, 2007.

———. *Sermons for Lent and the Easter Season*. Translated by Irene Edmonds. Cistercian Fathers Series 52. Kalamazoo, MI: Cistercian Publications, 2013.

———. *Sermons for the Autumn Season*. Translated by Irene Edmonds. Cistercian Fathers Series 54. Collegeville, MN: Liturgical Press, 2016.

———. *Sermons for the Summer Season*. Translated by Beverly Mayne Kienzle. Cistercian Fathers Series 53. Kalamazoo, MI: Cistercian Publications, 1991.

———. *St. Bernard's Treatise on Consideration*. Translated by A Priest of Mount Melleray. Dublin: Browne and Nolan, 1921.

———. *The Steps of Humility and Pride*. Translated by M. Ambrose Conway. Cistercian Fathers Series 13a. Kalamazoo, MI: Cistercian, 1989.

Casey, Michael, trans. *Cistercians and Cluniacs: St. Bernard's Apologia to Abbot William*. Kalamazoo, MI: Cistercian Publications, 1970.

Matarasso, Pauline, ed. *The Cistercian World: Monastic Writings of the Twelfth Century*. New York: Penguin, 1993.

Posset, Franz. *The Two-Fold Knowledge: Readings on the Knowledge of Self and the Knowledge of God Selected and Translated from the Works of Saint Bernard of Clairvaux*. Eugene, OR: Wipf and Stock, 2004.

Scholarship Pertaining to the Works of Bernard of Clairvaux

Altermatt, Alberich Martin. "Bernhard von Clairvaux: Sein Gottesbild im 5. Buch des Traktates '*De consideratione*.'" *Cistercienser Chronik* 77 (1970): 101–23.

Anderson, John D. "Paul in Book 5 of the *De consideratione* of Bernard of Clairvaux." *Cistercian Studies Quarterly* 42, no. 2 (2007): 137–50.

———. "Reconsidering De consideratione: Transition from Book 1 to Book 2." *Cistercian Studies Quarterly* 48, no. 2 (2013): 143–60.

Bennett, Jack Arthur Walter. "*Nosce te ipsum*: Some Medieval and Modern Interpretations." In *The Humane Medievalist and Other Essays in English Literature and Learning from Chaucer to Eliot*, edited by Piero Boitani, 135–72. Rome: Edizioni di Storia e Letteratura, 1982.

Bertrand, Dominique. "Bernardine Discernment: Between the Desert Fathers and Ignatius of Loyola." *Cistercian Studies Quarterly* 36, no. 3 (2001): 325–36.

Boissard, E. "S. Bernard et le Pseudo-Aréopagite." *Recherches de Théologie Ancienne et Médiévale* 26 (1959): 214–63.

Bouyer, Louis. *The Cistercian Heritage*. Translated by Elizabeth A. Livingstone. Westminster, MD: Newman Press, 1958.

Bredero, Adriaan H. *Bernard of Clairvaux: Between Cult and History*. Grand Rapids, MI: Eerdmans, 1996.

Brundage, James A. "St. Bernard and the Jurists." In *The Second Crusade and the Cistercians*, edited by M. Gervers, 25–34. New York: St. Martin's Press, 1992.

Bust, Richard ver. "Papal Ministry: A Source of Theology, Bernard of Clairvaux's Letters." In *Heaven on Earth: Studies in Medieval Cistercian History, IX*, edited by E. Rozanne Elder, 55–61. Cistercian Studies Series 68. Kalamazoo, MI: Cistercian Publications, 1983.

Casey, Michael. "Mindfulness of God in the Monastic Tradition." *Cistercian Studies Quarterly* 17, no. 2 (1982): 111–26.

———. "Bernard the Observer." In *Goad and Nail: Studies in Medieval Cistercian History X*, edited by E. Rozanne Elder, 1–20. Cistercian Studies Series 84. Kalamazoo, MI: Cistercian Publications, 1985.

———. *Athirst for God: Spiritual Desire in Bernard of Clairvaux*. Kalamazoo, MI: Cistercian Publications, 1987.

Cavadini, Catherine Rose. "Lips of Fear Kissed by Mercy: Expositions of *Timor Dei* in Cistercian Commentary on the Song of Songs." In *Saving Fear in Christian Spirituality*, edited by Ann W. Astell, 105–24. Notre Dame, IN: University of Notre Dame Press, 2020.

Châtillon, Jean. "L'Influence de S. Bernard sur la Pensée Scolastique au XIIe et au XIIIe Siècle." *Analecta Sacri Ordinis Cisterciensis* 9, nos. 3–4 (1953): 268–88.

Chapman, Alice. *Sacred Authority and Temporal Power in the Writings of Bernard of Clairvaux*. Turnhout: Brepols, 2013.

Clairmont, David A. "Medieval Consideration and Moral Pace: Thomas Aquinas and Bernard of Clairvaux on the Temporal Aspects of Virtue." *Journal of Religious Ethics* 41, no. 1 (2013): 79–111.

Constable, Giles. "A Report of a Lost Sermon by St Bernard on the Failure of the Second Crusade." In *Studies in Medieval Cistercian History: Presented to Jeremiah F. O'Sullivan*, edited by M. Basil Pennington, 49–54. Cistercian Studies Series 13. Shannon: Irish University Press, 1971.

Cvetković, Carmen Angela. *Seeking the Face of God: The Reception of Augustine in the Mystical Thought of Bernard of Clairvaux and William of St. Thierry*. Turnhout: Brepols, 2012.

Déchanet, Jean-Marie. "Aux Sources de la Pensée Philosophique de S. Bernard." *Analecta Sacri Ordinis Cisterciensis* 9, no. 3–4 (1953): 59–66.

Delaruelle, Étienne. "L'idée de croisade chez saint Bernard." In *Mélanges Saint Bernard: XXIVe Congrès de l'Association bourguignonne des Sociétes savantes 1953*, 53–67. Dijon: Association des Amis de Saint Bernard, 1954.

Delhaye, Philippe. *Le Problème de la Conscience Morale chez S. Bernard: Étudié dans ses Œuvres et dans ses Sources*. Namur: Éditions Godenne, 1957.

Dinzelbacher, Peter. "Bernhards Leben in chronologischer Übersicht." In *Sämtliche Werke, lateinisch/deutsch, Bd. I*, edited by Gerhard B. Winkler, Alberich Altermatt, Denis Farkasfalvy, and Polykarp Zakar, 38–41. Innsbruck: Tyrolia, 1990.

———. *Bernhard von Clairvaux: Leben und Werk des berühmten Zisterziensers*. Darmstadt: Wissenschaftliche Buchgesellschaft, 2017.

Doran, John. "Innocent III and the Uses of Spiritual Marriage." In *Pope, Church, and City: Essays in Honor of Brenda M. Bolton*, edited by Frances Andrews, Christoph Egger, and Constance M. Rousseau, 101–14. Leiden: Brill, 2004.

Dresser, Robert M. "Gradation: Rhetoric and Substance in Saint Bernard." In *Goad and Nail: Studies in Medieval Cistercian History X*, edited by E. Rozanne Elder, 71–85. Cistercian Studies Series 84. Kalamazoo, MI: Cistercian Publications, 1985.

Edgington, Susan B. "Albert of Aachen, St Bernard and the Second Crusade." In *The Second Crusade: Scope and Consequences*, edited by Jonathan Phillips and Martin Hoch, 54–70. New York: Manchester University Press.

Evans, G. R. *The Mind of St. Bernard of Clairvaux*. Oxford: Oxford University Press, 1983.

———. "The *De Consideratione* of Bernard of Clairvaux: A Preliminary Letter." *Cîteaux: Commentarii Cistercienses* 35 (1984): 129–34.

———. *Bernard of Clairvaux*. Oxford: Oxford University Press, 2000.

Farkasfalvy, Denis. "Bernard the Theologian: Forty Years of Research." *Communio: International Catholic Review* 17, no. 4 (1990): 580–94.

———. "Bernard's Concept of the Spiritual Life." *Analecta Sacri Ordinis Cisterciensis* 53 (1997): 3–14.

———. "Remarks and Suggestions Concerning the Critical Text of Saint Bernard's Treatise 'De Consideratione.'" *Analecta Sacri Ordinis Cisterciensis* 54 (2002): 285–310.

Flood, Bernard. "St Bernard's View of Crusade." *The Australasian Catholic Record* 47 (1970): 130–43.

Gasper, Giles E. M. "Bernard of Clairvaux, Material and Spiritual Order, and the Economy of Salvation." *Journal of Medieval History* 45, no. 5 (2019): 580–96.

Gilson, Étienne. *The Mystical Theology of St. Bernard*. Cistercian Studies Series 120. Kalamazoo, MI: Cistercian Publications, 1990.

Griggs, Daniel K. "Augustine's Influence on Bernard of Clairvaux's Teaching on Memory." *Cistercian Studies Quarterly* 32, no. 3 (1997): 475–85.

Hänsler, Basilius. "Die 'Pastoralregel' Gregors des Grossen und die Bücher Bernhards 'Über die Betrachtung.'" *Cistercienser Chronik* 16 (1904): 147–51.

Hiss, Wilhelm. *Die Anthropologie Bernhards von Clairvaux*. Berlin: Walter de Gruyter, 1964.

Holdsworth, Christopher. "Bernard of Clairvaux: His First and Greatest Miracle Was Himself." In *The Cambridge Companion to the Cistercian Order*, edited by Mette Birkedal Bruun, 173–85. Cambridge: Cambridge University Press, 2013.

Hufgard, M. Kilian. "Saint Bernard of Clairvaux: Friend or Foe of the Arts?" In *Heaven on Earth: Studies in Medieval Cistercian History, IX*, edited by E. Rozanne Elder, 62–71. Cistercian Studies Series 68. Kalamazoo, MI: Cistercian Publications, 1983.

Illich, Ivan. *In the Vineyard of the Text: A Commentary to Hugh's "Didascalicon."* Chicago: The University of Chicago Press, 1996.

Ivánka, Endre von. "La Structure de l'Âme selon S. Bernard." *Analecta Sacri Ordinis Cisterciensis* 9, no. 3–4 (1953): 202–8.

Jacqueline, Bernard. "Le Pape d'après le Livre II du *De consideratione ad Eugenium papam* de Saint Bernard de Clairvaux." *Studia Gratiana* 14 (1967): 221–39.

———. "Le Pape et les Romains d'après le *De consideratione ad Eugenium papam* de saint Bernard de Clairvaux." *L'Année Canonique* 17 (1973): 603–14.

James, Bruno S. *Saint Bernard of Clairvaux: An Essay in Biography*. London: Hodder and Stoughton, 1957.

Jordan, Mark D. "Thomas Aquinas on Bernard and the Life of Contemplation." In *Bernardus Magister*, edited by John R. Sommerfeldt, 449–60. Cistercian Studies Series 135. Kalamazoo, MI: Cistercian Publications, 1992.

Kahl, Hans-Dietrich. "Crusade Eschatology as Seen by St. Bernard in the Years 1146 to 1148." In *The Second Crusade and the Cistercians*, edited by M. Gervers, 35–48. New York: St. Martin's Press, 1992.

Kennan, Elizabeth T. "The 'De consideratione' of St. Bernard of Clairvaux and the Papacy in the Mid-Twelfth Century: A Review of Scholarship." *Traditio* 23 (1967): 73–115.

———. "Antithesis and Argument in the *De Consideratione*." In *Bernard of Clairvaux: Studies Presented to Dom Jean Leclercq*, edited by M. Basil Pennington, 91–109. Washington, DC: Cistercian Publications and Consortium Press, 1973.

———. "Rhetoric and Style in the *De Consideratione*." In *Studies in Medieval Cistercian History II*, edited by John R. Sommerfeldt, 40–48. Cistercian Studies Series 24. Kalamazoo, MI: Cistercian Publications, 1976.

Krahmer, Shawn M. "The Virile Bride of Bernard of Clairvaux." *Church History* 69, no. 2 (2000): 304–27.

———. "Adam, Eve, and Original Sin in the Works of Bernard of Clairvaux." *Cistercian Studies Quarterly* 37, no. 1 (2002): 3–12.

Köpf, Ulrich. *Religiöse Erfahrung in der Theologie Bernhards von Clairvaux, Beiträge zur historischen Theologie* 61. Tübingen: Mohr Siebeck, 1980.

Leclercq, Jean. *La spiritualité de Pierre de Celle (1115–1183)*. Paris: Librairie Philosophique J. Vrin, 1946.

———. "Origène au XIIe siècle." *Irenikon* 24 (1951): 425–39.

———. "Les manuscrits de l'abbaye de Liessies." *Scriptorium* 6 (1952): 51–62.

———. "Études sur Saint Bernard et le Texte de ses Écrits." *Analecta Sacri Ordinis Cisterciensis* 9, no. 1–2 (1953): 11–201.

———. "S. Bernard et la Théologie Monastique du XIIe Siècle." *Analecta Sacri Ordinis Cisterciensis* 9, no. 3–4 (1953): 7–23.

———. *The Interior Life*. Translated by Fergus Murphy. New York: P. J. Kennedy and Sons, 1961.

———. *Recueil D'Études sur Saint Bernard et Ses Écrits*. 4 vols. Rome: Edizioni di Storia e Letteratura, 1962–87.

———. "Theology and Prayer: The Education of Seminarians." *Encounter* 24, no. 3 (1963): 349–64.

———. "The Role of Monastic Spirituality Critically Discussed." *Worship* 39, no. 10 (1965): 583–96.

———. "La récréation et le colloque dans la tradition monastique." *Revue d'ascétique et de mystique* 43 (1967): 3–20.

———. "L'Art de la Composition dans les Traités de S. Bernard." In *Recueil D'Études sur Saint Bernard et Ses Écrits, Vol. III*, 105–62. Rome: Edizioni di Storia e Letteratura, 1969.

———. "Aspects Littéraires de L'Œuvre de S Bernard." In *Recueil D'Études sur Saint Bernard et Ses Écrits, Vol. III*, 13–104. Rome: Edizioni di Storia e Letteratura, 1969.

———. "Lettres de S. Bernard: Histoire ou littérature?" *Studi Medievali* 12 (1971): 1–74.

———. "Recherches sur la collection des lettres de S. Bernard." *Cahiers de Civilisation Médiévale* 14 (1971): 205–19.

———. "Modern Psychology and the Interpretation of Medieval Texts." *Speculum* 48, no. 3 (1973): 476–90.

———. "Experience and Interpretation of Time in the Early Middle Ages." In *Studies in Medieval Culture V*, edited by John R. Sommerfeldt, Larry Syndergaard, and E. Rozanne Elder, 9–19. Kalamazoo, MI: Western Michigan University Press, 1975.

———. "Psycho-history and the Understanding of Medieval People." *The Hanoverian* 6 (1975): 6–9.

———. "Psycho-history and the Understanding of Medieval People: Part III and Conclusion." *The Hanoverian* 7 (1975): 7–10.

———. *Bernard of Clairvaux and the Cistercian Spirit*. Translated by Claire Lavoie. Cistercian Studies Series 16. Kalamazoo, MI: Cistercian Publications, 1976.

———. *Nouveau Visage de Bernard de Clairvaux: Approaches psycho-historiques*. Paris: Les Éditions du Cerf, 1976.

———. "Psycho-history and the Understanding of Medieval People." *Cistercian Studies Quarterly* 11 (1976): 269–89.

———. "St Bernard and the Christian Experience." In *Aspects of Monasticism*, translated by Mary Dodd, 251–65. Cistercian Studies Series 7. Kalamazoo, MI: Cistercian Publications, 1978.

———. *Monks and Love in Twelfth-Century France: Psycho-Historical Essays.* Oxford: Oxford University Press, 1979.

———. *The Love of Learning and the Desire for God: A Study of Monastic Culture.* Translated by Catharine Misrahi. New York: Fordham University Press, 1982.

———. "The Renewal of Theology." In *Renaissance and Renewal in the Twelfth Century*, edited by Robert L. Benson and Giles Constable, 68–87. Cambridge, MA: Harvard University Press, 1982.

———. "Prayer at Cluny." *Journal of the American Academy of Religion* 51, no. 4 (1983): 651–65.

———. "Lectio Divina." *Worship* 58, no. 3 (1984): 239–48.

———. "L'Encyclique de Saint Bernard en Faveur de la Croisade." In *Recueil D'Études sur Saint Bernard et Ses Écrits, Vol. IV*, 227–46. Rome: Edizioni di Storia e Letteratura, 1987.

———. *Alone with God.* Translated by Elizabeth McCabe. New York: Farrar, Straus, and Giroux, 1989.

———. *A Second Look at Saint Bernard.* Translated by Marie-Bernard Saïd. Cistercian Studies Series 105. Kalamazoo, MI: Cistercian Publications, 1990.

———. "General Introduction to the Works of Saint Bernard (I)." *Cistercian Studies Quarterly* 40, no. 1 (2005): 3–25.

———. "General Introduction to the Works of Saint Bernard (II)." *Cistercian Studies Quarterly* 40, no. 3 (2005): 243–51.

———. "General Introduction to the Works of Saint Bernard (III)." *Cistercian Studies Quarterly* 40, no. 4 (2005): 365–93.

———. "Introduction to the Letters of Saint Bernard (II)." *Cistercian Studies Quarterly* 41, no. 3 (2006): 291–310.

———. "Introduction to Saint Bernard's Doctrine in the Sermons on the Song of Songs." *Cistercian Studies Quarterly* 43, no. 3 (2008): 309–25.

Martineau, Emmanuel. "Prudence et Considération: Un Dessein Philosophique de Saint Bernard de Clairvaux." *Les Études Philosophiques* 1 (1980): 23–45.

Mayr-Harting, Henry. "Two Abbots in Politics: Wala of Corbie and Bernard of Clairvaux." *Transactions of the Royal Historical Society* 40 (1990): 217–37.

McDonnell, Kilian. "Spirit and Experience in Bernard of Clairvaux." *Theological Studies* 58 (1997): 3–18.

McGinn, Bernard. "St Bernard and Eschatology." In *Bernard of Clairvaux: Studies Presented to Dom Jean Leclercq*, edited by M. Basil Pennington, 161–86. Washington, DC: Cistercian Publications and Consortium Press, 1973.

———. "Introduction." In *Three Treatises on Man: A Cistercian Anthropology*, edited by Bernard McGinn, 1–100. Cistercian Fathers Series 24. Kalamazoo, MI: Cistercian Publications, 1977.

McGuire, Brian Patrick. "Bernard's Life and Works: A Review." In *A Companion to Bernard of Clairvaux*, edited by Brian Patrick McGuire, 18–63. Leiden: Brill, 2011.

———. *Bernard of Clairvaux: An Inner Life*. Ithaca, NY: Cornell University Press, 2020.

Mellerin, Laurence. "*Oculus Simplex*: Discernment Spirituel et Progrès Éthique chez Saint Bernard." *Cîteaux: Commentarii Cistercienses* 63 (2012): 147–63.

Meschini, Marco. *San Bernardo e la Seconda Crociata*. Milan: Mursia, 1998.

Mews, Constant J. "The Council of Sens (1141): Abelard, Bernard, and the Fear of Social Upheaval." *Speculum* 77, no. 2 (2002): 342–82.

Michel, Bruno. "La considération et l'« *unitas spiritus* »." In *Saint Bernard et la Philosophie*, edited by Rémi Brague, 109–27. Paris: Presses Universitaires de France, 1993.

Morrison, Karl F. "Hermeneutics and Enigma: Bernard of Clairvaux's *De consideratione*." *Viator* 19 (1988): 129–52.

Paulsell, William O. "Virtue in St Bernard's *Sermons on the Song of Songs*." In *Saint Bernard of Clairvaux: Studies Commemorating the Eighth Centenary of His Canonization*, edited by M. Basil Pennington, 101–17. Kalamazoo, MI: Cistercian Publications, 1977.

———. "Bernard of Clairvaux as Spiritual Director." *Cistercian Studies Quarterly* 23, no. 3 (1988): 223–31.

Phillips, Jonathan. "St Bernard of Clairvaux, the Low Countries, and the Lisbon Letter of the Second Crusade." *The Journal of Ecclesiastical History* 48, no. 3 (1997): 485–97.

Pousset, Franz. "Bernard of Clairvaux as Luther's Source." *Concordia Theological Quarterly* 54, no. 4 (1990): 281–304.

Pranger, M. B. "Bernard of Clairvaux: Work and Self." In *The Cambridge Companion to the Cistercian Order*, edited by Mette Birkedal Bruun, 186–98. Cambridge: Cambridge University Press, 2013.

Radcke, Fritz. *Die eschatologische Anschauungen Bernhards von Clairvaux*. Greifswald, 1915.

Russell, J. Stephen. "Piety's Dance: The Cardinal Virtues in Bernard's *De consideratione*." *Cistercian Studies Quarterly* 49, no. 1 (2014): 27–42.

Scholl, Edith. "The Mother of Virtues: *Discretio*." *Cistercian Studies Quarterly* 36, no. 3 (2001): 389–401.

Sommerfeldt, John R. "Abelard and Bernard of Clairvaux." *Papers of the Michigan Academy of Science, Arts, and Letters* 46 (1961): 493–501.

———. "The Social Theory of Bernard of Clairvaux." In *Studies in Medieval Cistercian History: Presented to Jeremiah F. O'Sullivan*, edited by M. Basil Pennington, 35–48. Cistercian Studies Series 13. Shannon: Irish University Press, 1971.

———. "Charismatic and Gregorian Leadership in the Thought of Bernard of Clairvaux." In *Bernard of Clairvaux: Studies Presented to Dom Jean Leclercq*, edited by M. Basil Pennington, 73–90. Washington, DC: Cistercian Publications, 1973.

———. "Epistemology, Education, and Social Theory in the Thought of Bernard of Clairvaux." In *Saint Bernard of Clairvaux: Studies Commemorating the Eighth Centenary of His Canonization*, edited by M. Basil Pennington, 169–79. Kalamazoo, MI: Cistercian Publications, 1977.

———. "Epistemological and Social Hierarchies: A Potential Reconciliation of Some Inconsistencies in Bernard's Thought." *Cîteaux: Commentarii cistercienses* 31, no. 1 (1980): 83–92.

———. "Meditation as the Path to Humility in the Thought of Bernard of Clairvaux." *Mystics Quarterly* 15, no. 4 (1989): 177–83.

———. *The Spiritual Teachings of Bernard of Clairvaux*. Cistercian Studies Series 125. Kalamazoo, MI: Cistercian Publications, 1991.

———. "Bernard as Contemplative." In *Bernardus Magister*, edited by John R. Sommerfeldt, 73–84. Kalamazoo, MI: Cistercian Publications, 1992.

———. "Bernard of Clairvaux's Abbot: Both Daniel and Noah." In *Studiosorum Speculum: Studies in Honor of Louis J. Lekai, O.Cist.*, edited by Francis R. Swietek and John R. Sommerfeldt, 355–61. Cistercian Studies Series 141. Kalamazoo, MI: Cistercian Publications, 1993.

———. "Bernard on Charismatic Knowledge: The Truth as Gift." *Cistercian Studies Quarterly* 32, no. 3 (1997): 295–301.

———. "The Bernardine Reform and the Crusading Spirit." *The Catholic Historical Review* 86, no. 4 (2000): 567–78.

———. "Bernard of Clairvaux and the Trivial Arts: A Contemplative's Thoughts on Literature and Philosophy." In *Praise No Less than Charity: Studies in Honor of M. Chrysogonus Waddell, Monk of Gethsemani Abbey*, edited by E. Rozanne Elder, 141–59. Cistercian Studies Series 193. Kalamazoo, MI: Cistercian Publications, 2002.

———. *Bernard of Clairvaux: On the Life of the Mind*. Mahwah, NJ: Newman Press, 2004.

———. *Bernard of Clairvaux: On the Spirituality of Relationship*. Mahwah, NJ: Newman Press, 2004.

———. "Afterword: Looking Back at Bernard." In *A Companion to Bernard of Clairvaux*, edited by Brian Patrick McGuire, 369–74. Leiden: Brill, 2011.

———. "Contemplatives and Visionaries: Four Twelfth-Century Monastics." *Cistercian Studies Quarterly* 54, no. 2 (2019): 171–79.

Standaert, M. "La Doctrine de l'Image chez S. Bernard." *Ephemerides Theologicae Lovanienses* 23 (1947): 70–129.

Stepsis, Robert P. "Fulfillment of Self and Union with God in the Writings of Bernard of Clairvaux." *The American Benedictine Review* 24 (1973): 348–64.

Stiegman, Emero. "Humanism in Bernard of Clairvaux: Beyond Literary Culture." In *The Chimæra of His Age: Studies on Bernard of Clairvaux*, edited by E. Rozanne Elder and John R. Sommerfeldt, 23–38. Cistercian Studies Series 63. Kalamazoo, MI: Cistercian Publications, 1980.

———. "The Literary Genre of Bernard of Clairvaux's *Sermones super Cantica Canticorum*." In *Simplicity and Ordinariness: Studies in Medieval Cistercian History IV*, edited by John R. Sommerfeldt, 68–93. Cistercian Studies Series 61. Kalamazoo, MI: Cistercian Publications, 1980.

———. "A Tradition of Aesthetics in Saint Bernard." In *Bernardus Magister*, edited by John R. Sommerfeldt, 129–47. Kalamazoo, MI: Cistercian Publications, 1992.

———. "Bernard of Clairvaux, William of St. Thierry, the Victorines." In *The Medieval Theologians: An Introduction to Theology in the Medieval Period*, edited by G. R. Evans, 129–55. Malden, MA: Blackwell, 2001.

Stock, Brian. "Experience, Praxis, Work and Planning in Bernard of Clairvaux: Observations on the *Sermones in Cantica*." In *The Cultural Context of Medieval Learning: Proceedings of the First International Colloquium on Philosophy, Science, and Theology in the Middle Ages –September 1973*, edited by John Emery Murdoch and Edith Dudley Sylla, 219–61. Boston: D. Reidel Publishing, 1975.

Suraci, Antonio. "San Bernardo di Chiaravalle e Arnaldo da Brescia." *Analecta Sacri Ordinis Cisterciensis* 13 (1957): 83–91.

Verbaal, Wim. "Bernardus Philosophus." *Revista Portuguesa de Filosofia* 60, no. 3 (2004): 567–86.

———. "The Preaching of Community: Bernard of Clairvaux's Sermons and the School of Experience." *Medieval Sermon Studies* 48 (2004): 75–90.

Volz, Carl. "Martin Luther's Attitude toward Bernard of Clairvaux." In *Studies in Medieval Cistercian History: Presented to Jeremiah F. O'Sullivan*, edited by M. Basil Pennington, 186–204. Cistercian Studies Series 13. Shannon: Irish University Press, 1971.

White, Hayden V. "The Gregorian Ideal and Saint Bernard of Clairvaux." *Journal of the History of Ideas* 21, no. 3 (1960): 321–48.

Williams, Watkin. *Saint Bernard of Clairvaux*. Manchester: Manchester University Press, 1952.

Other Ancient and Medieval Works Cited

Latin Editions of Other Ancient and Medieval Works Cited

Aquitani, Prosperi. *Sententiarum ex operibus S. Augustini delibatarum*. In PL 51:427–534.

Augustine. *Confessions, Books IX-XIII*. Translated by William Watts. Cambridge, MA: Harvard University Press, 2000.

Augustini, Aurelii. *De doctrina Christiana*. Edited by Joseph Martin. Corpus Christianorum Series Latina 32. Turnhout: Brepols, 1996.

———. *De Trinitate libri XV (Libri I–XII)*. Edited by W. J. Mountain and Fr. Glorie. Corpus Christianorum Series Latina 50. Turnhout: Brepols, 1968.

———. *De Trinitate libri XV (Libri XIII–XV)*. Edited by W. J. Mountain and Fr. Glorie. Corpus Christianorum Series Latina 50a. Turnhout: Brepols, 1968.

Augustinus. *De civitate Dei, Libri I-X*. Edited by B. Dombart and A. Kalb. Corpus Christianorum Series Latina 47. Turnhout: Brepols, 1955.

Bingensis, Hildegardis. *Epistolarium*. Edited by L. van Acker. Corpus Christianorum Continuatio Mediaevalis 91. Turnhout: Brepols, 1991.

Boethius. *Contra Eutychen*. In *Tractates, The Consolation of Philosophy*, translated by H. F. Stewart, E. K. Rand, and S. J. Tester, 72–129. Cambridge, MA: Harvard University Press, 1973.

———. *De Trinitate*. In *Tractates, The Consolation of Philosophy*, translated by H. F. Stewart, E. K. Rand, and S. J. Tester, 2–31. Cambridge, MA: Harvard University Press, 1973.

Calcidius. *Timaeus, a Calcidio translatus commentarioque instructus*. Edited by J. H. Waszink. Leiden: Brill, 1962.

Cicero. *De finibus bonorum et malorum*. In *On Ends*, translated by H. Rackham. Cambridge, MA: Harvard University Press, 1989.

———. *Laelius de amicitia*. In *On Old Age, On Friendship, On Divination*, translated by W. A. Falconer, 108–210. Cambridge, MA: Harvard University Press, 1923.

———. *Topica*. In *De inventione, De optimo genere oratorum, Topica*, translated by H. M. Hubbell, 375–459. Cambridge, MA: Harvard University Press, 1976.

Dionysii Cartusiani. *De meditatione*. In *Opera omnia, Tom. XLI, Opera minora, IX*. Edited by Monachorum sacri ordinis Cartusiensis. Tornaci: Typis Cartusiae Sanctæ Mariæ de Pratis, Ex Editionibus Coloniae, 1912.

Gietl, Ambrosius M., ed. *Die Sentenzen Rolands nachmals Papstes Alexander III*. Amsterdam: Rodopi, 1969.

Gisleberti Pictauensis. *Expositio in Boecii librum primum de Trinitate*. In *The Commentaries on Boethius by Gilbert of Poitiers*, edited by Nikolaus M. Häring, 53–180. Toronto: Pontifical Institute of Mediaeval Studies, 1966.

Grégoire le Grand. *Homélies sur Ézéchiel, Tom. II*. Translated by Charles Morel. SC 360. Paris: Les Éditions du Cerf, 1990.

———. *La Règle pastorale, Tom. I*. Edited by Bruno Judic, Floribert Rommel, and Charles Morel. SC 381. Paris: Les Éditions du Cerf, 1992.

Gregorii Papae I. *Moralium libri sive expositio in librum B. Iob*. In PL 75:509–1160.

———. *Regulae pastoralis liber, ad Joannem episcopum civitatis Ravennae*. In PL 77:13–128.

Guigues II le Chartreux. *Lettre sur La Vie Contemplative (L'Echelle des Moines); Douze Méditations*. Paris: Les Éditions du Cerf, 1976.

Guillelmi de Conchis. *Glosae super Platonem*. Edited by Édouard Jeauneau. Corpus Christianorum Continuatio Mediaevalis 203. Turnhout: Brepols, 2006.

Haseldine, Julian, ed. *The Letters of Peter of Celle*. Oxford: Oxford University Press, 2001.

Häring, Nikolaus M., ed. "Die *Sententiae magistri Gisleberti Pictavensis (I)*." *Archives d'Histoire Doctrinale et Littéraire du Moyen Âge* 45 (1978): 83–180.

———. "Die *Sententiae magistri Gisleberti Pictavensis (II)*." *Archives d'Histoire Doctrinale et Littéraire du Moyen Âge* 46 (1979): 45–195.

Hildemarus. *Expositio regulae ab Hildemaro tradita*. Edited by Rupert Mittermüller. Cincinnati: Pustet, 1880.

Joannes Saresberiensis. *Polycraticus*. In PL 199:379–822.

Lombardi, Petri. *Sententiae in IV libris distinctae*. 2 vols. Spicilegium Bonaventurianum IV–V. Grottaferrata: Collegii S. Bonaventurae ad Claras Aquas, 1971–81.

Martin, Raymond M., ed. *Oeuvres de Robert de Melun*. 4 vols. Louvain: Spicilegium Sacrum Lovaniense, 1947–52.

Mauri, Rabani. *De clericorum institutione ad Haistulphum libri tres*. In PL 107:293–418.

Maximos the Confessor. *On Difficulties in the Church Fathers, The Ambigua, Vol. 1*. Translated by Nicholas Constas. Cambridge, MA: Harvard University Press, 2014.

Mikkers, E. "Un «Speculum Novitii» Inedit D'Etienne De Salley." *Collectanea Ordinis Cisterciensium Reformatorum* 8 (1946): 17–68.

Nequam, Alexander. *Speculum speculationum*. British Academy, 1988.

Pierre de Celle. *L'École du Cloître*. Edited by Gérard de Martel. SC 240. Paris: Les Éditions du Cerf, 1977.

Pulli, Roberti. *Sententiarum libri octo*. In PL 186:639–1010.

Radberti, Paschasii. *De fide, spe et charitate*. In PL 120:1387–1488.

———. *De vita s. Adalhardi*. In PL 120:1507–56.

Spannagel, Alfred, and Pius Engelbert, eds. *Smaragdi abbatis expositio in regulam S. Benedicti*. In *Corpus consuetudinum monasticarum*, VIII. Siegburg: Franz Schmitt, 1974.

Taio Cæsaraugust. *Sententiarum libri quinque*. In PL 80:727–989.

Taio Cæsaraugustanus. *Liber sententiarum*. Turnhout: Brepols, 2023.

Warnefridi, Pauli. *In sanctam regulam commentarium*. Montecassino: Abbot of Montecassino, 1880.

Weber, Robert, and Roger Gryson, eds. *Biblia Sacra Iuxta Vulgatam Versionem*. 5th ed. Stuttgart: Deutsche Bibelgesellschaft, 2007.

Wilmart, Dom André. *Le Recueil des pensées du B. Guigue*. Paris: Librairie Philosophie J. Vrin, 1936.

English Translations of Other Ancient and Medieval Works Cited

Abbot Suger of Saint-Denis. "The Illustrious King Louis [VII], Son of Louis [VI]." In *Selected Works of Abbot Suger of Saint-Denis*, translated by Richard Cusimano and Eric Whitmore, 127–83. Washington, DC: The Catholic University of America Press, 2018.

Abelard, Peter. "Prologue to the *Yes and No*." In *Medieval Literary Theory and Criticism c.1100–c.1375: The Commentary Tradition, Revised Edition*, edited by A. J. Minnis and A. B. Scott, 87–100. Oxford: Oxford University Press, 1988.

———. *Sic et non: A Critical Edition*. Edited by Blanche B. Boyer and Richard McKeon. Chicago: University of Chicago Press, 1976.

Allen, S. J., and Emilie Amt, eds. *The Crusades: A Reader*. 2nd ed. Toronto: University of Toronto Press, 2014.

Anselm of Canterbury. *Meditatio*. In *Complete Philosophical and Theological Treatises of Anselm of Canterbury*, translated by Jasper Hopkins and Herbert Richardson, 419–26. Minneapolis, MN: Arthur J. Banning, 2000.

———. *Proslogion*. In *Complete Philosophical and Theological Treatises of Anselm of Canterbury*, translated by Jasper Hopkins and Herbert Richardson, 88–112. Minneapolis, MN: Arthur J. Banning, 2000.

Aquinas, Thomas. *Summa Theologica*. 5 vols. Translated by the Fathers of the English Dominican Province. New York: Benzinger Brothers, 1948.

Aristotle. *The "Art" of Rhetoric*. Translated by John Henry Freese. Cambridge, MA: Harvard University Press, 1994.

———. *Metaphysics Books X–XIV, Oeconomica, Magna Moralia*. Translated by Hugh Tredennick and G. Cyril Armstrong. Cambridge, MA: Harvard University Press, 1997.

———. *Nicomachean Ethics*. Translated by H. Rackham. Cambridge, MA: Harvard University Press, 2003.

———. *Topica*. In *Posterior Analytics, Topica*, translated by Hugh Tredennick and E. S. Forster, 263–739. Cambridge, MA: Harvard University Press, 1960.

Athanasius. *Contra gentes*. In *Contra Gentes and De Incarnatione*, translated by Robert W. Thomson, 2–133. Oxford: Oxford University Press, 1971.

Augustine. *On Christian Teaching*. Translated by R. P. H. Green. Oxford: Oxford University Press, 1999.

———. *The City of God against the Pagans*. Edited by R. W. Dyson. New York: Cambridge University Press, 1998.

———. *The Magnitude of the Soul*. Translated by John J. McMahon. In *The Immortality of the Soul, The Magnitude of the Soul, On Music, The Advantage of Believing, On Faith in Things Unseen*, edited by Hermigild Dressler, 49–149. Washington, DC: The Catholic University of America Press, 1947.

———. *The Trinity*. Translated by Stephen McKenna. Washington, DC: The Catholic University of America Press, 1963.

Basil the Great. *On the Holy Spirit*. Crestwood, NY: St. Vladimir's Seminary Press, 1980.

Bellarmine, Robert. *The Mind's Ascent to God*. In *Spiritual Writings*, translated by John Patrick Donnelly and Roland J. Teske, 47–230. New York: Paulist Press, 1989.

Benedict. *The Rule of St. Benedict*. Edited by Timothy Fry. New York: Vintage Books, 1998.

Blund, John. *Treatise on the Soul*. 2nd ed. Edited by Michael Dunne and R. W. Hunt. British Academy, 2012.

Bonaventure. *Collations on the Six Days*. Translated by José de Vinck. In *The Works of Bonaventure*, vol. V. Paterson, NJ: St. Anthony Guild, 1970.

———. *The Journey of the Mind to God*. Translated by José de Vinck. In *The Works of Bonaventure*, vol. I, Mystical Opuscula. Quincy, IL: Franciscan, 1997.

———. *Soliloquy on the Four Spiritual Exercises*. Translated by José de Vinck. In *The Works of Bonaventure*, III, Opuscula, Second Series, 33–129. Paterson, NJ: St. Anthony Guild, 1966.

Brother Lawrence. *The Practice of the Presence of God*. New Kensington, PA: Whitaker House, 1982.

Calcidius. *On Plato's "Timaeus."* Translated by John Magee. Cambridge, MA: Harvard University Press, 2016.

Cassian, John. *Conferences*. Translated by Colm Luibheid. Mahwah, NJ: Paulist Press, 1985.

———. *The Institutes*. Translated by Boniface Ramsey. New York: Newman Press, 2000.

Chadwick, Henry, ed. *The Sentences of Sextus: A Contribution to the History of Early Christian Ethics*. New York: Cambridge University Press, 1959.

Chibnall, Marjorie, ed. *The "Historia Pontificalis" of John of Salisbury*. Oxford: Clarendon Press, 1986.

Climacus, John. *The Ladder of Divine Ascent*. Translated by Colm Luibheid and Norman Russell. Mahwah, NJ: Paulist Press, 1982.

Deme, Dániel. "The Letter of Isaac of Stella on the Soul." In *The Selected Works of Isaac of Stella*, 143–57. New York: Routledge, 2007.

Denis the Carthusian. *Meditation*. In *The Spiritual Writings of Denis the Carthusian*, translated by Íde M. Ní Riain, 273–98. Dublin: Four Courts, 2005.

Denzinger, Heinrich. *Enchiridion symbolorum*. 43rd ed. Edited by Peter Hunermann. San Francisco, CA: Ignatius Press, 2012.

Gottfried and Theodoric. *The Life of the Holy Hildegard*. Collegeville, MN: Liturgical Press, 1995.

Gregory the Great. *The Book of Pastoral Rule*. Translated by George E. Demacopoulos. Crestwood, NY: St. Vladimir's Seminary Press, 2007.

———. *Dialogues*. Edited by Edmund Garratt Gardner. London: Philip Lee Warner, 1911.

———. *Forty Gospel Homilies*. Translated by David Hurst. Kalamazoo, MI: Cistercian Publications, 1990.

———. *Homilies on the Book of the Prophet Ezekiel*. Translated by Theodosia Tomkinson. Etna, CA: Center for Traditionalist Studies, 2008.

———. *Moral Reflections on the Book of Job: Volume 1, Preface and Books 1–5*. Translated by Brian Kerns. Cistercian Studies Series 249. Collegeville, MN: Cistercian Publications, 2014.

———. *Moral Reflections on the Book of Job: Volume 3, Books 11–16*. Translated by Brian Kerns. Cistercian Studies Series 258. Collegeville, MN: Cistercian Publications, 2016.

Guigo II. *The Ladder of Monks*. In *Ladder of Monks and Twelve Meditations*, translated by Edmund Colledge and James Walsh, 65–86. Cistercian Studies Series 48. Kalamazoo, MI: Cistercian Publications, 1981.

Helmod, Priest of Bosau. *Chronicle of the Slavs*. Translated by Francis Joseph Tschan. New York: Octagon Books, 1966.

Hildegard of Bingen. "Letter 1 to Bernard of Clairvaux." In *The Personal Correspondence of Hildegard of Bingen*, edited by Joseph L. Baird, 17–20. Oxford: Oxford University Press, 2006.

Hugh of St. Victor. *De arca Noe morali*. In *Selected Spiritual Writings*, translated by A Religious of CSMV, 43–153. Eugene, OR: Wipf & Stock, 1962.

———. *De arca Noe mystica*. In *The Mystic Ark: Hugh of St. Victor, Art, and Thought in the Twelfth Century*, by Conrad Rudolph, 393–502. New York: Cambridge University Press, 2014.

———. *On Meditation*. Translated by Frans van Liere. In *Writings on the Spiritual Life: A Selection of Works of Hugh, Adam, Achard, Richard, Walter, and Godfrey of St. Victor*, edited by Christopher P. Evans, 381–94. Turnhout: Brepols, 2013.

Isidore of Seville. *Sententiae*. Translated by Thomas L. Knoebel. New York: Paulist Press, 2018.

Jolin, John J., trans. *Meditations of Guigo, Prior of the Charterhouse*. Milwaukee: Marquette University Press, 1976.

John of Salisbury. *Policraticus*. Translated by Cary J. Nederman. New York: Cambridge University Press, 1990.

Julianus Pomerius. *De vita contemplativa*. Translated by Sr. Mary Josephine Suelzer. New York: Newman Press, 1947.

Lombard,. *The Sentences*. Translated by Giulio Silano, 4 vols. Toronto: Pontifical Institute of Mediaeval Studies, 2007–10.

McCann, Justin, trans. *The Rule of Saint Benedict in English and Latin*. Fort Collins, Colo.: Roman Catholic Books, 1951.

McGarry, Daniel D., trans. *The Metalogicon of John of Salisbury*. Gloucester, MA: Peter Smith, 1971.

Odo of Deuil. *De profectione Ludovici VII in orientem: The Journey of Louis the Seventh to the East*. Translated by V. G. Berry. New York: W. W. Norton and Co., 1948.

Osbernus (Osbert of Bawdsey). *De expugnatione Lyxbonensi: The Conquest of Lisbon*. Translated by Charles W. David. New York: Columbia University Press, 1936.

Otto of Freising. *Chronica*. Edited by Adolf Hofmeister. Darmstadt, 1960.

———. *The Deeds of Frederick Barbarossa*. Translated by Charles Christopher Mierow. New York: Columbia University Press, 2004.

Peter of Celle. *The School of the Cloister*. In *Selected Works*, translated by Hugh Feiss, 63–130. Cistercian Studies 100. Kalamazoo, MI: Cistercian Publications, 1987.

Plato. *Phaedrus*. In *Euthyphro, Apology, Crito, Phaedo, Phaedrus*, translated by Harold North-Fowler, 405–579. Cambridge, MA: Harvard University Press, 2001.

———. *The Republic, Books I–V*. Translated by Paul Shorey. Cambridge, MA: Harvard University Press, 2000.

———. *The Republic, Books VI–X*. Translated by Paul Shorey. Cambridge, MA: Harvard University Press, 2000.

Plotinus. *Enneads, VI.6–9*. Translated by A. H. Armstrong. Cambridge, MA: Harvard University Press, 1988.

Pseudo-Dionysius. *The Celestial Hierarchy*. In *The Complete Works*, translated by Colm Luibheid, 143–91. New York: Paulist Press, 1987.

Puhl, Louis J., trans. *The Spiritual Exercises of St. Ignatius*. New York: Vintage Books, 2000.

Richard of St. Victor. *Selected Writings on Contemplation*. Translated by Clare Kirchberger. New York: Harper and Brothers, 1955.

Russell, Robert P., trans. *Divine Providence and the Problem of Evil: A Translation of St. Augustine's De Ordine*. New York: Cosmopolitan Science and Art Service, 1942.

Silvas, Anna M., trans. *The Rule of St. Basil in Latin and English*. Collegeville, MN: Liturgical Press, 2013.

Smaragdus of Saint-Mihiel. *Commentary on the Rule of Saint Benedict*. Translated by David Barry. Kalamazoo, MI: Cistercian Publications, 2008.

———. *Diadema monachorum: The Crown of Monks*. Translated by David Barry. Kalamazoo, MI: Cistercian Publications, 2013.

Stephen of Sawley. *A Mirror for Novices*. In *Treatises*, translated by Jeremiah F. O'Sullivan, 83–122. Kalamazoo, MI: Cistercian Publications, 1984.

Stewart, Alistair, ed. *The Gnomai of the Council of Nicaea (CC 0021)*. Piscataway, NJ: Gorgias Press, 2015.

Stump, Eleonore, trans. *Boethius's In Ciceronis Topica*. Ithaca, NY: Cornell University Press, 1988.

Tanner, Norman P. *Decrees of the Ecumenical Councils, Vol. 1, Nicaea I–Lateran V*. Washington, DC: Georgetown University Press, 1990.

Teresa of Ávila. *Interior Castle*. Translated by E. Allison Peers. New York: Image, 1989.

———. *The Way of Perfection*. Translated by Kieran Kavanaugh. Washington, DC: Institute of Carmelite Studies, 2000.

Ward, Benedicta, and Metropolitan Anthony, trans. *The Sayings of the Desert Fathers: The Alphabetical Collection*. Collegeville, MN: Liturgical Press, 1984.

William of St. Thierry. *Meditations*. In *On Contemplating God, Prayer, Meditations*, translated by Penelope Lawson, 75–190. Cistercian Fathers Series 3. Kalamazoo, MI: Cistercian Publications, 1970.

———. *The Nature of the Body and the Soul*. In *Three Treatises on Man: A Cistercian Anthropology*, edited by Bernard McGinn, 101–52. Cistercian Fathers Series 24. Kalamazoo, MI: Cistercian Publications, 1977.

William of Saint-Thierry, Arnold of Bonneval, and Geoffrey of Auxerre. *The First Life of Bernard of Clairvaux*. Translated by Hilary Costello. Cistercian Fathers Series 76. Kalamazoo, MI: Cistercian Publications, 2015.

William of Tyre. *A History of Deeds Done Beyond the Sea, Vol. I.* Translated by Emily Atwater Babcock and A. C. Krey. New York: Columbia University Press, 1943.

Wilson, Walter T., trans. *The Sentences of Sextus.* Atlanta: Society of Biblical Literature, 2012.

Wortley, John, trans. *Give Me a Word: The Alphabetical Sayings of the Desert Fathers.* Crestwood, NY: St. Vladimir's Seminary, 2014.

Scholarship Pertaining to Other Ancient and Medieval Works Cited

Andrée, Alexander. "Laon Revisited: Master Anselm and the Creation of a Theological School in the Twelfth Century." *The Journal of Medieval Latin* 22 (2012): 257–81.

Aust, Magdalena. "Was uns die Bibliothek von Cîteaux erzählen kann (2): Gregor der Große, Vater der zisterziensischen Mystik." *Cistercienser Chronik* 116 (2009): 17–34.

Bardot, Michael L., and Laurence W. Marvin, eds. *Louis VII and His World.* Leiden: Brill, 2018.

Barrow, Julia. "Religion." In *The Central Middle Ages: Europe 950–1320,* edited by Daniel Power, 121–48. Oxford: Oxford University Press, 2006.

Bavel, Tarcisius van. "No One Ever Hated His Own Flesh' Eph. 5:29 in Augustine." *Augustiniana* 45, nos. 1–2 (1995): 45–93.

Bell, David N. "Is There Such a Thing as 'Cistercian Spirituality'?" *Cistercian Studies Quarterly* 33, no. 4 (1998): 455–71.

Benson, Joshua, trans. "*Summa Sententiarum* I.15–19." In *Victorine Christology,* edited by Christopher P. Evans, 183–206. Hyde Park, NY: New City Press, 2019.

Berry, Virginia G. "The Second Crusade." In *A History of the Crusades, Vol. 1: The First Hundred Years,* edited by Marshall W. Baldwin, 463–512. Madison: University of Wisconsin Press, 1969.

Beumann, Helmut. "Kreuzzugsgedanke und Ostpolitik im hohen Mittelalter." *Historisches Jahrbuch* 72 (1953): 112–32.

Bliemetzrieder, F. "Anselms von Laon Systematische Sentenzen." *Beiträge zur Geschichte der Philosophie des Mittelaters* 18 (1919): 1–167.

Boschung, Peter. "Boethius and the Early Medieval 'Quaestio.'" *Recherches de théologie et philosophie médiévales* 71, no. 2 (2004): 233–59.

Bréhier, É. *Plotin: Ennéades.* Paris: Société d'Édition « Les Belles Lettres », 1924–28.

Bruteau, Beatrice. "On Being Observant." *Cistercian Studies Quarterly* 26, no. 1 (1991): 72–85.

Burchill-Limb, K.-Y. "The Actuality of Augustine's Distinction between *Uti* and *Frui*." *Augustiniana* 56, nos. 1–2 (2006): 183–97.

Burnett, Charles. "The Introduction of Aristotle's Natural Philosophy into Great Britain: A Preliminary Survey of the Manuscript Evidence." In *Aristotle in Britain during the Middle Ages*, edited by John Marenbon, 21–50. Turnhout: Brepols, 1996.

Bushlack, Thomas J. "Mindfulness and the Discernment of Passions: Insights from Thomas Aquinas." *Spiritus: A Journal of Christian Spirituality* 14, no. 2 (2014): 141–65.

Büttner, Roman. *Hrabanus Maurus und sein Wirken im Kloster Fulda*. Norderstedt: GRIN, 2006.

Chenu, M.-D. "Évangélisme et théologie au XIIIe siècle." In *Mélanges offerts au R. P. Ferdinand Cavallera, doyen de la faculté de theologie de Toulouse á l'occasion de la quarantiéme année de son professorat á l'institut Catholique*, 339–46. Toulouse: Bibliothéque de l'Institut Catholique, 1948.

———. *Nature, Man, and Society in the Twelfth Century*. Translated by Jerome Taylor and Lester K. Little. Chicago: University of Chicago Press, 1968.

Cipriani, Nello. "Memory." In *Augustine through the Ages: An Encyclopedia*, edited by Allan D. Fitzgerald, 553–55. Grand Rapids, MI: Eerdmans, 1999.

Colish, Marcia L. "The Sentence Collection and the Education of Professional Theologians in the Twelfth Century." In *The Intellectual Climate of the Early University: Essays in Honor of Otto Gründler*, edited by Nancy van Deusen, 1–26. Kalamazoo, MI: Medieval Institute Publications, 1997.

———. "Classicism and Catechesis in the Patriarch Treatises of Ambrose of Milan." *Rivista di Storia della Filosofia* 61, no. 1 (2006): 9–42.

Collins, Roger. *Visigothic Spain 409–711*. Malden, MA: Wiley-Blackwell, 2006.

Constable, Giles. "A Note on the Route of the Anglo-Flemish Crusaders of 1147." *Speculum* 28, no. 3 (1953): 525–26.

———. "The Second Crusade as Seen by Contemporaries." *Traditio* 9 (1953): 213–79.

Coon, Lynda L. "Collecting the Desert in the Carolingian West." *Church History and Religious Culture* 86, nos. 1–4 (2006): 135–62.

Corte, Daniel Marcel La. "Smaragdus of Saint-Mihiel: Ninth-Century Sources for Twelfth-Century Reformers." *Cistercian Studies Quarterly* 41, no. 3 (2006): 273–90.

Corrigan, Kevin. "'Solitary' Mysticism in Plotinus, Proclus, Gregory of Nyssa, and Pseudo-Dionysius." *The Journal of Religion* 76, no. 1 (1996): 28–42.

Courcelle, Pierre. "Plotin et saint Ambroise." *Revue de philologie, de littérature et d'histoire anciennes* 24 (1950): 29–56.

———. "Aspects varies du platonisme ambrosien." In *Recherches sur les Confessions de saint Augustin*. New ed. Paris: E. de Boccard, 1968.

Courtney, F. *Cardinal Robert Pullen: An English Theologian of the Twelfth Century, Analecta Gregoriana*, vol. 64. Rome: Pontifical Gregorian University Press, 1954.

Cowdrey, H. E. J. *Pope Gregory VII: 1073–1085*. Oxford: Oxford University Press, 1998.

Delhaye, Philippe. "L'Organisation Scolaire au XIIe Siècle." *Traditio* 5 (1947): 211–68.

de Lubac, Henri. *Medieval Exegesis, vol. 3, The Four Senses of Scripture*. Translated by E. M. Macierowski. Grand Rapids, MI: Eerdmans, 2009.

Dod, Bernard G. "Aristoteles latinus." In *The Cambridge History of Later Medieval Philosophy: From the Rediscovery of Aristotle to the Disintegration of Scholasticism 1100–1600*, edited by Norman Kretzmann, Anthony Kenny, and Jan Pinborg, 45–79. Cambridge: Cambridge University Press, 1982.

Dorter, Kenneth. "The Divided Line and the Structure of Plato's *Republic*." *History of Philosophy Quarterly* 21, no. 1 (2004): 1–20.

Dragnea, Mihai. *The Wendish Crusade, 1147: The Development of Crusading Ideology in the Twelfth Century*. New York: Routledge, 2020.

Edgington, Susan B. "The Lisbon Letter of the Second Crusade." *Historical Research* 69, no. 170 (1996): 328–39.

Engen, John H. Van. *Rupert of Deutz*. Berkeley: University of California Press, 1983.

Ernst, Stephan. *Ethische Vernunft und christlicher Glaube: Der Prozeß ihrer wechselseitigen Freisetzung in der Zeit von Anselm von Canterbury bis Wilhelm von Auxerre*. Münster: Aschendorff, 1996.

Evans, G. R. *Alan of Lille: The Frontiers of Theology in the Later Twelfth Century*. New York: Cambridge University Press, 1983.

———. *The Thought of Gregory the Great*. New York: Cambridge University Press, 1986.

Ferzoco, George. "The Origin of the Second Crusade." In *The Second Crusade and the Cistercians*, edited by M. Gervers, 91–99. New York: St. Martin's Press, 1992.

Fleteren, Frederick van. "Acies mentis." In *Augustine through the Ages: An Encyclopedia*, edited by Allan D. Fitzgerald, 5–6. Grand Rapids, MI: Eerdmans, 1999.

Floryszczak, Silke. *Die Regula Pastoralis Gregors des Großen*. Tübingen: Mohr Siebeck, 2005.

Forey, Alan. "The Siege of Lisbon and the Second Crusade." *Portugese Studies* 20 (2004): 1–13.

Freed, John B. *Frederick Barbarossa: The Prince and the Myth*. New Haven, CT: Yale University Press, 2016.

Garrison, Mary. "The Emergence of Carolingian Latin Literature and the Court of Charlemagne (780–814)." In *Carolingian Culture: Emulation and Innovation*, edited by Rosamond McKitterick, 111–40. New York: Cambridge University Press, 1994.

Gastaldelli, F. "Teologia Monastica, Teologia Scolastica e Lectio Divina." *Analecta Sacri Ordinis Cisterciensis* 46 (1990): 25–63.

Ghellinck, J. de. *Le mouvement théologique du XII*e *siècle*. Paris: Lecoffre, 1914.

Gibson, Margaret. *Boethius: His Life, Thought and Influence*. Oxford: Basil Blackwell, 1981.

Giraud, Cédric. *Per verba magistri: Anselme de Laon et son école au XII*e *siècle*. Turnhout: Brepols, 2010.

Gleber, Helmut. *Papst Eugen III (1145–1153) unter besonderer Berücksichtigung seiner politischen Tätigkeit*. Jena: Verlag von Gustav Fischer, 1936.

Graboïs, Aryeh. "The Crusade of King Louis VII: A Reconsideration." In *Crusade and Settlement: Papers Read at the First Conference of the Society for the Study of the Crusades and the Latin East*, edited by Peter W. Edbury, 95–104. Cardiff: University College Cardiff Press, 1985.

Green-Pedersen, Niels J. *The Tradition of the Topics in the Middle Ages: The Commentaries on Aristotle's and Boethius' "Topics."* Munich: Philosophia Verlag, 1984.

Hafner, Wolfgang. *Der Basiliuskommentar zur Regula S. Benedicti: Ein Beitrag zur Autorenfrage karolingischer Regelkommentare*. Münster: Aschendorff, 1959.

Hankey, Wayne J. "Mind." In *Augustine through the Ages: An Encyclopedia*, edited by Allan D. Fitzgerald, 563–67. Grand Rapids, MI: Eerdmans, 1999.

———. "*Ratio*, Reason, Rationalism." In *Augustine through the Ages: An Encyclopedia*, edited by Allan D. Fitzgerald, 696–702. Grand Rapids, MI: Eerdmans, 1999.

Häring, Nikolaus M. "The Case of Gilbert de la Porrée, Bishop of Poitiers (1142–1154)." *Mediaeval Studies* 13 (1951): 1–40.

Harkins, Franklin T. "*Lectio exhortatio debet esse*: Reading as a Way of Life at the Twelfth-Century Abbey of St. Victor." In *From Knowledge to Beatitude: St. Victor, Twelfth-Century Scholars, and Beyond, Essays in Honor of Grover A Zinn, Jr.*, edited by E. Ann Matter and Lesley Smith, 103–30. Notre Dame, IN: University of Notre Dame Press, 2013.

Hehl, Ernst-Dieter. "War, Peace and the Christian Order." In *The New Cambridge Medieval History, IV, c.1024–c.1198, Part I*, edited by David Luscombe and Jonathan Riley-Smith, 185–228. New York: Cambridge University Press, 2004.

Hiestand, Rudolf. "The Papacy and the Second Crusade." In *The Second Crusade: Scope and Consequences*, edited by Jonathan Phillips and Martin Hoch, 32–53. Manchester: Manchester University Press, 2001.

Holmes, George, ed. *The Oxford History of Medieval Europe*. Oxford: Oxford University Press, 1988.

Horn, Michael. *Studien zur Geschichte Papst Eugens III (1145–1153)*. New York: Peter Lang, 1992.

Houser, R. E. *The Cardinal Virtues: Aquinas, Albert, and Philip the Chancellor*. Toronto: Pontifical Institute of Mediaeval Studies, 2004.

Hunt, R. W. *The Schools and the Cloister: The Life and Writings of Alexander Nequam (1157–1217)*. Oxford: Oxford University Press, 1984.

Ivánka, Endre von. "*Apex Mentis*. Wanderung und Wandlung eines stoischen Terminus." In *Plato Christianus: Übernahme und Umgestaltung des Platonismus durch die Väter*, 315–51. Einsiedeln: Johannes Verlag, 1990.

Jong, Mayke de. "Growing Up in a Carolingian Monastery: Magister Hildemar and His Oblates." *Journal of Medieval History* 9, no. 2 (1983): 99–128.

Kardong, Terrence G. "The Earliest Commentator on RB: Smaragdus on Benedict's Prologue." *American Benedictine Review* 55 (2004): 171–93.

Katzir, Yael. "The Second Crusade and the Redefinition of *Ecclesia*, *Christianitas*, and Papal Coercive Power." In *The Second Crusade and the Cistercians*, edited by M. Gervers, 3–11. New York: St. Martin's Press, 1992.

Kolpacoff Deane, Jennifer. *A History of Medieval Heresy and Inquisition*. Lanham, MD: Rowman and Littlefield, 2011.

Küpper, Joachim. "*Uti* and *Frui* in Augustine and the Problem of Aesthetic Pleasure in the Western Tradition (Cervantes, Kant, Marx, Freud)." *MLN (Modern Language Notes)* 127, no. 5 (2012): 126–55.

Laistner, M. L. W. *Thought and Letters in Western Europe: A.D. 500 to 900*. 2nd ed. Ithaca, NY: Cornell University Press, 1966.

Lawn, Brian. *The Rise and Decline of the Scholastic "Quaestio Disputata": With Special Emphasis on Its Use in the Teaching of Medicine and Science*. Leiden: Brill, 1993.

Leathers Kuntz, Marion, and Paul Grimley Kuntz, eds. *Jacob's Ladder and the Tree of Life: Concepts of Hierarchy and the Great Chain of Being*. New York: Peter Lang, 1987.

Lees, Jay T. *Anselm of Havelberg: Deeds into Words in the Twelfth Century*. Leiden: Brill, 1998.

Lennox Conyngham, Andrew. "Ambrose and Philosophy." In *Christian Faith and Greek Philosophy in Late Antiquity: Essays in Tribute to Christopher George Stead*, edited by Lionel R. Wickham and Caroline P. Bammel, 112–28. Leiden: Brill, 1993.

Leinsle, Ulrich G. *Introduction to Scholastic Theology*. Translated by Michael J. Miller. Washington, DC: The Catholic University of America Press, 2010.

Lotter, Friedrich. *Die Konzeption des Wendenkreuzzugs*. Sigmarigen: Jan Thorbecke Verlag, 1977.

Lottin, Odom. "Nos. 1–282." *Bulletin de théologie ancienne et médiévale* 6 (1950): 5–88.

Luscombe, D. E. *The School of Peter Abelard: The Influence of Abelard's Thought in the Early Scholastic Period*. New York: Cambridge University Press, 1970.

Kienzle, Beverly Mayne. *Cistercians, Heresy and Crusade in Occitania, 1145–1229: Preaching in the Lord's Vineyard*. Rochester, NY: York Medieval Press, 2001.

Klosko, George. "The 'Rule' of Reason in Plato's Psychology." *History of Philosophy Quarterly* 5, no. 4 (1988): 341–56.

Krey, A. C. "William of Tyre: The Making of an Historian in the Middle Ages." *Speculum* 16, no. 2 (1941): 149–66.

Madec, Goulven. *Saint Ambroise et la Philosophie*. Paris: Études Augustiniennes, 1974.

Malcolm, John. "The Line and the Cave." *Phronesis* 7, no, 1 (1962): 38–45.

Mayr-Harting, Henry. "Odo of Deuil, the Second Crusade, and the Monastery of Saint-Denis." In *Culture of Christendom: Essays in Medieval History in Memory of Denis L. T. Bethel*, edited by Marc A. Meyer, 225–40. Rio Grande, OH: Hambledon Press, 1993.

Marenbon, John. "Carolingian Thought." In *Carolingian Culture: Emulation and Innovation*, edited by Rosamond McKitterick, 171–92. New York: Cambridge University Press, 1994.

Markus, R. A. *Gregory the Great and His World*. New York: Cambridge University Press, 1997.

McCracken, George E., ed. *Early Medieval Theology*. Louisville, KY: Westminster John Knox, 1957.

McGinn, Bernard. "Contemplation in Gregory the Great." In *Gregory the Great: A Symposium*, edited by John C. Cavadini, 146–67. Notre Dame, IN: University of Notre Dame Press, 1995.

McMahon, Robert. *Understanding the Medieval Meditative Ascent: Augustine, Anselm, Boethius, and Dante*. Washington, DC: The Catholic University of America Press, 2006.

McMinn Chambers, Frank. "Some Legends concerning Eleanor of Aquitaine." *Speculum* 16, no. 4 (1941): 459–69.

Merton, Thomas. "Blessed Eugenius III, Abbot of Tre Fontane, Pope." *Cistercian Studies Quarterly* 44, no. 2 (2009): 173–80.

Minio-Paluello, L. "Iacobus Veneticus Grecus: Canonist and Translator of Aristotle." *Traditio* 8 (1952): 265–304.

Morrison, Karl F. "Otto of Freising's Quest for the Hermeneutic Circle." *Speculum* 55, no. 2 (1980): 207–36.

Mulligan, Robert W. "*Ratio Superior* and *Ratio Inferior*: The Historical Background." *The New Scholasticism* 29, no. 1 (1955): 1–32.

Novikoff, Alex J. "Anselm, Dialogue, and the Rise of Scholastic Disputation." *Speculum* 86, no. 2 (2011): 387–418.

———. *The Medieval Culture of Disputation: Pedagogy, Practice, and Performance*. Philadelphia: University of Pennsylvania Press, 2013.

O'Callaghan, Joseph F. *A History of Medieval Spain*. Ithaca, NY: Cornell University Press, 1983.

O'Loughlin, Thomas. "Isidore of Seville as a Theologian." In *A Companion to Isidore of Seville*, edited by Andrew Fear and Jamie Wood, 135–52. Leiden: Brill, 2020.

Petersen, Joan M. "'Homo omnino Latinus'? The Theological and Cultural Background of Pope Gregory the Great." *Speculum* 62, no. 3 (1987): 529–51.

Pevarello, Daniele. *The Sentences of Sextus and the Origins of Christian Asceticism*. Tübingen: Mohr Siebeck, 2013.

Phillips, Jonathan. "The Murder of Charles the Good and the Second Crusade: Household, Nobility, and Traditions of Crusading in Medieval Flanders." *Medieval Prosopography* 19 (1998): 55–75.

———. *The Second Crusade: Extending the Frontiers of Christendom*. New Haven, CT: Yale University Press, 2007.

Pieper, Josef. *Leisure: The Basis of Culture*. Translated by Gerald Malsbary. South Bend, IN: St. Augustine's Press, 1998.

Pinckaers, Servais. *The Sources of Christian Ethics*. Translated by Sr. Mary Thomas Noble. Washington, DC: The Catholic University of America Press, 1995.

Ponesse, Matthew. "Smaragdus of St. Mihiel and the Carolingian Monastic Reform." *Revue Bénédictine* 116 (2006): 367–92.

Prozorov, Vadim. "Discipline and Mercy: Moses as a Pattern for Good Rulers in the Works of Pope Gregory the Great." In *The Christian Moses: From Philo to the Qur'ān*, edited by Philip Rousseau and Janet A. Timbie, 252–63. Washington, DC: The Catholic University of America Press, 2019.

Radice, Betty. "Chronology." In *The Letters of Abelard and Heloise*. New York: Penguin, 1974.

Rendsburg, Gary A. "*Lāśûaḥ* in Genesis XXIV 63." *Vetus Testamentum* 45, no. 4 (1995): 558–60.

Reuter, Timothy. "The 'non-crusade' of 1149–50." In *The Second Crusade: Scope and Consequences*, edited by Jonathan Phillips and Martin Hoch, 150–63. Manchester: Manchester University Press, 2001.

Riddle, John M. *A History of the Middle Ages, 300–1500*. Lanham, MD: Rowman and Littlefield, 2008.

Riley-Smith, Jonathan. *The Crusades: A History*. 2nd ed. New Haven, CT: Yale University Press, 2005.

Robertson, Duncan. *Lectio Divina: The Medieval Experience of Reading*. Cistercian Studies Series 238. Kalamazoo, MI: Cistercian Publications, 2011.

Robinson, T. M. *Plato's Psychology*. 2nd ed. Toronto: University of Toronto Press, 1995.

Rosemann, Philipp W. *The Story of a Great Medieval Book: Peter Lombard's "Sentences."* Toronto: University of Toronto Press, 2013.

Runciman, Steven. *A History of the Crusades, Volume II: The Kingdom of Jerusalem and the Frankish East 1100–1187*. Cambridge: Cambridge University Press, 1951.

Rydstrøm-Poulsen, Aage. "William of St. Thierry on the Soul." In *A Companion to William of Saint-Thierry*, edited by F. Tyler Sergent, 93–108. Leiden: Brill, 2019.

Savon, Hervé. "Saint Ambroise et la philosophie à propos d'une étude récente." *Revue de l'histoire des religions* 191, no. 2 (1977): 173–96.

Silvas, Anna. *Jutta and Hildegard: The Biographical Sources*. University Park: The Pennsylvania State University Press, 1999.

Smalley, Beryl. *The Study of the Bible in the Middle Ages*. Notre Dame, IN: University of Notre Dame Press, 1964.

Somfai, Anna. "The Eleventh Century Shift in the Reception of Plato's *Timaeus* and Calcidius's *Commentary*." *Journal of the Warburg and Courtauld Institutes* 65 (2002): 1–21.

Southern, R. W. *Scholastic Humanism and the Unification of Europe, Volume II, The Heroic Age*. Malden, MA: Blackwell, 2001.

Spatz, Nancy. "Approaches and Attitudes to a New Theology Textbook: The *Sentences* of Peter Lombard." In *The Intellectual Climate of the Early University: Essays in Honor of Otto Gründler*, edited by Nancy van Deusen, 27–52. Kalamazoo, MI: Medieval Institute Publications, 1997.

Straw, Carole. *Gregory the Great: Perfection in Imperfection*. Los Angeles: University of California, 1988.

———. "Gregory I." In *Augustine through the Ages: An Encyclopedia*, edited by Allan D. Fitzgerald, 402–5. Grand Rapids, MI: Eerdmans, 1999.

Stróżyński, Mateusz. "The Ascent of the Soul as Spiritual Exercise in Plotinus' *Enneads*." *Mnemosyne: A Journal of Classical Studies* 74, no. 3 (2021): 448–77.

———. "Spiritual Exercise in Plotinus: The Deictic Method." *Classical Philology* 117, no. 3 (2022): 495–517.

Stump, Eleonore. "Dialectic in Ancient and Medieval Logic." In *Boethius's "De topicis differentiis,"* translated by Eleonore Stump, 157–261. Ithaca, NY: Cornell University Press, 1978.

Taylor, Pegatha. "Moral Agency in Crusade and Colonization: Anselm of Havelberg and the Wendish Crusade of 1147." *The International Review of History* 22, no. 4 (2000): 757–84.

Taylor, W. R. "A New Syriac Fragment Dealing with Incidents in the Second Crusade." *The Annual of the American Schools of Oriental Research* 11 (1929–30): 120–30.

Teichman, Jenny. "The Definition of Person." *Philosophy* 60, no. 232 (1985): 175–85.

Tessera, Miriam Rita. "Philip of Flanders and Hildegard of Bingen: Crusading against the Saracens or Crusading against Deadly Sin?" In *Gendering the Crusades*, edited by Susan B. Edgington and Sarah Lambert, 77–93. New York: Columbia University Press, 2002.

Tweed, Roger G. "The Psychology of Gregory the Great (A.D. 540–A.D. 604)." *International Journal for the Psychology of Religion* 7, no. 2 (1997): 101–10.

Vandenberghe, L., and F. Costa Prado. "Law and Grace in Saint Augustine: A Fresh Perspective on Mindfulness and Spirituality in Behaviour Therapy." *Mental Health, Religion and Culture* 12, no. 6 (2009): 587–600.

Weisheipl, James A. "Science in the Thirteenth Century." In *The History of the University of Oxford*, vol. 1: *The Early Oxford Schools*, edited by J. I. Catto, 435–69. Oxford: Oxford University Press, 1984.

Wilford, F. A. "The Status of Reason in Plato's Psychology." *Phronesis* 4, no. 1 (1959): 54–58.

Wortley, John. "What *hêsychia* Meant to the Desert Fathers." *Cistercian Studies Quarterly* 54, no. 2 (2019): 159–70.

Young, Spencer. *Scholarly Community at the Early University of Paris: Theologians, Education and Society, 1215–1248*. New York: Cambridge University Press, 2014.

Zelzer, Klaus. "Überlegungen zu einer Gesamtedition des frühnachkarolingischen Kommentars zur Regula S. Benedicti aus der Tradition des Hildemar von Corbie." *Revue Bénédictine* 91, nos. 3–4 (1981): 373–82.

———. "Von Benedikt zu Hildemar: Zu Textgestalt und Textgeschichte der Regula Benedicti auf ihrem Weg zur Alleingeltung." *Frühmittelalterliche Studien* 23, no. 1 (1989): 112–30.

Contemporary Works Cited concerning Methodology, Spiritual Direction, and Psychotherapy

Aamar, Rola O., Angela L. Lamson, and Doug Smith. "Qualitative Trends in Biopsychosocial-Spiritual Treatment for Underserved Patients with Type 2 Diabetes." *Contemporary Family Therapy* 37, no. 1 (2015): 33–44.

Acklin, Thomas, and Boniface Hicks. *Spiritual Direction: A Guide for Sharing the Father's Love*. Steubenville, OH: Emmaus Road, 2017.

Alexander, Jeffrey, and Philip Smith. "The Strong Program in Cultural Theory: Elements of a Structural Hermeneutics." In *Handbook of Sociological Theory*, edited by Jonathan H. Turner, 135–50. New York: Kluwer Academic, 2002.

Ashley, Benedict. *Spiritual Direction in the Dominican Tradition*. New York: Integration Books, 1995.

———. "Spirituality and Counseling." In *The Ashley Reader: Redeeming Reason*, 291–303. Ave Maria, FL: Sapientia Press, 2006.

———. *Healing for Freedom: A Christian Perspective on Personhood and Psychotherapy*. Washington, DC: The Catholic University of America Press, 2013.

Ashley, Benedict M., Jean Deblois, and Kevin D. O'Rouke. *Health Care Ethics: A Catholic Theological Analysis*. 5th ed. Washington, DC: Georgetown University Press, 2006.

Avants, S. Kelly, Mark Beitel, and Arthur Margolin. "Making the Shift from 'Addict Self' to 'Spiritual Self': Results from a Stage I Study of Spiritual Self-Schema (3-S) Therapy for the Treatment of Addiction and HIV Risk Behavior." *Mental Health, Religion and Culture* 8, no. 3 (2005): 167–77.

Barry, William A., and William J. Connolly. *The Practice of Spiritual Direction*. 2nd rev. ed. New York: HarperCollins, 2009.

Bary, William Theodore de, ed. *The Buddhist Tradition in India, China and Japan*. New York: Random House, 1969.

Beck, Aaron T., Gary Emery, and Ruth Greenberg, *Anxiety Disorders and Phobias: A Cognitive Perspective*. Cambridge, MA: Basic Books, 1985.

Beck, Aaron T., A. John Rush, Brian F. Shaw, and Gary Emery. *Cognitive Therapy of Depression*. New York: Guilford Press, 1979.

Beck, Judith S. *Cognitive Behavior Therapy: Basics and Beyond*. 2nd ed. New York: Guilford Press, 2011.

Benestad, J. Brian. *Church, State, and Society: An Introduction to Catholic Social Doctrine*. Washington, DC: The Catholic University of America Press, 2011.

Berry, John. "Global, Indigenous, and Regional Perspectives on International Psychology." In *Caribbean Psychology: Indigenous Contributions to a Global Discipline*, edited by J. L. Roopnarine and D. Chadee, 45–68. Washington, DC: American Psychological Association, 2016.

Biglan, Anthony, and Steven C. Hayes. "Functional Contextualism and Contextual Behavioral Science." In *The Wiley Handbook of Contextual Behavioral Science*, edited by Robert D. Zettle, Steven C. Hayes, Dermot Barnes-Holmes, and Anthony Biglan, 37–61. Malden, MA: John Wiley and Sons, 2016.

Bonanno, George A. "Loss, Trauma, and Human Resilience: Have We Underestimated the Human Capacity to Thrive After Extremely Adverse Events?" *Psychological Trauma: Theory, Research, Practice, and Policy*, S, no. 1 (2008): 101–13.

Borneman, Tami, Betty Ferrell, and Christina M. Puchalski. "Evaluation of the FICA Tool for Spiritual Assessment." *Journal of Pain and Symptom Management* 40, no. 2 (2010): 163–73.

Bottaro, Gregory. *The Mindful Catholic: Finding God One Moment at a Time*. North Palm Beach, FL: Beacon Publishing, 2018.

Bowlby, John. *The Making and Breaking of Affectional Bonds*. New York: Routledge, 2005.

Brownell, Philip. *Spiritual Competency in Psychotherapy*. New York: Springer Publishing, 2015.

———. *Christianity and Gestalt Therapy: The Presence of God in Human Relationships*. New York: Routledge, 2020.

Bruford, W. H. *Culture and Society in Classical Weimar 1775–1806*. Cambridge: Cambridge University Press, 1962.

———. *The German Tradition of Self-Cultivation: 'Bildung' from Humboldt to Mann*. Cambridge: Cambridge University Press, 2010.

Brüssow, H. "What is Health?" *Microbial Biotechnology* 6, no. 4 (2013): 341–48.

Cadge, Wendy, and Julia Bandini. "The Evolution of Spiritual Assessment Tools in Healthcare." *Society* 52, no. 5 (2015): 430–37.

Carrington, Patricia, and Harmon S. Ephron. "Meditation as an Adjunct to Psychotherapy." In *New Dimensions in Psychiatry: A Worldview*, edited by Silvano Arieti and Gerard Chrzanowski, 261–91. New York: John Wiley and Sons, 1975.

Cashwell, Craig S., Paige B. Bentley, and J. Preston Yarborough. "The Only Way Out Is Through: The Peril of Spiritual Bypass." *Counseling and Values* 51, no. 2 (2007): 139–48.

Catechism of the Catholic Church. New York: Image/Doubleday, 1997.

Congregation for the Doctrine of the Faith. "Letter to the Bishops of the Catholic Church on Some Aspects of Christian Meditation." October 15, 1989. Available at www.vatican.va.

Cummings, Charles. *Monastic Practices*. Rev. ed. Collegeville, MN: Liturgical Press, 2015.

Daya, Roshni. "Buddhist Moments in Psychotherapy." In *Integrating Traditional Healing Practices into Counseling and Psychotherapy*, edited by Roy Moodley and William West, 182–93. Thousand Oaks, CA: Sage Publications, 2005.

Deci, Edward L. *Intrinsic Motivation*. New York: Plenum Press, 1975.

Dilthey, Wilhelm. *The Formation of the Historical World in the Human Sciences*. Princeton, NJ: Princeton University Press, 2002.

Ding, Yudan, Li Wang, Jindong Chen, Jingping Zhao, and Wenbin Guo. "Chinese Taoist Cognitive Therapy for Symptoms of Depression and Anxiety in Adults in China: A Systematic Review and Meta-Analysis." *Frontiers in Psychology* 11, no. 769 (2020): 1–12.

Dubay, Thomas. *Seeking Spiritual Direction: How to Grow the Divine Life Within*. Ann Arbor, MI: Servant Publications, 1993.

———. *Prayer Primer: Igniting the Fire Within*. Cincinnati, Ohio: Servant Books, 2002.

Engel, George L. "The Need for a New Medical Model: A Challenge to Biomedical Medicine." *Science* 196 (1977): 129–36.

Engku Kamarudin, E. M., W. S. Wan Sulaiman, N. H. Sarnon, and A. S. Amin. "The Clinical Application of the Biopsychosocial Model." *The American Journal of Psychiatry* 137, no. 5 (1980): 535–44.

———. "Data on Self-Awareness, Self-Determination, and Self-Efficacy of Opioid-Dependent Patients Receiving Methadone Treatment Before and After Getting Individual Psycho-educational (i-SEAZ) Intervention." *Data in Brief* 30 (2020): 1–6.

Fisher, Peter, and Adrian Wells. *Metacognitive Therapy*. New York: Routledge, 2009.

Francis, Pope. "General Audience: Catechesis on Prayer 31, The Meditation." April 28, 2021. Available at www.vatican.va.

Frankena, William K. *Ethics*. 2nd ed. Englewood Cliffs, NJ: Prentice-Hall, 1973.

Freud, Anna. *The Ego and the Mechanisms of Defence*. London: Karnac Books, 1993.

Freud, Sigmund. *A General Introduction to Psychoanalysis*. New York: Horace Liveright, 1920.

Frydenberg, Erica. *Coping and the Challenge of Resilience*. London: Palgrave Macmillan, 2017.

Fulton, Paul R., and Ronald D. Siegel. "Buddhist and Western Psychology: Seeking Common Ground." In *Mindfulness and Psychotherapy*, 2nd ed., edited by Christopher K. Germer, Ronald D. Siegel, and Paul R. Fulton, 36–58. New York: Guilford Press, 2013.

Gadamer, Hans-Georg. *Wahrheit und Methode*. In *Gesammelte Werke* 1. Tübingen: Mohr Siebeck, 1990.

———. *Truth and Method*. 2nd ed. Translated by Joel Weinsheimer and Donald G. Marshall. New York: Continuum, 2004.

Gallagher, Timothy M. *The Examen Prayer: Ignatian Wisdom for Our Lives Today*. New York: Crossroad Publisher, 2006.

Garzon, Fernando. "Christian Devotional Meditation for Anxiety." In *Evidence-Based Practices for Christian Counseling and Psychotherapy*, edited by Everett L. Worthington Jr., Eric L. Johnson, Joshua N. Hook, and Jamie D. Aten, 59–80. Downers Grove, IL: IVP Academic, 2013.

Geddes, John. "Evidence-Based Practice in Mental Health." In *Evidence-Based Practice: A Critical Appraisal*, edited by Liz Trinder and Shirley Reynolds, 66–88. Malden, MA: Blackwell Science, 2000.

Gelso, Charles J. *The Real Relationship in Psychotherapy: The Hidden Relationship of Change*. Washington, DC: American Psychological Association, 2010.

Gelso, Charles J., and Jean A. Carter. "Components of the Psychotherapy Relationship: Their Interaction and Unfolding During Treatment." *Journal of Counseling Psychology* 41, no. 3 (1994): 296–306.

Germer, Christopher, Ronald D. Siegel, and Paul R. Fulton, eds. *Mindfulness and Psychotherapy*. 2nd ed. New York: Guilford Press, 2016.

Giraldi, Tullio. *Psychotherapy, Mindfulness, and Buddhist Meditation*. Cham: Palgrave Macmillan, 2019.

Gold, Eva, and Stephen Zahm. *Buddhist Psychology and Gestalt Therapy Integrated: Psychotherapy for the 21st Century*. Portland, OR: Metta Press, 2018.

Goldberg, Lewis R. "An Alternative 'Description of Personality': The Big-Five Factor Structure." *Journal of Personality and Social Psychology* 59, no. 6 (1990): 1216–29.

Goldstein, Kurt. *The Organism*. New York: Zone Books, 1995.

Gonsiorek, John C., P. Scott Richards, Kenneth I. Pargament, and Mark R. McMinn. "Ethical Challenges and Opportunities at the Edge: Incorporating Spirituality and Religion into Psychotherapy." *Professional Psychology: Research and Practice* 40, no. 4 (2009): 385–95.

Gowans, Christopher W. *Self-Cultivation Philosophies in Ancient India, Greece, and China*. Oxford: Oxford University Press, 2021.

Graf, Peter, Laura L. Carstensen, Franz E. Weinert, and Richard A. Shweder. "Epilogue: Reflections and Future Perspectives." In *Interactive Minds: Life-Span Perspectives on the Social Foundation of Cognition*, edited by Paul B. Baltes and Ursula M. Staudinger, 430–40. New York: Cambridge University Press, 1996.

Groeschel, Benedict J. *Spiritual Passages: The Psychology of Spiritual Development*. New York: Crossroad, 1987.

Guggenbühl-Craig, Adolf. *Power in the Helping Professions*. Thompson, CT: Spring Publications, 2021.

Gunaratana, Bhante. *Mindfulness in Plain English*. Somerville, MA: Wisdom Publications, 2011.

Hahn, Thich Nhat. *The Miracle of Mindfulness: An Introduction to the Practice of Meditation*. Boston: Beacon Press, 1996.

Haidt, J. "Moral Psychology for the Twenty-First Century." *Journal of Moral Education* 42, no. 3 (2013): 281–97.

Hall, Calvin S., and Gardner Lindzey. *Theories of Personality*. New York: John Wiley and Sons, 1957.

Hathaway, William and Erica Tan. "Religiously Oriented Mindfulness-Based Cognitive Therapy." *Journal of Clinical Psychology: In Session* 65, no. 2 (2009): 158–71.

Hayes, Steven C., Victoria M. Follette, and Marsha M. Linehan, eds. *Mindfulness and Acceptance: Expanding the Cognitive-Behavioral Tradition*. New York: Guilford Press, 2004.

Heitler, Susan M. *From Conflict to Resolution: Skills and Strategies for Individual, Couple, and Family Therapy*. New York: W. W. Norton and Company, 1990.

Herdt, Jennifer A. *Forming Humanity: Redeeming the German Bildung Tradition*. Chicago: University of Chicago Press, 2019.

Hill, Clara E. *Helping Skills: Facilitating Exploration, Insight, and Action*. 4th ed. Washington, DC: American Psychological Association, 2014.

Hilty, Donald M. "Advancing Science, Clinical Care and Education: Shall We Update Engel's Biopsychosocial Model to a Bio-Psycho-Social-Cultural Model?" *Psychology and Cognitive Sciences* 1, no. 1 (2015): 1–6.

Hodgins, Holley S., and C. Raymond Knee. "The Integrating Self and Conscious Experience." In *Handbook of Self-Determination Research*, edited by Edward L. Deci and Richard M. Ryan, 87–100. Rochester, NY: University of Rochester Press, 2002.

Hwang, Kwang-Kuo, and Jeffrey Chang. "Self-Cultivation: Culturally Sensitive Psychotherapies in Confucian Societies." *The Counseling Psychologist* 37, no. 7 (2009): 1010–32.

John Paul II, Pope. *Vita consecrata*. Post-Synodal Apostolic Exhortation. March 25, 1996. Available at www.vatican.va.

Johnson, Susan M. *Attachment Theory in Practice: Emotionally Focused Therapy (EFT) with Individuals, Couples, and Families*. New York: Guilford Press, 2019.

Jones, Stanton L., and Richard E. Butman. *Modern Psychotherapies: A Comprehensive Christian Appraisal*. Downers Grove, IL: IVP Academic, 2011.

Kaam, Adrian van. *The Art of Existential Counseling*. Wilkes-Barre, PA: Dimension Books, 1966.

Kabat-Zinn, Jon. *Wherever You Go, There You Are: Mindfulness Meditation in Everyday Life*. New York: Hachette Books, 1994.

Kahn, Michael. *Between Therapist and Client: The New Relationship*. Rev. ed. New York: Henry Holt and Company, 1997.

Kernberg, Paulina F., Alan S. Weiner, and Karen K. Bardenstein. *Personality Disorders in Children and Adolescents*. New York: Basic Books, 2000.

Keyes, Corey L. M. "The Mental Health Continuum: From Languishing to Flourishing in Life." *Journal of Health and Social Research* 43, no. 2 (2002): 207–22.

———. "Promoting and Protecting Mental Health as Flourishing." *American Psychologist* 62, no. 2 (2007): 95–108.

Kitchener, K. S. "There is More to Ethics than Principles." *The Counseling Psychologist* 24, no. 1 (1996): 92–97.

Knabb, Joshua J. "Centering Prayer as an Alternative to Mindfulness-Based Cognitive Therapy for Depression Relapse Prevention." *Journal of Religion and Health* 51, no. 3 (2012): 908–24.

———. *Christian Meditation in Clinical Practice: A Four-Step Model and Workbook for Therapists and Clients*. Downers Grove, IL: IVP Academic, 2021.

Koons, Cedar R. *The Mindfulness Solution for Intense Emotions: Take Control of Borderline Personality Disorder with DBT*. Oakland, CA: New Harbinger Publications, 2016.

Kugelmann, Robert. "The Theory and Practice of Thomas Verner Moore's Catholic Psychiatry and Psychotherapy." *History of Psychology* 22, no. 2 (2019): 186–204.

Kvale, Steinar. "The Qualitative Research Interview: A Phenomenological and Hermeneutical Mode of Understanding." *Journal of Phenomenological Psychology* 14, no. 2 (1983): 171–96.

———. *Interviews: An Introduction to Qualitative Research Interviewing*. Thousand Oaks, CA: Sage Publications, 1996.

Laird, Lance D., Cara E. Curtis, and Jonathan R. Morgan. "Finding Spirits in Spirituality: What are We Measuring in Spirituality and Health Research?" *Journal of Religion and Health* 56, no. 1 (2017): 1–20.

Lamb, Matthew L. *History, Method, and Theology: A Dialectical Comparison of Wilhelm Dilthey's Critique of Historical Reason and Bernard Lonergan's Meta-Methodology*. Missoula, MT: Scholars Press, 1978.

Langberg, Diane. "The Spiritual Life of the Therapist: We Become What We Habitually Reflect." *Journal of Psychology and Christianity* 25, no. 3 (2006): 258–66.

Lee, Kin Cheung George. *Buddhist Counseling: An Introduction for Mental Health Professionals*. Saarbrücken: Lambert Academic Publishing, 2017.

Lief, Alfred, ed. *The Commonsense Psychiatry of Dr. Adolf Meyer: Fifty-Two Selected Papers*. New York: McGraw-Hill, 1948.

Lonergan, Bernard. "The Transition from a Classicist World-View to Historical-Mindedness." In *A Second Collection*, edited by William F. J. Ryan and Bernard J. Tyrrell, 1–9. Toronto: University of Toronto Press, 1974.

———. "Horizons and Transpositions." In *Philosophical and Theological Papers 1965–1980*, edited by Robert C. Croken and Robert M. Doran, 409–32. Toronto: University of Toronto Press, 2004.

Mackie, Alastair J. "Attachment Theory: Its Relevance to the Therapeutic Alliance." *British Journal of Medical Psychology* 54 (1981): 203–12.

Maddux, James E. "Self-Efficacy." In *The Encyclopedia of Positive Psychology*, edited by Shane J. Lopez, 874–80. Malden, MA: John Wiley and Sons, 2009.

Markowtitz, John C., and Myrna M. Weissman. "Interpersonal Psychotherapy: Principles and Applications." *World Psychiatry* 3, no. 3 (2004): 136–39.

Martin, Mike W. *From Morality to Mental Health: Virtue and Vice in a Therapeutic Culture*. Oxford: Oxford University Press, 2006.

Maslow, Abraham. *Motivation and Personality*. New York: Harper and Row, 1954.

———. *Toward a Psychology of Being*. 2nd ed. New York: Van Nostrand Reinhold, 1968.

McWilliams, Nancy. *Psychoanalytic Diagnosis: Understanding Personality Structure in the Clinical Process*. 2nd ed. New York: Guilford Press, 2011.

Merton, Thomas. *Spiritual Direction and Meditation*. Collegeville, MN: Liturgical Press, 1960.

Mikulincer, Mario, Phillip R. Shaver, and Ety Berant. "An Attachment Perspective on Therapeutic Processes and Outcomes." *Journal of Personality* 81, no. 6 (2013): 606–16.

Moncher, Frank J., and Craig S. Titus. "Foundations for a Psychotherapy of Virtue: An Integrated Catholic Perspective." *Journal of Psychology and Christianity* 28, no. 1 (2009): 22–35.

Moore, Thomas Verner. *Cognitive Psychology*. New York: Lippincott Company, 1939.

———. *The Nature and Treatment of Mental Disorders*. New York: Grune and Stratton, 1944.

———. *The Driving Forces of Human Nature and Their Adjustment*. New York: Grune and Stratton, 1950.

Morse, Janice M. "'Emerging from the Data': The Cognitive Processes of Analysis in Qualitative Inquiry." In *Critical Issues in Qualitative Research Methods*, edited by Janice M. Morse, 23–43. Thousand Oaks, CA: Sage Publications, 1994.

Nemeck, Francis Kelly, and Marie Theresa Coombs. *The Way of Spiritual Direction*. Collegeville, MN: Liturgical Press, 1985.

Niesser, Ulrich. *Cognitive Psychology*. New York: Appleton-Century, 1967.

O'Doherty, E. F. *The Priest and Mental Health*. Staten Island, NY: Society of St. Paul, 1963.

Olsen, Cyrus P. "Spirituality and the Health-Care Professional." *The Linacre Quarterly* 78, no. 4 (2011): 437–54.

Pargament, Kenneth I. *Spiritually Integrated Psychotherapy: Understanding and Addressing the Sacred*. New York: Guilford Press, 2007.

Pargament, Kenneth I., Nichole A. Murray-Swank, and Nalini Tarakeshwar. "An Empirically-Based Rationale for a Spiritually-Integrated Psychotherapy." *Mental Health, Religion and Culture* 8, no. 3 (2005): 155–65.

Pedersen, Lane D. "Mindfulness." In *Dialectical Behavior Therapy: A Contemporary Guide for Practitioners*, 118–24. Malden, MA: John Wiley and Sons, 2015.

Picciotto, Gabriela, Jesse Fox, and Félix Neto. "A Phenomenology of Spiritual Bypass: Causes, Consequences, and Implications." *Journal of Spirituality in Mental Health* 20, no. 4 (2018): 333–54.

Pilgrim, David. "The Biopsychosocial Model in Anglo-American Psychiatry: Past, Present and Future?" *Journal of Mental Health* 11, no. 6 (2002): 585–94.

Plante, Thomas G. "The 4 Ds: Using Ignatian Spirituality in Secular Psychotherapy and Beyond." *Spirituality in Clinical Practice* 4, no. 1 (2017): 74–79.

Propst, L. Rebecca. "Cognitive-Behavioral Therapy and the Religious Person." In *Religion and the Clinical Practice of Psychology*, edited by E. P. Shafranske, 391–407. Washington, DC: American Psychological Association, 1996.

Rennie, Thomas A. C. "Adolf Meyer and Psychobiology: The Man, His Methodology and Its Relation to Therapy." In *Papers from the Second American Congress on General Semantics*, edited by M. Kendig, 156–65. Chicago: Institute of General Semantics, 1943.

Reynolds, Stefan Gillow. *Living with the Mind of Christ: Mindfulness in Christian Spirituality*. Minneapolis, MN: Augsburg Books, 2020.

Rizzuto, Ana-Maria. "The Psychological Foundations of Belief in God." In *Toward Moral and Religious Maturity*, 115–35. Glenview, Ill.: Silver Burdett Company, 1980.

Rosin, Jessica. "The Necessity of Counselor Individuation for Fostering Reflective Practice." *Journal of Counseling and Development* 93 (2015): 88–95.

Rosmarin, David H. *Spirituality, Religion, and Cognitive-Behavioral Therapy: A Guide for Clinicians*. New York: Guilford Press, 2018.

Rubin, Jeffrey B. *Psychotherapy and Buddhism: Toward an Integration*. New York: Plenum Press, 1996.

Ruffing, Janet K. *Spiritual Direction: Beyond the Beginnings*. Mahwah, NJ: Paulist Press, 2000.

Rutter, Michael. "Psychosocial Resilience and Protective Mechanisms." *American Journal of Orthosychiatry* 57, no. 3 (1987): 316–31.

Seeman, Julius. "Toward a Concept of Personality Integration." *American Psychologist* 14, no. 10 (1959): 633–37.

Segal, Zindel V., J. Mark G. Williams, and John D. Teasdale. *Mindfulness-Based Cognitive Therapy for Depression*. 2nd ed. New York: Guilford Press, 2013.

Seligman, Martin E. P. *Flourish: A Visionary New Understanding of Happiness and Well-Being*. New York: Atria, 2011.

Sharf, Richard S. *Theories of Psychotherapy and Counseling: Concepts and Cases*. 6th ed. Boston: Cengage Learning, 2015.

Sheldon, Kennon M., and Tim Kasser. "Coherence and Congruence: Two Aspects of Personality Integration." *Journal of Personality and Social Psychology* 68, no. 3 (1995): 531–43.

Sheldon, Kennon M., Tim Kasser, Kendra Smith, and Tamara Share. "Personal Goals and Psychological Growth: Testing an Intervention to Enhance Goal Attainment and Personality Integration." *Journal of Personality* 70, no. 1 (2002): 5–31.

Shiah, Yung-Jong, and Kwang-Kuo Hwang. "Socialized Reflexivity and Self-Exertion: Mandala Model of Self and Its Role in Mental Health." *Asian Journal of Social Psychology* 22, no. 1 (2019): 47–58.

Shonin, Edo, William van Gordon, and Mark D. Griffiths, eds. *Mindfulness and Buddhist-Derived Approaches in Mental Health and Addiction*. New York: Springer, 2016.

Shweder, Richard A. "The Psychology of Practice and the Practice of the Three Psychologies." *Asian Journal of Social Psychology* 3 (2000): 207–22.

Siegel, Daniel J. *The Developing Mind: How Relationships and the Brain Interact to Shape Who We Are*. 3rd ed. New York: Guilford Press, 2020.

Sisemore, Timothy A., and Joshua J. Knabb. "Seeing Religions and Spiritualities from the Inside: Problems for Western Psychology That Can Be Addressed with an Indigenous Psychological Perspective." In *The Psychology of World Religions and Spiritualities: An Indigenous Perspective*, edited by Timothy A. Sisemore and Joshua J. Knabb, 3–28. West Conshohocken, PA: Templeton Press, 2020.

Skourteli, Marina Christina, and Clare Lennie. "The Therapeutic Relationship from an Attachment Theory Perspective." *Counseling Psychology Review* 26, no. 1 (2011): 20–33.

Smith, Amie E. M., Rachel M. Msetfi, and Laura Golding. "Client Self-Rated Adult Attachment Patterns and the Therapeutic Alliance: A Systematic Review." *Clinical Psychology Review* 30 (2010): 326–37.

Sperry, Len. "Integrative Spiritually Oriented Psychotherapy." In *Spiritually Oriented Psychotherapy*, edited by Len Sperry and Edward P. Shafranske, 307–29. Washington, DC: American Psychological Association, 2004.

———. "Integrative Spiritually Oriented Psychotherapy: A Case Study of Spiritual and Psychological Transformation." In *Casebook for a Spiritual Strategy of Counseling and Psychotherapy*, edited by P. Scott Richards and Allen E. Bergin, 141–52. Washington, DC: American Psychological Association, 2004.

Sperry, Len, and Jonathan J. Sperry. "Psychotherapy and Virtue: Positive Psychology and Spiritual Well-Being." In *Religion, Spirituality, and Positive Psychology: Understanding the Fruits of Faith*, edited by Thomas G. Plante, 145–58. Denver, Colo.: Praeger, 2012.

Stein, Edith. "The Separate Vocations of Man and Woman according to Nature and Grace." In *Essays on Woman*, 2nd ed., translated by Freda Mary Oben, 59–85. Washington, DC: ICS Publications, 1996.

Tapal, Adam, Ela Oren, Reuven Dar, and Baruch Eitam. "The Sense of Agency Scale: A Measure of Consciously Perceived Control over One's Mind, Body, and the Immediate Environment." *Frontiers in Psychology* 8 (2017): 1–11.

Tirch, Dennis, Laura R. Silberstein, and Russell L. Kolts. *Buddhist Psychology and Cognitive-Behavioral Therapy: A Clinician's Guide*. New York: Guilford Press, 2016.

Titus, Craig S. *Resilience and the Virtue of Fortitude: Aquinas in Dialogue with the Psychosocial Sciences*. Washington, DC: The Catholic University of America Press, 2006.

Torre, Mary Ann La. "Self-Reflection: An Important Process for the Therapist." *Perspectives in Psychiatric Care* 41, no. 2 (2005): 85–87.

Trader, Alexis. *Ancient Christian Wisdom and Aaron Beck's Cognitive Therapy: A Meeting of Minds*. New York: Peter Lang, 2012.

Vachon, Dominic O., and Albert A. Agresti. "A Training Proposal to Help Mental Health Professionals Clarify and Manage Implicit Values in the Counseling Process." *Professional Psychology: Research and Practice* 23, no. 6 (1992): 509–14.

Vansteenkiste, Maarten, and Kennon M. Sheldon. "There's Nothing More Practical than a Good Theory: Integrating Motivational Interviewing and Self-Determination Theory." *British Journal of Clinical Psychology* 45 (2006): 63–82.

Vergote, Antoine. *Psychologie Religieuse, Deuxième édition*. Brussels: Charles Dessart, 1966.

———. *The Religious Man: A Psychological Study of Religious Attitudes*. Dayton, OH: Pflaum Press, 1969.

Vijver, Fons J. R. van de, and Ype H. Poortinga. "Towards an Integrated Analysis of Bias in Cross-Cultural Assessment." *European Journal of Psychological Assessment* 13, no. 1 (1997): 29–37.

Vitz, Paul C., William J. Nordling, and Craig Steven Titus, eds. *A Catholic Christian Meta-Model of the Person: Integration with Psychology and Mental Health Practice*. Sterling, VA: Divine Mercy University Press, 2020.

Wallace, B. Alan, and Shauna L. Shapiro. "Mental Balance and Well-Being: Building Bridges between Buddhism and Western Psychology." *American Psychologist* 61, no. 7 (2006): 690–701.

Watson, David, and Lee Anna Clark. "Personality Traits as an Organizing Framework for Personality Pathology." *Personality and Mental Health* 14 (2020): 51–75.

Wells, Adrian. *Emotional Disorders and Metacognition: Innovative Cognitive Therapy*. New York: John Wiley and Sons, 2000.

Wertz, Frederick J. "Phenomenological Research Methods for Counseling Psychology." *Journal of Counseling Psychology* 52, no. 2 (2005): 167–77.

White, Victor. *Soul and Psyche: An Enquiry into the Relationship between Psychotherapy and Religion*. New York: Harper, 1960.

———. *God and the Unconscious*. Providence, RI: Cluny Media, 2021.

Wiggins, Marsha I. "Therapist Self-Awareness of Spirituality." In *Spirituality and the Therapeutic Process: A Comprehensive Resource from Intake to Termination*, edited by J. D. Aten and M. M. Leach, 53–73. Washington, DC: American Psychological Association, 2009.

Wilson, Kelly G. *Mindfulness for Two: An Acceptance and Commitment Therapy Approach to Mindfulness in Psychotherapy*. Oakland, CA: New Harbinger Publications, 2008.

Wood, Alex M., and Nicholas Tarrier. "Positive Clinical Psychology: A New Vision and Strategy for Integrated Research." *Clinical Psychology Review* 30 (2010): 819–29.

Yang, Kuo-Shu. "Monocultural and Cross-Cultural Indigenous Approaches: The Royal Road to the Development of a Balanced Global Psychology." *Asian Journal of Social Psychology* 3, no. 3 (2000): 241–63.

Index of Names

Index of Topics